Psychology and Religion

Psychology and Religion

Classical Theorists and Contemporary Developments

Fourth Edition

Andrew R. Fuller

ROWMAN & LITTLEFIELD PUBLISHERS, INC.
Lanham • Boulder • New York • Toronto • Plymouth, UK

ROWMAN & LITTLEFIELD PUBLISHERS, INC.

Published in the United States of America
by Rowman & Littlefield Publishers, Inc.
A wholly owned subsidiary of The Rowman & Littlefield Publishing Group, Inc.
4501 Forbes Boulevard, Suite 200, Lanham, Maryland 20706
www.rowmanlittlefield.com

Estover Road, Plymouth PL6 7PY, United Kingdom

British Library Cataloguing in Publication Information Available

Library of Congress Cataloging-in-Publication Data

Fuller, Andrew Reid.
  Psychology and religion : classical theorists and contemporary developments /
Andrew R. Fuller. — 4th ed.
    p. cm.
  Includes bibliographical references and index.
  ISBN-13: 978-0-7425-6022-2 (pbk. : alk. paper)
  ISBN-10: 0-7425-6022-8 (pbk. : alk. paper)
  1. Psychology and religion. 2. Psychoanalysis and religion. 3. Psychology,
Religious—History. I. Title.
  BF51.F84 2007
  200.1'9—dc22

                                                                2007020818

Printed in the United States of America

⊗™ The paper used in this publication meets the minimum requirements of
American National Standard for Information Sciences—Permanence of Paper
for Printed Library Materials, ANSI/NISO Z39.48-1992.

For Barbara, Susan, and Kaden

Contents

Preface ix

1 William James 1

2 Sigmund Freud 31

3 Carl Jung 65

4 Gordon Allport 105

5 Abraham Maslow 127

6 Alan Watts 167

7 Erich Fromm 195

8 Viktor Frankl 223

9 Developments 251

10 Feminist Psychology of Religion 277

11 Neuroscience and Religion 301

12 The Evolutionary Psychology of Religion 331

Index 353

About the Author 369

Preface

The present book surveys a wide range of viewpoints in the field of the psychology of religion. It includes a chapter on each of the following theorists, who, for want of a better term, will be referred to as "classical": William James, Sigmund Freud, Carl Jung, Gordon Allport, Abraham Maslow, Alan Watts, Erich Fromm, and Viktor Frankl. The orientations of these authors range from the descriptive (James, Allport) and the explicitly phenomenological (Frankl), through the psychodynamic (Freud, Jung) and the humanistic (Fromm, Maslow), to the Eastern (Watts). This wide range of approaches allows us a consideration of a wide range of issues. These eight psychologists, whose time was one of remarkable theoretical innovation and discovery, pioneered the investigation of any number of the major issues in the field, issues that remain of central concern in our day. Anyone interested in religious psychology will thus be interested in their work, from which something of value can always be gained.

Each of these authors drew our attention to something of significance in the rich domain of religious behavior: James, the rights of feeling and the priority of firsthand, personal religious experience; Freud, the wish-fulfilling character of immature, childish religion; Jung, the numinous as a "psychological fact" and the universal and never to be surpassed role of "symbols of transformation"; Allport, the difference between mature and immature religion, and the conscious and individual character of the former healthy religiousness; Maslow, the biological attunement of human nature to an ultimately spiritual cosmos, and the possibilities of human fulfillment through fusion with this cosmos; Watts, the experience of the interconnectedness, natural spontaneity, and rightness of the universe's

processes at all levels of their occurrence; Fromm, the opposed humanistic and authoritarian alternatives in religion and ethics and the human
ability to develop the powers of reason and love through the humanistic
alternative; and Frankl, human existence as a search for meaning, and indeed for ultimate meaning, in a realm beyond psychological processes of
all sorts.

The contributions of these eight psychologists, it is believed, are fundamental, lasting ones. Their accomplishments and their issues are not, of
course, the final word. Chapters 9 to 12 consider approaches essentially
subsequent to these classical ones, some of which are recent and still unfolding. Chapter 9 presents various developments in the psychology of religion. Included are Donald Winnicott, Ana-Maria Rizzuto, Paul Pruyser,
and Antoine Vergote on object relations theory and God-images; the research of Bernard Spilka and Daniel Batson and their colleagues on the scaling of religiousness; and, finally, newly added in this fourth edition,
Stanislov Grof on modern consciousness research and experiential psychotherapy. Chapters 10 through 12, with one exception (the section on
Sperry in chapter 11), contain all new material. Chapter 10 is an eclectic
overview of the feminist psychology of religion and includes Diane Jonte-
Pace's review of research in the field, Mary Daly's criticism of the masculine thrust of Western religion and the related victimization of women,
Carol Gilligan's approach to the moral development of women and an
"ethic of care," Majella Franzmann's thinking on the marginalization of
women in religious texts and practices, Naomi Goldenberg's critique of dualistic religion and her plea for a revival of the "maternal body," and Hetty
Zock's discussion of Erik Erikson's preference for a feminine-oriented psychology of religion. Chapter 11 considers developments in the intersection
of neuroscience and religion. It includes Roger Sperry on the determining
role of consciousness in neural processes and in the universe at large; neurophenomenology, a discipline launched in 1996 by Franciso Varela to unite
cognitive neuroscience and phenomenological philosophy; affective neuroscience and Tibetan Buddhist meditation, with special reference to Richard
Davidson; and James Austin on the interrelations between Zen Buddhism
and neuroscience. The concluding chapter 12 deals with the evolutionary
psychology of religion and includes Pascal Boyer on the psychological factors in the cultural evolution of religion and Daniel Dennett on including
cultural factors, alongside psychological ones, in that evolution.

These are a lot of views, and they are often found to conflict with one
another. This may not be a complete negative, however. Religious behavior may be compared to a vast park that one sets out to explore (compare
chapter 1, "Human Selectivity"). A problem and an opportunity immediately present themselves in such an endeavor. No explorer can survey the
entire park all at once, and so, he or she sets off on one or another path

through the larger territory. In this way, certain things come into view. This is the opportunity: to discover something. But taking a specific path means that certain other things never come into view, for the path doesn't pass their way. This is the problem: that one will miss a great number of things. The problem is not insurmountable, however, for another explorer takes a second path and, so, sees something the first explorer was unable to. And a third explorer takes a third path and discovers something missed by the first two.

The following attempts to formalize this metaphor of exploration. Certain "principles of interpretation" are specified, with an aim of locating the limits and validity of psychological theories, and of psychological theories of religion in particular. First, psychological theories are grounded in unprovable presuppositions. Such presuppositions or assumptions are acts of faith engaged in by the whole, feeling human being. Proof is thus consequent to personal commitment. General presuppositions concern the fundamental approaches and methods to be employed in psychological investigation and the aims to be pursued. Examples of specific presuppositions are the belief that unmasking the unconscious reveals important facts about an individual's motivation, that a description of actual life situations brings otherwise neglected dimensions of behavior into view, and that a consideration of the human potential is important for a complete understanding of people's actions. Second, such presuppositions—in the metaphor, the paths set out on to explore the territory of human behavior—yield an open space or horizon for the investigation of a certain domain of human behavior.

Third, a psychological theory finds its limits in the free space opened by its particular set of presuppositions. The validity of a psychological theory is precisely within such limits, which allow it to see what it does see and which prevent it, as a matter of principle, from seeing many other things, which are outside its reach. Fourth, any number of legitimate theoretical spaces is possible. The science of psychology is essentially historical and perspectival. There are, accordingly, several true psychological theories. Finally, depending on the behavioral domain being explored and the aims in view, certain ways of looking—certain paths—will be superior to others. It is important, then, that the appropriate theory be engaged in the particular case.

Certain consequences follow from these interpretive-critical principles. For one thing, no psychological theory has the right to deny the possibility of valid access to behavioral data through paths other than its own. No theory, in other words, has the right to decree that it has sole legitimacy in the investigation of human behavior. A map of the entire territory is not possible on the basis of one path. Positively, diversity and theoretical pluralism are ideals to be pursued. As many different paths are to be advanced in psychology as can fruitfully explicate behavior. Given the richness and complexity of human behavior, a great many such paths are possible. Religion is many things—there are many ways to be religious. Therefore, many psychologies of religion are necessary.

Ideally, it may be possible one day to map the entire territory of religious behavior, with all its paths and spaces. Reaching the goal of a comprehensive psychology of religion is by no means an immediate prospect, and this goal will always have its problems. In the meantime, all relevant and legitimate theoretical paths should be given their due. The chapters of this book feature a variety of *perspectives* on religious behavior, thus allowing different *aspects* of the "matter itself" of such behavior to come into view. Each such aspect represents something of the total territory to be taken into consideration in the development of a comprehensive psychology of religion. The various points of view represented here are all correct, within limits.

1

✛

William James

The unreasoned and immediate assurance is the deep thing in us, the reasoned argument is but a surface exhibition.

—William James

William James (1842–1910) was an American philosopher and psychologist of great originality and breadth. His influence, which continues to grow, has been felt well beyond his native land. James challenged the positivism of his day, opposing to it the active role of human interest and character in determining truth and, indeed, the very shape of the universe itself. Not a universe in itself, then, but a universe in process. Not objectivity and intellect alone, but subjectivity and the human heart as well. For James, science, representing only one human interest, is only one path to truth: science can never tell the whole truth. "Water," being "really" only two molecules of hydrogen and one of oxygen, may not exist for scientific interest, but, James insists, it does indeed exist for other human interests (1950, 656). These other interests open upon other orders of truth: perceptual, moral, esthetic, and religious truth.

James's concern is with religious questions of everyday existence, with a personal God of the heart. Neither the abstract God of intellectual categories and proofs nor the formalized God of ecclesiastical institutions holds any interest for him. Rather, God is an intimate matter of life and destiny. James's vision is indeed a pantheistic one: humans are internal parts of God, forming, through the subconscious, one field of consciousness with him. Truth, for James, is lived truth, truth that comes to pass in the struggle to live: truth happens to the idea of God in view of what belief in God brings to life. James's "pragmatic" approach to religious truth is a bold one, a challenge both to the positivist claim that religion has been replaced by science and to the rationalist claim that God is a matter for the intellect to resolve.

In a thinker as wide-ranging, penetrating, and iconoclastic as James, there is an inevitable blurring of the usual boundaries between disciplines. Religion holds an important place, moreover, in many of James's writings. The chapter opens with a summary of his classic essay, "The Will to Believe" (1956f), and closes with an overview of his seminal book, *The Varieties of Religious Experience* (1958). *The Varieties of Religious Experience* gives the place of honor to the description of rich and vivid case studies. This work has exerted a powerful influence on any number of psychologists of religion: Carl Jung, Gordon Allport, and Abraham Maslow, among others. In between these two works is considered James's pivotal notion of the selectivity of human life and its implications for the psychology of religion.

"THE WILL TO BELIEVE"

"The Will to Believe" was originally given as a lecture, being first published in 1896. This essay serves as a fitting introduction to James's writings, in particular to *The Varieties of Religious Experience*. He remarks at the outset of "The Will to Believe" that he is going to defend the right of the individual, in the absence of final proof, to adopt voluntarily "a believing attitude" (1956f, 1–2). James proceeds to define a "hypothesis" as anything proposed for our belief, and a "live" hypothesis as a hypothesis that lays a claim on us as having a real possibility of being true. The liveness of a hypothesis is seen to stand in proportion to our willingness to act on it, and maximum liveness is said to mean a willingness to act irrevocably. He says that such "willingness to act irrevocably" is, practically speaking, what he means by "belief" (1956f, 3).

James proceeds to inquire into the origin of belief as thus defined. Is intellect alone in determining belief, or does our "passional and volitional nature"—inarticulate tendencies deep within us—play its role? He comments that, in point of fact, we find ourselves believing "we hardly know how or why" (1956f, 9). Our "willing nature"—factors of belief including fear, hope, passion, prejudice, imitation, taking sides, and the like—for the most part determines which hypotheses are alive for us—which hypotheses lay a claim on our action—and which are dead.

James offers as an example the belief (willingness to act irrevocably) that we are able to discover truth. Our belief in truth, he says, is a "passionate affirmation of desire" (1956f, 9). We believe in truth not because of any defensible intellectual insight we might have into its discoverability but because we *want* it with a passion, because we want to believe that our investigations must continually advance us toward truth. What we have no use for, on the other hand, we reject in positive disbelief. Most scientists, aware, for example, that the fact of telepathic communication would jeopardize their basic working assumptions, and accordingly having no use for such communication, scoff at its least suggestion. "Passional tendencies and volitions," James says, precede ("run before") our beliefs (1956f, 11). Nonintellectual factors are thus seen to play a preeminent role in the origin of human belief.

James is neither a *skeptic*, who denies the possibility of attaining truth, nor an *absolutist*, who claims the certain attainment of truth, but an *empiricist*, who thinks that truth is attainable, but not the infallible knowledge of its attainment. Knowing something is one thing; knowing for certain that one knows it is another (1956f, 12). James the empiricist believes that our judgments, while forever open to reinterpretation and correction, through a continuing experiencing and a determined reflection on this experiencing, "grow more true" (1956f, 14).

James says that the finally convincing objective evidence so dear to the positivist—who will only believe if he or she sees—never quite manages its grand entrance (1956f, 16). The conviction that one's own particular evidence is of the "real objective brand," moreover, is, in his view, "only one more subjective opinion" (1956f, 16). Because the intellect has no "infallible signal" for assessing the truth of anything whatsoever with final objective certainty, he concludes that the trouble lies in the very nature of things. He resolutely refuses to give up his quest for truth, but he knows that it must forever remain just that—a quest. The point of origin of a hypothesis matters not. An empiricist judges a hypothesis to be true if it continues to be confirmed by the "total drift of thinking" (1956f, 17).

James remarks that some theorists, out of a positive dread of falling into error, and thus in order to avoid believing a lie, will to abstain from belief forever (1956f, 18). He rejects such an approach, which to him is but an expression of our "passional life," a fear slavishly obeyed. He simply does not think that making a mistake is the worst thing in the world. Better to risk error than forever hold one's mind in suspense!

James points out that the necessity to act is seldom so pressing in science that it is preferable to commit to a possibly false belief than to no belief at all (1956f, 20). The scientist thus has the luxury of being able to refrain from making up his or her mind until the objective evidence has become available. Because it makes no practical difference—because the truth the scientist may miss out on by not committing has no great bearing on life—the decision between hypotheses is safely postponed. The risk of immediate error is thus eliminated.

But, says James, we are not always able to wait safely for the absolutely convincing evidence. Science itself, in its very origin as science, does not hold back in this manner, but, consulting "her heart," fervently clings to the belief that the "infinite ascertainment of fact and the correction of false belief" are supreme goods for human life (1956f, 22). And when it comes to morality, James insists that, if we do not in our heart want "a world of moral reality," our head will never make us adopt one (1956f, 23). Morally committed individuals, moreover, are wholeheartedly convinced that their actions don't make a fool of them. Skeptics, for their part, adopting an attitude of doubt with their whole being, are no less dedicated to their vision than the morally committed (1956f, 23).

Our "passional nature," in James's view, thus has an inevitable bearing on our decisions between hypotheses not only as a matter of fact, but of principle. Playing such a role, James says, this nature is at times a "lawful determinant" of our choices (1956f, 19). As he puts it in another context, "our outer deeds and decisions" originate in the twilight "depths of personality," in the "dumb region of the heart," which is "our deepest organ of communication with the nature of things" (1956b, 62).

James further insists that faith in an undertaking is a major determinant of its success. As he remarks in his essay "The Sentiment of Rationality" (1956e), faith in a result brings about "a certain degree of subjective energy" and, hence, in part, the result itself: "the future fact is conditioned by my present faith in it" (97). The highest good, he proceeds to say, is achievable only through the "moral energy" generated by a faith that success will follow if we try hard enough. "This world is good, we must say, since it is what we make it—and we shall make it good" (1956e, 102). Faith, indispensable for the realization of its object, verifies itself. "Believing is seeing," Robert M. Pirsig writes in his novel *Lila* (1991, 336). A faith rooted in desire, bringing its object about, is thus said to be a lawful determinant of truths that depend on our personal action (1956f, 25).

Because faith in a fact helps bring that fact about—because faith is in on the creation of the fact's truth, which is to say, on its practical verification— James characterizes as insane a logic that outlaws as "shameful" and "the lowest depth of immorality" a faith that "runs ahead of" objective scientific evidence (1956e, 91–92; 1956f, 25). It is unreasonable to rule faith out as a path to truth, James says, when faith is part and parcel of truth's creation (1956e, 102). Concluding broadly, he remarks that "we cannot live or think at all without some degree of faith" (1956e, 95).

We now arrive at the central question: what about religious faith, what about belief in "eternal things"? First of all, James points out that religion claims to involve a decision that makes a momentous difference in our destiny. Religion proposes that we stand to gain or to lose immeasurably by our attitude of belief or disbelief. Second, he says there is no avoiding a choice in the matter. To play the skeptic and wait for more light is not to escape choosing. The agnostic's putting off of decision—"till all the evidence is in"—is itself a choice, a decision for a certain kind of risk: the decision that it is better to risk the loss of truth than the possibility of being in error (1956f, 26). Loss of truth is thus as certainly risked as it is by positive disbelief (atheism).

All in all, James concludes that agnostic skepticism, driven by a "passional" fear of error, is as active a bet as the religious hypothesis. It is not intellect (skepticism) against passion (theism) then, but intellect (skepticism) with its own dictatorial passion (fear). Religion might be true, and James does not want to give up his one chance of being on the winning side if it is. He wants, indeed he insists on, the right to choose his own form of risk. There is simply no proof, he says, that "dupery through hope" is worse than "dupery through fear" (1956f, 27). He rejects as irrational a thinking that closes off all possible access to certain kinds of truth. He refuses to keep his "willing nature out of the game" (1956f, 28).

Viewing religion concretely and in terms of our various options in its regard, James thus rebuffs putting a stopper on "our heart, our instincts, and our courage," only to wait and, thus, to act as if religion were clearly *not* true (1956f, 29). We have seen that James the empiricist is convinced that the absolutely final objective evidence will never make its triumphal appearance. He allows that we can wait if we want to—if we "will." But we act regardless, "taking our life in our hands" (1956f, 30). The skeptic, we have also seen, risks the loss of truth by his or her active bet. But, James says, the skeptic also assumes a certain position *against*. As he comments in another place, the individual who assumes the role of the skeptic on such matters as the existence of God, the rule of morality, and life after death "may again and again be indistinguishable from him who dogmatically denies them. Skepticism in moral matters is an active ally of immorality. Who is not for is against" (1956e, 109). James says the universe does not allow neutrality on any of a number of issues.

All in all, we have the right, in James's opinion, "to believe at our own risk any hypothesis that is live enough to tempt our will" (1956f, 29). James cautions, however, that such freedom to believe does not extend to matters that the intellect can adequately resolve on its own ground. He also points out that the person for whom the religious decision is a live one is never a believer in what is known to be untrue; he or she is not critically naive. Thus, while relativizing intellect's role in the pursuit of knowledge and truth to feeling and willing, James is by no means dismissive of intellect.

We can do no better to summarize James's overall conclusions on "the will to believe" than in the words in which he first announces his thesis: "Our passional nature not only lawfully may, but must, decide an option

between propositions, whenever it is a genuine option that cannot by its
nature be decided on intellectual grounds; for to say, under such circumstances, 'Do not decide, but leave the question open,' is itself a passional
decision—just like deciding yes or no—and is attended with the same risk
of losing the truth" (1956f, 11).

HUMAN SELECTIVITY

James thus insists in "The Will to Believe" that, faced with genuine options the intellect cannot adequately decide on its own, we are justified in
voluntarily believing that toward which our deepest and broadest—our
"passional"—self inclines. Faith, moreover, is said to play a crucial role in
the very rise of its chosen object, in this way making it true. Passion (feeling) and belief (willing), issuing in the very existence and truth of their
objects, codecide reality, are partners in the deciding of truth. Reality is
not fixed and constant, then, in James's view, but always being determined.

Human Selectivity and the Richness of Reality

There being no determinate reality for it to capture, human intellect is unable to function as ultimate knower or arbiter of the universe—not intellect, we have heard James remark, but the "dumb region of the heart" is
"our deepest organ of communication with the nature of things" (1956b,
62). With no given regulative truth, moreover, it must further be admitted
that reality has an inherently plural quality. "Life," James writes, "is confused and superabundant" (1971b, 23). Reality is so rich, in James's view,
that it overflows anything our perceiving or conceiving can ever make of
it. As there is always something more to be made of the universe, no single point of view can embrace or exhaust it. Reality there indeed is, in
James's opinion, and reality we can indeed get in touch with and know,
but reality as known is always limited, always partial. The real order of
the world is something we cannot help but "break." We break it, says
James, into the arts, into histories, and into sciences, thus making any
number of "separate serial orders of it" (1956d, 119). Our encounter with
the universe thus yields a variety of internally coherent accounts or por-
trayals (1956e, 76).

James maintains that there are "real, genuine possibilities in the world,"
real possibilities for us to determine the world and for it to undergo transformation. The way we approach things determines them, this way or
that. On the one hand, James's notion of indeterminism yields "a pluralistic, restless universe, in which no single point of view can ever take in

the whole scene" (1956a, 177). On the other, the richness James attributes to reality is such that any number of the most diverse points of view can all, and without contradicting one another, "get it right": perception, religion, philosophy, science, art, history, and so forth (compare below, "Religious Experience and Knowledge"). All in all, passion, vision, and belief decide truth in James's view. And yet, truth is a matter of "real, genuine possibilities in the world"—we do not invent reality; nor can we make it into anything we desire.

Selectivity of the Mind

James challenges the view of many of his colleagues according to which the human mind is "a passive, reactionless sheet of white paper" upon which reality registers itself (1956d, 129). The mind, to James, is no tabula rasa (John Locke). No passive mirror reflecting a sole truth of reality, the mind is inherently active and interested. According to Ralph Barton Perry, this eminently *selective* character of the human mind is the "one germinal idea from which [James's] whole thought grew" (James 1969, ix). Reality in its richness and availability for determination and change, and the human mind in its activity and directedness, its *selectivity*, are a perfect match for one another.

"In the total game of life," James writes, "we stake our persons all the while" (1956e, 94). The personal factor—our subjective and personal interests, the *demands* we put on things that they be one way or the other— enters into all our undertakings. The very thought of eliminating this factor is out of the question. To bid our "subjective interests be passive till truth express itself" out of the environing world is a futile undertaking, James argues, for truth never will (1956d, 130). It is altogether impossible to glimpse the world "in the unimaginable insipidity of its virgin estate"; our only hope of approaching the world, James comments, is to "operate" on it (1956d, 130).

Totalitarian Pretensions

James rejects no legitimate human endeavor, no science or philosophy. What he does reject, however, is the claim that this or that science or philosophy embraces the whole of reality in its formulations. James does not believe that any particular science or philosophy, having a corner on the truth, is in a position to declare other points of view—those of morality and religion, for example—lacking in legitimacy. James rejects the totalitarian pretensions of any point of view: no point of view has the right to act as if it is not a point of view born of human activity and interest (selectivity of the mind) and to swallow up other points of view; no point of view has the right to act as if points of view other than itself are closed off in principle from the attainment of truth.

James is highly critical of what he calls a "religion of exclusive scientificism." Certain positivists, he says, claim that all the gods have been deposed save one, the god of "Scientific Truth." This one remaining deity is seen to require the strictest obedience to the religion's single commandment: "Thou shalt not be a theist" (1956d, 131). Theism is thus barred, for to commit to theism is to yield to one's "subjective propensities," which, in the eyes of the "religion of exclusive scientificism," is "intellectual damnation" (1956d, 131).

James insists that philosophers of science who worship at the feet of the god of "Scientific Truth" forget that their condemnation of subjectivity in the name of objective analysis is but their subjective inclination: their personal vision of an emancipated world, their passion, and their choice (compare above, "'The Will to Believe'"). Such individuals are deluded, James says, in thinking they have escaped "subjective propensities" of their own. Sacrificing all other options, they have chosen to construct "the leanest, lowest, aridest result—namely, the bare molecular world" (1956d, 131). Reality conceived as "an army of molecules," James says, is able to satisfy perfectly the *appetite* of those who make the *demand* on the universe that it possess "immediate consistency" (1956d, 132).

Science, in James's view, is anything but a disinterested, purely objective observation of reality as it really and truly is in itself. Science is not a blank recording of what's "there": the mind is no tabula rasa, as we have seen, and reality no already finished, self-contained realm. Like everything human, science is grounded in desire, the desire to satisfy certain subjective interests and demands. As a directed (interested) activity of the human mind, science is selective. Science's account of the universe is thus necessarily partial and less than exhaustive. Other interests—religious, moral, and esthetic interests, for example—are, in James's view, no less valid than scientific ones. James insists on the right to give these other interests and demands their due. Science selects from the unbroken order of the world certain relations it deems essential, and the rest it ignores. James says that the chosen relations, while real enough, are "for our purpose," for the scientific ends of explanation and prediction. The relations ignored in the process are no less real and present, in James's view, and no less worthy of our attention (1956d, 119).

Selectivity of the Mind and Religion

The need many people have to believe that nature points to something spiritual and eternal, James remarks, is every bit as "strong and authoritative" as "the inner need of uniform laws of causation" can ever be for professional scientists (1956b, 56). Science being but *one* legitimate human interest, allowance must be made for other legitimate human interests. James insists that science simply has no authority to rule out religious demands, no right to ban religious belief, for science "can only say what is, not what is not" (1956b, 56). "The agnostic 'thou shalt not believe without coercive sensible evidence,'" he says further, is but an expression of a "private personal appetite for evidence of a certain peculiar kind" (1956b, 56). We have the right, in James's view, to believe whatever our deepest and broadest self inclines us to. The mind has a right to be interested in and want, to prefer and to select, not only scientific truth but religious truth as well. This is the argument of "The Will to Believe" (1956f), which is thus seen to be rooted in the notion of the selectivity of the mind (compare Perry's assertion, already cited, to the effect that this selectivity—the mind's active and interested character—is the key to the whole of James's thought).

"Human selectivity" thus has a greater bearing on "psychology and religion" than might first be suspected. In order for religious experience to be taken seriously on its own terms, certain "totalitarian pretensions" must be set aside, and reality conceived in terms that exceed the all-too-narrow limits of modern science: reality has to be expanded to embrace legitimate religious feeling. This James undertakes boldly and brilliantly, in part by showing the limitations of mere formula, in part by showing the interested (selective) dimension of all thought.

THE VARIETIES OF RELIGIOUS EXPERIENCE

James delivered the Gifford Lectures on Natural Religion in Edinburgh in 1901–1902. These lectures appear in book form as *The Varieties of Religious Experience* (1958). We turn now to the major themes of this relatively early classic in the field of religious psychology.

The Interest of Psychology in Religion

Religion has always held a central place in the determination of human behavior. James accordingly comments that the psychologist must find "the religious propensities of man . . . at least as interesting as any other of the facts pertaining to his mental constitution" (1958, 22). Even if the researcher does not actively participate in religion, James insists that such an important phenomenon as religion must not be rejected out of hand but given the full respect it deserves as a topic of investigation (1958, 98).

The Criterion for Judging Religion

James discusses the criterion he will use for evaluating the phenomena of religion in Lecture I. He rejects from the outset the view that religion is to be explained by reference to its—perhaps sexual, perhaps pathologically morbid—origins. There is no question, in his view, that religious phenomena have their history and organic background. He nevertheless refuses to accept the assertions of "medical materialism" that the more exalted experiences of our lives are "nothing but" the expression of organic disposition and that physiology will one day be able to render a full account of them as, say, the "perverted action of various glands" (1958, 29). From the vantage point of reductionism, St. Paul was *just* an epileptic, St. Theresa *only* a hysteric, and St. Francis of Assisi *merely* a "hereditary degenerate."

James points out that it is all too easy to turn the tables on the argument that religion is "nothing but" the expression of one or another organic disposition. Organic disposition can no less persuasively be made to account for the phenomena of atheism than for those of religion. Scientific theories, moreover, are as fully conditioned organically as religious emotions (1958, 29–30). In fairness to the rules of logic and consistency, then, ruling out religious mind-states in view of their organic base entails an equivalent exclusion of science's claim to know reality.

James, thus dismissing "the bugaboo of morbid origin," says he will focus instead on the workings of religion as a whole, across the full range of its variations, in all its "varieties." His criterion for judging religion will not be its origins and early stages, "interesting as these may be," but exclusively its results, and in particular the results it is seen to produce in the lives of deeply religious individuals. James is interested, then, in religion's "more completely evolved and perfect forms" (1958, 22). He will accordingly concern himself with the writings of articulate individuals from among the "most accomplished in the religious life." James has little interest in "your ordinary religious believer," whose religion originates secondhand through tradition, imitation, and habit (1958, 24). It was indeed "religious geniuses," for whom religion was an "acute fever" rather than a "dull habit," who set the pattern, in James's view, for the merely communicated and more habitual forms of religion. It is to the original determining experiences of such religious geniuses to which James will attend in the present lectures.

James freely admits that religious leaders, perhaps even more than geniuses in other fields, have fallen prey to "abnormal psychical visitations" (1958, 24). He nevertheless points out that it would be unthinkable in the sciences to discredit a theory by reference to its originator's "neurotic disposition." The same, James argues, must hold for religious convictions.

Their value is to be ascertained not in view of the psychopathology of the individual who entertains them but by "spiritual judgments" bearing directly upon them (1958, 32). The standards James proposes for judging religious viewpoints are "immediate luminousness," "philosophical reasonableness," and "moral helpfulness." Expressed succinctly, James's general criterion for judging religious phenomena is "By their fruits ye shall know them, not by their roots" (1958, 34).

Circumscribing the Topic

Circumscribing his topic in Lecture II, James rejects the generality that all religion has a single essence or core, such as a feeling of dependence or fear. He regards religion, on the contrary, as highly personal and individual, with a variety of characters alternately assuming an equivalent importance (1958, 39). Given that there are truly different types of religious experience and that spiritual lives exhibit great diversity, he finds no ground for assuming at the core of every religious experience a single, distinct, and elementary religious sentiment. Religious objects, he remarks, arouse the variety of our many natural feelings (1958, 98).

James finds the "inner disposition" of the individual to form the center of personal religion (1958, 41). Personal religion moves the individual to initiate personal, as opposed to ritual, acts. A direct heart-to-heart relation is found to exist between the individual and his or her God, with the ecclesiastical institution and such mediating go-betweens as priests and sacraments occupying a decidedly secondary position. James says he will bypass the institutional and theological dimensions of religion in these lectures and limit himself, to the extent he can, "to personal religion pure and simple" (1958, 41). "Religion" means for James "the feelings, acts, and experiences of individual men in their solitude, so far as they apprehend themselves to stand in relation to whatever they may consider the divine" (1958, 42). And "the divine" means "only such a primal reality as the individual feels impelled to respond to solemnly and gravely, and neither by a curse nor a jest" (1958, 47).

The Personal Nature of Religion

James discusses the personal nature of religion in a variety of connections throughout the lectures. In this section are gathered together some of his views on this most central of topics. He points out that a positivist conception of science renounces the personal point of view in favor of an ideal of impersonality. Individual life and personality, on the basis of such an ideal, are "nothing but" the passive outcome of the impersonal and general workings of elementary physical and chemical forces, processes that natural science has been most adept at mastering (1958, 105; compare above, "Totalitarian Pretensions"). Subjective elements of experience are suppressed in a scientistic account of this sort in favor of objective, impersonal factors. But those individuals undergoing religious experience have always reported the personal or subjective dimension as a prominent factor in it. A positivist philosophy of science is thus led to argue that religion is obsolete, that it represents a stage in human development that enlightened humanity has now outgrown (in favor of science), and that religion is a mere anachronistic survival (1958, 371).

Rejection of the View That Religion Is Obsolete

James concedes that our ancestors did indeed confuse facts with dreams, hallucinations, and cock-and-bull stories (1958, 374). It is pointed out, however, that it is only recently that the distinction between conjecture and fact, the personal and the impersonal, was first suspected or conceived at all. James says it is hardly to be expected that our ancestors could have anticipated the results of modern science. Nor could our predecessors have found a more promising avenue to the knowledge of nature, he argues, than its richer animistic elements (1958, 376). He points out that the religious individual has always favored the personal over the impersonal. What excites the religious person about the sun is not impersonal abstractions about its physical nature but the personal meaning it holds, the beauty and promise of the dawn, for example. James insists that the same holds for religious individuals to this day. They are not impressed by the physical laws things obey but by "the terror and beauty of phenomena," "the 'sublimity' of the stars," and the thunder's "voice" (1958, 376). Even today the devout individual says that he or she meets God in solitude and that God is always there to provide the support needed.

The "survival theory" of religious phenomena answers, "Pure anachronism!" (1958, 376). But James, deeming the impersonality of the scientific attitude shallow, rejects the theory that religion is obsolete. He knows full well that religion has always emphasized the personal and richer aspects of life, but it is precisely such personal and private phenomena that he considers to be realities in the most complete sense (1958, 376–77).

James argues that the general and the impersonal are symbols of reality, not reality itself. The reality of each individual's destiny and subjective experience—reality in the complete sense, in James's view—is bypassed when exclusive stress is placed on impersonal factors. Menu entries are symbols of reality. "Sirloin steak" is not a steak but refers to a steak, and not to a particular steak but to any of a number of steaks in the restaurant's kitchen. James says that insisting on the sole validity of the objective and the general is like saying we must content ourselves forever with the menu of reality, with symbols of reality, rather than reality itself. Interpreting reality with all the "various feelings of the individual pinch of destiny" left out, James says, is like serving the menu for the meal (1958, 377).

James insists, then, that our description of the world retain its individual aspects. He thinks we become profound precisely when we entertain questions of individual destiny, with everything these questions imply (1958, 378). Our responsibility is with our private destiny. Such concern James defines as a religious one, and such religious concern, he says, plays a crucial and irreplaceable part in life.

The Primacy of Personal Religion

James's interest in these lectures is with personal religion; with original—*the* original—religious experiences; with the firsthand experiences of individuals. He presses the distinction between religion as an "individual personal function" and religion as an "institutional, corporate, or tribal product" (1958, 261). He points out that the word "religion" can refer either to a personal experience or to an ecclesiastical institution. Many, however, take the word only in its institutional sense. It happens often enough, then, that the very mention of "religion" serves to trigger the image of a particular church and certain of its associates, along with immediate thoughts of hypocrisy, superstition, meanness, and tyranny (1958, 262). Unaware that "religion" need not refer to a church, many denounce religious phenomena quite in general. It is important to note that in these lectures James almost always uses "religion" in its personal sense and hardly ever in its institutional sense.

James generalizes along the following lines about the historical development of churches. Personal contact with the divine is what originally gives the founders of religion their power. A genuine, firsthand, personal religious experience is the primary thing. Religious geniuses spontaneously attract followers (1958, 261). The situation tends to develop naturally in the direction of increased organization and formalization, and the ecclesiastical institution is born. But then politics and "the lust of dogmatic rule" are likely to make their entrance and "contaminate the originally innocent thing" (1958, 262).

When in the course of time new original religious experience occurs, it appears as unorthodox to the established church, which, according to James, was born of just such experience. Should the teaching that becomes attached to the new experience spread, it is recognized as a definite heresy and is condemned. If it triumphs, the new doctrine becomes the established ecclesiastical wisdom. But then has come into being another institution like the one overcome. "The day of inwardness is over: The spring is dry." The members of the new church live a secondhand religion and "stone the prophets in their turn" (1958, 263). The new church will try to stifle any fresh manifestation of the spontaneous religious spirit. And so it goes. James holds that charges against religion should be leveled not against religion proper—personal experiential religion—but against "religion's practical partner, the spirit of corporate dominion" (1958, 263).

In the development of religion, then, the individual experience of the divine is held to be primary, and organized religion secondary (1958, 42). Theological formulas (dogmas) are thus viewed as deriving from religion's deeper source; religious ideas are subordinate to religious feeling (1958, 329). "The spontaneous intellect of man," James writes, "always defines the divine which it feels in ways that harmonize with its temporary intellectual prepossessions" (1958, 346). It is James's hope that his inquiries in these lectures into personal religion will yield a number of general formulations acceptable to other researchers of similar open mind. James thus intends to play a part in the establishment of a "science of religion" (1958, 331). The general facts he hopes to discover are to be derived from the richness of primary personal religious experience and not from the secondarily generated myths, superstitions, creeds, and theologies of the various religious denominations.

The General Nature and Function of Religion

James begins his third lecture, "The Reality of the Unseen," by characterizing the religious attitude in broad and general terms as the belief that an "unseen order" exists and that our highest good lies in achieving harmony with this order (1958, 58). The seen world, from the religious point of view, stands in a relationship of dependence upon the unseen order. James remarks that the psychology of his day supposes that an original knowledge of reality is gained only through the five senses. But he discovers in human consciousness the experience of an unseen dimension, a "sense of reality, a feeling of objective presence, a perception of something 'there'" that is deeper and more general than the experience of reality provided by sense experience (1958, 61). James argues, moreover, that contact with this unseen reality, which is to say, religion, has effects on the individual's life. "Spiritual energy" becomes active, and "spiritual work" is done (1958, 361). Religion excites, adding a new zest to life, expanding personality, renewing the powers of life, and giving a new meaning and glory to the common things of life (1958, 381). The religious individual attains a feeling of safety and peace. Love governs interpersonal relations.

Yielding to the unseen "objective presence" is seen to lead to an attitude of joy (1958, 73). James comments that religion has had far more to do in the course of the centuries with joy than with fear—which is not to deny the perennial role of fear, or of sadness and personality contraction, in religion broadly considered (1958, 73–74). James remarks that truly religious individuals never experience the service of the highest reality as a burden (1958, 49). The great Christian saints, for example, actively accepted the universe. No mere Stoical agreement, theirs was a passionate assent to reality. This marks a very important difference, in James's eyes, between religious individuals and everyone else. Religion confers an enchantment on life that nothing else can. James declares this extra dimension of emotion, this enthusiastic espousal, to be a positive meaning of religion (1958, 54). Religion, rather than the manifestation of one or another particular emotion (see above, "Circumscribing the Topic"), thus turns out to be the very "excitement of emotion" itself, the excitement of vital positivity, of what James terms the "yes-function."

Religious happiness, James remarks, is characteristically no escape: "It cares no longer for escape" (1958, 55). The religious attitude, rather, is sacrificial. In the final analysis, he insists, our dependence on the universe is absolute. Humans have no choice but to sacrifice and to surrender in one way or another. The positive espousal of surrender and sacrifice that is seen to occur in the religious life thus "makes easy and felicitous what in any case is necessary" (1958, 56). And, rather than causing sadness and resignation, religion brings happiness. James thus sees religion as playing a vital role in human life, a role it alone can. If we disregard theological affirmations and view religion as a purely personal and subjective experience, religion is seen to have had an extraordinary influence and endurance throughout history. James believes that, for these reasons, religion serves as one of humanity's most important "biological functions" (1958, 382). Religion brings richness to life—the religious impulse is indeed said to be the very love of life itself. The total absence of faith, of religious feeling, on the other hand, is said to spell collapse (1958, 381).

Healthy-Minded and Morbid-Minded Religion

James draws a contrast in Lectures IV through VII between "The Religion of Healthy-Mindedness" (Lectures IV and V) and "The Sick Soul" (Lectures VI and VII). This contrast serves to lead into a discussion of "The Divided Self, and the Process of Its Unification" in Lecture VIII and a treatment of "Conversion" in Lectures IX and X. "Healthy-mindedness" is James's term for that tendency that sees all things only as good (1958, 83). States of high religious excitement, "invasive moral states and passionate enthusiasms," he says, make it simply impossible for some individuals to experience evil. The ordinary distinction between good and evil seems to be swallowed up in these lives "in an omnipotent excitement which engulfs the evil" (1958, 84). Walt Whitman, who is seen to have excluded "all contractile elements" from his writings and to have voiced only feelings "of the expansive order," is cited as exemplifying this healthy-mindedness incapable of apprehending evil (1958, 80–81).

Exactly opposite to such healthy-minded minimizing of evil is a morbid-minded maximizing of it. "Morbid-mindedness," James remarks, discovers life's evil aspects to be of its very essence and holds that the world is best understood when these aspects are given their full due (1958, 114). For morbid-mindedness, sin and evil abound, and feelings of guilt, sadness, hopelessness, and fear predominate. The morbid-minded assessment of reality discovers only failure everywhere. Individuals plagued with morbid-mindedness dwell on their mistakes and misdeeds, their vocational inadequacies and possibilities lost. "Every pound of flesh exacted," James writes, "is soaked with all its blood" (1958, 119). A style of experiencing that finds human nature to be rooted in failure, moreover, is painfully aware of the fact that old age and its infirmities have the last word and that we are in the end, every last one of us, mercilessly blotted out. The cases James considers in this connection alternately reveal "the vanity of mortal things," "the sense of sin," and "the fear of the universe" (1958, 136).

Healthy-minded individuals, their world a "one-storied affair," need to be born just once. The sick soul, by contrast, to gain peace, has to be born twice. The world of the twice-born, James remarks, is a "double-storied mystery" (1958, 140). The morbid-minded individual, knowing in the depth of his or her being that natural good has simply too many enemies, finds it necessary to lose his or her natural life in order to participate in the spiritual life. In brief, while certain individuals are seen to have been born with a harmonious inner constitution, the character of the twice-born seems to be psychologically grounded in a constitution that is incompletely unified (1958, 141).

A religiously inclined individual, possessed of a sensitive conscience and besieged by a chaos of competing higher and lower tendencies, is said to undergo, during the difficult period of attaining a unified personality, an unhappiness characterized by a sense of inner wrongness, worthlessness, guilt, and of standing in "false relations" to his or her Creator (1958, 143). Unification, on the other hand, once achieved, is seen to usher in enormous happiness and relief, and never more so than when the unification is of a specifically religious character. James says the process of unification often transforms, easily and successfully, intolerable misery into deep and enduring happiness (1958, 146). Something—"a faith," "an excitement," "a force that re-infuses the positive willingness to live" (1958, 155)—wells up inside and gets the better part of sadness.

While healthy-mindedness considers the morbid-minded way of "the sick soul" to be diseased, morbid-mindedness finds healthy-minded optimism to be shallow and blind. Giving his own overall assessment of the contrasted attitudes, James finds morbid-mindedness to be closer to the full range of human experience. The healthy-minded turning away from evil, while more than satisfactory in good times, may indeed fail to serve, given a tragic turn of events (1958, 137). James adds that it might turn out that evil facts are our one access to some of reality's deepest truths (1958, 138). James points out that evil events are in any case as genuine a part of reality as good ones. The most complete religions, in his view, will therefore be the ones in which the pessimistic elements are the most fully developed (1958, 139). Buddhism and Christianity are the best known of these. Both emphasize deliverance and the attainment of rebirth by way of a death of sorts.

Conversion

James points out that the process of unification, which may come about either gradually or suddenly, has been called "being converted" and, alternatively, "receiving grace" and "experiencing religion." To say that someone is converted means that once peripheral religious ideas now take center stage. Everything else recrystallizing around them, religious aims thus come to form the "habitual center" of "personal energy" of the individual undergoing conversion (1958, 162). Such a change in personal equilibrium is seen to be intensely individual.

James points out that merely passing through a crisis of sudden conversion does not certify "twice-bornness." The truly patient and selfless "child of God," he says, may indeed never have passed through such a crisis at all (1958, 192). The unequivocally "genuine child of God," in his view, is "the saint" (see below, "The Characteristics and Value of Saintliness"), not "the instantaneous crisis convert."

The sudden conversion experience, James remarks, be its "fruits for life" truly outstanding or largely insignificant, permanent or transient, is nevertheless always of an "extraordinary momentousness" to the individual undergoing it. Conversion experiences are filled in their occurrence, on the one hand, with feelings of personal powerlessness and bankruptcy and, on the other, with a sense of control by a "higher power" (sense of grace), accompanied by feelings of peace, harmony, and "a willingness to be." Worry is replaced by the sense that all is well. "A passion of willingness, of acquiescence, of admiration," "a sense of clean and beautiful newness," and "the ecstasy of happiness" are all said to characterize the conversion experience (1958, 199, 203).

James is of the opinion that the discovery of the subconscious mind was an event of the greatest importance for the science of psychology (1958, 188). The fact of the subconscious mind is said to mean the existence, at least in some individuals, not only of consciousness but also of a set of thoughts, feelings, and memories outside of consciousness altogether. It means, in other words, that there is more life in our total "mind" than we are ever aware of (1958, 386). As James remarks in another context, "My present field of consciousness is a center surrounded by a fringe that shades insensibly into a subconscious more. . . . Every bit of us at every moment is part and parcel of a wider self" (1971a, 259).

According to James, certain contents are elaborated in the subconscious mind, only later making their entry into consciousness. Such incursions into consciousness, whose source the subject may never suspect, assume a variety of forms: impulses to act, inhibitions of action, delusions, obsessive ideas, and hallucinations (1958, 189). James thinks that subconscious mental activities must be regarded as conscious facts of some sort: that is, that the subconscious mind is a sub-*consciousness*.

James believes it is the subconscious that takes the lead in the sudden shifting of personal centers of energy in evidence in conversion experiences. He says that the new center of personal energy that takes over and around which everything comes to recrystallize is "incubated subconsciously," the results "hatching out" at full term (1958, 172, 186). A conspiring of the higher and the lower emotions is often found to take place: a subconscious ripening of the higher, happy, and excited mind, simultaneously with an exhaustion of the lower, despairing, and anxious mind. James remarks that what characterizes the sudden, as opposed to the gradual, convert is not—at least not necessarily—the favor of a divine miracle but the psychological peculiarity of a large region in which subliminal mental work can take place and from which invasions abruptly upsetting the balance of the "primary consciousness" can proceed (1958, 191).

Psychology and religion, James points out, are in perfect agreement up to this point. Both accept forces outside the conscious mind that bring redemption to life (1958, 173). Psychology defines these forces as "subconscious" and speaks of their workings, for example, in terms of an "incubation." Psychology neither supposes nor requires that these forces transcend the life of the individual, while Christian theology does. James points out that one of the tasks of a science of religion is to find a mediating term between science and religion—in order to account, for example, for the impression of outside influence conveyed by "instantaneous crisis conversion." James feels that such a term is available in the psychologist's concept of the subconscious self (1958, 385–86). On the one hand, this concept has given science an important access to the understanding of primary religious phenomena. On the other, support is given to the claims of the various institutional religions that the individual is influenced by something outside himself or herself, which is to say, outside consciousness (1958, 195).

James points out that the idea of the subconscious does not necessarily exclude the notion of "a higher penetration" (1958, 195). But, if there is a miraculous operation of God's grace, James thinks it likely that such grace makes use of the "subliminal door" (1958, 215). James's ideas on the subconscious are further considered below ("Lower Mysticism," "Religious Experience and the Subconscious," and "Conclusions").

The Characteristics and Value of Saintliness

Lectures XI, XII, and XIII are devoted to the topic of saintliness. James finds there to be a common core of characteristics displayed by saints, that is, by those beneficiaries of grace who live in a relatively permanent state of spiritual excitement, of yes-saying that dissolves every cowardly, stingy, and lazy "no" (1958, 212). Saints, living in the religious center of personal energy, are described as motivated by spiritual enthusiasm. They are, James comments, like a breed apart. A composite picture of saintliness, said to be identical in all religions, contains the following features: (1) the sense of living in a world that is wider than the usual one, the immediate experience of a "higher power"; (2) voluntary and passionate abandonment of self to this "higher power," known to be in "friendly continuity" with one's individual life; (3) a diminution of self, accompanied by great elation and freedom; and (4) a shifting of balance toward "loving and harmonious feelings," toward the "yes" and away from the "no" (1958, 216–18).

Saints are seen, in consequence of these "inner conditions," to display ascetic harshness toward themselves, strength of soul, purity, and charity. They are magnanimous, humble, and at peace with themselves. Geared to doing or being, saints often discard their possessions. James remarks that such lives are freer than lives grounded in having. With every dollar we have to guard, he comments, "sloth and cowardice creep in" (1958, 250). The religious ecstasy experienced by saints is said to be a unifying state of mind, in which "the sand and grit of the selfhood" tend to disappear and tenderness to predominate (1958, 221). The joyousness displayed by saints is said to be an expansive emotion. This joyousness is self-forgetful, tender, and kindly. The love manifest in the lives of saints may be so unifying as to abolish all the usual barriers.

The essence of the twice-born philosophy is found to be in evidence in saintly asceticism. Asceticism, James says, is an expression of the conviction that there is something truly wrong with the world in its present state and that something has to be done about this wrongness, beginning with oneself (1958, 280–81). James remarks that the characteristics of saintliness form a cluster that seems "to flow from the sense of the divine as from its psychological source" (1958, 285). These characteristics are thus found to possess clear religious significance.

James, passing from description to appraisal, discusses "The Value of Saintliness" in Lectures XIV and XV. James reminds the reader that his primary concern is with private religious experience and not with religion's institutional forms (1958, 262). Disavowing final and absolute knowledge in the religious sphere and claiming instead only "reasonable probability," James gives his assessment of personal religion in terms of the fruits found to bear in the lives of saints (1958, 260–61). His summary conclusion is that the results yielded by religious experience at its best are the best things human history has to record (1958, 207). It is precisely in the name of religious ideals, he says, that charity, trust, patience, bravery, and devotion have evidenced themselves in the annals of history at their highest pitch. James asserts that "in a general way and on the whole," religion, judged by the criterion of its results in the lives of saints, deserves a towering place in history. The cluster of saintly characteristics, he says, is "indispensable to the world's welfare" (1958, 290).

Saints are said to be perceived for what they are. Their strength and greatness, their goodness, and their sense of mystery about things are apparent in everything they undertake. They are bigger than life. James finds the "strong men of the world" to be dry, hard, and crude by comparison (1958, 290). He says saints increase the amount of goodness in the world. Believing in the sacredness of all human life, they are said to be forerunners leading the way. Because "the world is not yet with them," saints often strike people as preposterous (1958, 277). Saints nevertheless kindle a fire in others, stirring to life otherwise dormant "potentialities of goodness." Without the trust in the worth of human life manifested by saints, James writes, "the rest of us would lie in spiritual stagnancy" (1958, 277). Saints are thus seen to constitute a "genuinely creative social force." James holds religious or saintly experience to be a natural experience, like fear, for example, and, as such, to be potentially available to all.

Mystical States of Consciousness

James discusses "Mysticism" in Lectures XVI and XVII. He proposes that personal religious experience has its "root and center" in mystical states of consciousness (1958, 292). Given James's preoccupation with personal religion, mystical states thus serve as a vital center for his entire project. Mystical experiences are described as both real and of paramount importance. Mystical states excite the "yes-function." They leave behind a profound sense of their significance, changing inner lives long after their occurrence. Mystical states of consciousness are said to share a number of features: (1) ineffability—one has to experience these states oneself to gain a true appreciation of their value; (2) transiency—they last perhaps half an hour, almost never more than two hours; (3) passivity—the will in abeyance, one is seized by a "higher power"; and (4) noetic quality—there occurs an insight into depths of truth otherwise unavailable (1958, 292–93).

The final characterization of mystical experiences as noetic locates them among states of knowledge. Mystical experiences are said to convey a strong impression of being revelations of new levels of truth (see below, "Religious Experience and Knowledge"). James comments that mystical knowledge of God is patterned more after immediate feeling than after abstract logical judging; insight into mystical truth is more like perceptual than conceptual knowledge. Mystical knowing would be perception of a special sort, however, for the mystic insists that the senses play not the least part in the distinctive truth attained. Mystical knowledge, having no specific conceptual or sensible content of its own, is thus said to be neither intellectual nor sense knowledge. Mystical states "repudiate articulate self-expression." They are nevertheless said to "assert a pretty distinct theoretic drift" (1958, 319). James remarks that most mystical experiences support the philosophical positions of optimism and monism. Irrespective of variations in geographical location and theological belief, James finds the mystical tradition to speak with one voice down the centuries.

Religious mysticism pure and simple involves a sudden realization of the immediate presence of God. The limited individual, upon such a realization, feels himself or herself to be absorbed by the unlimited, to be immersed in the "infinite ocean of God" (1958, 305). As is written in the Upanishads, "An invisible and subtle essence is the Spirit of the whole universe. That is Reality. That is Truth. THOU ART THAT" (Mascaro 1965, 118). The falling of the usual barriers between the individual and the Absolute, James remarks, is "the great mystic achievement" (1958, 321). The universe is said to be experienced as a "living Presence," and God to be "here" (1958, 307). The eternal is experienced as now. James points out that the whole thrust of mystical experience, in close kinship to "twice-bornness," is decidedly antinaturalistic in its thrust.

James describes the transition from ordinary to mystical states of consciousness as going "from a less into a more," from a smallness to a vastness, and from a state of unrest to one of rest (1958, 319). He writes of this experience elsewhere: "There are . . . possibilities [in us] that take our breath away, of another kind of happiness and power, based on giving up our own will and letting something higher work for us, and these seem to show a world wider than either physics or philistine ethics can imagine. Here is a world in which all is well" (1971a, 266).

Mystical states as thus described are remote from the everyday life of most people. Let us review, then, the more familiar experiences James cites as having features in common with mystical states (1958, 294–96). Among these more ordinary plunges into mystical consciousness are the feeling that one has been through an experience before (the déja vu experience), the deep emotions produced by music, and the sense that everything in life is meaningful. Nature, moreover, is seen to possess a special power to awaken mystical moods—a sense of awe, for example, before its majesty (1958, 302–303). A further step into mystical experience is the consciousness produced by "intoxicants and anesthetics," especially alcohol. James thinks that alcohol holds the power it does over humanity precisely because of its ability to stimulate our mystical faculties. "Sobriety diminishes, discriminates, and says no; drunkenness expands, unites, and says yes. . . . The drunken consciousness is one bit of the mystic consciousness" (1958, 297). Drunkenness, "the great exciter of the yes-function," seems to unite us, for a time, with truth. James nevertheless remarks that, on the whole, alcohol is a "degrading poisoning."

James further singles out nitrous oxide as a powerful stimulant of mystical consciousness. Experiences with this gas, he says, reveal that our ordinary conscious state is but one special kind of consciousness, and that other, entirely different forms of consciousness exist. Though we may be completely unaware of these other forms, James insists that any account of the universe that disregards them must prove less than final (1958, 298; see below, "Religious Experience and Knowledge"). James says that his personal use of nitrous oxide furnished him with an insight to which he ascribes a sort of metaphysical significance. The essence of this insight he describes as an experience of the reconciliation of the world's universally troublesome opposites: the overtaking of the inferior opposite by its nobler and better partner, the monistic absorption of evil into good.

Lower Mysticism

James remarks that religious mysticism—"religious mysticism proper"—is only half of the story of mysticism. "The other half has no accumulated traditions," he says, "except those which the textbooks on insanity supply" (1958, 326). James thus indicates a "lower or diabolical mysticism" that makes its appearance in certain forms of psychosis. Both higher and lower forms of mysticism are said to arise from the subconscious. James points out that there is in lower mysticism the same sense of being controlled by powers outside the individual, the same voices and visions and missions, and the same sense of revelation and importance. But pessimism, abandonment, and gloominess dominate, and the powers are unfriendly to life. Lower mysticism, James says, is like classical or higher mysticism turned upside down.

The subconscious, James comments, houses all sorts of things, both "the snake and the seraph." Origination there is no certification of worth. James insists that we must test and confront all that announces itself from the subconscious, as we do what presents itself through the senses. Critical intelligence is crucial.

Religious Experience and Knowledge

James thinks it probable that, at some point in their lives, religious individuals all went through a personal crisis in which they "saw the truth" (1958, 67). Such experiences are said to bring certainty and to have a powerful effect. They are as convincing as sense experience and generally much more convincing than logical argument (1958, 71–72). Rationalism is found to reject such "vague experiences" in favor of intellectual clarity and articulateness. But James thinks that the reasoned argument is secondary, that nonrational "instinct," feeling, the unreasoned—"our passional nature" of "The Will to Believe" (1956f)—is the deeper thing in us. "Instinct leads," he writes; "intelligence does but follow" (1958, 73).

James remarks that the world is interpreted by different individuals according to varying systems of ideas, yielding each time some "characteristic profit" (1958, 107). Science is grounded in reason, religion in mystical experience. He believes that science and religion, as different as they are from one another, both provide genuine access to an incredibly rich universe (1958, 107; see above, "Selectivity of the Mind").

Mystical states, experienced as insight into truth and indeed as important illuminations, are said to provide a direct challenge to the authority of nonmystical consciousness, even to the point of breaking that authority down. James remarks that mystical states show rationalistic consciousness—consciousness grounded in the senses and intellect—to be but one form of consciousness. Mystical states, like the perceptions of worldly objects, are experienced as direct "perceptions" of fact. James remarks that mystical experience may very well open upon a greater and more inclusive world, thus constituting a perspective on reality superior to that of our ordinary experience (1958, 327).

Mystical states thus point to the possibility of "other orders of truth" altogether (1958, 324). It may just be, James suggests, that the supernaturalism ("belief in an unknown world" and in its significance for our life—James 1956b, 51) and the optimism conveyed by mystical experiences are "the truest of insights into the meaning of this life" (1958, 328). James similarly comments in another context that our specifically religious experiences, presenting us with the "strangest possibilities and perspectives," suggest that our ordinary experience "may be only a fragment of real human experience" and that an intellectual logic that ignores such experiences will never be able to "reach completely adequate conclusions" (1971a, 266–67). No matter what our final judgment on the truth afforded by mystical states of consciousness, James says that, at the very least, they provide us with hypotheses. The wider world glimpsed in mystical experience would have its heavenly regions, but its hellish ones as well (see above, "Lower Mysticism").

James undertakes to determine whether objective truth can be ascribed to the sense of divine presence experienced by the greatest saints (1958, 329). His conclusion is that mystical states, though "entirely willing to corroborate religion," are altogether too private in their "utterances to be able to claim a universal validity" (1958, 329). Private mystical revelations, while "absolutely authoritative" for those who have them, carry no authority for those who do not. The religious revelations so convincing to the mystic are simply unable to yield a generally convincing statement of their truth. Thus, with regard to the truth of religion, such considerations leave James not with the certainty of objective knowledge but with a "maybe."

Truth and the Task of Religious Philosophy

James deals with certain questions of religious "Philosophy" in Lecture XVIII. He insists once again upon the primacy of feeling over intellect in religious matters. Regarding the proofs of God's existence, for instance, he comments that people who already believe in God find these arguments convincing, while those who don't do not (1958, 334).

James concludes this lecture by asserting it to be beyond the capabilities of intellect (philosophy) to assure us of the objective truth or falsity of religious phenomena (compare above, "Religious Experience and Knowledge"). Conceptual processes, he says, class and interpret facts but can neither produce facts nor reproduce their individuality. "There is always a *plus*, a *this-ness*," he writes, "which feeling alone can answer for. Philosophy in this sphere is thus a secondary function" (1958, 346). He simply does not share with traditional intellectualism the belief that concepts are the ultimate key to reality. He thus reaches the conclusion that philosophy, as "critical science of religion," is left with the task of mediation, of effecting a consensus on the phenomena of religion. Such a task is to be fulfilled by extending the efforts of the present lectures, that is, by a further separating out of the common and essential elements in religion from its individual and accidental ones.

James has reached the conclusion in these lectures that neither an all-too-private mysticism nor a philosophy that trades in concepts can provide objective certainty in the religious sphere. Such certainty, he says, is apparently forever beyond our reach. But absolute certainty is not what James is after in any case. His interest from the outset and all along has been in personal experience, not in the impersonal and finally convincing formula, the general argument to be made, in the concreteness of individual destiny, not in the abstractness of merely signified reality. We recall at this juncture the positive evaluation that James, applying his criterion of fruitfulness, has placed on the personal religion of saints. "We have wound our way back," he writes, "after our excursion through mysticism and philosophy, to where we were before: the uses of religion, its uses to the individual who has it, and the uses of the individual himself to the world, are the best arguments that truth is in it" (1958, 348). He is quite content to return to his "empirical" philosophy: the true is what works well on the whole. He thus ends where he begins, with the truth of life and feeling.

Religious Experience and the Subconscious

James takes up "Other Characteristics" of religious experience in Lecture XIX. Among these other features are the esthetic dimension, prayer, and the subconscious. In view of the importance of the topic for a psychology of religion, in this section are reviewed James's further reflections on the subconscious (see also above, "Conversion" and "Lower Mysticism," and below, "Conclusions").

The subconscious is the larger region of the mind. Invasions into consciousness are said to be prepared there. We don't experience the hidden source of such invasions, which simply confront us. All sorts of things are said to originate in the subconscious: intuitions, hypotheses, hallucinations, delusions, fixed ideas, hysterical accidents, and telepathic cognitions. The subconscious is the source of dreams. And it is said to be the fountainhead of much that nourishes religion (1958, 366). Religious (mystical) experiences originate in the subconscious. Incursions from the subconscious take place in conversion and prayer. James speculates that the opening, or door, to the subconscious must be especially wide in religious individuals. All in all, emanations from the subconscious are seen to have exercised a powerful influence on religious history.

James remarks that it is virtually impossible to find a religious leader, regardless of background, who has not experienced "automatisms" of one sort or another: visions, voices, raptures, and guiding impressions (1958, 362). Religious geniuses, sensitive individuals that they are, are said to be particularly susceptible to such invasions from the subconscious. A voice from heaven or a vision makes a powerful impression, increasing conviction and corroborating belief (1958, 362). The sense of being used by a higher power, James points out, has been called "inspiration."

Conclusions

James devotes Lecture XX to "Conclusions." Religion's essential is once again located in feeling, in "an excitement of the cheerful and expansive order which renews our vital powers," in the "love of life" (1958, 381–82). When an intellectual content comes into association with religious feeling, it is likely to get stamped with truth, which, says James, explains the passionate devotion of religious people everywhere to the smallest details of their varying creeds (1958, 382).

James concludes that the world's religious creeds share a common nucleus (1958, 383). This common deliverance consists in what James has called "twice-bornness": salvation from a sense of wrongness about oneself. In the more developed minds studied by James, the experience of salvation assumes a mystical coloring. The religious individual experiences the transition from a less to a more. When salvation—the solution—comes, the individual is said to identify his or her real being with the higher and better part of himself or herself undergoing development in the subconscious.

"The believer is continuous," James writes in "A Pluralistic Universe," "with a wider self from which saving experiences flow in" (1971a, 267). The individual realizes that this wider and higher self with which one is continuous is itself "continuous with a More of the same quality" at work in the universe outside oneself, that one is able to maintain a working relationship with this More outside, and that this More holds the promise of salvation when one's "lower being has gone to pieces" (1958, 384). James comments further in "A Pluralistic Universe," "Those who have had such experiences . . . have had their vision and they *know*—that is enough—that we inhabit an invisible spiritual environment from which help comes, our soul being mysteriously one with a larger world whose instruments we are" (1971a, 267).

James describes salvation as the surrender of one's lower being, the experience of redemption as a gift coming from an outside helping power, and immediate union with that power. The experience is, all in all, one of reconciliation and unification. Differences in detail, attributable in part to theological reflection, are said to mark the various institutional creeds. James remarks that not all theologies agree that "the More" is personal in quality. All agree, however, that "the More" exists, that it really does something, and that this something is for the better when one gives in to it.

James hypothesizes that "the More," this wider and higher self contacted in religious experience, "whatever it may be on its farther side," on this side is "the subconscious continuation" of our conscious life (1958, 386). James thus asserts that it is the higher faculties of the subconscious mind that are at work in religious experience (see above, "Conversion," "Lower Mysticism," and "Religious Experience and the Subconscious"). This agrees with the widespread belief in a power higher than the conscious individual. James points out that psychology, with its concept of the subconscious, and religion, with its belief in the supernatural, are thus in agreement that the experience of salvation is accomplished by forces outside consciousness.

James's personal "creed" is that there indeed exists a dimension of existence different from that yielded by our senses and intellect. The subconscious is said to plunge into this other dimension. He believes that this unseen or mystical dimension produces effects, first in us and then through us in the everyday world around us. Higher energies flow into our life in mystical states of consciousness and transform our personality (1958, 389). The inner change for the better leads to changed conduct in the external world and to corresponding changes in that world. According to James, that which works effects in another reality must itself be termed a reality. The mystical world is thus seen to be a real one. Mystical experience, no less than ordinary consciousness, is said to be real and to have a significance.

James uses the commonly accepted name for the supreme reality: "God." He believes that we humans and God have business with each other and that we become better or worse to the extent that we meet or do not meet the demands God makes on our lives. If we are open to God, our deepest destiny takes a turn for the better, and we are fulfilled. Applying his pragmatic criterion, James argues that, in view of the real effects God produces, God is real (1958, 389). God's real effects are said to be exerted on our personal centers of energy and through these on the external world. Mystical revelations may be private, but, James points out, their consequences for life are not. God may be unseen, but the effects God produces in the world are not.

The "maybe" of religion's truth is thus turned, on pragmatic—and not objective—grounds, into a decided "yes" on James's part: "Divine facts exist" (1958, 391). The world of our present consciousness, he affirms, is but one of many worlds of consciousness that exist. Our ordinary conscious lives are limited forms of awareness within a larger conscious whole. We are said to be already one with this larger consciousness, with God. James analogizes that we humans stand in the same relation to the total universe as our pets do to us. Our dogs and cats are engaged in events whose significance transcends their understanding. We, too, are said to be engaged, without our comprehension, in "the wider life of things." James records elsewhere his firm disbelief that human experience is the "highest form of experience extant in the universe" (1963b, 131).

James's "yes," transcending the categories of intellect, is a matter of faith. Religious truth has a personal, not conceptual, character. "The total expression of human experience," he says, urges us on to an affirmation of life's religious dimension. We may well believe, he writes in another context, "on the proofs that religious experience affords, that higher powers exist and are at work to save the world on ideal lines similar to our own" (1963b, 131–32).

Reality is still in the process of being decided, in James's view, and we humans have a part in deciding it (compare above, "Selectivity of the Mind"). We are God's partners in determining the contours of what is yet to come. Human activity, energized by belief, is a creative force in reality, codeciding the future course of an unfinished universe. James writes elsewhere, "To cooperate with [God's] creation by the best and rightest response seems all [God] wants of us. In such co-operation with his purposes . . . must lie the real meaning of our destiny" (1956b, 141).

EVALUATION AND CONCLUSIONS

"The Will to Believe" has an existential ring to it: "to choose not to choose is a choice" (Maurice Merleau-Ponty), and faith is a legitimate decision arising out of one's total being (feeling). James thus elevates the rights of the individual above the "truth" of the "experts." His emphasis on the personal and individual, feeling character of faith, moreover, taken together with his emphasis on the essentially active, determining character of the mind, has affinities with the contemporary hermeneutic preference for the diverse and the plural. While thus emphasizing the role of subjectivity in all human undertakings, James's concern with the world's multiple possibilities, coherences, and legitimacies nevertheless leaves no doubt as to his empiricist faith in truth. James insists he is not a skeptic: the determination of truth may be personal and practical, and truth may not preexist in itself, but truth there is.

James's rejection of the preeminence of mere concept is an important one. Not dry and abstract, truth is a process in which the human being is passionately involved. Not eternally finished, truth is ever to be determined. Priority in life and religion is thus ceded to feeling and becoming. Subordinating intellect and preconception to feeling and faith, James clears an important path for experiential approaches in general in the psychological study of religion.

For James, the dismantling of positivism teems with practical consequences. Were positivism true, faith in the divine would be impossible, with determinable bad consequences in the world. The positivist's exclusive devotion to objective facts, moreover, necessitates a reductionistic psychology of religion. James rejects any system of thought whose chosen preconceptions make the very real facts of experience, religious or otherwise, vanish before one's very eyes. Finally, he insists, positivists aren't themselves passive recorders of evident facts but men and women of faith actively shaping their results.

James makes an important distinction in *The Varieties of Religious Experience* between personal and institutional religion. His conclusion, however, that authentic religiousness is essentially of a mystical-personal character seems unwarranted. Isn't there a valid religiousness more ordinary than the mystical? Haven't many members of institutional religion personalized their religion without being mystics in the narrow sense of the term? It would seem that there are different forms of genuine religiousness and that, here as elsewhere, pluralism is to be given preference.

James's notion of a culture-free religious (mystical) experience, moreover, is open to question. All human experience, permeated by language, would seem to bear a cultural stamp. If there is thus no uninterpreted experience, traditional theological formulas are integral, and not incidental, to the experience of the divine: they not only arise from such experience but shape it as well. Religious geniuses and reformers were introduced to their God through the language of their community. The experience of Jesus is not that of the Buddha; the Kingdom of God is not Nirvana; Christian love is not Buddhist compassion. While reducing religion to its sociocultural conditions fails to do justice to religion's proper meaning, it must nevertheless be recognized that religion always bears a cultural-historical stamp.

Allowing for the ambiguities and mysteriousness of existence, James gives the psychologist of religion room to breathe. He reproaches dogmatism wherever he finds it, scientific dogmatism and religious dogmatism alike. He defends the right of the individual to pursue an ideal of meaning and truth in the very nitty-gritty of life. Remarking that the "dumb region of heart" is "our deepest organ of communication with the nature of things," moreover, James points to a preconscious intelligence or openness to being. Feeling not only has its right, in James's view, but its light as well. James, with a voice truly his own, is remarkably contemporary.

REFERENCES

James, W. *The Principles of Psychology*, 2 vols. New York: Dover, 1950.

———. "The Dilemma of Determinism." In *The Will to Believe and Other Essays in Popular Psychology*, 145–83. New York: Dover, 1956a.

———. "Is Life Worth Living?" In *The Will to Believe and Other Essays in Popular Psychology*, 32–62. New York: Dover, 1956b.

———. "The Moral Philosopher and the Moral Life." In *The Will to Believe and Other Essays in Popular Psychology*, 184–215. New York: Dover, 1956c.

———. "Reflex Action and Theism." In *The Will to Believe and Other Essays in Popular Psychology*, 111–44. New York: Dover, 1956d.

———. "The Sentiment of Rationality." In *The Will to Believe and Other Essays in Popular Psychology*, 63–110. New York: Dover, 1956e.

———. "The Will to Believe." In *The Will to Believe and Other Essays in Popular Psychology*, 1–31. New York: Dover, 1956f.

——. *The Varieties of Religious Experience.* New York: New American Library, 1958.

——. "The Meaning of Truth." In *Pragmatism and Other Essays,* 133–184. New York: Washington Square Press, 1963a.

——. "Pragmatism." In *Pragmatism and Other Essays,* 1–132. New York: Washington Square Press, 1963b.

——. "Introduction." In *Collected Essays and Reviews,* ed. R. B. Perry, vi–xxv. New York: Russell and Russell, 1969.

——. "A Pluralistic Universe." In *Essays in Radical Empiricism and a Pluralistic Universe,* ed. R. B. Perry, 121–284. New York: Dutton, 1971a.

——. "Essays in Radical Empiricism." In *Essays in Radical Empiricism and a Pluralistic Universe,* ed. R. B. Perry, 3–120. New York: Dutton, 1971b.

Mascaro, J. (trans.). *The Upanishads.* New York: Penguin, 1965.

Pirsig, Robert M. *Lila: An Inquiry into Morals.* New York: Bantam, 1991.

2

+

Sigmund Freud

Religion is but a reflection of the dynamic conflicts between the ego, the id, and the superego.

—Sigmund Freud

Sigmund Freud (1856–1939), who once described himself as an "infidel Jew," firmly rejected the "material" truth of religion and its supernatural interventions, harboring a special dislike for the unthinking religion of the masses (1963[1919], 271). Freud was nevertheless drawn to the topic of religion time and again, treating of it at length in several of his writings and taking it up a last time shortly before his death in the book *Moses and Monotheism* (1967[1939]). Freud was a serious student of religion, moreover, developing elaborate and coherent psychological and historical accounts of it. His personal honesty and courage in this regard, as in others, are widely recognized.

Freud was emblematic of the positivism of his time. Early in his career, he espoused the ideal of accounting for all psychological processes objectively, in terms of physical and chemical processes. Humans are no more in a special category, he thought, than any other natural process. Copernicus denied that the sun revolves around the earth, Darwin that humans are an immediate creation of God, and now Freud that humans govern their own fate. Human actions, mechanistically driven by unconscious forces, are no more free than a pebble falling to earth.

Freud invokes causal factors from the past to explain human behavior. The more temporally remote the determining factor, moreover, the more powerful its influence is said to be. Events in childhood have a greater bearing on behavior than those of last week; events in the childhood of the species determine childhood events today; the first emergence of life on earth gave rise to the first and most fundamental of instincts, the instinct to cancel life out: "the aim of life is death." Behind this belief in the past's overwhelming hold on the present is Freud's belief that nature forever strives for the lowest possible degree of energy. Psychologically, this striving is the search for tension reduction and underlies both the pleasure principle and the death instinct. Life, like nature, runs backwards.

This theoretical bondage to the past notwithstanding, Freud offers individuals the therapeutic hope of a release from repression and, with that, a measure of psychic wholeness. He offers an analogous hope to humanity as a whole. But, first, religion will have to be given up—religion results, in Freud's view, from the perseverance in adulthood of childhood relations to the father. The future belongs to reason, according to Freud, not to faith. An early influence on Freud was Ludwig Feuerbach (1804–1872), who viewed God as a projection of everything of value in human nature.

Whatever one's final judgment on Freud's work, his legacy is enormous. We owe much of the way we think and talk today to him. It is because of Freud that the unconscious is a common cultural acquisition. Before post-modern deconstruction, moreover, was the Freudian "hermeneutics of suspicion" (Ricoeur 1970, 32). Challenges to Freud, of course, are legion in our day and have been for some time. But such challenges are precisely reactions to him. Freud was and remains a beginning. As is said, if he had never existed, we would have had to invent him.

Freud, as already suggested, explains the phenomena of religion through lingering childhood ties to the father. In this regard, Freud's efforts at a psychology of religion display a certain unity. Freud nevertheless presents us with several accounts of religion, which will be considered in turn in this chapter: religion as continuation of childhood ego-experiencing (see below, "Religion and the Oceanic Feeling"), religion as wish fulfillment (see below, "Religion as Illusion"), religion as compulsion (see below, "Religion as 'Universal Compulsive Neurosis'"), religion as historically motivated delusion (see below, "Religious Doctrines as Delusions"), and religion as service of the divine pair, Eros and Logos (see below, "Freud and Eros"). The first four views are explicitly Freud's own. The fifth is an interpretation based on Freud's developing theory of the destructive and constructive energies held to be everywhere at work in the universe.

RELIGION AND THE OCEANIC FEELING

Freud describes the "oceanic feeling" as a subjective feeling of an indissoluble bond, or oneness, with the whole of the universe, a feeling of something limitless (infinite) and a sensation of eternity (1962[1930], 12). The oceanic experience has also been called "mystical experience" (William James), "the experience of the self" (Carl Jung), "realization of the Supreme Identity" (Alan Watts), "cosmic consciousness" (Richard Bucke), and "peak experience" (Abraham Maslow).

Freud, who never doubted the origin of religion in the child's relationship with the father (see below, "Religion as Illusion" and "Religion as Historical Truth"), says he was troubled by the position of a number of thoughtful scholars that religious phenomena originate in the oceanic feeling (1962[1930], 12–13). Freud remarks that he was never able to discover anything like an oceanic feeling in himself. Nor, he remarks, does science find it easy to deal with something as intangible as an oceanic feeling. He surmises that this feeling is in fact subordinate to a thought—the thought of indissoluble oneness with the universe—which it accompanies and to which it is adequate (1962[1930], 12).

And so, the thought of oneness with the universe would be fundamental and original, and the feeling of oneness secondary. Freud the rationalist thus gives theoretical preference to ideational content over direct experience, to thought over feeling. Indeed, the whole idea that an immediate feeling gives individuals a suggestion of their connection with the universe, and that such is its very purpose, struck Freud as so strange that he undertook to give the oceanic feeling a genetic explanation: that is, an account in terms of its genesis.

Freud points out that there is ordinarily a more or less clear and sharp boundary between the ego and its surrounding world. Such, in any case, is how it is with adults. But an infant does not yet distinguish between the two. Rather, it is, says Freud, that the ego of an infant is all-embracing (1962[1930], 15). Ego and world are thus intimately connected in the experience of the infant. The ego is said to accomplish the "separation off of the external world from the ego" only later. Adult, or differentiated ego, feeling is much more limited than childhood ego feeling, then, "a shrunken residue" of a much more inclusive feeling (1962[1930], 15).

Freud has no difficulty acknowledging the existence of an oceanic feeling. It would be the persistence in some individuals of an earlier phase of ego feeling, the continuation alongside the adult ego, with its sharper and clearer boundaries, of the more inclusive and, indeed, all-embracing feeling of the childhood ego. Freud thus traces the oceanic feeling of infinity and eternity experienced by some adults back to a persisting earlier stage of ego feeling. He points out that a persistence of this sort is not unusual in the mental realm; what is primitive, he says, is often preserved alongside the "transformed vision," which originates in it (1962[1930], 15). He deems the ideas appropriate to such a persisting earlier phase of ego feeling to be precisely those of limitlessness and an immediate bond with the universe (1962[1930], 15).

It's not the existence of the oceanic feeling that Freud has difficulties with, but its interpretation. He is unable to bring himself to accept this feeling as the source of religious phenomena. A feeling has to be the expression of a strong need, in Freud's view, for it to be a source of energy. The child's need for the father's protection is such a strong need (and source of energy). Freud indeed says that there is no need in childhood stronger than that for fatherly protection (1962[1930], 19). Religious needs originate, according to Freud, in infantile weakness and helplessness and from "the longing for the father" engendered by such weakness and helplessness (see below, "Religion as Illusion"). The religious needs and feelings of adults are all said to center around and aim at the father.

Freud suspects that the oceanic feeling of oneness and the phenomena of religion were originally unconnected, linking up only later. The thought that we are one with the universe, the ideational content of the oceanic feeling, on the other hand, seems to him to be a "first attempt at a religious consolation," a bid at neutralizing the threatening dangers of the universe (1962[1930], 19). In summary, Freud's main points on the oceanic feeling and religion would appear to be the following. The oceanic feeling is not the source of the need for religion but the persistence of a developmentally earlier—undifferentiated—ego feeling, the feeling of the intimate bond between ego and world prior to their separation off from one another in the course of development. The persisting experience in some adults of an immediate bond with the environment, while originally devoid of religious significance, sometimes assumes a religious character later on, through the mediation of the idea or thought of such a bond.

Primary in the oceanic feeling is not the all-embracing childhood feeling, then, but the ideational content later coming into association with it and (incorrectly) identifying it as a literal oneness with the whole universe, as an actual immersion in the infinite and the eternal—that is, *as* the oceanic feeling. The thought of actual "oneness with the universe" is an attempt at "religious consolation" in the face of the manifold dangers of an uncaring universe. The persisting childhood feeling of oneness with the environment, while secondary to the thought of a literal bond with the universe, is nevertheless adequate to it. Hence the conjunction of feeling and idea, idea reinforcing itself and its ability to console by bestowing a religious interpretation on persisting feeling: "If I am one with the universe, even to the point of feeling my oneness with it, how can the universe be all that dangerous?" Logically, the sequence would be thus: Adult Weakness and Helplessness vis-à-vis a Threatening Universe → Religious Needs → Idea of a Consoling Bond between the Individual and the Universe → Association between Persisting Undifferentiated Ego Feeling and Consoling Idea of Oneness with the Universe.

RELIGION AS ILLUSION

Where William James goes to great length investigating personal or mystical religious experience, Freud disposes of the oceanic feeling and mysticism in a few pages, deeming it lacking in original religious significance. Where James investigates religious geniuses, Freud turns to the religion of the common folk, the masses. Where James finds religion to be of enormous positive significance in human life, Freud thinks we'd be better rid of it altogether. James rejects science's claim to universal validity, thus rebuffing Freud's positivist view that science (Logos) is destined to replace religion. James looks to religion expectantly, exercising a "hermeneutics of recollection" (Paul Ricoeur), which brings a certain range of phenomena into view. Freud looks at religion skeptically, practicing a "hermeneutics of suspicion" (Ricoeur), which provides access to certain other phenomena. We turn now to Freud's view of average, everyday religion as wish fulfillment: that is, as imaginative activity reshaping reality to gratify human need. The father occupies a central position in this account. The full role the father is held to play in religion, however, will only become apparent later in the chapter (see below, "Religion as Historical Truth").

The Nature of Religious Doctrines as Illusions

Freud finds religion to be an illusion—he also characterizes it, as we shall see, as a psychotic delusion and a neurotic compulsion. Illusions, Freud points out, are not inherently contrary to fact. Delusions contradict reality; illusions may or may not. And illusions may or may not be capable of realization. What characterizes an illusion, by Freud's definition, is its derivation from a wish: a belief is an illusion when a wish fulfillment is "a prominent factor in its motivation" (1964[1927], 47–48). Wishing, or wish fulfillment, is the activity of imagining an appropriate tension-reducing object. Illusions are thus seen to arise from the life of the imagination. Freud comments that one wishes when one stands in need of something and that one wishes by imagining an object that, in the past, satisfied the need in question: that is, by remembering a formerly satisfying object. Wish fulfillment also goes by the name of "primary process thinking"; "secondary process thinking," by contrast, refers to the ego's reality-oriented dealings with the environment. Dreaming of drinking water is an example of primary process thinking or wishing; actually obtaining a glass of water is an example of secondary process thinking.

It has already been suggested that Freud, in defining illusion, intentionally brackets the question of an illusion's bearing upon reality. What we long for and "dream up" sometimes has a corresponding object in reality—the glass of water of our dreams, for example—and sometimes not—paradise on earth, for example. Wishing, moreover, is remembering: recalling an object that once played a tension-reducing role in our lives, whatever distortion or embellishment the shaping activity of our imagination may presently cause our former experience to undergo. Dreaming of drinking water, we recall water; dreaming of paradise, we recall happier days. The latter daydream of paradise entails considerable revision of earlier experiencing; the former night dream of water relatively little.

Applying the notion of primary process thinking (wishing) to religion, Freud says that religious ideas are "fulfillments of the oldest, strongest and most urgent wishes of mankind" (1964[1927], 47). The teachings of religion, derived neither from experiences of the matters they speak of nor from serious thinking on such matters, are illusions. The power of illusions is seen to lie in their ability to satisfy needs and, thus, to reduce tension (a painful increase in the organism's energy level). All religious ideas are illusions, in Freud's opinion, products of the imagination that bring enormous relief from tension, satisfactions of pressing needs open neither to proof nor to disproof (1964[1927], 49–50).

The Need Pressing for Fulfillment

Freud describes the need that the illusions (doctrines) of religion fulfill along the following lines (1964[1927], 20–22). Life is difficult. Civilization forces us to renounce basic satisfactions. Others harm us. Nature threatens us with its untamed forces. Death and the darkness of the grave await us. Good goes unheralded, even as evil reaps ample rewards. No matter where we turn, the terrors of life and the universe leap out at us. Our damaged self-esteem requires repair. Our curiosity demands answers.

Adult human beings are thus said to suffer from weakness and helplessness. But, Freud says, we were weak and helpless once before: as children. When young, although we feared the father, and "with reason," we could count on his protection and care—such ambivalence toward the father is crucial in Freud's psychology of religion. The child's need for the father's protection is aroused by terrifying helplessness, said to be the strongest need of childhood. The childhood and adult situations of weakness and helplessness are seen to be fundamentally related: our helpless situation as adults is simply the continuation of its "infantile prototype," our helpless situation as children (1964[1927], 23). Childhood helplessness, in Freud's view, is destined to plague us all our life.

The Nature of the Wish

Freud says that we learned as children to establish a personal relation with those we seek to influence (1964[1927], 31). We are seen to call on this early lesson of life when in adulthood we personify the threatening forces of nature. Given the tremendous superiority of these forces, however, justice would not be done them if they were merely made into equals, and so, says Freud, we bestow on them the character of the father, of that person who in childhood was every inch a god (1964[1927], 24). According to Freud, we turn the forces of nature into gods, after the model of the father. The superior forces of nature and the godly father thus come to be assimilated to one another. The father, in this view, is the first and original god, the model for every subsequent god of religion. These later gods, by Freud's account, are indeed "god-like": they are in the image of the original god, like the human father. Man isn't made in the image of the God of religion, then, as the book of Genesis has it, but the other way around: the God of religion is in the image of the father. All gods are fatherlike, in Freud's view, not all fathers godlike.

The immediately preceding accords with what Freud has to say about the "infantile prototype" of childhood helplessness. Childhood helplessness and its associated terror arouse the need for the father's "protection through love" (1964[1927], 47). As helpless children, we could always count on the father for security and love. The father, it has been remarked, was a godly figure, so much larger and stronger than we, capable of allaying all our fears and insecurities. Was there anything this superior figure couldn't do? The father was a most satisfying presence indeed, remedying our inherent helplessness, comforting us, and bringing good feelings. Confronted with nature's superior forces, adults stand in a similar situation of helplessness, in desperate need of protection. This need for protection is the motive behind the already mentioned conversion of the forces of nature into gods, after the image of the father. Freud says we never really left the father behind, this divine figure of childhood satisfaction and protection.

Still helpless, still in need, adults still cling to the father, still long for the father and his "protection through love." Helpless and still clinging to the father's memory, we imagine his presence and his protection from the dangers threatening us at every turn. We wish: we picture the father to be as big and strong, as much a god, as ever. We remember him to be as powerful as we experienced him to be as children, and, indeed, as more powerful still, as omnipotent. Our needs are relieved, our tensions are reduced, through wishing, through illusion. What "would be nice," what would cancel out our helplessness before the terrors of life and nature and make us happy, has become a "fact," through the activity of our imagination. The father of memory and the present forces of nature have been imagined into one another. We are now able to relate to the forces of nature as persons—"the gods"—and, through subservient religious practices, win them over and influence them.

Freud thus argues that the way the child deals with helplessness, through reliance on the father, also characterizes the adult's reaction to admitted helplessness. Freud says that this reaction, the assimilation through wishing of the infantile and the adult situations of helplessness, is the formation of religion. The father, in Freud's view, is the model for all of humanity's gods. Freud makes the case, moreover, that the origin of the gods out of "the longing for the father" not only has an "infantile prototype" but a "phylogenetic prototype" as well (1964[1927], 24; see below, "The Historical Truth of Religion"). The father was the original mighty one and protector—the original god—in our prehistoric childhood, just as he is in childhood today. This prehistoric father is seen, in the course of religious development over the centuries, gradually to have made his return and reclaimed his title as God and Lord of heaven and earth.

Freud thus finds religion to derive from childhood helplessness and the related dependence on the father, as continued by adult helplessness and the related "longing for the father." Human beings, grown up but still helpless, are said to return time and again to the memory image of the father (1965[1933], 163). The effective strength of this image, associated with the satisfaction of important childhood needs, in conjunction with persisting adult weakness and need for protection, in Freud's view, sustains human belief in God. All in all, the recognition that childhood helplessness is destined to remain with us all our life institutes a lifelong clinging to the father, now projected onto the forces of nature outside, now more powerful and exalted than ever. We are thus, in the course of development, said to create for ourselves our gods, gods we dread and try to win over, gods we entrust with our protection (1964[1927], 35). A benevolent Providence, projected out of our longings for a caring, protective father, now watches over us.

The positive feelings of the child toward the father have been prominent in the above. It is precisely such feelings, the longing for the father's protection through love, that are evoked by human helplessness. In point of fact, however, and as already suggested, Freud finds male children and adults to be profoundly ambivalent toward the father: loving, yet fearing and even hating him, at one and the same time—Freud defines ambivalence as the "coincidence of love and hate towards the same object" (1946[1913], 202). One has reason to hold the father in high esteem for his omnipotence, but this same omnipotence gives one reason to be wary of and to distrust him as well (1946[1913], 68). It is thus to be expected, Freud says, that the God arising out of "longing for the father" will be feared, no less than admired and loved—thus our dread of the gods and our need to win them over. Ambivalence toward the divine, Freud insists, is found in all religions.

The Further Development of Religion

Freud observes that, with the rise of science, nature became a realm in its own right, losing its personal characteristics. Nature was no longer seen, for example, to possess emotions and purposes. But human beings are said to have remained helpless and to have continued to long for the father, and so for the gods (1964[1927], 24). And the gods retained their age-old functions: reconciling human beings to the cruelties of fate and, especially, death; compensating for the sacrifices required by civilization and, in particular, for the sacrifice of aggressive instinct; and depriving nature of its terror. In the course of time, moreover, the gods came to be more and more associated with morality, overseeing, for example, the execution of civilization's rules, which presumably derived from the gods themselves.

Freud sees the gods of polytheism (belief in many gods) as eventually becoming condensed into one God (monotheism). This development is seen as a return to the beginnings in history of the idea of God and makes it clear that the father had always been the concealed nucleus of every divine figure (1964[1927], 27; the theme of the historical origin of religion in prehistoric events centering around the father will be discussed at length below in the section "Religion as Historical Truth"). People are now able to relate to God as intimately and intensely as children do to their human father. Freud remarks that, even to this day, the average person has no choice but to imagine a concerned Providence "in the figure of an enormously exalted father." Such a God understands needs and hears prayers. Freud is pained to realize that most people will never outgrow this childish view of reality (1962[1930], 21).

The Doctrines of Religion

Civilization, Freud remarks, has created a set of religious ideas. These doctrines, born of the need to soften the blows that accompany adult weakness and helplessness, are said to be constructed by primary process thinking out of memories dating back to the time of childhood weakness and helplessness, out of the adult's memory image of the father (1964[1927], 25).

The system of religious illusions (religious doctrines), with which civilization furnishes its members, ready-made and without the need for effort on their part, is seen to include beliefs in a benevolent and superior intelligence, life after death, moral laws governing the universe, and the rewarding of good and the punishment of evil (the idea of a "moral world-order"). Freud remarks that consoling ideas such as these neutralize human helplessness and its associated pains. A superior intelligence is believed to ordain events "down here," with a view to our ultimate satisfaction. We are assured that whatever we might miss out on on earth will be made up for a thousandfold in heaven. Answers are provided to such troubling matters as the problem of evil and the meaning of existence. Death is held to be but the transition to a new and more glorious life. Superior wisdom, infinite goodness, and divine justice, attributed to the God or gods that created us, are considered to be everywhere at work in the universe. Beliefs such as these take the bite out of life's terrors, hardships, and sufferings, bringing enormous relief (1964[1927], 27); as St. Paul remarks, "Oh death, where is thy sting?" Without the illusions of religion, Freud remarks, countless individuals, losing their one consolation in life, wouldn't be able to go on (1964[1927], 57).

The Failure of Religion

Freud says that religion, through such injunctions as "Thou shalt not kill!" has done civilization a great service (1964[1927], 60). But religion is seen not to have done enough. Having dominated human life for thousands of years, and thus having had ample opportunity to prove itself, religion, in Freud's considered opinion, has not succeeded in producing happiness, comforting people, or civilizing them. He finds evidence for this in the large numbers of his contemporaries dissatisfied with civilization. Nor does Freud have reason to suppose that people were any happier when religion ruled supreme in human life; they certainly weren't any more moral (1964[1927], 61)! He points out, moreover, that religion has, in the course of human history, provided as much support for immoral undertakings as for moral ones (1964[1927], 62). On the whole, then, he thinks that religion has been a failure.

The Price Paid for the Illusions of Religion

Living in religious illusion, Freud thinks, cripples our human powers. He finds a depressing contrast between the "radiant intelligence of a healthy child" and the "feeble intellectual powers of the average adult" (1964[1927], 77–78). He attributes this "relative atrophy" to a religious education. He is not surprised to find weakness of intellect in those who have unquestioningly adopted the doctrines of religion, with all their absurdities and contradictions (1964[1927], 78). He finds the greater risk not in giving religion up but in holding on to it (1964[1927], 57).

The Development of an Adult Attitude

Freud is confident that the "infantilism" in evidence in religious belief will be overcome. We cannot remain children forever (1964[1927], 81). He thinks that people will be able to venture out into "hostile life" and face things as they are, rather than as they imagine them to be. People will become resigned to reality and learn to rely on their own resources. When that happens, when people turn from a fancied other world to the one right in front of them, it is believed that sufficient energies will be liberated to make life tolerable for all.

Freud's hope is for intellect to become dictator in human life. While such a "primacy of the intellect" may be a long way off in the future, Freud nevertheless thinks it attainable. In all likelihood, he remarks, intellect will try to achieve the very things presently expected of God: the love of humankind and the decrease of suffering. Freud asserts that "our God Logos" will attain these aims to the extent nature allows (1964[1927], 88–89).

Freud is of the opinion that, en route to the future reign of intellect, religious beliefs will have to be set aside. He says that, in the long run, reason and experience must win out over religion and its obvious contradictions (1964[1927], 89). Intellect (science) is to conquer imagination (illusion). History is said to show that the more that knowledge is gained, the less religious beliefs govern life. Only science is able to provide knowledge of external reality, in Freud's view; only reason (Logos) can be our guide. Freud allows of no court of appeals above reason (1964[1927], 43).

RELIGION AS HISTORICAL TRUTH

Freud says that he was more concerned in *The Future of an Illusion* (1964[1927]) with what common people understand by their religion than with religion's deepest sources, with the "manifest" motivation of the average person's religious behavior than with its "latent" motivation (1962[1930], 21). He occupied himself in that work, he remarks further, with the already established body of culturally communicated religious doctrines, with doctrines as finished products, ready-made for adoption by the masses. He says that his earlier *Totem and Taboo* (1946[1913]), on the other hand, was devoted to a consideration of the origin of religion in view of the more "concealed part," in terms of the "deeper" rather than the more "manifest" motives.

The Historical Truth of Religion

Freud comments that, while he placed an essentially negative evaluation on religion in *The Future of an Illusion*, in *Totem and Taboo* he locates a power in religion in the "truth" it is found to contain (1963[1925], 138). Religious doctrines are said to tell the *historical* truth (1964[1927], 69). Such historical truth, in Freud's view, is by no means a *material* truth about real beings and events in a realm above nature: religious doctrines are not to be taken at their face value. We turn our attention now to Freud's considerations of religion's "deeper part" and to the manner in which religion is said to harbor the historical truth.

Totemism

Freud asserts that totemism is a primitive phase through which every culture passes (1946[1913], 140). Ultimately, according to Freud, it is always an animal that is honored in totemism (1963[1925], 127). The clan claims to have descended from the honored animal: the animal is the clan's totem (1946[1913], 5). Most striking to Freud were the similarities between the taboos of totemism—not to kill the totem animal and not to have sexual relations with the women of one's clan—and the male child's two Oedipal desires—to kill the father and to have sex with the mother. These similarities led Freud to conclude that the totemistic system, with its taboos, originated in a situation structurally identical to the Oedipus complex.

The clan, attributing its descent to the totem animal, honors the animal as its father. Freud is of the opinion that the true nucleus of totemism—its *latent* content—and the "starting-point in the formation of religion" was a historical killing of an actual human being (1963[1925], 128). The human being thought to have been killed was a father, the original prehistoric father. Freud expressed this opinion in print many times, as early as 1913 and as late as 1939. His theory is detailed and carefully constructed and tied in at critical points to the central Oedipus complex. It does not represent a passing fancy on Freud's part.

Freud speculates as follows about the prehistory of the human species. Originally, before the rise of civilization, human beings lived in any number of relatively small groups. Presiding over each such "primal horde" was a "primal father," a violent and despotic ruler who reserved all the women for himself (1946[1913], 162)—Freud adopted the notion of the primal horde from Charles Darwin. The primal father's sons, unhappy, as one might expect, with the existing order, represented dangerous rivals to the father. Should the sons arouse jealousy in the father, Freud says the father had them killed or castrated or driven out (1967[1939], 102). The father was thus clearly someone to fear and keep an eye on. The sons could nevertheless count on the father's favors and protection—so long as they remained "obedient sons." One day it came about, however, that the sons banded together, overwhelmed and killed their father, and then proceeded to consume his flesh (1963[1925], 129). In this way, says Freud, the expelled brothers brought an abrupt end to the "father horde" (1946[1913], 183).

The sons had always been ambivalent toward their father—mention has already been made of the importance of ambivalence in Freud's psychology of religion. On the one hand, the sons feared and hated the man who thwarted their "sexual demands" and pursuit of power (1946[1913], 184). On the other, they loved and admired him, "longed" for him ("longing for the father") and looked up to him. Ambivalence—tenderness and hostility together, the coinciding of love and hate toward the same object (1946[1913], 202)—is thus seen to be of the essence of the father-son relationship (1967[1939], 172). The sons' fear and hatred of the primal father, their resentment, led them to murder him. Their love and admiration led them to the literal incorporation of his flesh into their flesh; thereby did they identify with and acquire a portion of the strength of this man they so greatly admired (1946[1913], 183).

But now, Freud's narrative continues, modeling themselves after their violent father, "the envied and feared model for each of the brothers," the brothers began to get in each other's way and to fight one another (1946[1913], 183). Not only that, but tender feelings toward the missing father, feelings suppressed at the time of the murder, began to mount in the brothers. Freud comments that the sons' hatred and fear having culminated in the father's assassination, their "suppressed tender impulses"—the other side of their ambivalence—"had to assert themselves" (1946[1913], 185). Such tender feelings announced themselves in the remorse the brothers began to feel over their action. The sons came to share a common guilt for their misdeed.

Sorely pressed, on the one hand, by their failed rivalry with one another—each seeking to gain all the women for himself after the model of the father, but, lacking the father's strength, each failing (1946[1913], 186)—and by their remorse and guilt, on the other, the sons brought matters to a certain resolution. This solution, Freud says, coincides with the formation of totemism. Banding together as a clan of brothers, the sons installed a totem animal before themselves in the place of honor. The totem animal was thought of both as the clan's ancestor and as its guardian and protector, helping in times of illness and giving the tribe "premonitions and warnings" (1946[1913], 5, 136). The totem animal, in short, was a father substitute, the father restored.

Freud remarks that the sons solved the problem of their guilt, in effect "undoing" their act of murder, through the taboo against killing the totem animal (father substitute). The sons instituted at the same time the taboo against choosing women of their own clan as sexual partners, thus renouncing one and all the ideal of the father's absolute dominance

(1967[1939], 104). With the help of these two taboos of totemism, originating out of "the sense of guilt of the sons," the competing sons are said
to have transformed themselves into a society of brothers (1963[1925],
129). The two taboos, as already pointed out, correspond to the two repressed wishes of the Oedipus complex.

Freud is of the opinion that the sons' reaction of remorse to their murder of their father marks the beginnings of social organization, morality,
and religion. Society is said to be based on "complicity in the common
crime," religion on "the sense of guilt and the consequent remorse," and
morality jointly on "the necessities of society" and the expiation demanded by the sense of guilt (1946[1913], 188–89).

Humanity's "original sin," in Freud's version of human prehistory, is
the sons' killing of the primal father, with its attendant sense of guilt.
Totemistic religion is said to have issued from the sons' attempt to soften
this guilt and to reconcile with the father through subsequent obedience.
In Freud's view, all later religions are attempts to solve the very same
problems. They are all reactions aiming at one and the same event that is
at the origin of culture and that has been driving humanity ever since
(1946[1913], 187). The human sense of guilt, traceable to the original sin of
parricide, is, in Freud's opinion, "the most important problem in the development of civilization" (1962[1930], 81).

Totemism, Freud further remarks, marks the achievement of a kind of
compromise. The father substitute would take care of the sons. All the
sons had to do was honor the father's life (1946[1913], 186). The father
substitute, the sons pledged, would not die the way the original father
had. Freud nevertheless reminds us of totemism's solemn ceremonies, the
whole point of which was the killing and consumption of the totem animal (1946[1913], 137). These ceremonies were in fact a "feast of triumph"
celebrating the sons' victory over their father (1967[1939], 104–105). No
single brother would dare take it upon himself to kill the sacrificial animal. Only the whole clan, and only under the proper circumstances,
could undertake the otherwise forbidden act. Freud remarks that the clan
conceived of itself as of one blood, one substance, with their God, the
totem animal. This realistic fellowship of blood had to be renewed from
time to time—thus the necessity of the sacrificial meal, the ritual killing
and eating of the totem animal. By eating the animal, Freud says, the clan
members maintained their "material identity" with one another and with
their God.

The periodic killing and eating of the totem was thus of central importance in totemism. But there's more. The ritual murder of the totem was
followed by a period of compulsive lamentation, the immediate origin of
which was fear of retribution, but whose underlying goal, says Freud, was
the removal of the guilt incurred by the original killing of the primal fa-

ther (1946[1913], 181). A festival celebration, during which no human impulse was denied gratification, came after this period of mourning. Acts normally forbidden were now allowed. The fact that the totem was a father substitute accounts, in Freud's view, for a sacrificial killing of it that evokes contradictory intense mourning and holiday mood. The ambivalence characteristic of the sons' relations to the father—exultation over being rid of him (hate), regret over having killed him (love)—extended to the father substitute. The totem feast commemorated and repeated the signal event of father-murder, with which began "social organization, moral restrictions, and religion" (1946[1913], 183).

The final words of *Totem and Taboo* are from Goethe: "In the beginning was the deed" (1946[1913], 207). Freud admits that his narrative account of the origins of religion is hypothetical. He speaks, for example, of "the uncertainties of our assumptions" and "the difficulties of our conclusions" (1946[1913], 203). Freud nonetheless holds to his account, returning to and elaborating upon it a number of times in the course of more than thirty years. Freud's version of human prehistory enables him to bring the origin of religion within the sphere of the pivotal Oedipus complex, to base the former upon the very ambivalence in evidence in the latter. Totemism was the result, he says, of the conditions that underlie the Oedipus complex (1946[1913], 171). The Oedipus complex of male children today is a reenactment, according to Freud, of events dating back to human prehistory.

Every male child of today is thus said to undergo one and the same drama undergone by the sons of old. The operative factors (love and hate directed at the father), Freud remarks, have undergone no change at all down the ages. What seems to have so fascinated Freud about the theory of the primal father's murder is its ability, on the one hand, to provide a historical antecedent of the Oedipus complex and, on the other, to explain the multiple phenomena of religion, and, thus, to lay bare the previously hidden connections between human prehistory, the Oedipus complex, and the origins of religion. "In the beginning was the deed!"

Love and the Origin of the Superego

We have heard Freud to the effect that "social organization, moral restrictions, and religion" all originated in the murder of the father and the sons' reaction of guilt (1946[1913], 183). Humans feel guilty when they transgress certain "moral restrictions." Freud says this is owing to the psychic agency of the superego, or "conscience." The primal father, however, knew neither "moral restrictions" nor guilt, nor did his sons, at least prior to their horrendous deed. Morality—"moral restrictions"—first appeared only *after* the sons killed the father. The superego, the "authority" behind both "moral restrictions" and the guilt that follows their violation, first arose in the sons precisely in reaction to their act of murder.

Freud thus assumes that the inner sense of guilt (superego) shared by humans springs from the Oedipal situation, being first acquired historically after the sons banded together and killed their father (1962[1930], 78). But how did the sons come to feel guilt over their misdeed in the first place if they weren't already in possession of a superego, if the superego, which gives rise to guilt, first arises precisely in reaction to this misdeed? Freud's answer is as follows. The first guilt indeed goes back, "as a special case of remorse," to the killing of the primal father (1962[1930], 79). After the sons satisfied their hatred by murdering the father, Freud says that their love, their tender feelings, came forward in the remorse or guilt they felt over the deed and "set up the superego by way of identification with the father" (1962[1930], 79).

Thus, the first appearance ever in human history of "moral restrictions." All in all, it is not "moral restrictions" that give rise to the sons' guilty feelings but the sons' tender feelings. Love, in conjunction with its murderous counterpart (destructiveness or hate), gives rise to the first guilt ("as a special case of remorse") and to the superego and its "moral restrictions." The first guilt was not due to the superego, but the superego to the sons' ambivalence towards their father and the guilt this ambivalence cannot help but engender.

The superego arises as an internalization of the father and the external coercion formerly exercised by him. Reacting—in guilt, itself due to love—to their impious deed, the sons will now respect the father's wishes and refrain from killing him and from having sex with the women of their clan (1964[1927], 69). These "moral restrictions" of the superego—the taboos of totemism, later generalized as civilization's "prohibitions against murder and incest" (1964[1927], 33)—were originally the father's self-serving and brutally enforced rules. The "special mental agency" of the superego thus continues the will of the father.

History, Repression, and Religion

The murdered primal father is said to constitute the original image upon which all later generations modeled their figures of God (1964[1927], 69). God is always and everywhere, in Freud's view, constructed on the model of an earthly father: God is an idealized father, "nothing but an exalted father" (1946[1913], 190). Freud sees the phenomena of religion, in all their variety, as the return of important historical occurrences centering on the prehistoric murder of the father. Because of the pain (guilt) involved, the sons are said to have repressed these events on their way to becoming a clan of brothers. This is an important observation on Freud's part. Religious phenomena, like the neurotic symptoms of individuals, are said to be "the return of the repressed" and, thus, to constitute a form of remembering of rejected material from the past.

Repressed material is said to bring with it enormous power upon its return—precisely because it is the repressed that is making its return. Freud expressly locates the tremendous power of religious phenomena here, in the upward urgency of the repressed. The expulsion from consciousness, by reason of the pain involved (guilt as a "special case of remorse"), of the sons' desires (to kill the father and seize the women) and related historical events is what accounts for the compulsive character of religious phenomena, for their immense hold on humanity. Their historical truth, Freud says, is what makes them effective.

Freud remarks that it is typical in neurosis for a period of latency to intervene between the earlier traumatic event and the later appearance of the illness (1967[1939], 97). Neurosis, he says, is a "delayed effect of the trauma." The later illness, he comments further, can be considered an attempt to cure the psychic split brought on by the trauma, to reconcile the ego with the part that has been split off, thus unifying and strengthening the ego and rendering it a more effective agent in its dealings with the surrounding world (1967[1939], 97).

The threat of castration directed at the male child (by the father) for his attempts at intimacy with the mother and at getting rid of the father (Oedipus complex) is said to be the earlier traumatic event. Repression of these occurrences, including a renunciation of instinct, is the child's defense against the threat of castration and the "castration anxiety" it engenders. Repressed material, rather than obediently holding its place, retains its power, however, and continues to press for conscious expression: the repressed strives to make its return. The neurotic symptom, "the return of the repressed," represents the later disturbance or illness (1967[1939], 164). Freud proposes the following sequence in the development of a neurosis: trauma → repression → latency → outbreak of the neurosis → "return of the repressed" (1967[1939], 101).

Religion as "Universal Compulsive Neurosis"

Neurosis, religion, society, art, and ethics, remarks Freud, all originate in the Oedipus complex (1946[1913], 202). Freud's claim, in short, is that religion, growing out of the very factors operative in the Oedipus complex, is a neurosis, that the phenomena of religion are to be understood by analogy to neurotic symptoms. Trauma, defense, latency, outbreak of illness, and "return of the repressed": all these are said to characterize not only neurosis in general but the neurosis of religion in particular. Freud specifies the neurosis of religion as compulsive neurosis: religion has the status of a mass compulsive neurosis of humanity, its grandiose powers being due to the very factors operative in Freud's compulsive patients (1967[1939], 68). The present section explores the analogy drawn by Freud between compulsive neurosis and religion.

Humanity as a whole, says Freud, in its early development, fell into a state analogous to neurosis, and for the same reasons that individuals become neurotic. The weak intellect of the child makes it necessary, in Freud's view, for affective means—pain—to accomplish the restriction of instinct required for communal existence (1964[1927], 70). Children must go though a phase of neurosis in order to become civilized. Pain (castration anxiety) in the childhood of the individual leads to repression. And pain (guilt due, on the one hand, to the sons' impiety and, on the other, to their love) leads to something like repression in the childhood of the species (human prehistory). Repression gives rise to its "formations" (symptoms = "the return of the repressed"). The "formations" due to prehistoric repression would be the variety of religious phenomena that have become attached to civilization, with all their characteristic compulsiveness. "Religion," Freud writes, "would thus be the universal compulsive neurosis of humanity" (1964[1927], 70–71). Humanity's mass neurosis, like the compulsive neurosis of childhood, arises out of the Oedipus complex, "out of the relation to the father."

Freud points out the specific parallels between the compulsive acts of neurotics and the religious observances of the pious in a relatively early essay entitled "Obsessive Acts and Religious Practices" (1963[1907]). Compulsions, Freud says, function as protective devices: a certain ritual must be performed, or disaster will surely follow. By expressing unconscious motives, compulsive acts afford a measure of satisfaction, and indeed of the very satisfaction these acts also serve to prevent. The satisfaction cannot take its original form, to be sure, and indeed only a psychological expert can make it out in its symptomatic disguise. The symptom represents a necessary compromise between the satisfaction sought and its prevention. Compulsive acts, Freud says, are compromises. Freud sees the primary resemblance between compulsive acts and religious practices in the "fear of pangs of conscience" that follows the omission of the required ceremony and "in the conscientiousness with which the details are carried out" (1963[1907], 19).

Religion, like compulsive neurosis, is seen to be founded on the giving up of instinct. Because religion is less than fully successful in accomplishing the suppression of instinctual impulses, there remains, as in the neurosis, a continuing temptation to act on them. There is in both religion and the neurosis the same anxious expectation of misfortune—punishment by God, in the religious case. The knowledge of the pious that they are "miserable sinners in their hearts" is said to parallel the sense of guilt of compulsive neurotics (1963[1907], 23).

Religious observances, moreover, like compulsive actions, are seen to serve as protections. The pious religious observances, prayers, and invocations with which the believer begins each of his or her daily activities, Freud says, are "defensive and protective measures" (1963[1907], 23). Petty rituals, through the same displacement by which trivial matters assume the utmost importance in compulsive neurosis, are gradually seen to become the essential thing in religious practice. As protective measures, religious observances are meaningful. As symptomatic compromises, however, their true meaning remains hidden to the believer. Freud remarks that compromise, a fundamental feature of compulsive acts, is clearly in evidence in the religious compulsion, when religious individuals engage, in the very name of the divine and all that is holy, in the very violence they decry.

Freud thus finds that the analogy between religion and compulsive neurosis works quite well and that many of the "peculiarities and vicissitudes" found in the developmental history of religion can be understood in the light of the neurosis (1964[1927], 72). In view of the similarities discovered, Freud concludes with the now familiar words that religion is a "universal compulsive neurosis" (1963[1907], 25). He also reverses this formula and says that compulsive neurosis is a "pathological counterpart to the formation of a religion, a private religious system" (1963[1907], 25). Or, as he writes in another context, "The ceremonials and prohibitions of compulsive neurotics drive us to suppose that they have created a private religion of their own" (1963[1919], 225). Freud remarks that his neurotic patients are attempting to address the very needs and to solve the very conflicts that the masses do by way of institutional religion. This squares with Freud's assertion that religious individuals, in adopting the universal solution—the "universal compulsive neurosis"—are spared the personal one. Freud thus describes compulsive neurosis as a religion. But it is a religion only of sorts, for Freud is also moved to remark that compulsive neurosis is a "tragi-comic travesty of a private religion," a distortion of religion, "a caricature of a religion" (1946[1913], 96; 1963[1907], 19). Freud says that compulsive neurosis differs from religion in its privateness, apparent senselessness, and individual variability (1963[1907], 19).

Further Reflections on Religion and Neurosis

Freud renews his reflections on the analogy between religion and compulsive neurosis in other writings, and most notably in *Totem and Taboo* (1946[1913]), a book published some six years after "Obsessive Acts and

Religious Practices" (1963[1907]). In *Totem and Taboo*, Freud compares compulsive neurosis and the particular religion of totemism. Freud, it will be recalled, holds totemism to have been the first religion and a universal stage in the development of culture.

The compulsive act, we have seen, is a compromise between the present enactment of renounced instinct and the present forbidding of it by the father in the form of the internalized agency of "moral restrictions," the superego. The taboos of the religion of totemism originated, according to Freud, in the sons' renunciation of the very gratifications the father had denied them while still among them. This act of renunciation was a repression of sorts of the sons' fundamental instinctual desires to kill the father and possess the women of the horde. Rejected, these desires retained fullness of force and continued to seek expression, in direct opposition to the internalized will of the father in the superego. The phenomena of totemism are compromises serving, on the one hand, to express the desires of the sons and, on the other, to keep them in check. Behind a taboo, Freud comments, is a "forbidden action" strongly desired by the unconscious (1946[1913], 44). Offered in proof that the sons, now a clan of brothers, continued to seek gratification of their instinctual desires is the totem feast, at which the father substitute was ritually killed and eaten and a festival declared giving free rein to all impulses.

In sum, the compulsive character of religious phenomena is held to derive from the fact that the strongest human desires, on the one hand, retain their instinctual power and upward pressure and, on the other, have an outlaw status. These desires seek fulfillment with the force of nature itself, in Freud's view, but direct fulfillment is denied them. The dynamics found in religion—the compulsiveness and compromise everywhere in evidence in totemism and religion in general—thus parallel the dynamics found in the neurosis.

Like the taboos of totemism and like neurotic prohibitions, moreover, "self-evident" moral prescriptions of all sorts originate, on the one hand, in "the will of the father" as "a command of conscience" and, on the other, in the continued urge to violate that will. All three are compromise formations. Freud points out, however, that this true origin of moral prescriptions in repressed instinct making its return is generally not understood. Morality is thought to issue from God, either directly by way of his revealed word or indirectly through the natural law inscribed by him in the human soul. Freud sees this "divine necessity" of the moral law as testifying to its compulsive or compulsory character, thus reinforcing his belief that the origin and dynamics of morality lie in repressed instinct. Freud comments that everything "mysterious, grandiose, and mystically self-evident" about ethical precepts results from their origin in the will of the primal father (1967[1939], 156). The taboos of totemism, neurotic prohibitions, and moral prescriptions (ethics, morality) are thus all said to originate in repressed instinct. All three, with the symptoms of religion and the compulsions of neurotics in general, owe their status as compromises—and thus their compulsiveness—to this fact.

Freud says that the taboos of totemism eventually became "'organized' as a piece of inherited psychic property" (1946[1913], 43). They became part of what Freud calls the "archaic heritage," psychic traces of human experience down the ages. Thus passed on from generation to generation by way of a hereditary mechanism, these prohibitions touch all succeeding human beings. Freud is thus able to assert that totemism makes its reappearance in the developmental history of children today (1946[1913], 43). Every child today is destined to remember and reenact ancient human prehistory. But so, too, is humanity collectively destined, in the phenomena of religion. Individual neurotic and collective religious outcomes obey the same dynamics stemming from a common prehistoric origin.

The works in which Freud first drew the analogy between neurotic compulsion and religion were early—"Obsessive Acts and Religious Practices" dates from 1907 and *Totem and Taboo* from 1913. One may well ask whether Freud later came to modify his views. He did not, as can be seen from one of his last works, *Moses and Monotheism*, whose publication dates from 1939. He remarks there that his convictions, if anything, have grown stronger since *Totem and Taboo*. He says that from that work on he never doubted that religion—as the return of repressed human prehistory, as compulsively controlling behavior by reason of the historical truth contained—is to be understood on the model of neurotic symptoms (1967[1939], 71).

Religious Developments after Totemism

After varying periods of time, from the very short, in the case of totemism, to the very long, in the case of recent and current developments, the repressed events of human prehistory are said to have returned, after the fashion of the compulsions of neurotic patients, in the form of the compulsive phenomena of religion. The repressed memories returned as the world's religions. In the meantime, between the original repression and the later outbreak of religious symptoms (phenomena of religion): that is, during the period of latency, the memories of the former events are said to have formed part of the archaic heritage already mentioned. The archaic heritage is what makes it possible, in Freud's scheme of things, for the mass phenomena of religion to occur many years after the repression of prehistoric times. People have always known, Freud remarks, that they once had a primal father and that they killed him (1967[1939], 129).

In summary, Freud assumes that, in the course of its early development, humanity as a whole developed conditions resembling a neurosis

(1964[1927], 71), that certain key events were repressed early on in the life of the species, and that the phenomena of religion, in all their variety and even to this day, represent the gradual return of this repressed prehistory. Repression is said to account for the compulsive character in evidence in religion's rites, doctrines, and moral prescriptions. The brothers' murder of their father, Freud remarks, left "ineradicable traces" in human history, expressing itself more frequently in "substitute formations" the further it receded from conscious memory (1946[1913], 200).

Between Totemism and Monotheism: Polytheism

Freud says that all religions are attempts at solving the same problems: reduction of the sense of guilt resulting from the primal father's murder, and reconciliation with the father through subsequent obedience (1946[1913], 187). Totemism and all later religions have one and the same content of "obliterating the traces" of the sons' primeval crime and of "expiating [that crime] by bringing forward other solutions of the struggle between the father and the sons" (1963[1919], 226). Freud holds "the longing for the father" to be "the root of all religious evolution" (1946[1913], 191). The gods are in every case modeled after the father; our personal relation to them depends on our relation to our human father (1946[1913], 190).

The initial return of the father, motivated by the sons' longing for him, took the form of the totem animal (father substitute). Freud says that a "humanizing" of the animal divinity of totemism first made its appearance with polytheism: the divine regains human form as "the gods" (1967[1939], 105). Polytheism is thus cited as a major step toward a more proper representation of the original god, the primal father (1967[1939], 105). Polytheism's masculine gods, which are numerous, share authority, and occasionally render obedience to a "higher god," are said to reflect the situation as it existed in patriarchical times (1967[1939], 106).

Freud accounts for the religious development from the father substitute of totemism to the gods in human form of polytheism along the following lines (1946[1913], 191–92). The sons killed the father in an attempt to become like him, but none was successful in attaining the father's "perfection of power." With the passage of time, the bad feelings toward the father gave way to an enormously increased longing for him. There arose, with this increased "longing for the father," an ideal with the content of "the fullness of power" and the 'freedom from restriction" of the murdered father (1946[1913], 191–92). The brothers revived the "old father ideal" by making those among them who "had distinguished themselves above the rest" into gods.

The idea was hardly foreign to antiquity, Freud comments, for a human being to become a god. Freud deems the deification of the murdered father in the form of "the gods" "a much more serious attempt at expiation" than the brothers' former treaty with the totem animal (1946[1913], 192). People came to believe, moreover, that the world was created by a being like a man, idealized, however, to the point of being superior in every way to any human being, a superman or superfather (1965[1933], 162). Freud finds it interesting that, though there were many gods, only one was held to be the creator and that this creator was an idealized human being. This "god-creator," Freud says, was "undisguisedly called 'father'" (1965[1933], 163).

Moses and Monotheism

Both totemism and polytheism, in Freud's opinion, are manifestations of repressed material. Both are neurotic symptoms, bringing with them a portion of the historical truth. Totemism brings back, in the form of the animal who must not be killed, the memory of the father who was killed. Polytheism returns to God (the father) his human form. Eventually, according to Freud, after totemism and after polytheism, belief in a single omnipotent father-God developed. Monotheism, restoring to God his full figure as father, is said to be a further return of the long-hidden historical truth. Freud judges this recovery by the primal father of his historical rights to have been a momentous step forward for humanity (1967[1939], 109).

Freud has written at some length about this next and crucial step in "the return of the repressed" in *Moses and Monotheism* (1967[1939]). He proposes in this late work a number of striking hypotheses about the figure of Moses, his life and accomplishments. At the heart of Freud's reflections, which he attempts to support with textual and historical material, is the notion that the historical Moses was in fact an Egyptian nobleman who attempted to impose on the Jews the Egyptian religion of the pharaoh Ikhnaton.

The religion in question was a strict monotheism that refused itself the tempting beliefs in magic and a life after death. Moses hoped, as Freud has it, to found a new empire by freeing the Jews from Egypt and passing on to them the new religion—a religion now disdained by the Egyptians, who placed a high value on the afterlife. Having "stooped" to the Jews, Freud says, Moses made them his people; they were his "chosen people" (1967[1939], 55). The Jews are said to have repaid Moses for his high-minded efforts with rebellion: Freud says they murdered their "enlightened despot." Moses's newly adopted people found the highly spiritualized religion of Ikhnaton no more to their liking than had the Egyptians of the Eighteenth Dynasty (1967[1939], 58). Freud remarks that Ikhnaton's religion was unable to satisfy their needs: it represented too much of a burden—compare the biblical story of the golden calf—and so, they threw the burden off.

Having rejected Moses's highly spiritual religion and having even killed Moses himself, Freud hypothesizes, the Jews took up the worship of an altogether new god, Jahve (Jehovah). Freud says that Jahve, a "volcano God," "an uncanny, bloodthirsty demon" who avoids the light of day and walks at night, was very much like any of the gods worshiped by neighboring tribes and peoples at the time (1967[1939], 39).

Later, however, the monotheism taught by Moses, after centuries of lurking in darkness and obscurity, is said to have returned with a great force. This force is attributed to the fact that the monotheistic "one, true God of all," along with the godlike father figure of Moses, had been subjected to something akin to the repression that underlies neurosis. Freud remarks that Jahve, the intervening god of the Jews, came to be fused with the returning god of Ikhnaton and Moses. Jahve thus became purer, taking on a resemblance to the old Mosaic god. The entire Jewish people came to recognize Jahve as the only god, and he became the focus of all their interests. Freud thus says that remaining in the background across the centuries between Moses's introduction of the monotheistic god and that god's later return was the conception of this older, this other, more spiritual god, a single god who embraced the whole world, a god "as all-loving as he was all-powerful," a god opposed to magic and ritual, and one who established as humanity's highest ideal "a life of truth and justice" (1967[1939], 61–62).

No matter, then, that the teaching of Moses had been rejected. The tradition of this "more spiritual conception of God" that "the Egyptian Moses" had given "to one part of the people" itself remained, its influence eventually attaining Moses's original aim (1967[1939], 61–62). In time, the forgotten god of Moses, the god whose place was taken by Jahve, is said to have outgrown Jahve in strength (1967[1939], 62). The prophets, Freud says, "seized by the great and powerful tradition which had grown in darkness," diligently preached Moses's old doctrine of a god who rejects ceremonial and sacrifice, a god who demands but belief "and a life of truth and justice" (1967[1939], 63). The prophets' efforts are seen to have been successful, reestablishing "the old belief," which became the "permanent content of the Jewish religion" (1967[1939], 63).

Freud, true to form, explains the delayed effect of the earlier doctrine of the "one, true God" by analogy to neurosis, as the return, after a period of latency, of a long-forgotten event. Freud thinks it was precisely repression, followed by latency and return, that gave the later monotheism its enormous power over people. The Jews close to the original events are said to have "repressed" the killing of their leader and lawgiver (1967[1939], 85). And for a long time, no trace was indeed to be found of the monotheistic religion. Jewish monotheism and "traumatic neurosis," Freud says, correspond on the feature of latency (1967[1939], 84–85).

Bridging the generations when no vestige of monotheism was anywhere in evidence was the archaic heritage. Moses's religion had not perished from the earth. There survived rather, says Freud, an "obscured and distorted" memory of it. The "tradition of a great past" continued to exercise its effects "from the background" (1967[1939], 159–60). The tradition gradually grew in force until, according to Freud, it finally changed Jahve into the God of Moses and brought back the long-forsaken monotheistic religion (1967[1939], 159–60). The monotheistic ideal, "the religion of the primal father," thus seizes hold of the Jews after a long period of latency, coming to be their most treasured possession (1967[1939], 108).

The murder of the primal father, on the one hand, and Moses's monotheism and murder, on the other, are intimately associated, in Freud's view, in the archaic heritage, the latter deriving their meaning and power from the former. "The one true God" of monotheism, he says, was no one else but the returned murdered father, and Moses an "eminent father substitute" (1967[1939], 113). Awakening among the Jews the memory of the primal father stored in the archaic heritage, according to Freud, was "a recent real repetition of the event," the murder of Moses (1967[1939], 129–30). Freud conjectures that, without this murder, monotheism would never have gained a foothold. Monotheism was later able to make the powerful impression it did on the Jews because, in killing the "eminent father substitute," Moses, they had repeated the great primeval crime (1967[1939], 113). Through the murder of Moses, the "original crime" thus paid a return visit. This murder is said to form an important link between the murder of the primal father and the reappearance of that father as the "one, true God" of monotheism (1967[1939], 114). In adopting monotheism, the Jews denied the earlier events surrounding Moses, such as Freud claims to have retrieved (1967[1939], 85).

As in neurosis, so in the father's return in monotheism is a compromise struck in which something is remembered, but incorrectly. The father is brought back in Jewish monotheism but not properly identified as the primal human father. As in neurosis, so in the religious case is there the characteristic compulsiveness: "great psychic intensity" and independence of the demands of reality and logic (1967[1939], 96).

Christianity

Despite the enormous advance made in the history of religion with monotheism and the return of the father-God, Freud points out that aspects of the "prehistoric tragedy" still remained buried. The return of the repressed, Freud says, is a "slow" one. By reason of the general upward movement of the repressed, these remaining aspects continued to press for recognition. Freud detects in the Jewish people's mounting sense of guilt the precursor of a further advance into consciousness of repressed human prehistory. The apostle Paul, Freud says, seized upon this sense of guilt and traced it back to its origin (1967[1939], 109–11). Paul called it original sin, identifying it as an offense against God himself that only a death could expiate. Freud comments that Paul was indeed right, up to a point, but that he was unable to make the final identification of the offense as the murder of the primal father. The original deed thus remained in the forgotten background, "the fantasy of expiation" taking its place in consciousness in the form of the good news of humanity's salvation: by sacrificing himself on the cross, a son of God had taken upon himself the whole world's guilt.

Christianity represents, in Freud's view, a further major advance of repressed human prehistory back into human awareness. Humanity now admits, in Christian doctrine, its "original sin," correctly acknowledging it as an offense against God. Much of the truth of the events of human prehistory, Freud comments, is thus owned up to. The teachings of Christianity are sufficiently revelatory, moreover, for Freud to decipher the true character of the original offense. Christianity is said, in other words, to make the tacit admission that humanity's primal sin was an actual murder of the original God, the historical primal father, now "God the Father." Christianity holds the death of Christ to be a complete expiation releasing humankind from original sin, thus, in effect, admitting the original sin as a murder of the primal father: the sin has to fit its expiation, the crime its punishment. Freud comments that only the "sacrifice of another life" can atone for a murder and that the "self-sacrifice" indicates a "blood-guilt" (1946[1913], 198). From the necessity of the death of Christ to reconcile humanity with its father, Freud surmises the true character of the sons' prehistoric crime. Freud thus works backwards: since it was a son, and indeed the very son of God, who had to atone for humanity's guilt, that guilt must be due to an actual murder of the primal father.

Freud locates the historical truth in Christ's resurrection in the idea that the risen Christ is the returned father, transformed and put in his place. Here, then, is one of God's sons who, after all this time, has achieved the primal father's fullness of power, who, become a God like his father, has finally taken the father's place. In this way, Freud comments, are the sons' original wishes against the father fulfilled (1946[1913], 199). "The religion of the son," Freud says, succeeds that of the father (1946[1913], 199)—it is possible to make out in Freud's own deification of human reason ("Our God Logos") a further development in this religion of the son.

The killing of Moses, we have seen, prepared for monotheism's later return and acceptance by the Jews. Freud detects a parallel in the case of Christ. The killing of Christ prepared the way for the apostle Paul to create a new religion and thus to further the unveiling in consciousness of the events of human prehistory. Christ, Freud says, was Moses's "substitute and successor" (1967[1939], 114). The transfigured (resurrected) Christ is a son taking his father's place, at one and the same time "the resurrected Moses" and "primeval father" making his return (1967[1939], 114). Christianity is thus seen to mark an enormous progress in the repressed's return (1967[1939], 111–13).

Freud sees the totem feast surviving, moreover, with only slight distortion, in the Christian Eucharist. He remarks that "the children of God" consider themselves, in the sacrament of the Eucharist, to be eating God's very flesh and to be drinking his very blood (1963[1925], 130–31). Christian Communion is viewed at bottom as a renewed setting aside of the father—a repetition of the original crime which made expiation necessary in the first place (1946[1913], 199)—and the installation of human beings in the place of God. Intended as a propitiation of the father-God, the Eucharist ends by dethroning the father and setting him aside (1967[1939], 111). The very ritual that restores the father—in the person of Christ, the father's substitute—to his place of honor and authority is a defiant reenactment of his cruel removal.

Religious Doctrines as Delusions

Freud views the phenomena of religion as "survivals" and "revivals" of the past, the forgotten returned after the fashion of neurotic symptoms. Each part that makes its return is seen as bringing with it tremendous power and influence, like anything that has undergone repression and later comes back. Religious phenomena, like, and indeed as, psychopathological symptoms, are "the return of the repressed" (1967[1939], 164)—thus, according to Freud, the compulsive quality found in religious doctrine, ritual, and morality.

Religious rituals are compulsions—serving to protect against expected misfortune and, thus, to allay anxiety. The moral prescriptions of religion are prohibitions—serving to hold temptation at bay and, thus, to prevent a renewal of the sense of guilt. Religious doctrines, according to Freud, are delusions. A delusion, it will be recalled, is an idea that contradicts reality, a belief held counter to all available evidence. A delusion, Freud says, always harbors some portion of forgotten historical truth. Freud views the compulsiveness characteristic of delusional beliefs as issuing from the core of unconscious truth at their base.

Thus, while religious doctrines have not the least foundation in external reality, they nevertheless bear within them a kernel of returning historical truth, which is what makes people believe them (1967[1939], 108). Freud says his realization that religious doctrines contain the essence of the historical truth increased his respect for religion. Such truth as makes its return in delusions, however, always undergoes distortion and misrepresentation. Freud remarks that the historical truth contained in religious doctrines has been so systematically disguised that only a few have been able to discern it. As the disguised return of the repressed—distorted returning truth—religious beliefs are compromises, like religious rituals and moral injunctions.

What returns with enormous power and influence in the doctrines of religion, in Freud's view, is humanity's "original sin," which is why these doctrines demand belief and withstand every logical objection (1967[1939], 107). This process, Freud is saying, is to be understood in terms of the delusions occurring in certain psychotic conditions. The monotheistic ideal of the "one, true God," for example, is the disguised return of humanity's repressed past, a distorted memory that people have no choice but to give their credence to upon its return (1967[1939], 167). As a revival of the past, the belief in one God is truth, historical (and not "material") truth. As a distortion of the truth of the past, this belief is a psychotic delusion. Freud thus views religion not only as a mass compulsive neurosis but as a mass delusional psychosis as well.

The Future of Religion

Freud's hope that enlightened reason (Logos) will come to displace the religion of illusion has already been alluded to (see above, "The Development of an Adult Attitude"). Freud holds that religion, grounded in repression and functioning as compulsion, has served humanity well in restraining instinct and, in particular, human violence. The renunciation of instinct, Freud remarks, is a cornerstone of civilization. He is nevertheless of the opinion that the time has come for the replacement of the irrational workings of repression by the "rational operation of the intellect," exactly as happens in psychotherapy. Intellect is destined to replace affect—thus manifests itself once again Freud's belief in the superiority of reason over feeling (compare above, "Religion and the Oceanic Feeling"). Reason is to overcome repression first by undoing its hidden hold on human life—by rendering that hold conscious—and then by taking over from repression the control of unruly human instinct and by establishing rules for communal living (1964[1927], 73).

Freud welcomes the full exposure of the repressed to conscious awareness. Become conscious, our unseemly prehistory would lose its power to stage its return ("the return of the repressed") as the phenomena of religion (mass neurotic and psychotic symptoms). The full disclosure in consciousness of primal human history would thus spell the end of religion. Freud holds that compulsiveness in the form of the world's religions—mass religion viewed in its deeper motivation—must be brought to an end for humanity's sake, in the interest of the liberation of human powers currently in bondage to repression.

Freud sees religion as a transitional stage between the childhood and the adult phases of human development (1964[1927], 69–73). He points out that the compulsive neuroses of childhood, to which he has likened religion, tend to disappear spontaneously in the course of development. He thinks that a parallel growing out of the "universal compulsive neurosis" is inevitable and, indeed, that humanity is presently in the midst of just such a stage of growth (1964[1927], 71). Religious phenomena, Freud says, are "religious relics" (1964[1927], 72).

FREUD AND EROS

Freud undertook, late in life, a radical revision of his instinct theory. We now turn to this development in Freud's thinking. Freud generally viewed the constructive elements in human life as a sublimation of sexuality. Immediacy of discharge (tension reduction or pleasure), the original—and still underlying—aim of the sexual instinct, by this account is said to become inhibited ("aim-inhibited sexuality"), and other, higher aims, such as tenderness, group cohesion, and work, to be pursued in its stead. Constructive aims are thus said to be secondary to the original and more fundamental, pleasure-seeking instinctual aim—the aim of eliminating tensions from the organism.

At various points in his later writings, however, when Freud takes up a discussion of Eros, the "sexual" as distinguished from the destructive instincts, he moves away from basic tenets of his standard tension-reduction model. He proposes, for example, that Eros holds everything in the world together (1965[1921], 30)—such a state of affairs presumably existed before the first appearance of human beings and, thus, before sublimation. Eros, moreover, is said to break the peace by producing tensions—such an activity is directly counter to the aim of reducing organismic tension. And civilization is said to serve Eros, whose aim is "to combine single human individuals, and after that families, then races, peoples and nations, into one great unity, the unity of mankind" (1962[1930], 69); Eros has the aim "of uniting and binding," of making more than one into one (1960[1923], 35; 1962[1930], 55). Finally, Freud calls Eros "the preserver of all things" (1959[1920], 92)—this task of preservation presumably extends to tense states of affairs. Eros, continually accomplishing ever more far-reaching combinations of living particles, is thus seen to have the goal of making life more complex and of preserving it in all its intricacy (1960[1923], 30).

The conservative aim said to be characteristic of instinct in general is thus not found to govern Eros, the love instinct: Freud says he is unable to apply to Eros his formulation that instincts tend to bring back an earlier, more restful state of the organism (1949[1940], 21). Freud discovers, to the contrary, a striking opposition between the never-ending tendency of Eros toward extension and the conservative character of instinct. He remarks that this opposition "may become the starting-point for the study of further problems" (1962[1930], 65n).

The aim of Freud's destructive instincts is the literal destruction of things, their tearing apart, the undoing of connections (1949[1940], 20). In addition to "the instinct to preserve living substance and to join it into ever larger units," Freud writes that there is a second, "contrary instinct" that seeks to take these units apart and return them to "their primeval, inorganic state" (1962[1930], 65–66). The destructive instincts—like Eros, said to be everywhere at work in nature—seek the destruction of any and all bodily cells and, thus, the literal death of the organism. As Freud succinctly puts it, "The aim of life is death." The destructive instincts thus constitute a "death instinct."

The death instinct, working to reinstate the more peaceful state of affairs that prevailed before the first appearance of life and its greater tensions, clearly manifests the conservative character attributed by Freud to instinct in general. Freud's earlier instinct theory—before the introduction of Eros as the enhancer and conserver of an expanding life—generally opposed pleasure-seeking (unsublimated) sexuality to destructiveness, taking them together as the two great forces at work in the organism (instincts). An increase in sexual tension is experienced as irritating, its decrease (tension reduction) as pleasurable. The organism thus seeks the reduction of sexual energy (tension reduction), an undoing of sexual energy amounting to a death of sorts, "a little death." The pleasure-seeking sexual instincts would thus appear in Freud's earlier theory to belong to the death or destructive instincts, at least in what concerns their original and, in the final analysis, still underlying aim. The backwards course of sexual instincts to a prior state of affairs (lower state of tension) can only be under the sway of the conservative destructive instincts which serve to undo connections and dissolve things.

While Eros introduces new and disturbing tensions into life and works to preserve them, the destructive or death instincts, conforming to "the inexorable pleasure principle," do what they can to annihilate these same tensions, and even life itself (1949[1940], 109; 1960[1923], 36–37). The death instincts, Freud remarks, under the prompting of the pleasure principle, work to subdue Eros, "the mischief-maker," and thus to reinstate a more original state of peace (1960[1923], 49). Destructive instincts and pleasure-oriented sexuality (Freud's earlier instinct theory), said by Freud to be two, apparently come down to the same thing, a single instinct of destructiveness—Freud's late assertion of the conservative nature of all instinct would thus represent the lingering hold of his earlier instinct theory (1949[1940], 19–20). Destructive instincts and the Eros of Freud's later theory, on the other hand, are true opposites.

Eros, as Freud described it later in life, is something new. It does not obey the conservative law said to govern instinct in general. Its original aim is not tension reduction: it is not pleasure-seeking sexuality, either unsublimated or sublimated. Eros is rather a cosmic principle of creation, expansion, unification, and preservation, full partner to a cosmic principle of destruction (death or destructive instincts). Love and hate constitute, in Freud's later theory, nature's two primal forces.

With the death instinct a universal principle of destruction, with Eros a universal principle of construction, and with both principles active "in every particle of living substance," Freud has arrived, in his attempt to discover the instinctual foundations of human behavior, at a cosmic struggle of opposites (1960[1923], 31). Freud himself called this struggle the "battle of the giants." Freud arrives at a vision that transcends human life and, indeed, connects with various religious traditions: with Christianity, for example, and its dualism of good and evil (God and the devil); with Taoism and its harmonizing of yin and yang. Freud has, in any case, struck out on a new and promising path in his later theorizing: leaving behind the "contrast" between pleasure-seeking sexuality and destructiveness, he has outlined the myth of an all-determining, transhuman, primal pair.

EVALUATION AND CONCLUSIONS

The influence both of Freud's general psychology and of his psychology of religion has been enormous. First, some critical remarks regarding his general assumptions. Contrary to people's experience of themselves as engaged in a network of meanings or values surrounding them at every turn, Freud views human life—and religion—to be an intrapsychic struggle among ego, id, and superego. This internal battle between conscious and unconscious, between the mind and a "mind behind the mind," is a legacy of Cartesian philosophy. The mind, René Descartes said, was *res cogitans*: an inner, closed, and private domain confined to its own states and, thus, without any direct access to the world outside it. Mind and meaning, for Descartes, as for Freud, are inside. This intrapsychic location of mind (ego, id, and superego) is a metaphysical assumption on Freud's part, an act of faith taken over from the modern philosophical tradition. The time is ripe, it is suggested, for psychology to set aside metaphysical approaches of all sorts—including the objectivism by which Freud equated the workings of the entire universe with physical and chemical operations (the Cartesian *res extensa*)—in favor of more modest approaches.

The immediately following paragraphs comment on Freud's several psychological attempts to account for the phenomena of religion. Freud's treatment of the oceanic experience, so central in the work of William James, Carl Jung, Abraham Maslow, and Alan Watts, seems more an attempt to dispose of a theoretically troublesome matter than to come to serious terms with it. Freud's established understandings, it seems, prevented him from considering the mystical experience of oneness on its own ground, and so, he reduced it, as was his wont, to its past.

Where Freud's handling of the oceanic feeling reveals his disdain for feeling as a legitimate path to knowledge (compare James's opposed attitude), his theory of illusion manifests his low estimation of the role of imagination in human life (compare the opposed view of Jung). Freud indeed wanted to see dismantled all "primitive" products of the imagination, all myths and other such illusions. Whether or not one is willing to go that far, by unmasking childish, parent-oriented, wish-fulfilling religious behavior, Freud has made an important contribution to the psychology of religion.

Freud's coherent and intriguing theory of the ultimate origins of religion in the murder of the primal father is fanciful at best. If anything, Freud's accounts in this regard embrace too much, are too coherent, too ingenious. And, indeed, a frequent charge leveled against Freud is that he drew historical conclusions well beyond the evidence—consider, for example, his version of the "Egyptian Moses" or his idea that every culture passes through a totemistic phase. It is difficult to avoid the suspicion that Freud was so beholden to the Oedipus complex that he was driven to find "historical" confirmations of it.

Freud reminds us of the important role of suspicion in the psychology of religion. And, to be sure, there are wish-fulfilling and compulsive forms of religion. The problem is that Freud takes into account only such forms. Just as there is an immature, sick religion, so, too, is there a mature, healthy one (Allport, ch. 4). There are indeed many ways to be religious.

Freud's late theory of Eros seems worthy of further exploration. One wonders what Freud might have made of Eros had he been able to break with nineteenth-century positivism. What if, for example, Freud had considered the oceanic feeling of oneness with the universe as a manifestation of Eros? Freud viewed Eros as all-embracing and all-uniting, indeed as holding everything in the universe together. Why not the oceanic experience as an experience of Eros in its cosmic dimension?

REFERENCES

Feuerbach, L. *The Essence of Christianity*. New York: Harper, 1957.

Freud, S. "Obsessive Acts and Religious Practices." In *Character and Culture*, ed. P. Rieff, 17–26. New York: Collier, 1963 (first published in German in 1907).

———. *Totem and Taboo: Resemblances between the Psychic Lives of Savages and Neurotics*. New York: Random House, 1946 (first published in German in 1913).

———. "Psychoanalysis and Religious Origins." In *Character and Culture*, ed. P. Rieff, 222–27. New York: Collier, 1963 (first published in German in 1919).

———. *Beyond the Pleasure Principle*. New York: Bantam, 1959 (first published in German in 1920).

———. *Group Psychology and the Analysis of the Ego*. New York: Bantam, 1965 (first published in German in 1921).

———. *The Ego and the Id*. New York: Norton, 1960 (first published in German in 1923).

———. *An Autobiographical Study*. New York: Norton, 1963 (first published in German in 1925).

——— *The Problem of Anxiety*. New York: Norton, 1936 (first published in German in 1926).

———. *The Future of an Illusion*. New York: Doubleday, 1964 (first published in German in 1927).

———. *Civilization and Its Discontents*. New York: Norton, 1962 (first published in German in 1930).

———. *New Introductory Lectures on Psychoanalysis*. New York: Norton, 1965 (first published in German in 1933).

———. *Moses and Monotheism*. New York: Random House, 1967 (first published in German in 1939).

———. *An Outline of Psychoanalysis*. New York: Norton, 1949 (first published in German in 1940).

Jung, C. G. *Memories, Dreams, Reflections*, ed. A. Jaffe. New York: Random House, 1961.

Ricoeur, P. *Freud and Philosophy: An Essay on Interpretation*. New Haven: Yale University Press, 1970.

3

✛

Carl Jung

The innermost self of every human being and animal, of plants and crystals, is God.

—Carl Jung

The psychology of Swiss psychiatrist Carl Gustav Jung (1875–1961) is a psychology of religion to its core. Like Sigmund Freud's, Jung's psychology is a psychodynamic one, focused on relations of power between conscious and unconscious. Jung acknowledges a great debt of gratitude to Freud for his pioneering explorations of the unconscious. He indeed says that Freud, by exploring "those dark places" called complexes—a "complex" is an autonomous set of emotionally charged psychic contents—was the true discoverer of the unconscious. Jung remarks that those who resisted Freud were in actuality resisting what was beyond their control in themselves: "fascinating" and "terrifying" complexes. When complexes take over, Jung says, the precious freedom of the ego comes to an abrupt end (1969c, 104). Complexes are so important, in Jung's view, that he considers them, and not dreams, to be the "royal road" to the unconscious.

Despite his indebtedness to Freud and his close association with him for a number of years, Jung was never able to bring himself to accept Freud's belief in the overwhelming importance of sexuality in human life. Particularly objectionable to him was Freud's reduction of spirituality to repressed instinct (1961b, 149). Jung in fact finds there to be not only an instinctual unconscious but a spiritual one as well. The mind, he says, is possessed of specific principles of its own, archetypes that, expressing themselves in consciousness in the form of universal symbols or myths, first give rise to consciousness, structure all its experiences, and initiate its far-reaching transformations. Charged with archetypal power, symbols introduce the zest of the divine into consciousness, turning every human life into a spiritual adventure of meaning. Jung indeed defines religion as careful consideration of the symbols reaching us from the unconscious. Spirit, then, has a life of its own, according to Jung, and is every bit as universal as instinct. Together, archetypes and instincts form what Jung calls the "collective unconscious." All in all, says Jung, our life, our ideas, and our behavior "spring from something greater than the personal human being" (1961a, 333).

Jung, committed to the exploration of the life of the spirit on its own terms, finds an ally in William James. Jung says he greatly admires James's psychology, citing his "psychological vision and pragmatic philosophy" as his guides on "more than one occasion." James's "far-reaching mind," Jung comments, made him realize that psychology's horizons "widen into the immeasurable" (1969c, 125).

THE REALITY OF THE PSYCHE

Jung uses the term "psyche" for the totality of all psychic processes. As such a totality, the psyche or mind contains that limited consciousness that goes by the name "ego." The psyche, Jung says, sets the limit for human experience. Everything we know or come in contact with is mediated through the mind: the human psyche is the "starting-point of all human experience" (1969c, 125). All objects of immediate experience are "the contents of consciousness" (1969c, 139–40). Such contents occur in the form of images: the human being, "enveloped in a cloud of changing and endlessly shifting images," lives "immediately only in the world of images" (1969c, 327–28). Put simply, "image *is* psyche" (Wilhelm and Jung 1962, 130). We live in a world of images created by the psyche.

Jung thus emphasizes the reality of the psyche. "Psychic experience" being the only realm we know immediately, the surrounding world is virtually nonexistent unless it takes the form of a psychic image (1969a, 480–81). The psyche is seen to generate knowledge—scientific knowledge, for example—which, then, is rooted in the psyche. The psyche, Jung writes, is the "womb of all the arts and sciences" (1966, 86). Art, science, and the very world itself are thus all a function of the psyche, the "'sine qua non' of all existence" and the reality par excellence. If there is anything more real than the psyche, Jung says, it is impossible to imagine what that could possibly be—anything imagined, of course, is itself a psychic image.

The psyche is thus found to be a phenomenon in its own right and, indeed, to be "superlatively real" (1968a, 173–74). Jung rejects any attempt to understand or try to explain the psyche as an epiphenomenal product of "matter," in his view, a "thoroughly metaphysical concept" which uncritical individuals have turned into a substance (1969a, 477). It was the nineteenth century, he says, that first "discovered" matter and drew the conclusion that everything arises from material causes operating through chemical action (1969c, 340–41). Psychic happenings thus came to be reduced to glandular activity and thoughts to the brain's secretions (1969c, 343). In this way, the psyche—the avenue to all knowledge—was pushed to the point of virtual nonexistence (1969c, 169). Jung sees in the omnipotent matter of nineteenth-century materialism the Creator God of old, no longer in personal, but in conceptual, form. Jung remarks that the rise of materialism was by no means the first time in history that the gods have undergone transformation (1969c, 340–41).

Jung adopts a phenomenological approach to the psychological realm. He claims to have no theory but simply to be giving an empirical description of the self-presenting phenomena of the psyche. He says that we must have the courage in our day to undertake a psychology with the psyche left in, which is to say, a psychology based on the psyche as an independent "spiritual principle" (1969c, 344). Outwardly, the human being is a living material body—human being as "living being"—but inwardly it is a series of images of its activities—human being as "mind" or "spirit" (1969c, 326). Material body and field of images, body and mind, are a pair of opposites, in Jung's view, two sides of the same coin. Jung suspects that their very division may be the separation, in the interest of conscious discrimination, of a single reality.

The psychic images, which alone we are in contact with, are said to be anything but a random "picturing" of vital activities but to form instead an overall self-regulating structure, full of purpose and meaning (1969c, 325–26). Jung gives the name "analytical psychology" to his approach. Analytical psychology, refusing to break psychic phenomena down into their supposed elements, concerns itself with the psyche as a self-regulating whole (1969c, 363). The term "analytical" is thus not to be misunderstood.

THE UNCONSCIOUS

The psyche consists of both conscious and unconscious contents. There are said to be no clear boundaries between the two: the psyche is a "conscious-unconscious whole" (1969c, 200). The far vaster portion of the psyche, according to Jung, is unconscious. "Unconscious," for Jung, means "unknown." The unconscious psyche is thus "the unknown psyche," the unknown within us. The unconscious is not one thing or another, then, but "the Unknown" in its immediate bearing on us (1969c,

68). The unconscious psyche is described as the original form of everything psychic.

"The unknown psyche" is said to embrace as content everything we
know but are not thinking of at the moment; everything we have forgotten; perceptions or impressions that have insufficient energy to become
conscious and thus remain subliminal; sets of ideas that are too weak and
undefined to reach consciousness; everything we want, feel, think, remember, and do, but without paying conscious attention to; the total
range of future things that are presently taking shape in us and will later
become conscious; and everything that won't fit in with the conscious attitude (1969c, 185, 310).

The Personal Unconscious

Jung says that there is a psyche outside of consciousness "whose contents
are 'personal'" in character (1968a, 7). He calls this psyche the "personal
unconscious." The contents of the personal unconscious are the results of
experience, having been acquired during our lifetime. The personal unconscious is said to consist of contents that we would rather forget and
not acknowledge, everything that we would rather believe is not the case
(1969a, 571). The contents of the personal unconscious are integral to the
individual personality, however, and so could just as well be conscious
(1968a, 7). Jung gives the name of "the shadow" to the personification of
the personal unconscious.

The Collective Unconscious

Jung regards the personal unconscious as forming but the top layer of the
unknown psyche within (1969a, 573). There is, in addition, said to be an
unconscious psyche with contents of an impersonal character. This psychic domain is Jung's "collective unconscious." The collective unconscious is described as the depths and foundation of the psyche (1969c,
148); humanity's "unwritten history" from time immemorial (1969a, 188);
the powerful deposit of experience accumulated by our ancestors over
millions of years; and a timeless, eternal world-image (1969c, 376). Instincts and what Jung calls "archetypes," as has already been indicated,
make up the contents of the collective psyche.

Jung says that the collective or impersonal psyche, unlike the personal
unconscious, has nothing to do with individual experience (1969c, 148).
The collective unconscious is thus not acquired during our lifetime. This
"all-embracing One" is said to be present, rather, in each and every one of
us from the beginning. The collective unconscious is the one "psychic sub-
stratum" common to all (1969a, 277). Its contents are "universal and of

regular occurrence" (1969c, 134)—thus its "collective" (impersonal, universal) character. Unknown and, indeed, altogether beyond the reach of our understanding, it is "unconscious." The collective unconscious is the unknown psyche common to all human beings.

The collective unconscious is said to be inherited, its essential structure transcending all differences of culture and individual character (1958, 308). The collective psyche, as Jung sees it, is no less biologically determined and part of our evolutionary development than the body: in common with the human body, the human mind bears traces of its "phylogenetic development" (1969c, 248). The collective unconscious is always there in advance of consciousness as a "system of inherited psychic functioning" passed on from earliest times (1969c, 350). Embedded in the structure of the human brain and the nervous system, according to Jung, lies "a deposit of world-processes" (1969c, 376).

When such a brain begins functioning, it is said to do so in all the "differentiated perfection" it has developed down the ages, producing without fail the very results produced time and again before (1969c, 371). A human child today, Jung remarks, is born with a brain inherited from his or her ancestors, not with the brain of an ape or hippopotamus, with a brain predetermined to specifically human modes of behavior, not to those of an ape or a hippopotamus (1969c, 226–27). The psyche, in Jung's view, is thus anything but a "tabula rasa," but the "deposit" of all that humans have experienced from their earliest beginnings (1969c, 157). The cumulative experience of our ancestors thus survives and plays an active role in the lives of all human beings.

By reason of the basic uniformity of the unconscious psyche, unconscious processes are found to show themselves everywhere in forms that are astonishingly the same (1969c, 110). This is seen especially in the fundamentally identical myths that arise everywhere and at all times throughout the world, without the slightest possibility of cultural transmission. The agreement found among the world's myths is produced, in Jung's view, by the disposition passed down by inheritance to react the same way everywhere and at all times (1969c, 111). "Fantastic mythological motifs and symbols" are said to appear quite spontaneously in consciousness. Jung calls these archetypal motifs or symbols, which are the natural language of the unconscious, "primordial images," saying they belong to the unconscious psyche's "primordial stock" (1969c, 112). Primordial or archetypal images are "pathways" laid down in the course of the experience of our ancestors (1969c, 53).

The collective unconscious is thus said to contain "latent dispositions towards certain identical reactions," "common instincts of imagination and action" (Wilhelm and Jung 1962, 87). Conscious imagination and action first developed, Jung remarks, on the basis of primordial or archetypal images and never lose touch with them altogether. The collective unconscious arranges the material of consciousness into definite patterns, structuring our experience of the world and our behavior towards it. We don't *learn* to be human. Contained in the unconscious, rather, are all the patterns of human existence and activity inherited from our ancestors and shaping "reality" itself (1969c, 349). The way the world appears to us, our sciences, and the very gods we believe in—Jung indeed refers to the collective psyche as the realm of the gods (1971, 192)—are said to be a function of the collective unconscious, the matrix of all conscious phenomena (1969a, 478).

The collective unconscious thus predisposes us to see things as we in fact do, and, indeed, so unobtrusively that we naively take things as being in reality the way they appear to be. Mythological motifs and symbols spontaneously appear in fantasies, dreams, visions, and other unusual mind-states having nothing to do with personal acquisition or cultural influence—the collective unconscious is said to be akin to an "unceasing stream" of images (primordial images) that "drift into consciousness" in dreams and abnormal states of mind (1969c, 350). Before consciousness first arises, then, the human child is outfitted with an existing "system of adapted psychic functioning" (1969c, 349). The collective unconscious predisposes the human being to the full range of human experience, both instinctual and spiritual.

Jung says that the collective unconscious is a natural phenomenon. It contains everything to be found in human life: good and evil, the profound and the silly, the light and the dark, and the beautiful and the ugly (1968b, 94). It can be dangerous, but need not be. In any case, Jung asserts that it should not be made the object of a parlor game (1956, 124). Jung says the collective unconscious contains traces of all the stages life has ever traversed. It would indeed be possible theoretically, in his view, to "peel" the collective unconscious layer by layer, right back to the psychology of the most primitive organisms (1969c, 152).

"Archetypes," the contents of the symbol-producing collective unconscious, are said to be "imprints" in the psyche. Preexisting and conditioning experience, archetypes are the inherited forms of the psyche's functioning; structural forms of what becomes conscious and, indeed, of what can become conscious; forms for perceiving and conceiving: archetypes organize ideas and images, arranging conscious materials into definite patterns of experience and determining the content and course of all psychic processes (1961b, 347; 1969a, 149). Jung says we have not the least direct knowledge of archetypes, inferring their existence, instead, from their effects, from the characteristic direction and shape of human experience, which is to say, from the organization archetypes can be detected to confer on human life (1969a, 518–19; 1969c, 231). Just as instinct regularly and uniformly regulates conscious *action*, archetype regularly and uniformly regulates conscious *perception* (1969c, 136).

Archetypal images are those images—primordial images—possessed of a dynamism that cannot be attributed to the individual (1969a, 319). We don't control archetypal power, Jung insists, but are "possessed" by it. Jung points to mental disturbances characterized by intrusions of the unconscious as the most striking evidence of a store of primordial images. Found in schizophrenia, for example, are "unmistakable mythological images" (1969c, 138).

An archetype manifests or expresses itself in consciousness as a symbol. Jung thus sees a symbol as an archetype making its appearance in consciousness. A symbol is an emotionally charged image possessed of an essentially mythological—universal and transhuman—character. Symbols imply something vague and hidden. Bridges to an unknown shore, Jung says, symbols "mean more than they say" (1966, 76–77). Symbols function to express unconscious contents that were never conscious and that have no other way of reaching consciousness (1969c, 175). Symbols play a compensatory, teleological role in psychic self-regulation: they provide consciousness with precisely what it is lacking at the moment.

Intensity of emotion gives the symbolic archetypal product its numinosity: that is, its distinctive possessive or obsessive quality (1961b, 347). Real forces with a specific energy of their own, archetypes are "powers" within us—independent centers possessed of enormous emotional intensity—capable of interfering with the conscious will and disturbing its intentions (1956, 80; 1961b, 352; 1969c, 313). Archetypes thus have an overpowering, even divine, character (numinosity). Archetypes, in their symbolic manifestations before consciousness, convey an impression of eternity (timelessness) and indefiniteness to the conscious mind (1969a, 490–91). Archetypes are said to account for the experience of unity found in all mystical experience.

Archetypes have a psychic life of their own, then, in Jung's view, producing changes in consciousness with purpose and spontaneity. Archetypes are indeed said to possess some sort of consciousness and free will of their own, some sort of personal form (1969a, 362), to be beings characterized by personality and full of meaning (1969c, 122). Otherwise stated, archetypes are seen to have a certain "effulgence" about them—"numinosity," Jung writes, "entails luminosity" (1969c, 191)—and are seen to behave like consciousnesses (1969c, 229). Citing in evidence dreams and psychopathology, Jung says the unconscious psyche sets goals, feels, perceives, intuits, and thinks, just like the conscious psyche (1969c, 349). Unconscious processes are indeed said to have an intelligence and subtlety superior to the insights of the conscious mind (1969c, 334).

The unconscious is the great unknown, in Jung's view, knowable only through its effects on consciousness (1969c, 368). Archetypes are themselves irrepresentable, announcing themselves only through symbolic ideas and images (1969c, 214). To gauge the importance of these irrepresentable factors in the collective psyche, Jung says we have only to consider the religions of the world and their role in human behavior. All important ideas in history—religious, scientific, philosophical, and ethical—are held to derive from the archetypes (1969c, 158).

Archetypes are, all in all, psychic patterns dating from time immemorial, nature in its pure form (1969c, 149), nature being simply "the given" (1969c, 210). Jung offers the following suggestions regarding the origin of archetypes (1969c, 153–54). Primitives live in a "mystical identity" or "participation" (*participation mystique*, Lucien Levy-Bruhl) with their world, being bound to it in a compulsive—"magical" or "mystical"— manner by a system of projections and introjections (1969c, 265). The primitive does not experience the distinction between subject and object: what is outside is experienced inside, and what is inside is experienced outside. Unconscious identity with the object prevails, the unconscious being projected into the object and the object being introjected into the subject (Wilhelm and Jung 1962, 123).

Plants and animals are thus experienced as behaving like human beings, while human beings experience themselves as animals as well as humans. The surrounding world is alive with ghosts and gods. Everything is exciting and miraculous. The daily rising, course, and setting of the sun, for example, must have had a profound impression on the primitive mind, *imprinting* themselves on the psyche in the form of an image from primordial time: a "primordial image"—archetypes, we recall, are called psychic "imprints" by Jung. Jung speculates that our original human identity ("mystical participation") with the world would have led, in similar fashion, to the whole internal world of archetypes—to the archetypes of the mother, the child, rebirth, the shadow, and the like.

LIBIDO AND ITS TRANSFORMATION

Psychic energy, in Jung's view, is a specific version of the broader "life energy," or libido. Psychic libido is found to be nothing concrete, nothing definable. It is not reducible to a single unchanging "substance," such as sexuality (Freud). The energy of the psyche can undergo any number of transformations that are genuine—life can take on any number of forms that are truly new. Spiritual pursuits are no less real and genuine manifestations of life for Jung than instinctual ones (1969c, 38).

Jung says symbolic events, such as rites of spring and rites of initiation, fire the imagination with new conscious goals and thus serve as stepping-stones to new kinds of activity (1969c, 48). Symbols transform energy, are "symbols of transformation" of energy (1969a, 503; 1969c, 45). Giving libido a new and equivalent expression, the symbol offers a steeper gradient for the channeling of energy. By thus giving rise to new and higher forms of activity, symbols do spiritual work. The archetypes of the collective unconscious are autonomous centers of energy, "powers," which act on consciousness through symbols, archetypal emissaries. Jung cites the emotional charge of symbols as evidence of their archetypal origin and power. It is precisely this archetypal charge that enables symbols to excite and transform consciousness, to change and increase humanity's consciousness. Symbols energize altered patterns of behavior.

The psyche thus grows and becomes differentiated, in Jung's view, by the ego's relationship to the contents of the collective unconscious (archetypes), as these contents take on symbolic form before the conscious psyche. Jung remarks that "symbols of transformation" are most clearly in evidence in a living religion. Collective (institutional) religion allows people to curb instinct (sublimation) and to engage in all manner of worthwhile activities. Opposing spirit to nature, collective religious belief enables a cultural attitude to develop in opposition to pure instinctuality (1969c, 60). Such, Jung says, has been the historical function of all religions: to effect the transformation of human beings into new, future human beings and to make it possible for the old to fade away and die (1969c, 393).

ARCHETYPES AND MYTH

Archetypes constitute, with instincts, the one unknown psyche common to all: the collective unconscious. This collective psyche represents in condensed form untold years of human experience, constituting in each of us the sum total of the psychological functioning of our ancestors (1969c, 280). Archetypes are the "inherited powers of the imagination," giving rise in consciousness to symbols, emotionally charged images (1956, 75). These symbols, constituting in their totality a "natural world-image," have a mythological character: they express the primordial "mystical identity" of experiencer and experienced ("mystical participation"), the unity of experience before the advent of ego-consciousness, and the differentiation of subject and object from one another (1969c, 280). Archetypes, said to form a whole spiritual world within us, generate our religions and our philosophies (1968b, 68). All ideas about humanity and the

world, past, present, and future, derive, in Jung's view, from the archetypal "mythological matrix" of human experience (1969c, 280).

Archetypes thus forever express themselves in the symbolic form of
myth. Humanity's myths, which Jung calls "miracle tales," are essentially
rooted in the pregiven archetypes of the collective unconscious: archetypes are structures reproducing the same mythical ideas over and over
again, wherever human life is to be found (1968a, 35). Myths are universal images. It is not we who invent our myths but myth that addresses us,
presenting itself as the very "Word of God" (1961b, 340). Myths shape,
even invent, us. No one escapes mythological involvement, in Jung's
view, and least of all those who denounce myth in the name of enlightened progress.

Myths, Jung remarks, are psychological facts (1969c, 37). He says that
the mythical fantasies his patients recounted to him "came" to them from
the unconscious. The similarity of myths from primitive times and the
fantasies of twentieth-century patients indicate to Jung their common origin in the collective unconscious. Projected from the unconscious, the
same "myth-motifs" recur wherever humans are found. Mythological images and motifs are typical psychological phenomena, to be understood
in terms of psychological imprints, archetypal traces of the most common
functions of the human psyche (1971, 169).

The Function of Myth

Myth is an expression, then, in Jung's view, of the archetypes of the collective unconscious, their natural, primordial language (1968d, 25). The
unconscious always shows itself to the conscious mind in the symbolic
form of emotionally charged images. The symbols constitutive of myths—
but also of fairy tales, folklore, rituals, and religious doctrines—channel
the contents of the collective unconscious to consciousness for integration
there. The symbolic language of myth is the necessary "intermediate stage
between unconscious and conscious cognition" (1961b, 311). Modern consciousness may seem infinitely far removed from the archaic world of
myth, but, in Jung's opinion, its roots are undeniably mythological.

Reason is said to be limited in comparison to myth. Purely rational formulations are far too narrow, in Jung's view, to do justice to human experience as a whole. The "primordial language" of myth is richer and broader
and can express life more precisely than science (1961b, 3). While the rational enterprise of science is general and abstract, myth is individual and
concrete. Jung thus locates the power of the symbolic language of myth in
its ability to speak to the whole human being. Life and existence have their
ground, in Jung's opinion, beyond reason. And yet, he insists, the irrational
aspects of life—those aspects beyond, but not against, reason—have an

equal right to be lived. Here myth plays its specific role. Myth, by no means mere fiction or illusion, expresses best the eternal aspects of human life (1969a, 409): myth is an "all-embracing vision," the disclosure of a "divine life" in us (1961b, 340). By adequately expressing the "dynamism underlying our individual entanglement in things," myths have a "'saving,' therapeutic significance" (1961b, 320).

To sum up, the collective unconscious, with its archetypes, is the myth-making mind, "the matrix of eternal images and meanings" (1971, 167). Myths are a necessary stage from unconsciousness to consciousness and constitute a broader vision than science.

The conscious mind originated in the collective unconscious and derives its life from it. By keeping ego-consciousness in contact with our roots, myth is a kind of "mental therapy" (compensation) for the overall problems of life (1968b, 68). Jung says that, in the final analysis, all collective ideas, deriving from the collective unconscious, are religious in character, archetypal compensations for life's major problems (1971, 220). Primordial images (archetypes) are viewed as deposits resulting from a struggle for existence and adaptation that has been going on for an untold number of years (1971, 221). Whenever any human is confronted with a major life experience, this deposited treasure is necessarily constellated. Jung comments that the mythic imagination has unfortunately all but vanished in our age. Having thus lost contact with our roots, we are said to be in serious trouble.

A tireless advocate of the role of myth in human life, Jung nevertheless points out that myth may be equivocal and even demonic. Critical intellect is not to be repudiated (1961b, 341). Reason is needed to test the mythic visions arising from the collective unconscious. Greater insight, for example, might have prevented the myth of the "master race" from bewitching an entire nation and creating a living nightmare for millions of people.

The Universality of Mythical Themes

Jung says that archetypes account for the fact, already alluded to in the above, that the same motifs appear in the folk tales and myths of peoples everywhere (1969a, 50). Typical mythological images are "autochthonous"—native to the human psyche—appearing regularly in the legends of gods and heroes, in stories that tell of the coming and going of spirits, and in the notion of a magic substance or power (1969c, 137). The same mythic themes found in ancient times repeat themselves throughout the world today. They reappear in the dreams of Jung's patients, as well as in the fantasies of psychotics, which are virtually identical with those to be found in primitive peoples (1969c, 372). Jung views the migration of myths from culture to culture (cultural transmission) to be highly improbable (1969a, 490). As the natural symbolic expressions of archetypes transmitted by heredity to all human beings, however, humanity's myths would be expected to show the observed uniformity.

Over the course of his scientific lifetime, Jung made an intensive comparison of the symbols found in the symptoms of psychotics, in the world's religions, in mythology, in his own powerfully influential dreams, folklore, fairy tales, Gnosticism, alchemy, literature, and the dreams of neurotics. Such a comparative method was his way of scientifically establishing the hypothesis of the similarity of the human mind to which he gave the name "collective unconscious" (1968d, v). Jung insists that he did not posit the collective unconscious in advance but arrived at it empirically by surveying the multiplicity of relevant cross-cultural phenomena. The collective unconscious is inferred from the data as that unknown psychic region necessary to account for the variety of uniform conscious outcomes.

Jung thus begins with myths, fairy tales, the experiences of neurotics and psychotics, and his own dreams and discovers a region of the unknown (unconscious) psyche deeper than Freud's id, one that is not reducible to the operation of material-instinctual forces, a spiritual foundation for humanity's most fundamental experiences. The collective unconscious, with its archetypes, becomes for Jung a necessary postulate if the data of consciousness (myths, fairy tales, dreams, and the like) are to be adequately understood. Jung does not claim to know what archetypes are, only what they do.

INDIVIDUATION

Jung defines individuation as the process by which an individual living being becomes what it is meant to be from the beginning: the acorn an oak, the calf a cow, and the child an adult (1969a, 467–68). Human individuation is one's unfolding as a human being like all other human beings, but in one's own unique and destined way. Our task in life, in Jung's view, is thus, on the one hand, to actualize our extensive common humanity and, on the other, to become differentiated from everybody else and stand on our own two feet (1961b, 343). Individuation reaches its ultimate goal in the experience of what Jung calls the "self."

The "self" is the totality of consciousness and unconsciousness, the personality in its wholeness. To attain the self is for the center of gravity of the personality to shift from the fragmentary and limited ego to a "hypothetical point" midway between consciousness and the unconscious (1970b, 45). To attain the self, the center of the total personality, is for the ego now to revolve around it as the earth does around the sun (1956, 252; 1968a, 23–25). The self's reality is infinitely wider than that of the ego, which is small in scope and intensity by comparison, "like a smaller circle within a larger one" (1969a, 258).

The typical expression in consciousness of the archetype of the self is said to be the mandala, the circular symbol of order and wholeness (1961b, 335). The mandala is a "uniting symbol," able to integrate all aspects of the personality (1969a, 79, 199). The mandala represents "the struggle and reconciliation of opposites" (1961b, 335): the self is indeed defined as a union of all opposites, embracing both conscious and unconscious, male and female, good and evil, spirit and instinct, and so forth (1968d, 19). The self, in accordance with mandala symbolism, is thus not only the center, or midpoint, of personality, but its circumference as well, embracing both conscious and unconscious, everything psychic (1968b, 41). The self is thus the all-embracing totality of the conscious and the unconscious, the essence of the wholeness of the psyche.

Individuation, synonymous in Jung's terminology with the realization or actualization of the self, is said to be the goal of our biological and psychological development. Every life is destined from the first to be the actualization of a whole: that is, of a self (1968d, 222). With the actualization of the self, Jung says, the original tendency toward wholeness becomes a psychic happening. Individuation is thus the production and unfolding of our previously potential original wholeness. Not only does the ego evolve out of the self as its exponent, not only does "I" happen to my "self," but the ego is directed to the self as its highest goal as well (1968a, 223). Such making real of the self is held to be our strongest urge and a veritable law of nature. Jung comments that the archetype of the self turns up everywhere in mythology, but also in the fantasy life of individuals in the twentieth century (1969c, 317).

Jung describes becoming a self—becoming a whole psychically—as a process of development consisting in integrating the contents of the unconscious into consciousness (1969c, 223). Such integration (individuation) brings about far-ranging transformations in the ego-personality (1969c, 223–24). Unconscious contents, which themselves change upon attaining conscious status, vitalize and enrich the ego. Conscious will subordinates itself to the new and greater figure of wholeness being realized. With the attainment of conscious wholeness or self, the ego preserves its intrinsic structure and qualities (1969c, 225n). And yet, the experience of the self embraces infinitely more than the ego ever could: the ego, all other selves, and indeed the whole cosmos (1969c, 226; see below, "The Microcosmic Character of the Self").

Jung comments that individuation necessarily implies the uniqueness of the individual. To attain the self is to achieve one's true individuality and destiny, to become the single and definite being one is. As life's true goal, the self alone makes sense out of life. Individuation is extricating oneself from the domination of both external (social) and internal (archetypal) figures and achieving one's true individuality within the context of the whole psyche. Individuation comes to pass, Jung comments, regardless of external circumstance.

Time and space are said to be relative in the collective unconscious: no definite temporal or spatial limits apply to the self (1968a, 167–68). The experience of the self is consequently often found to bring with it an experience of timelessness, a feeling of eternity or immortality. The self is said to mean higher consciousness. Jung suspects that the creation of this superior personality leads to a consciousness detached from the world, as a natural preparation for death (1958, 340–41). The process is said to begin at the middle of life, around the age of thirty-five. With life then becoming "life towards death," dying is said to begin well before the moment of death, and death to be the fulfillment of life's meaning. Jung says that religions used to be schools for forty-year-olds but that today they are not up to the task. As a result, people are left to their own devices.

The second half of life is every bit as meaningful as the first half, in Jung's view, only its meaning is different (1956, 84). Life's two halves are each to be lived in accordance with its proper meaning (1969c, 399). The meaning of life's morning is said to lie in coming to grips with the external world, raising a family, and the like—a young person misses out on the first half of life if unwilling to take on the world and fight for one's life with all one's might. But taking such a program over into life's afternoon is done only at the price of inflicting inner damage on oneself—an older person misses out on the second half of life if unable to listen to the "secrets of the brooks" coursing down from the peaks to the valleys. From the middle of life onwards, one is truly alive, in Jung's view, only if one admits death into life, only if one is willing to "die with life" (1969c, 407). It is more in accord with humanity's "collective psyche," Jung remarks, to view death as fulfilling life's meaning, as its true goal rather than its mere termination (1969c, 410). Jung says that the unconscious doesn't make a big deal out of the fact of death but that it has a definite interest in how we die, in how, for example, we settle our affairs with others.

ARCHETYPES AS GODS

Jung describes "the numinous" (*numinosum*), a term already referred to, as "the inexpressible." The numinous approaches consciousness as scarily fascinating: mysterious and inviting, on the one hand, terrifying and repelling, on the other (Otto 1977). The numinous is that which is beyond conscious control, that which has an emotional charge that seizes control of consciousness. The numinous is experienced as an agent with an existence outside consciousness, a compelling power that overtakes the ego and transports it into a state of "will-less surrender," or rapture (1969c, 186).

Because archetypes are outside the ego and independent of it, they qualify, in Jung's opinion, as the possessors of a numinous—or "divine" or "spiritual" or "magical" or "mystical"—quality when they approach consciousness in the form of symbols. Archetypes are "numinous factors," producing feelings of uncanniness and strangeness. Fascinating and possessive, archetypes can force themselves on consciousness and extensively change it (1956, 80). There are, then, according to Jung, superior powers in the psyche. Reason (the ego) is only one psychic function—rationalism, Jung says, is getting stuck in the stage of the son.

Archetypes are, accordingly, of immense significance to the field of religious psychology: the experience (through symbols) of the archetypes is the experience of the numinous, but the numinous is the experience of the divine; therefore, archetypal experience is the experience of the divine, of "the gods." Archetypes often put the ego under their spell, inducing high states of passion and occasioning a surrender that is freely given because of the richness of meaning (spiritual character) they bring with them (1969c, 205–206). Jung comments that archetypes have been known to initiate philosophical and religious convictions in those considering themselves farthest removed from such beliefs.

Despite the immense spiritual meaningfulness of archetypes, Jung says that people are, quite properly, afraid of their menacing power. Archetypes entail a loss of control, that central and hard-won possession of the ego. When contents of the collective unconscious become activated, consciousness is disturbed and confusion ensues. Jung points out that the breaking in of alien contents from the unconscious—visitation by strange and even monstrous thoughts, marked changes in the way the world appears, and distortions in people's faces—characterizes the onset of some forms of psychosis (1969c, 311–12). If psychological processes in the unconscious of a whole people become activated, Jung says one can justifiably compare the mental state of that people to a psychosis. If what is thus activated is successfully communicated to the people, on the other hand, it can have a redeeming effect (1969c, 314–15). Unconscious forces are then channeled into consciousness in a manageable form and a new source of power (libido) is attained by the people.

Jung points out that beings with the characteristics of the archetypes—that is, with numinosity (powerful emotional value, the "psychically powerful")—have always been called divine, "gods" (1967b, 64). And, indeed, according to Jung, "God" is an appropriate name for the numinous, for overwhelming emotion. "God" is "an impulse of the soul": a mental image equipped with numinosity, a symbol in which an archetype makes a rather startling advance to consciousness, a power of a very personal nature with an irresistible influence (1958, 350). "God" is said to be as close as it is possible for an essentially unknown or irrepresentable archetype to present itself directly to consciousness. All in all, "God" is, in Jung's view, a psychological fact of the first order.

Numinous archetypes are thus "ruling powers, the gods" (1956, 105). The collective unconscious, Jung says, houses an internal world of gods: it is a living pantheon, the place of residence—and origin—of all humanity's gods. Spirits and gods, says Jung, belong to the inner psychic realm of the collective unconscious—spirits and gods are indeed said to be one and the same as the collective unconscious (1969a, 525). Jung indeed uses the term "God" as a synonym for the collective unconscious. "The gods," Jung says, are personifications of unconscious contents (1969a, 163).

By identifying archetypes and the divine—archetypes and "the gods"— Jung is admitting the superiority of power of archetypes relative to the ego. The universal presence in human experience of an omnipotent God is evidence, moreover, in Jung's view, for the universal presence of the archetypes of the collective unconscious. Jung says he limits his statements to what reaches people from within the psyche, which is not to deny a God outside the psyche: his comments, he insists, are not to be taken as extending to what might be the case outside the psyche.

Jung rejects repression as an appropriate response to the unconscious. He nevertheless feels that the lines between the conscious and the unconscious, "between what is ego and what is non-ego," should be most sharply drawn. The collective unconscious is to be recognized consciously as "other," that which the ego is not (1956, 83). Jung says the gods were originally experienced as living a life of their own outside the psyche. These gods were projections in space of powers that are still alive and active in the unconscious psyche. And Jung remarks that God may be experienced within one's psyche even today. But God is in no sense a property of the ego. According to Jung, God remains and must remain outside the ego. God is the ego's "living opposite," its "other," an archetypal manifestation (1956, 120). In sum, God is seen to exist within the psyche but outside the ego. For Jung the divine has nothing human about it; God is not, for example, a magnified father (Freud).

Jung says that God is the psychological fact representing one's "supreme value," the greatest power in one's life, the "overwhelming psychic factor" (1969a, 81). Should someone refuse to admit God consciously, then only the names change. "God" now assumes another title— perhaps that of some ideology or "ism"—but "God" demands the same belief, fear, and surrender that any projected God ever did. Every mythology, every religion, and every "ism" is archetypal in its essence (1969c, 206). In Jung's view, something always presses the ego into its service.

Sex is said to have been Freud's God, something numinous religiously observed: "sexual libido," with all the "divine qualities" that have always been attributed to the "psychically stronger agency," functioned as a "hidden God" in Freud's life and theory (1961b, 151–52). To the extent that sex, or whatever, possesses someone, determining his or her actions and thoughts, that person can properly be said to have "made a god of it." Respectability is seen to be "our real god" today (1976, 684). Jung thus says that, when God is rejected on a conscious level, an unconscious substitute simply takes his place. Jung feels it is better to give conscious recognition to the tremendous influence of the collective unconscious relative to the ego and call it "God," the name it has always had (1956, 81).

THE SELF AS AN IMAGE OF GOD IN THE PSYCHE

For Jung, God is neither an idea in need of proof nor an object to be blindly believed in but an "obvious psychic fact" (1969a, 464). God is an experience, the most immediate and certain of all experiences (1961b, 62). Jung argues that no one would talk of God if God were not such a psychological fact of immediate experience: the idea would never have crossed people's minds in the first place, much less taken control of their lives. Jung thus views God as a fact valid in itself. As for proof, he thinks that one can no more prove God than one can prove the beauty of a sunset (1961b, 92). Both simply *are*. As for belief, Jung claims to know God rather than to "believe in" him; he says he believes only what he knows (1969a, 44). He remarks that God and the boundless and unified cosmos that constitutes "God's world" are realities of his experience.

God, for Jung, is an inner experience, the experience of the self. The archetype of the self is described as indistinguishable from the image of God spoken of by early Christian thinkers as imprinted in the human soul at creation (1969a, 157); in the words of the Bible: "God created man in his image. In the image of God he created him" (Genesis 1:27). The experience of the self, Jung says, is an experience of this likeness, the image of God imprinted in the human psyche (1956, 250; 1961b, 334). The self is thus a "manifestation of the ground of the psyche," of the "God within us." The God-image or self, this imprint in the depths and center of human life, is said to be the collective expression from the beginning of time of the immense power over consciousness of "unconscious concentrations of libido" (1971, 243).

When no longer projected as a God distinct from the psyche and inhabiting external space, the self is described as a supreme union of opposites.

Jung says that the supreme union of opposites manifesting itself in consciousness, the experience of the self, and the immediate experience of the
divine within are empirically all one and the same experience (1969a, 261).

Included within the unity and wholeness of the self or inner God-image
is the multiplicity of "the gods" (see above, "Archetypes as Gods"). The
dissociability of the primitive mind shows itself in the belief in several
souls and any number of gods (1969c, 104). Jung points out that spirits
and gods weren't mere topics of discussion for the primitive, as they tend
to be for us, but living experiences. The universal belief in spirits, Jung
says, follows directly from the structural feature of the unconscious by
which it gives rise to complexes (1969c, 101); indeed, he comments, if
there were no tendency toward dissociation in the psyche, no one would
talk of gods or spirits at all (Wilhelm and Jung 1962, 111). Primitives are
thus said to have personified contents of the unconscious as spirits and
gods and to have sought to meet the requirements of these personified
contents by "sacred and magical rites" (1969c, 369). When assimilated, the
gods formerly projected in space become conscious ideas, losing their autonomy and personality (Wilhelm and Jung 1962, 110–11).

All the archetypes are said to be arranged in a concentric order around
the self, the midpoint and circumference of personality: everything in the
psyche revolves around the all-embracing self (1969a, 573). Symbolizing
in consciousness the archetype of the self, the mandala has religious significance in Jung's psychology (1969a, 81). This circular representation expresses the wholeness of the self—the completeness of the psychic
ground—or, in mythological terms, the God incarnate in human life
(1961b, 335). Mandala symbolism thus manifests the God within and the
unity of God and man: mandalas bring the divine totality before consciousness. Jung considers the mandala to be the ultimate in the way of
symbols of the self and his final discovery. Like the mandala, Christ is a
symbol of the self, of God incarnate in human life.

Jung says that one can do no better in the attempt to verbalize the numinous experience of the union of all opposites than the biblical "God is
love" (1961b, 353). Love is a "unified whole." Representing not only thesis and antithesis but synthesis as well, the self is described as having a
thoroughly paradoxical character (1968d, 19). The experience of this par-
adox is said to be the experience of the highest reality: of the God that is
love, of the love that is God, of the God that constitutes the foundation,
center, and circumference of the human psyche.

Attaining the self, we have seen, is becoming individuated, which is to
say, gaining one's true individuality. Since the self is an imprint of the divine in the psyche (God-image), attaining one's individuality in attaining
the self is said to be attaining God, attaining divine status. True individuality is thus inextricably bound up, in Jung's view, with what everyone

calls "God." The fulfillment of the finite lies not in one's beauty or wealth or talent but in one's relation to the infinite.

The God-image is said to be an experience that spontaneously springs up from the collective unconscious. Jung says that this experience is so tremendously effective that people feel it establishes the existence of divine figures—of Christ, for example, or of a creator-God—outside the psyche (1969a, 363). Jung insists, however, that a psychological approach must be critical. The God-image is to be taken as a psychic event. While the experience seems to point to the divine figures, Jung does not see it as establishing their extrapsychic existence.

It is thus naive, in Jung's view, to identify the experience of the self, of the God-image, with a God beyond and separate from the psyche. Jung says it is empirically impossible to determine whether or not there is such a God. Thus, when Jung uses the word "God," he is referring to a psychic event, an archetypal experience, and nothing more. In thus granting "God" a place in the psyche preexisting consciousness, Jung is denying that "God" is an invention of consciousness, but he is not making any affirmations about "God's" true nature (1961b, 347–48). All in all, then, Jung neither denies nor affirms a divine being *beyond* the psyche, but he does indeed grant a place *in* the psyche to a superior force, a force ultimately defined by its indefinability.

Jung says his critics frequently confuse the terms "God" and "God-image" and, so, hearing him say "God" when he is in fact saying "God-image," rank him among the theologians (1969c, 278). Jung insists that talk about "God" is metaphysical speculation—about what might be the case outside the psyche—and altogether beyond the psychologist's competence. Jung refuses to hypostatize the God-image. Talk about the "God-image," on the other hand, is talk about a certain range of psychological facts (experiences) and properly within the psychologist's sphere (1969c, 279). The God-image is a definite fact the psychologist can and must reckon with (1969c, 278). Jung remarks that the idea of God didn't fall from heaven. Its primordial essence is contained, rather, in the human psyche, and no amount of "enlightened progress" will dispel it.

THE MICROCOSMIC CHARACTER OF THE SELF

Jung views archetypes as the equivalent of the world outside the psyche and as complementing that world: what lies outside has its counterpart within; what happens outside also happens within (1968a, 196). Archetypes thus have a cosmic character, which is why they are experienced as numinous and "godlike." The collective unconscious is described as a microcosm— "the small world," the universe in miniature—within us, as wide and universal as the universe itself. We are sons of the macrocosm—"the great world," the universe in its totality. The mandala, the major symbol of the self, is said to express this microcosmic nature of the self (1961b, 196).

Jung remarks that the experience of the psyche's essential archetypal character as an imprint of God (God-image) is an experience of the imprint of the whole universe, an experience of the universe from its very center. The experience of the self, the center and essence of the collective unconscious and of the personality in its totality, is, in other words, an experience of being at the very center of the universe, an experience of our midpoint as the midpoint of all existence (1969a, 288). We have heard Jung to the effect that archetypes are arranged in a concentric order around the self: everything in the psyche revolves around the oneness and wholeness of the self (1969a, 573). But so, too, Jung is saying, does the entire universe. The experienced midpoint that is the self is of truly cosmic significance. Having the same essence as the universe and being its very center, the psyche in its structural totality (self) is held to be in agreement with—to "correspond" to—that of the cosmos: what happens in the macrocosm likewise happens in the microcosm (1961b, 335).

RELIGION

Jung defines religion as the linking up of consciousness with unconscious psychic processes possessed of a life of their own (1958, 117). Religion, Jung says, is "dependence on and submission to the irrational facts of experience." Religion is a "careful consideration and observation" of "dynamic factors" that are "powers"; of unconscious forces—archetypes (see above, "Archetypes as Gods")—and of the symbols that express the life of these forces; of the numinous, which is to say, of the "dynamic agency" beyond conscious control (1969a, 7–8, 596; 1970a, 256). Religion is thus said to connect us with the eternal myth, creating in the process a balance between ego and non-ego. Religion is further characterized as the way consciousness is changed by contact with the numinous (1969a, 8).

The way to reach God, and therefore wholeness, is said to be through the daily exploration and following of the will of God (1961b, 46). This is what constitutes a religious attitude, in Jung's opinion, what religion is all about. Jung insists that one finds one's true individuality not through collective religious practices but through individuation (actualization of the self), by evolving a religion "of an individual character." Jung says there is no disputing religious experience (1969a, 104). Religious experience brings meaning, vitality, and satisfaction to life, causing everything to appear in a new splendor.

Conscious one-sidedness—Western rationalism, for example—may well occasion the development of a dangerous counterposition in the unconscious. Jung says invasions from the unconscious in revenge for the violence consciousness (reason) does it bring with them "intense spiritual suffering." Thus besieged, consciousness faces the serious danger of being undermined and coming under unconscious possession. Religion and magic were developed, in Jung's opinion, to meet just such a possibility and to repair the damage done. Religions are "systems of healing for psychic illness" (1969a, 344).

The Symbols of Religion

Since the Enlightenment, Jung comments, religions have come to be rationalistically misconstrued as philosophical systems "concocted out of the head" (1969a, 408–409). The presumption has been that someone invented God and the various religious dogmas one day and, wielding enormous suggestive power, convinced those around him of his "wish-fulfilling" image of reality (1969a, 409). Jung challenges this view by arguing that it is not the head that thinks up religious symbols at all but the heart, the unconscious region of the psyche, which is precisely why these symbols, a complete mystery to consciousness, come upon us as "revelations."

Religious symbols, Jung says, are "natural" psychic manifestations, with an organic life and development of their own down the centuries (1969a, 409). It is pointed out that even today we find authentic religious symbols springing up, like flowers, from the unconscious. These symbols are said to show themselves, both in form and content, as arising from the same unconscious psyche at the origin of the great world religions. The universality and effectiveness of religious symbols are due to the "adequate expression" they give to the unconscious from which they spring. Religious truths are thus viewed as belonging to our essential psychological constitution.

Codified religious ideas (dogmas), rather than being conscious inventions blindly passed on by tradition, originate in the "careful consideration" of the archetypes—Jung's definition of religion—which they thus express (1969c, 221). Archetypes, forever exercising their effects, don't need to be *believed* in. Their meaning and import are rather said to be intuited (1969c, 221–22). By keeping us in contact with our unconscious roots, the symbols of religion serve their original purpose of warding off the dangers of a potentially vengeful unconscious. Through these symbols, moreover, the collective unconscious offers the promise of redemption to a consciousness wounded by the struggles of life.

The Doctrines of Religion

Theological preaching, says Jung, is a "mythologem," a set of archetypal images giving a fairly "exact description of the unimaginable transcendence" (1976, 682). Jung says that every religious creed (system of doctrines or teachings) arises, on the one hand, on the basis of an experience of the numinous and, on the other, on the basis of trust in the experience and the change this trust produces in consciousness. Creeds are formalizations (codifications) of original religious experience arising from contact with the unconscious (1969a, 8–9). That archetypes are the equivalents of religious dogmas, Jung maintains, can be empirically demonstrated (1968d, 17).

Original religious experience is said to be powerful (numinous) and yet to be idiosyncratic and lacking in conceptual precision. It takes centuries of reflection and working over by a great many people before a purity of formulation is attained that overcomes the peculiarities, shortcomings, and flaws of individual religious experience (1969a, 50). Doctrinal symbols serve to excite consciousness by expressing and depicting before it the archetypes of the collective unconscious. Jung remarks that creeds, though far removed from the original experience, may serve their function as connecting links with the unconscious for thousands of years. Jung's psychology is primarily concerned with original religious experience, the personal religious experience of the individual. Part of his program, however, is to trace the path from such experience to codified religious dogma (1969a, 9).

Religious dogmas are "sacred history," a condensed and formalized rendering of the "myth of the divine being and his deeds" (1968a, 179). Dogmas—of the Trinity, for example, or the Incarnation, or the descent of the Holy Spirit on Pentecost—are said to present in vivid conscious imagery the spontaneous life-processes of the unconscious. Jung remarks that no abstract theory could possibly express the irrational as well. Doctrines are found to be more enduring than theories and to possess a surprising liveliness. Jung finds sufficient reason for this in the power doctrines have to reveal the life of God in the psyche and to put us in contact with that life, and thus to bring meaning to human life. Because doctrines keep the lines of communication open between conscious and unconscious, the unconscious is found to show its friendly, instead of its vengeful, face. So long as doctrines validly express the unconscious, Jung comments, the unconscious recognizes itself in them and cooperates with the conscious mind. Religious doctrine thus fulfills a task that science is unable to.

Jung insists that in engaging in a discussion of religious symbols he is not raising the question of their possible truth or falsity. He claims to deal with facts, not hypotheses. A symbol, he says, is the statement of an unconscious fact that reason can neither substantiate nor refute. Jung treats all metaphysical statements about a realm transcending human experience and verification as psychic phenomena ultimately deriving from and referring to the unconscious (1969a, 476). Psychology, he says, isn't concerned with things "in-themselves" but with what people think about such things, not with the real existence, for example, of a Heavenly Father watching over us but with the fact of the experience of such a figure and of its significance for life (1969c, 309n). Jung warns us not to conclude that, just because people talk about metaphysical objects, these objects actually exist outside the psyche: talking about God does not establish the existence of God (1970b, 548).

Metaphysical statements are important to Jung not because of the suprasensible world they portray but because they are statements of the psyche, because they manifest the psyche. Jung says a God that is absolute and beyond all experience means nothing to him. But a God that is a "powerful impulse" of the soul (unconscious) most certainly does because such a God can influence his life (Wilhelm and Jung 1962, 129). Jung does not claim to know whether the content of religious doctrines is true or false; he has nothing to say about the extrapsychic reality of the metaphysical objects and events depicted. But he emphatically denies that myth, as found in doctrinal symbols, is mere fiction.

Myth is no more false, than, say, a flower. Neither, in Jung's opinion, is to be judged by the rational categories of truth or falsehood. Both, rather, precede reason. Jung insists that psychic processes really do exist and that psychic contents are as real as any plant or animal (1970b, 455). The (psychological but not metaphysical) validity of doctrines is proved, he says, to the extent that "the agreement of mankind" allies itself with them. Jung remarks that a religion needs a myth. He thus opposes "demythologization," the attempt to purify Christianity of such mythical elements as the Virgin Birth and the Resurrection. Since the function of religion is precisely to keep people in touch with the "eternal myth"—and not to justify itself in a "scientific" age—a religion without a myth is said to be pointless (1969a, 409).

Jung cites Catholic Christianity as an example of a religion possessed of powerful mythical elements (1969c, 156). There is belief in a trinity of divine persons: Father, Son, and Holy Spirit. There is a family, with Christ as bridegroom and the Church as his bride and the mother of Christians. The baptistery serves as "the womb of the Church": there Christians are born into the Church and, with that, into union with the bridegroom, Christ. The pope is the "Supreme Pontiff," serving as "medicine man" or "mana personality." Jung says that all the archetypes are in play in Catholic doctrine, with all their psychic power, recapitulating the whole of humanity's ancestral experience of father and mother and child, husband and wife, mana personality, and rescue from great danger. These projections, Jung remarks, furnish the believer with a tangible experience of the collective unconscious. One needs to search no further, for the timeless is always within easy reach. Such religion makes life unconditionally meaningful and keeps one whole.

Religious Rituals

Whereas doctrines are symbolic *statements*, rituals are symbolic *actions*. Like symbols in general, Jung sees rituals as spontaneously springing up from and expressing an unconscious source. In rituals, Jung comments, people put themselves at the disposal of an "autonomous and 'eternal' agency" outside consciousness and its categories (1969a, 249). Rituals are seen to act like containers receiving unconscious contents (1969a, 350). Many rituals, he notes, have the single purpose of producing numinous effects (1969a, 7). Rituals, thus serving as symbolic mediators between the unconscious and the conscious, are said to be a safe way to deal with the unconscious (1969a, 47). They make the unconscious available to the conscious mind, thus protecting against the dangers of a potentially vengeful unconscious. But they do so in a measured way, thus ensuring that the unconscious does not overwhelm consciousness.

PSYCHOLOGY AND CHRISTIAN DOCTRINES

Historically, the two most important Christian doctrines have been the Trinity—three persons forming one God—and the Incarnation—the becoming man of the second divine person. Jung claims to approach both dogmas as psychological symbols: that is, as expressions of dynamic relationships between the collective unconscious and the ego. Jung sees these doctrines as expressing the psyche and its transformation, both over the centuries and in the life history of individuals. The teachings are said to be in remarkable correspondence with the archetypes they manifest: Christian doctrines are found to formulate the "working principles" of the collective unconscious with great precision (1969b, 29). Essential Christian teaching thus contains the secrets of psychic life. Major points of Jung's psychological descriptions of the Christian doctrines of the Trinity and the Incarnation are presented in the following paragraphs.

The thrust of the Christian doctrine of the Trinity is the existence of one God in three persons: Father, Son, and Holy Spirit. The doctrine portrays the Father, the first divine person, as generating the Son, and Father and Son as together breathing forth the Holy Spirit, who thus expresses the love of Father and Son for one another. God the Father represents the unconscious, in Jung's analysis, the original psychic unity, the self in its not yet differentiated form. Jung speaks of "Father" as the "state of unreflecting awareness," the state of merely being aware of what is given (1969a, 182). Father is the childhood state both of humanity and of the individual.

Psychologically, the generation by God the Father of the Son, the second divine person, represents the generation of the ego by the self: the Son is said to be to the Father as the ego is to the self, "as the moved to the mover" (1969a, 259). Jung views ego-consciousness as proceeding or evolving from the unconscious by way of differentiation from it. God the Son represents this process: the emergence of consciousness, its tremendous increase in the course of evolution, and its achievement of independence from the Father (the unconscious). The Son stands for criticism, conscious differentiation, and discrimination.

The Son is thus, in Jung's view, a higher state of reflection than the Father: "Son" is a "reflective and rational state of consciousness" (1969a, 182). By assuming human form in the person of Jesus (doctrine of the Incarnation), moreover, the Son (consciousness) is said to find himself removed from his Father (the unconscious), a distancing that reaches its peak on the cross when the Son cries out, "My God, My God, why have you abandoned me?" This experience is an ordeal for the human being. "Son," Jung points out, is a transition stage, standing for the intermediate state between child and adult, for a growing consciousness increasingly removed from its source in the unconscious (1969a, 182). "Son" is described as "a conflict situation par excellence." The Son eventually has to be reunited with his Father.

The Holy Spirit, in the Christian doctrine of the Trinity, is the third divine person. As the life common to Father and Son, their reciprocal bond of love, Jung says the Holy Spirit restores the original unity by overcoming the split from the Father that the Son had to undergo in order to achieve higher consciousness. The Holy Spirit, Jung writes, "rounds out the Three and restores the One" (1969a, 135). By incarnating in human life (consciousness), the original One entered into opposition to itself, the Son in opposition to his Father. The tension reaches its climax in the suffering of the Son on the cross and in his admission of abandonment by God (1969a, 136).

Jung says that, as man, the Son is apparently so far removed from the Father that he can only find him by an act of absolute self-surrender (1969a, 251). In the sacrifice of the crucifixion, the Son returns to the Father. Seized by the Holy Spirit, the reconciler of the opposites, the Son is reunited with the Father, consciousness with the unconscious. The Holy Spirit, the answer to the suffering God on the cross, thus restores the original world of the Father and its unity, but with a noteworthy difference:

the world of the Father has now been brought into human experience and reflection.

The first stage is the unconsciousness of the world of the Father. The second is the consciousness of the Son, which is at a distance from the world of the Father, where consciousness originated. The third stage, that of the Resurrection, is the reconciliation represented by the Holy Spirit, who unites Son with Father once more. There is in the third stage a recovering of the original state of the Father but no reversion to unconsciousness, for the conscious discrimination and reflection gained in the second stage are preserved intact (1969a, 182–83). The Son—ego—sacrifices itself to the Father—self—and "dies," but the Son remains, with his differentiated consciousness, only now fully integrated into the psychic wholeness of the Father. The ego is preserved, but now in the context of the self, its point of origin and destination.

Jung says the doctrines of the Trinity and the Incarnation, taken purely psychologically, refer to the differentiation of the psyche. The psyche was originally only unconsciousness, but, according to Jung, everything unconscious wants to become conscious. The psyche differentiates itself, increasing in consciousness, through the play, tension, and eventual reconciliation of opposites. Ego-consciousness must eventually surrender to the unconscious to regain unity with it. The ego has to give up its centrality of position and exclusive independence, must suffer and die to itself (1969a, 183). Then, the self, and not the ego, becomes the midpoint of personality. The third stage means that ego-consciousness has entered into its proper, which is to say, its subordinate, relationship to the superior and infinitely more comprehensive totality that is the self, the microcosmic likeness of God that is the ground of the psyche, the God-image (1969a, 185).

The advance to the third stage means a conscious recognition of the unconscious—a recognition on the part of the Son of the Father's priority—and a reconciliation of consciousness with the unconscious through the archetypal manifestation of the Holy Spirit. The psyche thus becomes one again, only now it is conscious as well as unconscious. An advance has been made, as original unconscious oneness yields to differentiated oneness: the Father wakes up to find himself not only Father but Father and Son in the unity of the Spirit, one differentiated life in the supreme unity of all opposites, the self (compare chapter 6, "Identity").

When Christ is seen as a symbol of the self—of the Son, with his heightened consciousness, restored to his original unity with the Father—the Holy Spirit is seen as symbolizing the realization of the self: the reconciling of opposites, the resolution of the suffering in the Godhead that Christ personifies (1969a, 176). The Holy Spirit reunites Christ and the Father, consciousness and the unconscious. The living spirit, Jung writes, is a "mediator and uniter of opposites" (1968a, 86–87)—Jung points out that the Holy Spirit has the same formula as the Father: a union of opposites (1969a, 186).

All in all, as a psychological symbol, the Trinity is said to express the "essential unity of a three-part process" of psychic maturation taking place both within humanity at large and within the individual (1969a, 193). In the Middle Ages, Jung comments, one turned to the Trinity in order to grasp the structure of the psyche, but today one turns to the psyche in order to understand what the doctrine of the Trinity can possibly mean (1969a, 147). The three persons of the Trinity are said to be personifications of the three phases of a natural psychic occurrence that always tends to express itself through the medium of myth (1969a, 193). In the doctrine, all three persons share one and the same nature. This is necessary symbolically, Jung says, since it is one and the same psyche that undergoes the progressive transformations. The Trinity is a symbol of the differentiation of human consciousness and the eventual reconciliation through the Holy Spirit of the conscious (Son) and the unconscious (Father). The primary transformations are produced by the archetypes.

THE CONTINUING INCARNATION, CRUCIFIXION, AND RESURRECTION

Jung points out that in Christian doctrine the Holy Spirit descends on humanity after Christ's departure, taking up residence in human beings and including them in God's sonship (1969a, 158). God thus continues to incarnate through the Holy Spirit. Only now, the activity of the Spirit is not limited to effecting the incarnation of God in Christ but does so in the human species as a whole (1969a, 414).

At first, Jung remarks, the gods lived on the tops of mountains or in caves, seas, and woods (1969a, 84). Later they came together to form one God. Then, that God became man in the person of Jesus Christ (the Father attaining consciousness; stage of the Son). But nowadays, the God-man is seen to have disappeared into the unconscious and to be absent. We could say, "God is dead," and the question becomes where we shall find him again. Today, in Jung's opinion, the God-man has left his throne and is "dissolving himself in the common man" (1969a, 84).

In psychological terms, the Christian doctrine of the descent of the Holy Spirit on Pentecost is said to represent the entry of the unconscious into consciousness, the raising into consciousness of conflicts that were previously unconscious but now have to be faced. Consciousness has to separate the opposites joined in nature in order for it to be aware, for the essence of consciousness lies in telling differences, in discrimination. Jung comments that this coming to consciousness or incarnation of God in human life necessarily means the suffering of opposites. Incarnation is the conscious experience of the terrible contradiction within the psyche. It is the experience of good and evil, light and darkness.

Christ's suspension between good and bad thieves is said to tell us that the growth and differentiation of consciousness inevitably lead to the crucifixion of the ego (the Son), to the intense suffering necessitated by our suspension between "irreconcilable opposites" (1968a, 44). We have to be crucified with Christ. We are involved, Jung says, in a moral suffering of opposites fully equivalent to physical crucifixion. Jung enjoins us not to repress the painful states of consciousness resulting from the manifestation of the separated opposites but to experience them fully. Only thus is consciousness expanded and made whole. The ego is what has to be sacrificed. It must "let go" and give up its centrality of position. Consciousness (the Son) must let itself be set aside so that the unconscious (the Father) can have the opportunity it needs.

The life of Christ, Jung remarks, is the story of a human being transformed by his destiny. The events in Christ's life are the story of the psyche and happen everywhere. Jung views our present age as a stage in the development of the psyche. We modern Westerners are far removed from God (the unconscious), and our ego must die to itself to reach God. This is said to be foretold in the crucifixion of Christ.

But Christ dying anticipates Christ rising: self-surrender announces reconciliation with the Father. Jung says that Christ is the typical God who dies and transforms himself and is the model of human destiny in our times (1969a, 89). Christ rises again on the third day and, his humanity transformed, is reunited with his Father through the agency of the Holy Spirit (1969a, 90). Jung says that the opposites between which we are presently torn can be reconciled by the Holy Spirit, the archetypal symbol of reconciliation. The Spirit can effect a balance between the opposites. According to Jung, the suffering of the opposites spells an important increase in consciousness. It means we are on the way to our lost wholeness and an experience of the God within. Jung comments that when wholeness is attained, we shall have found God again the only way God can be found: as a numinous totality embracing both good and evil. We shall have attained the self, our creator, our totality, and our goal. And the self—God, the God-image—will have achieved consciousness. Just as we humans were once manifested out of God, Jung remarks, God will be manifested out of us (1969a, 179).

All in all, then, psychic wholeness is achieved through enduring the opposites (1968d, 20). The suffering of the opposites is a necessary step on the way to the reconciliation of differentiated opposites in the unity and wholeness of the self: the path to resurrection is through suffering and death. Incarnation—individuation—is complete when human life attains the divine realm, and God descends into the human (1969a, 162). Jung comments that the ego's isolation is then overcome, consciousness is broadened, the conflict ceases, and the unconscious shows its favorable side. Evil is then included in the psychic totality of the self and, balanced by good, loses its destructive power.

The Holy Spirit, Jung remarks, is an "autonomous psychic happening," a "reconciling light" in the darkness of the mind, with the power to transform chaos into order (1969a, 176). When God is not projected, Jung says he can be found within, where he is presently slumbering. Individuation, our relation with the God within and our true individuality, is attainable. Jung thus views the present state of divided opposites and darkness as preliminary to a future union of God's opposites, a union that will amount to no less than the realization of the saying "You are gods." The attainment of individuation is a relation to the infinite, which is said to be our life's true goal (1961b, 325). If we fail in this regard, we throw ourselves into things that have no real final importance. We become taken, for example, with our beauty or our cleverness.

Life seeks completeness, says Jung, not perfection. A complete life is said to be the work of the Holy Spirit, who leads into all kinds of dangers and, at the same time, into consciousness—the wider consciousness created by the Holy Spirit is the very goal of God's incarnation. Without error and sin, there is said to be no experience of union with God. This, says Jung, is what it means to serve God: to be an active participant in the emergence of light out of darkness, to further God's becoming conscious of his creation and the human being's becoming conscious of his or her self (1961b, 338). We meet the God yet to be transformed when we confront the unconscious. Jung finds in the progressive incarnation of God in human life the real history of the world.

SPIRIT

Psychologically, Jung says, the phenomenon of spirit is an autonomous psychic complex (1969c, 335). Like every such complex, spirit appears as having an "intention" superior, or at least equal, to that of the ego. To do justice to this superiority of spirit, we might speak of a "higher" consciousness and not merely of the unconscious. Spirit, like complexes in general, presents itself to consciousness as a personal being (1969c, 335). We have seen, for example, that in Christian doctrine spirit is portrayed as the third person of the Trinity. In any case, Jung insists, spirit is certainly no idea that someone sat down and formulated one day. In its purer manifestations—its working principle inscrutable, the origin of its intentions obscure, and its aim effectively enforced—spirit presents itself rather as a "higher" consciousness possessed of a life of its own (1969c, 335–36).

Jung describes archetypal spirit as a "dynamic and half-substantial" agency, "the dynamic principle." Spirit moves one as does the wind. In the New Testament, for example, spirit is said to "blow where it wills"; compare also the Pentecostal wind (1968c, 210). In keeping with its wind-nature, spirit is vivifying, firing, stimulating, inciting, and inspiring. Spirit is always an "active, winged, swift-moving being" (1968c, 212). In addition to its characterization as wind, spirit is also said to be breathed into one. Various traditions indeed view spirit as both wind and breath (1976, 156). Jung comments that spirits manifested themselves spontaneously to primitives, visiting them while they were awake, and that thoughts appeared to them like hallucinations. On all sides, Jung says, the unconscious "jumps out" at them, "alive and real" (1975a, 26). Jung remarks that, if these things happened to us today, we'd be declared insane.

It is the deep impression of superiority that spirit makes on consciousness that gives it its "revelatory character" and absoluteness of authority (1969c, 336). Jung cautions, however, that spirit represents danger, for what strikes us as "higher" is not always higher from the standpoint of accepted morality. Nor are the manifestations of spirit always superior intellectually. Jung concludes, therefore, that it would probably be more accurate to regard spirit—this "hypothetical consciousness"—not as "higher" but simply as "wider." Jung says that life needs to be lived in a certain spirit, needs to be taken hold of and possessed by the wider consciousness that is spirit for the fulfillment of its destined potentialities (1969c, 333). Life needs the superiority of independent, dominant spirit, the inspiration that spirit alone can bring. Spirit gives life meaning and allows it its fullest unfolding. Mere ego existence, on the other hand, is dull for all concerned.

Spirit typically appears in the symbolic form of the "wise old man," the "superior master and teacher" (1968c, 35). The wise magician or medicine man, Jung comments, penetrates the "chaotic darkness of brute life with the light of meaning" (1968c, 37). Spirit thus represents the "pre-existent meaning" lying hidden in life's chaos (1968c, 35). Spirit, Jung states, is the archetype of meaning, and the spiritual is that toward which life moves as to its goal. Spirit inspires us with good and creative ideas, fills us with enthusiasm, and spurs us on (1968c, 214).

Reason is judged incapable of giving adequate expression to spirit and its workings, to the spirit of an age, for example (1969c, 325, 336). For that, Jung says, a symbol is needed: symbolic images, neither defining nor explaining but pointing beyond themselves to a meaning that escapes our grasp and that words cannot encompass, are the best possible expression for spirit and its obscure character. Jung indeed virtually identifies the symbolic life with the spiritual life, symbol with spirit. "Symbols," he writes, "are spirit from above" (1968c, 24). Spirit—archetype of meaning (almost like saying "archetype of archetypes"), inspiring agency (issuing in psychic transformations), union of opposites (see above, "Psychology and Christian Doctrines"), and at one with the symbolic life—comes close to capturing the essence of the life and dynamism of the collective unconscious.

Spirit, which fragile human concepts are unable to exhaust, is a complex that holds within it "the seeds of incalculable possibilities." The manifestations of spirit, Jung comments, are indeed marvelous, as various as the universe itself (1969a, 347). Spirit is said to characterize the lives of those who look askance at this world and its happinesses (1976, 584). Spirit is "another world" within this one. Adulthood, Jung comments, does not consist in identifying with various groups but in giving oneself over to the spirit of one's proper independence (1969a, 184). Creativity is described as an original spiritual undertaking: great artists are said to be governed by a creative power greater than themselves (1974, 115). Jung remarks that in the Middle Ages people thought in terms of spirit but that today we always begin with matter, deeming it real and spirit unreal (1976, 799). Jung challenges such materialistic assumptions. Spirit and matter, he says, may well be forms of the same "transcendental being," mind and body "one and the same life" (1968c, 213).

A spiritual life—a life lived according to an ideal in which one resolutely chooses one's own way—demands a life beyond social, moral, religious, political, and philosophical conventionality. God's "true sons" are said to be those who break with convention and take the "steep and narrow path" that leads into the unknown (1974, 175). Such a life, Jung remarks, has been called a "vocation," breaking with the herd and sacrificing oneself to one's "calling." The individual has been "called" to follow his or her own star, to obey his or her own law, to listen to the whispering voice of his or her own inner spirit (1974, 176). There is said to be no universal blueprint for living: the only meaningful life is one lived in pursuit of its own realization (1974, 181; 1977, 41).

Jung remarks that the "inner voice" "calling" to individual wholeness is an extrahuman one belonging to a "powerful objective psychic factor" (collective unconscious), one that happens of itself and has always been given a divine name (1974, 182). Fleeing this call to actualize the law of one's being, and thus realize life's meaning, may result in a neurosis (1974, 183). Neurosis is a "developmental disturbance" of the personality (1974, 184). Faithfulness to one's essential individuality, by contrast, has a therapeutic effect. The inner voice, representing the highest and lowest, the good and the bad, is a call to "a fuller life," to "a wider, more comprehensive consciousness" (1974, 184).

PSYCHOLOGY AND EASTERN RELIGIONS

Jung's views on Christianity have been presented above ("Psychology and Christian Doctrines" and "The Continuing Incarnation, Crucifixion, and Resurrection"). This section samples his views on Eastern religious traditions.

The Opposites and the Mediating Symbol

The problem of the opposites, along with redemption from the clash of opposites through a mediating symbol, the unification of the opposites, is an age-old one. The uniting symbol, Jung points out, appears differently in Eastern and Western religions (1971, 194). Western religions are said to locate the middle term that mediates between the opposites outside the psyche in the form of a God or Messiah. Jung judges these religions to be more primitive than their Eastern counterparts because they lack insight: they tell a childish story of an external, mediating God, a figure of projection, who, in the form of a kindly and solicitous parent, puts an end to our division when he sees fit and for reasons we are not let in on. In the East, everything is different. Jung comments that the East, having struggled with the problem of opposites for thousands of years, has developed a psychological way of deliverance *within* human knowledge and capability. The religions of China and India, he says, offer a "redemptive middle way" that can be attained through a certain conscious attitude. Release from the opposites and redemption are thus available in the East without the intervention of projected family members.

The Redemptive Middle Way between the Opposites in India

The purpose of classical Indian religion, as expressed in the Upanishads, is deliverance from the opposites plaguing human nature from within and union with and new life in Brahman (1971, 197). Jung points out that Brahman is at one and the same time God—world-ground and world-creator—and a psychological state of redemption: Brahman is both divinity itself and atman, the self as a union of opposites, a psychological state beyond changing affects (the tension of opposites). Atman, or self, is thus essentially identical with Brahman, or God; the self as "originating ground of the psyche" does not differ from the world-ground. The human being "*in* the self" is God (1969a, 580–81). Atman, or self, is true reality: "that which breathes through me," that which, like Tao, is in all beings, a "totality superordinate to consciousness" (1975a, 464; see below, "The Middle Path between the Opposites in Chinese Philosophy"). The experience of the self (atman), the "higher totality," lifts us out of the play of opposites ("Maya").

To become thus freed from the opposites entails liberation from every emotional state and tie to objects (1971, 118). Jung remarks that withdrawing libido from all contents and supplying it to the self results in a complete state of introversion. Through detachment from the object, there is said to be formed in the self "an equivalent of objective reality," an identity of inside and outside, of self (atman) and world, a fusion of subject and object, known technically as "That art thou." The concept of Brahman, Jung remarks, is only slightly different from the concept of atman: the notion of the self is not given in Brahman, which is "a general indefinable state of identity between inside and outside" (1971, 118–19). The Indian aim, then, is the establishment of a mediation from which redemption—liberation from the opposites—will emerge. Brahman thus involves redemption, deliverance from affect (including suffering). The psychological result for the individual is the attainment of Brahman as a state of bliss: Brahman's disciple incarnates Brahman.

Jung remarks that Brahman is identified with "Rta," a libido symbol that is said to convey "order, regulation, destiny, sacred custom, statute, law, right, truth," "fixed direction and regularity, the idea of a predetermined, ordered path or process" (1971, 211). Brahman is thus portrayed through the libido symbolism of a creative, dynamic principle (1971, 201). Jung points out, moreover, that the word "Brahman" itself derives from the word "to swell." The very term is thus said to indicate a psychological state in which libido is concentrated; compare, for example, our manner of speaking of someone as "bursting with emotion" (1971, 202). Jung comments that practitioners of Yoga seek to withdraw attention from both external and internal worlds—from the opposites—in order to allow an accumulation of libido to occur. The goal is to effect a basic transformation of personality, to realize the self in experience (1977, 102). Unconscious contents of a suprahuman and cosmic character, primordial images that have always and everywhere symbolized the generative power that moves the cosmos, are said to become activated in the process. Such generative power, Jung says, is in fact the projection of the living essence of humanity, of libido (psychic energy).

Jung does not believe that morality was thought up one day, only then to be legislated for human life (1971, 212). Morality is rather viewed as essential to the "laws of life," to libido and its "path." The natural flow of psychic energy, the "middle path" mediating between and embracing the opposites, means complete obedience to the spiritual laws governing human life. The highest moral principle, Jung says, is "harmony with natural laws" guiding libido toward some vital maximum (1971, 213).

Jung remarks that the Upanishads describe the middle path, which is no easy task, with great depth and "astonishing psychological accuracy" (1971, 213). Our Western haughtiness in regard to this Eastern wisdom is said to reveal how barbaric we really are. We are so undeveloped, in Jung's view, that we continue to turn to a (projected) "Father in Heaven" to give us external rules to live by. Jung remarks that we are unable to trust ourselves and the laws of our nature. Why is this so? Because, according to Jung, beneath a thin veneer of Christianity there lurks within us the unreformed "wild beast." Having never mastered our barbarism, we have never won, through the conflict of opposites, the freedom of a morality whose roots lie within.

Brahman and a certain psychological state—the self as a union of opposites—are one (1971, 200). But more generally than that, Brahman-atman is the "universal Ground from which all creation proceeds." The process of uniting with Brahman is a cosmogonic one. All things find the "right way" in Brahman, the "universal ground" and "creative universal essence," and are "eternally dissolved and recreated" (1971, 120). Brahman is altogether beyond our understanding: the opposites come into being through Brahman and must be overcome—united and dissolved—in Brahman, which nevertheless stands outside them.

The Middle Path between the Opposites in Chinese Philosophy

The ancient Chinese philosophy of Taoism provides a middle way between the opposites in its notion of Tao (1971, 214). Not appearing to our senses, Jung remarks, Tao isn't any thing in particular. Tao is no thing, nothing, nothing appearing in the world: Nothing. Tao is instead the world's organizer, the law obeyed by both the cosmos (outer world, macrocosm) and human life (inner world, psyche/microcosm) (Wilhelm and Jung 1962, 10–11). Tao is method, principle, natural or life force, the regulated processes of nature, the idea of the world, the prime cause of all phenomena, the good, the right, and the moral order.

Tao is the "primal law," the "undivided one," the "Way" (the conventional translation). It is the final world principle antedating the emergence of any and all opposites (yang and yin), and hence reality as we know it (Wilhelm and Jung 1962, 11, 12, 17). Tao, motionless, is "the means of all motion and gives it law": Tao is the "immutable, eternal law at work in all change," the law governing change and giving it meaning (Wilhelm 1967, lv–lvi), the "latent 'rationality'" operative in all things and rendering them knowable (1969c, 487–88), and "transcendental meaning." Richard Wilhelm translates Tao, brilliantly, in Jung's view, as "Meaning" (1969c, 486). Tao, Jung says, symbolizes the archetype of the self.

Tao is "the reign of law" and the "right way." Liberated from the opposites, but able to unite them in itself, Tao is the middle road between them (1971, 120). The condition of Tao is the "beginning of the world" before anything has begun, a condition that "superior wisdom" can attain (1971, 215; 1976, 119). Tao is the "creative process," that in which all things have their beginning and end (1971, 215). The concept of Tao in China is said to be closely allied to those of Brahman and Rta in India (1971, 215). This affinity is said to be due not to cultural transmission but to their common archetypal origin. The primordial image or archetype informing Brahman (Rta-Brahman-atman) and Tao is found everywhere as a primitive notion of energy or "soul force" and makes its appearance in Jung's psychology as the concept of libido.

Jung remarks that Tao divides into the fundamental pair of opposites, yang—heaven, light, warmth, and maleness—and yin—earth, darkness, cold, and femaleness. "Yin" is the cloudy, the yielding, the negative (the "no"), and the feminine; "yang" is the bright, the strong, the positive (the "yes"), and the masculine. The basic idea, as Wilhelm points out, is that out of the change and interplay of opposing forces—yang and yin—arises the world of being (Wilhelm 1967, lvi). Taoism views human life as a microcosm symbolizing the coincidence of the opposites, of yang and yin, heaven and earth (1971, 271).

Taoist ethics sets as its goal the liberation from the clash of the opposites and a return to Tao, a union of opposites (1971, 215). The sage seeks harmony with Tao in order to avoid falling into extreme attitudes and thus becoming entangled in the conflict of the opposites. Freed from the opposites and seeing them in their inevitable connectedness and alternation with one another, the true disciple of Tao is one with it (1971, 216). Such an individual is said to undergo the same redeeming and uplifting transformation as the disciple who has united with Brahman (1971, 216).

Jung says Tao, Christ, the Buddha, and atman all express the one self of humanity (1975a, 410). The mediating or uniting symbol of the self, of "psychic wholeness," necessarily arises, in Jung's view, when opposites attain a sufficient degree of tension. There is one truth, but it is said to speak in many tongues.

MEISTER ECKHART AND THE RELATIVITY OF GOD

Jung cites the writings of the thirteenth-century Roman Catholic mystic Meister Eckhart as an important step in the direction of his own psychological approach to religious phenomena. Eckhart proposes a relativity of God to human life, a notion of human closeness to God akin to the view of the Upanishads (1971, 242). The thrust of Eckhart's notion of the relativity of God is that the divine is not "absolute" and "cut off" from human life; that while the human being is a "function" of God, God is also a "function" of the human being; that, in a certain measure, God depends on human life (1971, 243).

Eckhart distinguishes between "God" and "Godhead" (1971, 254). Godhead, which neither knows nor possesses itself, "is all," the "All-oneness," "all-pervading creative power." The soul (unconscious) is said to be a function of the Godhead, and God a "function of the soul." God thus springs from the soul and, ultimately, from the Godhead. In Jung's terminology, God first comes to exist in an "act of conscious differentiation from the unconscious," whereby the ego, separating out as subject from the "dynamis" or "power" of the unconscious, becomes aware of this "dynamis"—that is, becomes aware of God as object (1971, 255).

God is thus seen to arise in an act of differentiation of conscious and unconscious (1971, 254–55). In this act, the ego as subject distinguishes itself from God as object: "God becomes," along with ego-consciousness (1971, 255). God ceases to exist, on the other hand, when the soul immerses itself once again in the "dynamis" of the unconscious: the "breakthrough" of which Eckhart speaks occurs when the ego breaks with the world and becomes identical once again with the unconscious "dynamis," or Godhead. God, no longer distinguishable from the subject, is then no longer experienced as an object. Eckhart's assertion of the relativity of God thus implies the withdrawal of projected unconscious contents from external objects and their discovery as belonging to the subject, which is to say, it implies an awareness of God as implicated in unconscious processes (1971, 243–44). God, for Eckhart, is a psychological value, the highest or supreme value in the psyche (1971, 246). Eckhart, like Jung himself, is thus said to assume a wholly psychological viewpoint in which God personifies an unconscious content (1971, 248).

When the psychodynamic state that is God is projected onto an object, Jung remarks that the object seizes power over the subject, something of the world assuming the role of God. Eckhart's view is that God is to be withdrawn from objects and realized psychologically (1971, 248). The formerly projected excess libido thus accrues to the revitalized subject: God takes up residence in the unconscious (the soul) as an autonomous complex. A "oneness of being" between conscious and unconscious and a feeling of ecstatic bliss occur. The supreme value thus in the unconscious, the ego virtually disappears in favor of the self (1971, 249). The self is the state of the child, Jung says, of the primitive, of paradise. Things now proceed of their own accord, accumulated libido joyfully flowing forth without effort. Such is the experience of the self.

EVALUATION AND CONCLUSIONS

Jung, with the whole modern philosophical and psychological tradition, regards human experience as a closed inner realm of psychic occurrences. Our gods, our science, all our knowledge, and our very world are said to arise for us precisely and only as images: "Image *is* psyche." Jung thus asserts that we move exclusively within a domain of psychic images with no direct access to extrapsychic reality—thus the legacy of René Descartes in the work of Jung. If consciousness is an inner realm (*res cogitans*) for Jung, so, too, is the unconscious. This is an immediate consequence of the Cartesian legacy in Jung's thought. If consciousness is an inner domain, where else could the unconscious be but inside too, below or behind consciousness, a "mind behind the mind"? Freud, it has been seen, shares essentially the same view (see chapter 2, "Evaluation and Conclusions").

The divine, in accordance with Jung's view of the essentially inner character of the mind, like everything else, occurs as an intrapsychic image. God is an (intra)psychic force appearing to consciousness in symbolic form. Given the superiority of power of the unconscious—explicitly equated with the divine—Jung says we have no choice but to be religious, no choice but to pay attention to the images arising from the deepest depths of the "mind behind the mind": that is, from the collective unconscious. Religion, for Jung, is a relation, within the psyche, between consciousness and unconscious archetypal forces. Freud's view is similar, only the intrapsychic relation is between consciousness and unconscious *instinctual* forces. Jung's God is a supreme concentration of psychic energy or libido. It is the distribution of energy in the psyche that determines our fate, in Jung's view, not we ourselves. Divine archetype rules. Archetypes, with a constantly present, specific charge or energy, are extremely powerful causal factors. Better indeed to heed them!

Jung claims to limit himself to what takes place within the psyche and to leave undecided the possible existence of divine beings outside the psyche. And yet, Jung speaks condescendingly of believers who worship extrapsychic divine figures, such as Christ. Asserting that such figures are projections of the God in the psyche or God-image, Jung reduces them to the psyche. This is psychologism. Jung claims to know that divine figures outside the psyche do not exist, claims to know what does *not* exist outside the psyche. Despite his disclaimers, Jung has quite a lot to say about conditions outside the psyche. Through his doctrine of the microcosmic character of the psyche, moreover, Jung identifies individual human life with the universe as a whole. By defining the individual in cosmic terms, Jung leaves far behind the modest claims of an empiricist only interested in the phenomena. Jung's psychology turns out in fact to be pantheistic metaphysics. Both Jungian pantheism and Freudian objectivism, attempting to account for the whole of everything, say far too much.

The point is neither to reject Jung out of hand, as academic psychologists have tended to do, nor to make a cult figure out of him, as some of his followers have, but to locate his lasting contribution to the psychology of religion. Having criticized Jung's metaphysical presuppositions, what of his legacy? It is suggested that this legacy consists in his detailed and wide-ranging descriptions of the symbolic life. Through these descriptions, Jung introduces the important dimension of the magical into psychology: the mythical and the dreamlike, the mysterious and the mystical, the ambiguous and the paradoxical, meaning, spirit.

Symbols are "symbols of transformation" of consciousness, the mythical background from which springs the variety of human endeavors. Windows on the numinous and the magical, symbols liberate us from the literal, the seeming objective. The living spirit liberates from the dead letter. It is this preoccupation with the original value of the psyche, its spiritual or symbolic character, that marks Jung's contribution to psychology. Jung follows human life forward into the future of its spiritual unfolding.

REFERENCES

Jung, C. G. *Two Essays on Analytical Psychology*. New York: Meridian, 1956.

———. *Psyche and Symbol*, ed. V. deLaszlo. New York: Doubleday, 1958.

———. *Freud and Psychoanalysis*. Princeton: Princeton University Press, 1961a.

———. *Memories, Dreams, Reflections*, ed. A. Jaffe. New York: Random House, 1961b.

———. *The Spirit in Man, Art, and Literature*. Princeton: Princeton University Press, 1966.

———. *Alchemical Studies*. Princeton: Princeton University Press, 1967a.

———. *Symbols of Transformation*. Princeton: Princeton University Press, 1967b.

———. *Aion*. Princeton: Princeton University Press, 1968a.

———. "Approaching the Unconscious." In *Man and His Symbols*, ed. C. G. Jung, 1–94. New York: Dell, 1968b.

———. *The Archetypes and the Collective Unconscious*. Princeton: Princeton University Press, 1968c.

———. *Psychology and Alchemy*. Princeton: Princeton University Press, 1968d.

———. *Psychology and Religion*. Princeton: Princeton University Press, 1969a.

———. *The Psychology of the Transference*. Princeton: Princeton University Press, 1969b.

———. *The Structure and Dynamics of the Psyche*. Princeton: Princeton University Press, 1969c.

———. *Civilization in Transition*. Princeton: Princeton University Press, 1970a.

———. *Mysterium Conjunctionis*. Princeton: Princeton University Press, 1970b.

———. *Psychological Types*. Princeton: Princeton University Press, 1971.

———. *The Psychogenesis of Mental Disease*. Princeton: Princeton University Press, 1972.

———. *The Development of Personality*. Princeton: Princeton University Press, 1974.

———. *Civilization in Transition*. Princeton: Princeton University Press, 1975a.

———. *Letters: 1951–1961*, ed. G. Adler, in collaboration with A. Jaffe. Princeton: Princeton University Press, 1975b.

———. *The Symbolic Life*. Princeton: Princeton University Press, 1976.

———. *The Practice of Psychotherapy*. Princeton: Princeton University Press, 1977.

McGuire, W. (ed.). *The Freud/Jung Letters: The Correspondence between Sigmund Freud and C. G. Jung*. Princeton: Princeton University Press, 1974.

Otto, R. *The Idea of the Holy*. New York: Oxford University Press, 1977.

Wilhelm, R. *The I Ching [Book of Changes]*, trans. C. F. Baynes. Princeton: Princeton University Press, 1967.

Wilhelm, R., and C. G. Jung. *The Secret of the Golden Flower: A Chinese Book of Life*, trans. C. F. Baynes. New York: Harcourt, Brace and World, 1962.

4

✛

Gordon Allport

I venture the opinion that all of the animals in the world are psychologically less distinct from one another than one human being is from other human beings.

—Gordon Allport

Gordon W. Allport (1897–1967) was a major figure in the development of the psychology of personality in the twentieth century. Adopting an eclectic and pluralistic approach, his intentions were to supplement the findings of psychoanalysis and learning theory. A hallmark of Allport's work is his concern with individual uniqueness, which he tried to balance against universal law, psychology's principal preoccupation in his day. Allport devoted a small book, *The Individual and His Religion* (1950), to the psychology of religion. The work's aim, as its title suggests, is to explore religion's place and development in the life of the individual, and in particular in the lives of mature and productive individuals—Allport indeed criticizes previous theories for failing to attend to psychologically healthy religiousness. Thus oriented to the religion of the individual, Allport, like William James, does not discover a single origin or essence of religion.

Allport makes the important distinction in *The Individual and His Religion* between intrinsic, or mature, religion and extrinsic, or immature, religion. He eventually came to develop (with J. M. Ross) an Intrinsic-Extrinsic Religious Orientation Scale to measure the meaning of religion in the life of the individual (1968, 237–68). Whereas intrinsic religion is religion lived for its own sake—sacrificial, loving religion—extrinsic religion is religion used by people—self-serving, comfort-seeking religion.

Intrinsic religion is carried over into the totality of life; extrinsic religion is not. Intrinsic religion is an integrating factor; extrinsic religion is given to compartmentalization and fragmentation.

Allport's distinction between intrinsic and extrinsic religion is not the one made by James between personal and institutional religion: a participant in institutional religion may manifest either intrinsic or extrinsic religiousness, as may a nonparticipant. The psychoanalytic critique of religion, Allport points out, may be brought to bear on extrinsic religion but not on the intrinsic version. Intrinsic religion has a predominantly conscious character, being central to the life of the one who practices it.

Allport insists on the dynamic, growing character of human personality, thus the title of his classic book *Becoming* (1955). Personality is not finished in childhood but, acting on, as well as reacting to, its environment, continues to develop throughout life. New motives, unique in pattern to the individual, arise. New facts and expanding horizons call for integration. Religion plays an important role here: mature religiousness, Allport holds, has the never completely finished task of meaningfully relating the individual to the whole of being.

In a challenge to empiricist—"Lockean"—psychological approaches, such as radical behaviorism, Allport turns to modern phenomenology and its theory of intentionality: behavior is always trying to bring something about, always reaching out and relating to something. Healthy behavior, including healthy religious behavior, has its intrinsically valuable others. It is not governed by environmental causes. Life is indeed a dynamic process, in Allport's view, not a mechanical chain of inputs and outputs—not a mechanism of any sort.

MATURE RELIGION

Central to Allport's approach to human personality, and hence to religion, is the notion of sentiment—alternatively, an interest-system or outlook. A "sentiment" is defined by Allport as an organization of thoughts and feelings that are directed to a valued object (1950, 18). A sentiment is a style of existence, a way of relating oneself to life. Though complex in nature, sentiments are seen to be relatively unchanging components of personality. The "mature religious sentiment" is said to be a readiness formed through experience to react favorably to certain objects and principles that are regarded as central and permanent in reality and are of ultimate importance in one's life (1950, 64). The mature religious sentiment is charged with making sense of everything in reality that truly matters. This sentiment has the task of accommodating "every atom of experience" referred to it (1950, 61).

As it plays such a role in life, Allport says it is easy to see why the religious sentiment can never be completely successful. There is always something more for it to accomplish. Allport points out that this is a reason why the religious sentiment is able to forge things together: it is precisely the unfinished task, in his view, that motivates and integrates human activities (1950, 105; 1955, 91). This sentiment, moreover, may include inconsistencies (1950, 64). And the individual may not always live up to it. Allport nevertheless insists that the construction and maintaining of a mature personality depends on such a mature religious outlook.

The task of the mature religious sentiment, as already suggested, is to form a meaningful whole of all experience. The mature religious sentiment provides the forward thrust that enables us, at each stage of our development, to relate ourselves meaningfully to the totality of "Being" (1955, 96). This sentiment is thus to be comprehensive, an integral system that directs our life as a whole. The mature religious sentiment is said to be at the very heart of life. The individual's religion, according to Allport, is an attempt to get in touch and harmony with reality and its Creator. It is our ultimate attempt to round out our personality by finding "the supreme context" in which we rightly belong (1950, 161). The religious sentiment is that segment of our personality that, arising at the core of our life, is "directed toward the infinite" (1950, 161).

Allport finds the general object of the religious sentiment to be so vast that, while the sentiment remains fairly stable over time, numerous particular objects and values come to be taken into account one after the other. As an openness to all facts and values, the mature religious sentiment necessarily belongs to the mainstream of things (1950, 61). It cannot, as a consequence, be doing its job and be the mere product of an imagination that is providing an escape from reality (wish fulfillment).

In the healthy personality, which is ordered and unified, one sentiment is ordinarily found to hold the dominant position. When such a dominant sentiment is religious in character, the individual is seen to have a sense of affiliation with all of reality. This, Allport says, makes for an especially integrated and ordered personality. The mature religious sentiment brings meaning and peace. Allport points out that some people need to love God for the sake of the completeness and intelligibility of their lives. He acknowledges that religion's final truths are unknown, but he insists that a psychology that blocks the understanding of the religious potentialities of human life hardly merits the title "Logos of the human psyche" (1955, 98).

The Individual Character of Religion

The mature religious sentiment is described as unique and varied. It is essentially individual in character. The emphasis on individuality, as we have seen, is a hallmark of Allport's psychology. For example, he does not think that all religion has one religious emotion at its core, such as a feeling of absolute dependence, as suggested by Friedrich Schleiermacher, or an experience of the numinous, as proposed by Rudolf Otto. Allport suspects that such an attribution of the various phenomena of religion to a single essential religious feeling is in fact the projection of the characteristic religiousness of the individual researcher. He insists that there are many truly different kinds of experiences to be found in religion. The religious sentiment is characterized more by the customary manner in which the individual reaches out beyond himself or herself than by any special feature of the experience itself (1950, 5; see below, "Intentionality and Religious Behavior"). Nor, of course, are religions always seen to share the same conceptual framework. Some believe, for example, in life after death and in a personal God, while others do not.

Not only is there no common core of feeling or thought characteristic of religion in general, in Allport's view. Neither is there a common origin. Religion does not universally originate, for example, in the repression and sublimation of sexuality (1950, 7–8). Allport points out, for example, that religion is sometimes seen to thrive when repression is simply out of the question. There are said to be too many conscious factors in evidence in the determination of religious behavior, moreover, for a comprehensive account of religion in terms of the unconscious (1950, 9). Nor does Allport discover a "religious instinct" at the root of religious behavior.

Allport points to several factors at work in the origin and development of religion:

1. organic desire (1950, 10)—unfulfilled desires, for example, for safety, play a role in the development of religion; people often pray for what they are lacking;
2. temperament (1950, 13)—the individual's optimism or pessimism, for example, influences the development of the religious sentiment;
3. psychogenic desires and spiritual values (1950, 14)—people are curious and locate knowledge outside themselves, calling it truth or justice; these become values one wants to see flourish;
4. the pursuit of meaning (1950, 17)—that people are in wonder before reality and want to know its meaning is one of the most common origins of religious thought; religious systems take up the questions time and again of the purpose of creation and the meaning of evil, and when satisfactory solutions are found, life becomes meaningful;
5. culture (1950, 25)—conformity to culture, especially in childhood, contributes to the origin of religion; rituals and doctrines are at first accepted without question or understanding.

These are said to be the formative influences that come to be integrated into the religion of the individual. Religion has so many roots, which weigh and influence in so many different ways, and there are so many different rational interpretations possible of "things in general" that a uniform outcome in the religious dimension of our life is said to be inconceivable (1950, 29). The uniqueness of the individual's religion is instead guaranteed. There are, in Allport's view, as many kinds of religious experience as there are religious individuals. According to Allport, the individual's "religious quest" is a solitary one from start to finish (1950, 161). No one can provide the individual with the faith that he or she alone can evolve.

A number of desires, such as fear, gratitude, and curiosity, are seen to contribute to the origin of religion. People vary enormously in their ability to grow out of the religion of their childhood and to develop a "well-differentiated mature religious sentiment" (1950, 161). This, Allport remarks, is a major reason for the tremendous variability of the religious sentiment from individual to individual. This sentiment is seen to vary in breadth and depth, as well as in content and mode of functioning. It is seen to be fragmentary, superficial, and trivial in some individuals. In others it is mature: differentiated, deep, pervasive, and integrated into the total personality.

The Criteria of Mature Religion

Allport describes the mature religious sentiment as characteristically well differentiated, dynamic, persistently directive of behavior, comprehensive, integral, and heuristic. The mature religious sentiment is well differentiated (1958, 65). Many interests and beliefs are articulated and ordered to form the singleness of pattern of such a sentiment. The sentiment is nevertheless seen to take a critical stance toward the material integrated into it. There is an appropriate attitude to each belief and moral position entering into the pattern. Allport points out that the mature sentiment is bound to undergo reorganization as personality develops and knowledge is acquired. The integration of new facts and experiences into the religious sentiment is seen to be a lifelong task that only the individual himself or herself can accomplish.

The mature religious sentiment is dynamic (1950, 71). As we have seen, religion originates, at least in part, in organic desire. The mature sentiment is seen to become independent of its origins, however, and to serve ends that are properly the individual's own—this is Allport's important notion of "functional autonomy." New meanings and motives emerge in the course of the development of the mature religious sentiment. The sentiment thus undergoes transformations as it develops. Like the oak tree, the mature religious sentiment "shatters and discards the acorn" that originally nourished it (1950, 72).

Allport contrasts functional autonomy with "geneticism" (derived from the word "genesis"), the view that behavior is determined either by inheritance or by the earliest of learning experiences. Geneticism sees a person's motives, even in middle age, as altered versions of a "primary material" (1960, 137). Allport remarks that this primary material has been given different names: instincts, reflexes, drives, and id. Sublimation (Sigmund Freud) and conditioning (John Watson) are two of the modifications such a primary material is said to undergo in the course of development. Allport's notion of functional autonomy shifts the focus of motivational theory away from the varieties of geneticism to the "present 'go' of interests" that are currently initiating and sustaining behavior (1960, 140). Adult motives, "functionally independent" (functionally autonomous) of the former systems out of which they grew, are varied, "self-sustaining contemporary systems" (1961, 227). With the notion of functional autonomy, Allport is proposing that genuine transformations of motivation occur in the course of human development, that there is life and development after childhood and, indeed, all one's life.

In Allport's view, the energy involved in the functionally autonomous mature religious sentiment now belongs to this sentiment alone and is not drawn from the self-interested desires that helped launch it. A decided break with the past has occurred. The mature religious sentiment is thus no longer a servant of the desires at its origin but exists as a need in its own right, harboring within itself the power it needs to live itself forward and further its own ends. This sentiment is a growing frame of reference for the interpretation of reality. When central to the individual, it is a powerful influence in the personality, with the ability to transform lives.

The mature religious sentiment is persistently directive of behavior (1950, 74). It sustains moral standards and provides moral zeal. The mature religious sentiment is comprehensive (1950, 76). It represents the synthesis of a great many factors. The function of this comprehensive attitude, in Allport's view, is to relate the individual in a meaningful way "to the whole of Being" (1955, 94). The mature religious sentiment, seeking "a theory of Being" in which all the fragments are meaningfully ordered, never rests content until it embraces all the central facts of reality. The mature religious sentiment necessarily covers more ground than any other sentiment. Its horizon is broader, embracing matters that it alone can.

The mature religious sentiment is integral, forming an overall pattern that is a homogeneous whole (1950, 79). Comprehensive, on the one hand, this sentiment is harmonious in design, on the other. The mature religious sentiment can neither ignore nor oppose science but, in Allport's view, must rather coexist with it. Moral theology has learned from psychology, for example, that compulsions sometimes seize control of people's actions and deprive them of free will, which is not to deny that, if we believe we are free, we are able to use our resources more flexibly and successfully than if we believe we are in chains (1950, 80). Allport points out that a major issue the mature religious sentiment must come to grips with and integrate is the problem of evil.

The mature religious sentiment is heuristic (1950, 81). A heuristic belief, Allport says, is one that is held tentatively until it is confirmed or replaced by a better one. People often accept the authority of a revelation, for example, not because it can be empirically proven but because it helps them find answers to life's troublesome questions. Faith, as Allport sees it, is a working hypothesis, belief based on a probability (see below, "Faith"). The faith that we will be alive next week is cited as an example of a valuable hypothesis. We live our lives on the basis of probability, in Allport's view, not certainty. Faith generates the energy that makes success possible. Every human accomplishment is said to result from a risk taken in the absence of advance certainty (1950, 82).

Faith is thus viewed as a risk it is impossible to avoid. The mature religious sentiment is shaped in "the workshop of doubt" (1950, 83). The mature believer knows the uncertainty of his ground, says Allport, but does not want to become a skeptic when faith might be a valid avenue to truth, and so long as it is a major determinant of human success (compare chapter 1, "'The Will to Believe'"). Both the believer and the agnostic are able to acknowledge that the nature of Being is unknowable. But believers, basing their decision to believe on a probability, discover the value of their decisiveness in the energy generated, the understandings developed, and the positive meanings fostered. The mature religious individual, knowing full well why some are skeptics, is seen to prefer his or her own bet. In the religious sphere, the wager of faith is often seen to turn despair into resolve. So long as the probability of truth remains, Allport rules out the possibility that faith is a mere wish-fulfilling illusion.

FAITH

When very young, Allport points out, we believe almost everything we are told (1950, 114). Words and facts are virtually interchangeable to the child (1950, 139). This "credulity" is also found in inexperienced adults and in situations of suggestibility toward a speaker. "Doubt" is a reaction of hesitancy. It is said to result from a clash between beliefs or between evidence and a belief. "Disbelief" is negative. It is a rejecting attitude or response (1950, 139). Disbelief usually comes with experience. Disbelief is seen to be more definite than the doubt as which it begins.

Developmentally, doubt soon replaces credulity. Allport remarks that even young children test reality. Without such testing, a hopeless immaturity would prevail. Doubt is a necessary lesson to learn. A great many people are said to have mastered this first lesson of higher education, which is to say, not to be taken in. But Allport remarks that this is the only lesson a great many learn, that never finding their way forward to affirmation, many people's education breaks off here (1950, 117). Because religion tries to embrace so much—to bind "fact, value, and ultimate reality"—it is said to be the most controversial mental activity, the one most given to doubt (1950, 117).

"Belief" is an affirmation of the existence of the object of a sentiment (1950, 113). Mature belief, a third stage following credulity and doubt, is seen to develop painfully out of successive doubts and affirmations (1950, 138). Belief tends to lead to actions that fit the sentiment in question. A belief, even an uncertain one, can generate a great deal of energy. "Faith" is defined as a belief based on a probability (1950, 157). Faith sets up an intended relationship with a religious object. Faith is the belief that a goal is valid and attainable. Doubt always remains a possibility, however. Allport says that we normally continue to believe in an object only if there is a measure of independent support. A belief is properly called a delusion if it is deprived of sense perception, rational support, and the beliefs of others (1950, 156–57).

The highest degree of faith is seen in the conviction of the mystic that his or her immediate experience establishes the existence of God once and for all. On the other hand, Allport remarks that we can be "half-sure without being half-hearted" (1950, 157). Even a relatively low degree of faith can generate an enormous amount of activity. Our faith in the United Nations may be incomplete, yet we can still give it our total support. The religious sentiment, according to Allport, has the "longest-range intentions" and is consequently able to integrate personality to a marked degree (1950, 161). It can bring meaning and peace in the face of the "tragedy and confusion of life."

RELIGION AND SCIENCE

Allport affirms that science has proven to be "brilliantly productive." Even so, he points out, science presents itself to the mature religious individual as an essentially limited enterprise (1950, 128). Allport remarks that such human endeavors as our moral and political commitments, our choice of goals, and the preference of love over hate are grounded not in science but in concrete probabilities. The scientist is seen to prefer certainty to adequacy. Religion does not pretend to argue from certainty, basing its case instead on the legitimacy of its attempt to discover "reasonable certitude within the domain of adequacy" (1950, 130). Allport finds the world of private experience an acceptable test of love, one that neither science nor, for that matter, any other endeavor is able to furnish. If the scientist would systematically unite the facts known with the values held, Allport says his or her frame of reference would undergo an enormous expansion, approximating the religious.

Allport thinks that a time may be coming when religion will no longer be regarded as the no-longer-interesting point of origin of the brilliant light of science. Religion might indeed come to be viewed as just the "fresh and sparkling insight" that a science that prides itself on knowing nothing about values needs to complete and correct itself (1950, 133). People may wake up to the realization that intellect alone is not up to the task of surmounting the very real difficulties of a harsh reality. For that, faith and love are also said to be needed. Religion lives in the realm of faith and love, as well as in that of reason.

Allport is of the opinion that both religion and psychology need to broaden their outlooks. Science narrowly conceived and religion narrowly conceived can make no progress with each other. Allport sees our historical task as uniting the realm of science with that of purpose and value. Science by itself is seen to be unable to generate the enthusiasm necessary to realize the beneficial possibilities that exist within its discoveries. Allport says that an individual with a religious sentiment that is mature tries to accommodate science within religion, properly expanded (1950, 132).

INTENTIONALITY AND RELIGIOUS BEHAVIOR

Allport is of the view that the individual's religion can only be understood with the help of phenomenology's theory of "intentionality" (1950, 142). According to this theory, human life is essentially characterized by mental acts, and a "mental act" is an intending, aiming at, or stretching to an object that is the goal of our intention. The intentional object—the object aimed at in the mental act—is necessarily implicated in every act of intending. The individual, Allport says, is thus always *trying to do* something (1950, 143). People are always engaged in understanding, perceiving, judging, imagining, feeling, and the like. And they are always trying to do *something*, always engaged in understanding something, perceiving something, judging something, and so forth.

Allport believes that phenomenology, with its theory of intentionality, more adequately handles religious phenomena than traditional behaviorism, with its emphasis on observables and the priority of the environment.

In the realm of religious behavior, the subjective thrust of the mind toward an object is judged to be of the greatest importance. Paramount in mature religion, says Allport, is what the individual is actively trying to bring about, the sense he or she is trying to make of things, and not the way the environment is shaping behavior. Visible (observable) behavior in the religious realm is said to tell very little (1950, 143). When it comes to religious behavior, then, it is Allport's view that the notion of an organism that actively structures its world is preferable to that of a passive and empty organism whose total structure issues from the environment. Mature religious behavior is preeminently active. Classical behaviorism can only miss the point of such behavior.

In terms of intentionality, a sentiment is a dynamic source of intentions that aim at actualizing the values integral to the sentiment (1950, 144). The theory of intentionality thus renders explicit the dynamic, organizing character of sentiments. Mature sentiments are never at the mercy of their situation. Neither are such sentiments driven, in Allport's view, by unconscious forces. The mature religious sentiment, for example, is the result of much conscious thought.

Allport states that an intention's object (goal) is in every case present as an idea. Sometimes the object—the mall I intend to visit this afternoon, for example—also exists externally as well. But the goals of our intentions are not always that clear (1950, 145). Such is the case with religious objects. The intentions generated by the religious sentiment are said to be more important, however, than the clarity of their object. Allport refers to the medieval philosophy of the Scholastics to make his point: it is more important, they said, to love God than to know him.

Allport also considers the notion of intention important for the psychology of religion because of its emphasis on the future (1950, 147). A mature sentiment is always geared to bringing about some state of affairs. Intentions with the longest ranges are said to be best able to bring ordered unity to life. Allport comments that, in order to understand people, we have to know what they are trying to accomplish. In his view, psychology has not fared very well in this regard: while people tend to busy themselves "leading their lives into the future," psychology has busied itself with "tracing them into the past" (1955, 51).

Allport locates the inadequacy of most definitions of religion in their manner of focusing on one intention or another—worshiping the "wholly other," for example, or seeking the strength to maintain one's ideals—to the exclusion of all others. About all that can be said in this regard, says Allport, is that religion is an attempt of one sort or another to actualize cherished values (1950, 149). He thinks it better to bear in mind the enormous individual variations in the religious sentiment than to search for a common core. Pressed to single out a common feature of all religious intentions, however, Allport would nominate the mystical goal of oneness (1950, 151).

CONSCIENCE

Allport remarks that in the course of social living there is no getting away from forming a conscience and that the capacity for conscience exists in virtually everyone (1950, 99). He cites the following key facts about conscience: (1) the universality of conscience, except in rare pathological instances, regardless of culture; (2) the variability of the contents of conscience in different cultures—a variability Allport suggests is probably overestimated; and (3) the slow and painful acquisition of conscience through learning.

As children we do not know why we "must" do this or that thing. The conscience of childhood, consisting of a number of unrelated and arbitrary "musts" externally imposed, is said to be fragmentary (1955, 78). With growing maturity, however, people are seen to make the moral reasons for their behavior their own. "Musts" become "oughts" (1950, 100). "Musts" still exist, as when "I 'must' go shopping for food." But "oughts" dominate the mature individual's moral life. "I 'ought' to visit a relative in the hospital" is said to be quite different from "I 'must' visit a relative in the hospital."

Allport thus sees the "must" of the superego as being replaced in the mature individual by the "ought" of the "mature conscience." The mature conscience is no longer seen as depending upon external enforcement but upon the values of maturity, which characteristically differ markedly from the values of childhood (1950, 101). Adults discard culturally imposed codes in favor of codes of their own. "Oughts" come into being, Allport says, that were never "musts." Even though educated to prejudice, for example, we may come to believe we "ought" to treat all people as equals. Nor do all "musts" become "oughts." As adults we may not feel we "ought" to go to church according to the schedule that was a "must" of childhood. Allport says that adults feel guiltiest not when they violate "tribal taboos" or "parental prohibitions" but when they act against their personal moral codes (1955, 71). What triggers guilt in adults may indeed have little or nothing to do with childhood patterns of obedience.

Allport states that conscience in adults is properly expected to be adult in character, keeping pace with the individual's age and experience. Adult (mature) conscience is a process that controls passing impulses and merely expedient actions in favor of long-range aims and the consistency of our self-image (1955, 68). Mature conscience is a guide in the determination of values, relating the individual to reality as presently conceived.

The voice of conscience, "a present guide to conduct" and no mere vestige of childhood, no superego, speaks *now* in the mature individual. Functionally autonomous of its origins, adult conscience is the "arbiter of adult values" (1950, 101).

Allport remarks that the religious sentiment produces a conscience appropriate to its values. The conscience of most religious people is seen, for example, to have "more to do with love than with fear." Saying that mature religious people do things, or refrain from doing things, out of fear of God's punishment is a travesty of their experience (1955, 72–73). All in all, individuals with a mature religious sentiment are described as adopting a style of life that demands discipline, love, and reverence. Someone who does the right thing merely because of the fear of punishment is said to have a childish conscience, a conscience arrested in its development.

When we violate our sentiments, Allport says, we feel guilty. Guilt is said to be "a sense of violated value" (1955, 73). According to Allport, conscience indicates whether or not our actions are in accord with our values. It speaks when the integrity of a sentiment is being challenged by our conduct. A mature conscience is thus to be heeded, in Allport's view, in the interest of the mental unity that has been fashioned, in the course of a lifetime, on the one hand, out of impulse and, on the other, out of aspiration. Many "irreligious" individuals, Allport says, have a highly sensitive conscience (1950, 101). It is pointed out that psychology and religion agree that, in most cases, the conflicts leading to mental disturbances are between impulse and moral obligation (1950, 97–98).

PRAYER, RITUAL, AND DOCTRINE

Prayer, ritual, and dogma are all seen as ways to focus the religious intention for a time (1950, 151). Allport remarks that prayer is not necessarily directed to a God who is expected to advance the supplicant's worldly position. Prayer, moreover, can assume a variety of forms. Allport states that the solitary religious quest tends to become burdensome. Most people want to share their religious insights with others "under a common set of symbols" (1950, 153). As a consequence of this desire, ritual and dogma come to be developed. Allport remarks that rituals tend to bring to the fore intentions that would otherwise remain dormant. Doctrines are seen to be an attempt to improve upon the formulations of individuals and to achieve a statement common to many. Since people are unique individuals, however, no single doctrinal formulation is able to serve everyone (1950, 154). If we value the individual, Allport says, religious tolerance is essential.

NEUROSIS

Allport remarks that present-day religion would say that the neurotic is living a life that, in some respects at least, is extremely self-centered (1950, 106). Neurosis is thus said to be hooked up with pride and self-preoccupation. When the neurotic stops focusing on himself or herself and begins to concentrate instead on selfless goals, Allport comments, an immediate improvement occurs. A more becoming humility on the neurotic's part, especially if integrated into an overall religious framework, would bring movement in the direction of a more mature conscience and, with that, improved mental health (1950, 106; compare above, "Conscience").

MYSTICAL EXPERIENCE

Allport suspects that immediate mystical experience is the most commonly accepted way in which people validate their religion (1950, 158). Such experience is as convincing to the mystic as perceptual experience is to the average individual.

RELIGIOUS LANGUAGE

Allport points out that a difficulty with the language of religion is that it has no other words to use than those that are also used by science. Images based on space and time, for example, are commonplace in the Bible (1950, 135). Christ is described as ascending, as going up in space, to heaven. Hell, on the other hand, is pictured as down. Such spatial imagery is meaningless to modern science. Evolutionary theory speaks in terms of millions of years, the Bible in terms of a few thousand. Certain numbers, such as twelve or forty, have a symbolic significance in the Bible. In science they are just numbers. A day of Creation is one thing, an astronomical day another.

Religious language is thus problematic in our scientific age. There is no alternative but for doubt and confusion to arise, Allport remarks, when properly religious and properly scientific discourse are uncritically mixed, as though the terms were equivalent in the two discourses. Examples of such illegitimate mixing are "Each of the six days of creation lasted twenty-four, sixty-minute hours" and "While God and heaven are up among the clouds, hell and the damned are down below the earth's surface."

Allport points out that the fact of the matter is that religious doctrine, like religious ritual, means much more than it seems to (1950, 136). Religious language is said to refer to realities of cosmic dimensions. Words invoked to express ultimate realities are necessarily used with the greatest possible latitude. It is impossible to demonstrate or accurately specify their objects. Citing A. N. Whitehead, Allport remarks that words were apparently invented to facilitate discrimination between the tangible things of everyday life, not to forge a single unified meaning out of the whole of everything. But it is exactly this latter task that religious language is seen to have set for itself. Religion simply does not concern itself, Allport says, with mere facts and ordinary purposes. Religious language signifies, in the first place, ideals and the preference and striving for a certain way of life. It signifies the desired "completion of knowledge" and "perfection of one's own nature" (1950, 137). Religious language and ordinary mundane language are thus worlds apart. The standards for the one are not to be applied to the other.

RESPONSES TO SOME OBJECTIONS TO RELIGION

In the course of his reflections on the individual's religion, Allport answers a number of objections psychologists have raised against religion. This section summarizes these answers.

Religion Causes Mental Breakdown

Preoccupation with religion may be an effect of mental breakdown, says Allport, rather than its cause. Perhaps religious language best represents to a disturbed person the mysterious forces that have taken over one's life (1950, 94).

Religion Is a Magical Phase in Humankind's Development

Some propose that "primitives," children, and uneducated people engage in religious practices as a general means to resolve problems. This is to say that human beings pass through a magical phase of development that has now been outgrown and is to be replaced by science. Allport points out, however, that even "primitives" have no difficulty distinguishing between the domains of science and religion (1950, 22). "Primitives" are seen to be realistic and empirical when things can be controlled but not so when they cannot (Bronislaw Malinowski). It is further pointed out that religions have made significant historical contributions to the development of logic, mathematics, and science.

Religious Optimism Is Wishful Thinking

Allport views as superficial the charge that the religious bias in favor of optimism is wishful thinking. This claim is seen to overlook the fact that

religious hope and religious beliefs have very little to do w
wishes of everyday life (1950, 24). The great religions of the
demand self-denial, discipline, and surrender. One has to lose
order to find it. This has little to do with mundane and transparently self-
centered wish fulfillment, daydreaming, and rationalization.

The normally intelligent, healthy individual knows that the problems
of life cannot be solved by wishing (1955, 94). The nonreligious person,
moreover, is also seen to seek cognitive unity and coherence and, in the
absence of certainty, also "plans for a happy landing." Working principles
that lead to success, Allport points out, always depict life as friendly to
human aspirations. It comes as no surprise, then, that religion does so too.
Allport admonishes those who brand religious thinking as illusory not to
examine their own working principles too carefully (1950, 25).

Religion Is the Product of Culture

Some argue that the religious sentiment of the individual faithfully du-
plicates the cultural model. Allport points out, however, that not a few individuals question, and even reject, the very beliefs that have ever so carefully been instilled in them. Allport goes on to argue that individuals who
adopt a certain religious custom do so for their own good reasons (1950,
28). People do not conform, for example, in the interest of "social cohe-
siveness."

Religion Is Rooted in the Longing for the Father

Sigmund Freud's view that adult religion is universally the repetition of
childhood experiences having to do with the father is found to be a trivial
one. The fact that some children carry over the image of their human father
to a father in heaven is no proof that all religious adults do likewise (1950,
94). The argument that belief in God is but the projection of positive feelings of dependence and love toward one's earthly father, moreover, finds
its logical parallel in the affirmation that disbelief in God (atheism) is but
the projection of ambivalence or hatred toward the father (1950, 118). Allport thinks that both belief and doubt occasionally contain elements of unconscious attitudes toward parents. He points out further that atheism is
not always the opposite of religion. Fervent atheists are seen to display a
profound interest in religion (1950, 118). Finally, some people are called
atheists simply because their concept of God is not the conventional one.

Religion Is a Rationalization of Our Longings

We have seen that religious strivings often originate in organic desire, the
pursuit of meaning, and the concern for the fulfillment of values. Some

critics of religion propose that, in the pursuit of gratification, we "rationalize our longings" through fabricated religious beliefs (1950, 123). Allport points out that citing origins as the reason for the phenomena of religion is too easy and, as already suggested, can justly be turned against itself: background can be used to explain disbelief no less effectively than belief (1950, 124). Allport says that origins simply tell us nothing about a belief's validity. One must understand, rather, the part the belief plays in the present life economy of the individual. It is pointed out that Freud never takes the religious sentiment at its face value. A more balanced view, in Allport's opinion, is that sometimes we can, and sometimes we cannot, take this sentiment at its face value (1960, 104). A judgment can only be made in view of the individual whose sentiment it is.

When the individual in question has evolved a guiding philosophy of life in which the religious sentiment is consistently directive of behavior and makes sense of the whole of life, then, in Allport's view, it is a dominant motive and to be accepted at its face value. A religious sentiment of this sort is said to be the result of a great deal of reflection and criticism, and attributing it to rationalization is unjustified. When religion is a cover for egocentricity, on the other hand, we are faced with a form of religion that resembles neurosis, a religion that serves as a defense against anxiety and exists solely for personal advantage. A religion of this sort is not a dominant need in its own right (functional autonomy) but serves other needs—such as for security, status, and self-esteem. Such religion, Allport says, is not to be taken at its face value. The error of the psychoanalytic theory of religion is said to lie in its location of religious belief in the ego's defensive maneuvering rather than "in the core and substance of the developing ego itself" (1955, 96).

IMMATURE RELIGION

We have seen that Allport does not find all religion to be mature and beyond criticism. Some religion is indeed immature. Attaining a certain chronological age is no guarantee of the maturity of any sentiment. Religious becoming at times suffers arrest, in which case the individual may be left with infantile—self-serving and superstitious—religious beliefs (1955, 96). Allport points out that society does not pressure for religious maturity as insistently as it does for maturity in other areas of life. Religion is generally regarded as a private matter, and so, individuals may be left to their egocentric, magical, and wish-fulfilling type of religion. As a result, it is asserted, there are more residues of childhood in adult religious attitudes than in any other region of the personality (1950, 59).

The maturity of a sentiment depends, in Allport's view, on its keeping pace with relevant experience. The religious sentiment suffers arrested development when people find their childhood religion comforting and, so, resist moving beyond it. Childhood religion is often hung on to in order to preserve pleasant childhood memories and to guarantee comfort and social status. For such a religion to confront science, suffering, and criticism would be an enormous, perhaps insurmountable, challenge (1950, 60).

Allport does not find most criticism of religion to be criticism of religion proper but of immature religion, of religion that has not grown beyond the gratification of impulses (1950, 61). Immature religion is seen either to be wish fulfilling or to serve as a tranquilizing agent. It remains self-justifying and self-centered. It is unreflective. It fails to find the supreme context in which the individual can meaningfully locate his or her being. Nor does it enable the individual to judge his or her conduct in perspective. It excludes vast segments of experience. It is incapable of uniting the personality. Immature religion, engaging magical thinking, is seen to be in pursuit of material comfort. Not functionally autonomous of its origins, its motive force thus remains organic desire.

Religion functioning as an escape from adult responsibility is seen to be common enough. Some religious beliefs indeed have a childish character: unquestioning, irrational, and authoritarian. A faith geared to self-advantage, Allport says, is bound to come undone (1950, 120). The religious sentiment must transcend personal whim. Allport comments that mature religion affirms God, whereas immature religion insists that God is exactly as it pictures him to be (1950, 78). Allport argues that if Freud had been "more perceptive," he would have noticed that only religion in its immature version resembles a neurosis (1968, 149).

RELIGION AND LOVE

Allport affirms that, so long as we are healthy, we always want more love in our life, that we can never love or be loved enough (1960, 205). And when we imagine "a perfect state of being," Allport says that we invariably imagine "the unconditional triumph of love" (1960, 205). He thinks that people align themselves almost universally with religion because all of the world's major religions offer a framework for a basic love relationship with an all-embracing principle and affirm the ideal of the solidarity of all human life. Many individuals need "a sense of cosmic affiliation" in order for their lives to be "complete, intelligible, right" (1950, 92–93).

Allport generalizes that hatred of humanity results from frustrated relationships with others. A rejected or threatened desire for love, he says, "turns to anxious fear" (1960, 205–206). Misanthropy is seen to be universally "a matter of frustrated affiliative desire and the attendant humiliation to self-esteem" (1960, 205–206). Hostility has a secondary character, then, according to Allport, developing when there is a disturbance in the security generated by genuine love (1950, 91). Allport believes that a major obstacle to the improvement of human relations is the ease with which the human mind generates categories (1960, 212). We find it all too easy to lump others into a category and then to view "them" as inferior to "us."

RELIGION AND PREJUDICE

Allport defines ethnic prejudice in his book, *The Nature of Prejudice,* as "an antipathy based upon a faulty and inflexible generalization" (1958, 10). Prejudice may be only a matter of feeling, or it may be expressed as well. It may be directed toward a group as a whole or toward an individual as a member of that group. Some religious people, Allport comments, are deeply prejudiced, while others regularly practice universal love. Religion seems to be in large measure responsible, he goes on to say, both for the prejudice of the one group and for the tolerant love of the other. Allport has investigated this question and concludes that the difference in behavior is due to differences in religiosity between the two groups. He distinguishes two forms of religious orientation.

On the one hand, there's "extrinsic religion" (compare above, "Immature Religion"). Extrinsic religion is something people use, not something they live. It's a "dull habit" or a "tribal investment" used for "occasional ceremony, family convenience, and personal comfort" (1968, 148). Extrinsic religion is a self-serving, self-protecting, and utilitarian outlook on life. It brings comfort and salvation at the expense of other groups. Religion is not a value in itself but is used to serve other needs. This form of religion is a mode of conformity, a crutch, and a tranquilizer. Prejudice is easily accommodated, Allport points out, within extrinsic religiosity. Prejudice brings status and social support and, so, is useful. Prejudice brings feelings of security and comfort, moreover, by viewing all virtues as belonging to the in-group and all vices to the out-group.

"Intrinsic religion," on the other hand, is mature religiousness, a longing for and a commitment to "an ideal unification of one's life" under the guidance of "a unifying conception of the nature of all existence" (1968, 151; compare above, "Mature Religion"). Intrinsic religion characterizes the lives of those who have made all aspects of a religion's creed their own. Such people do not hold back, do not exclude the commandment to love others, whoever they may be. They subordinate their needs to their overall commitment to religion. Love, humility, and compassion have been made their own. There is no room for prejudice and contempt for others in such religiousness.

The distinction between extrinsic and intrinsic religion is seen to clarify the empirical finding that people who attend church are more prejudiced than those who do not. A close look at the data shows that a significant minority of the attenders is less prejudiced than the nonattenders (1968, 237). It is the casual, irregular, fringe members who are found to be high in prejudice. The religious motivation of these members is extrinsic in character. Members whose religion is intrinsic, on the other hand, are seen to be low in prejudice. A further study found that, in six groups of church-goers, there was a significant trend for members with an extrinsic religious orientation to be more prejudiced than those with an intrinsic one (1968, 245–60).

All in all, then, the sort of religion the individual has appears to be an important determining factor in the development of a tolerant or a prejudiced outlook. Allport concludes that the words "religion" and "religious" are too broad for discriminating use (1968, 260). He cautions that, should the terms continue to be used, important distinctions need to be made.

EVALUATION AND CONCLUSIONS

Allport presents us in *The Individual and His Religion* (1950) with a psychological overview of religion that is both sage and on target. He challenges one-sided outlooks—those with an exclusive emphasis on early life, for example, or the workings of the environment or the unconscious. He insists on the active and conscious role of the individual in shaping his or her religion. The individual's motivation is recognized as his or her very own. There is a healthy, mature religiousness, as well as a sick, immature one. Mechanisms, of whatever sort, are not to be invoked in accounting for mature religion, which instead belongs to the very "core and substance of the developing ego itself" (1955, 96). No common origin or core is to be attributed to all religion. All in all, in the interest of fairness and balance, Allport has prescribed a judicious program of correctives for the further development of the psychology of religion.

An important feature of Allport's work is his descriptive or phenomenological approach. Mature religious behavior is found, in the final analysis, to be an attempt to actualize cherished values. This primary emphasis on values, noticeably absent in so much of psychology (but see, for example, chapters 5 and 8 on Abraham Maslow and Viktor Frankl), is an important one. Allport returns us to the actual structure of behavior. He thus aligns himself with those psychologists who believe that progress in psychology will come not from blindly adopting the procedures of physics but from taking the proper measure of human life (see, for example, Koehler 1947, ch. 2). Allport supported empirical research and engaged in it himself. A principal concern, however, was that psychology attain a proper conceptualization of its subject matter. Attention to actual human behavior, Allport finds, reveals not only its fundamental orientation to value but its active, structuring character as well.

Freudian rationalism sought straightforwardly to bring to light the unconscious motive power behind religion and thus to deprive it of its pernicious hold on humanity. Enlightenment, it was hoped, would eliminate myth and mystery from the face of the earth, ultimately issuing in the victory of "Our God Logos." Allport, for his part, acknowledged a necessary role of ambiguity in human life. Like James, he recognized faith's role in the success of human endeavors. Human actions are based on probabilities, says Allport, not final certainties. And doubt always remains a possibility, and never more so than in matters of religious faith. The intentions the religious sentiment gives rise to, moreover, are said to be more important than the clarity of the objects aimed at. Finally, religious language has a symbolic, not a literal, character, and can never adequately specify its objects.

In a more critical vein, Allport's account of mature religion seems in some respects to be overly intellectual and optimistic—consider, for example, religion's role of making sense of every atom of experience referred to it. Allport's psychology of religion, moreover, like that of James and of Carl Jung, is highly individualistic: individuals evolve an adult religiousness essentially on their own, seeking out the company of others only afterward for the common expression and further development of their faith. Allport eventually admitted that he had failed to take "ecological, social, and situational factors" sufficiently into account and that "inside and outside systems" need to be more adequately related (1968, 63).

All in all, however, Allport's clarity, incisiveness, and deep humanism have made him an important figure in American psychology. In addition to his distinction between mature and immature religiousness, particularly significant for the psychology of religion has been his work on the scaling of religious orientation and values (Allport 1968; Allport, Vernon, and Lindzey 1970).

REFERENCES

Allport, G. W. *Personality: A Psychological Interpretation*. New York: Holt, 1937.
———. *The Individual and His Religion*. New York: Macmillan, 1950.

———. *Becoming.* New Haven: Yale University Press, 1955.

———. *The Nature of Prejudice.* New York: Doubleday, 1958.

———. *Personality and Social Encounter.* Boston: Beacon Press, 1960.

———. *Pattern and Growth in Personality.* Boston: Beacon Press, 1961.

———. *The Person in Psychology.* Boston: Beacon Press, 1968.

Allport, G. W., and J. M. Ross. "Personal Religious Orientation and Prejudice." *Journal of Personality and Social Psychology* 5 (1967): 432–43.

Allport, G. W., E. Vernon, and G. Lindzey. *Manual, Study of Values: A Scale for Measuring the Dominant Interests in Personality.* Boston: Houghton Mifflin, 1970.

Koehler, W. *Gestalt Psychology.* New York: New American Library, 1947.

5

✢

Abraham Maslow

What isn't worth doing, isn't worth doing well. What needs doing, is worth doing even though *not* very well.

—Abraham Maslow

Abraham Maslow (1908–1970) seeks to renew psychological science by extending it into directions long shunned in American psychology. Reproaching orthodox psychology—Sigmund Freud, for example—for identifying the sick and the evil with the true essence of human nature, Maslow sets before us, for our emulation, healthy human beings, self-actualized individuals able to show others what they are capable of. The human being, Maslow says, need not remain a mere fragment, cut off from others and their "real self"—from the creativity and vitality of the unconscious, for example—but can be whole.

Health and wholeness are intimately associated, in Maslow's view, with the spiritual life and the sacred, the ultimate values of "Being" (Being-values). God, Maslow says, is being defined anew in our time as a possibility within human nature. Maslow thus concludes that human life is self-transcending—that the eternal, transhuman values of the cosmos (Being-values) are inscribed in the very depths of human nature: that is, that human life as a whole is oriented to the Good, the Beautiful, the True, the Just, and the like. In this way does Maslow identify inside and outside: possessed of the ultimate defining characteristics of the universe itself, human life is the universe in miniature, a microcosm. Health and wholeness, Maslow concludes, are gained precisely through the realization of our inner affinity with the universe that gave us birth. Maslow's humanistic psychology, it turns out, is a transhumanistic psychology. Maslow thinks of his attempts at expanding psychology's horizons as picking up where Freud left off: exploring those biological needs neglected by Freud, higher and, in the final analysis, spiritual needs. In addition to following Freud's pioneering lead, Maslow draws from whatever source advanced his psychological understanding: Kurt Goldstein, Carl Jung, Gordon Allport, Erich Fromm, existentialism, Eastern philosophy, Gestalt psychology, behaviorism, and so on.

Guided by what he judged to be the actual facts of human life, Maslow challenges accepted dogma. Finding the biological essence of human life to be neutral or good, he rejects traditional doctrines of original sin and the id. Finding human life to be oriented to intrinsic values rather than governed by extrinsic stimuli, he parts company with radical behaviorism. Finding "value-free" science to be a positive danger, he repudiates it. Taking his lead from the givens of human life as he saw them, Maslow has the courage to espouse unpopular views. Where other psychologists become nervous at the very mention of the divine and the sacred, Maslow puts them at the very center of his psychology. Where other psychologists turn their back on phenomena that don't fit the available methods, Maslow says the method should be adapted to the phenomena. Where other psychologists adhere to reductive theories of motivation, Maslow admits the full range of human desire.

Maslow's psychology focuses on the higher or "farther reaches of human nature." He is nevertheless acutely aware of the power of evil in human life; he indeed describes himself in his *Journals* as possessed of an overwhelming "tragic sense of life and evil" and anything but "unrealistically optimistic" (1979, 200). Maslow is nevertheless able to give an account of evil in terms of our higher and deeper nature. Evil, he says, has a reactive character. There is no inborn inclination to murder and be violent, no innate desire to rape and plunder. These result not from the thwarting of our true—biological—nature, not from its free expression.

No more than evil does Maslow neglect the necessary role of discipline and hard work in the attainment of human health and success. Self-actualization, he says, has to be earned, which means it is something that can be learned and, so, taught to our children. Maslow's psychology is decidedly not of the armchair variety: based on what is judged the best available evidence, it is a call to action, to the furtherance of the values of Being in our schools, our offices, our homes, our hospitals, our government, and society in general.

PLEA FOR AN EXPANDED SCIENCE

Maslow finds valuelessness to be the "ultimate disease" of our time (1970b, vii; see 1970c, 5–10). No longer does there seem to be anything to admire and be awed by, to live or die for (1970c, 42). The certainties that prevailed before World War I are seen to have given way to chaos, relativism, and widespread despair. When the traditional values collapsed, Maslow says there were no commonly accepted ones to take their place.

But, Maslow insists, the longing for some kind of certainty remains. Affluence, revealing the spiritual hunger of people when they have everything, has made the problem of values stand out in its full clarity (1970c, 37–38). When there is something to reach for, Maslow says, life is meaningful. But when one lacks nothing, then what? We are seen to be in that transitional period in which the old values no longer serve but in which we cannot yet agree on the answer to "then what?" Maslow's psychology is an attempt to arrive at an answer to just this question. It is based neither on authorities nor on tradition but on the rigorous attitude of science. Maslow's hope is to find answers that people can agree on when given thoughtful consideration.

Value-Free Science's Contribution to Valuelessness

Maslow points out that "orthodox nineteenth-century science" is of no help in the task he has set himself and that conventional science has in fact aggravated the problem of valuelessness (1970c, 11–12). In its quest for objective certainty, orthodox science self-consciously determined to be value-free. Facts, and facts alone, were to constitute its realm. Values were considered arbitrary and to have nothing to do with facts. The concern of value-free science, value-free psychology included, did not extend, then, to values and the life of value. At one extreme, Maslow says, psychology even rejects personal experience, arguing that, because such experience is private (subjective) rather than public (objective) in character, it is not open to scientific scrutiny. Freudian psychoanalysis, for its part, is seen to have opted for the position that the "higher life" and its values serve only "to defend against the instincts," that the highest values in life are nothing but disguised versions of the lower cravings of human nature (1970c, 7). Maslow remarks that psychoanalysis comes close to being nihilistic.

Maslow thus sees value-free science as having no theory of the criterion of human growth, no theory of what is intrinsically worth pursuing, as knowing nothing about ultimate values, the ideal, and the mysterious (1970c, 41). Maslow says this amounts to saying that science can only deal with what is, with facts, and that the goals and purposes of life, life's values, are beyond the range of natural knowledge, beyond science's capabilities. It is to say that values cannot be understood in a satisfactory manner, the way facts are. Maslow firmly believes that the value-free paradigm of science inherited from the physical sciences is unsuitable for the science of life, and even more so for the science of human behavior (1971, 5). If psychology's goal is to understand people, Maslow says personal values, plans, and purposes must be taken into account (1971, 5).

The Sickness of Value-Free Science

Many intellectuals are seen to lose faith in the way of life of "positivistic, nineteenth-century science," just as they do in religious orthodoxy (1970c, 43). Maslow says this is not without its reasons. Science has proven positively dangerous to human life in our times (1971, 172). Such becomes the case, Maslow says, when science, excluding personal experience, declares it has nothing to say about the values and goals of life. When science affirms that values are arbitrary, Stalin's murderous deeds cannot be proved wrong; being a good scientist is compatible with being a good Nazi; and science is an instrument to be used by anyone for any end (1969, 120; 1970c, 16). All in all, science becomes sick, in Maslow's view, when it rules out values. It comes as no surprise, then, that in our day many people are afraid of science, seeing in it a threat to everything they hold sacred. Maslow thus views the traditional value-neutral philosophy of science as both wrongheaded and dangerous. It is not just amoral, in his judgment, but antimoral (1971, 21).

Value is what is important to people, what motivates their behavior and what they live for. Value-free science is accordingly unsuited to deal with human questions. Maslow says it was quite proper for science to deny the existence of purpose in things—in the stars, for example. But people act, make plans, and are involved (1969, 2). Maslow argues that a theory of science that excludes so much that is real lacks comprehensiveness and, so, must fail in its attempts to come to an understanding of human behavior (1970c, 43).

The Proposed Expansion of Science

Maslow is convinced that what we need today is an expanded science, one "with larger powers and methods," a science able to investigate values and to instruct people in their regard (1970c, 17), a science that does not intentionally set out to desacralize everything in its path in the fashion of orthodox science (1969, 137), a humble science capable of awe in the face of the mystery of reality (1979, 390). Maslow thinks that science needs to expand into all those dimensions of life that, until now, have been excluded from serious consideration. Some of these areas are values, goals, and ends; the sacred, the mysterious, and the ambiguous; and the unconscious (1970c, 40–47). Such a science would necessarily be one with the psyche and personal experience left in; the whole person must be taken into account (1969, xiii, 7–8, 18). Maslow remarks that what we stand in urgent need of today is a personal science whose aim is not making people more predictable and amenable to scientific control, but less so (1969, 40). He feels that a psychological science expanded along such lines would be a much more powerful instrument than conventional science (1969, 47).

Science needs to embrace all that is real and that can be naturalistically observed, to acknowledge and describe "all of reality, all that exists, everything that is the case" (1968, 72). Maslow insists that science can ask any question, and that, once asked, its investigation must be governed by procedures that measure up to its character and particularities and not by ones arbitrarily prescribed in advance. Methods will have to be created as needed, the old ones derived from the physical sciences being judged inadequate to the task. The beginnings of an expanded science will be sloppy, Maslow admits, but as later stages develop, greater rigor will be demanded; an adequate psychological science will gain in precision in due course (1969, 14, 56–57). Maslow remarks that a science expanded along these lines would encompass much that has been called religious.

Maslow believes that values can be studied naturalistically, like any of nature's secrets. Such a naturalistic study of values forms the heart of Maslow's project. The values by which we are to live are held to lie within human nature, for the discovery. Values are to be derived, then, from our essential biological essence. It is not a matter of fabricating or constructing them. Maslow is firmly convinced that the only teaching that can serve us now is "empirical, naturalistic knowledge," taken in the broadest possible sense (1970c, 10). Ultimately, our only hope is advancing in knowledge through a greatly expanded science (1971, 4). Only truth can be our foundation, he says, and not blind trust in anything—only knowing, not believing. Maslow's goal is to enlarge science, not abolish it (1969, xvi). It is thought that an expanded comprehension of human nature will help people fulfill their longing for certainty as to how to live.

ASSUMPTIONS OF MASLOW'S PSYCHOLOGY OF HEALTH

Maslow thinks that what psychology calls "normal" is in fact "a psychopathology of the average" resulting from the indiscriminate lumping together of both healthy and pathological behavior (1970b, 122). Maslow lists the following basic assumptions of his new conception of human health and sickness (1968, 3–4): each of us has an essential inner nature that is biologically based; this inner nature is in part unique, in part specieswide; this nature can be scientifically investigated; this inner nature seems not to be "intrinsically or primarily or necessarily" evil; because this nature is good or neutral, it is to be encouraged rather than suppressed; if this nature is suppressed, the individual becomes sick—psychopathology is in general the result of "the denial, frustration or the twisting of essential human nature" (1970a, 269); this essential inner nature is weak, delicate, and easily overwhelmed, especially in its higher reaches; and there is no successful avoiding of discipline, pain, and tragedy. These assumptions are elaborated upon in various sections of this chapter.

THE BASIC NEEDS

Related to values are needs: whatever people truly need is, for that very reason, an intrinsic good to them: that is, a value. When we are hungry, for example, and need food, food is a value, intrinsically valuable to us at the moment. Maslow thus reasons that, if we succeed in determining our "basic needs," we will also have discovered basic human values, values intrinsic to our biological constitution.

One approach to the problem of fundamental human needs is through psychopathology. In their attempts to discover the origins of neurosis, Freud, Jung, and Alfred Adler are all said to have discovered biological needs that were neglected or violated early in life. Maslow argues that the psychologist can take a lesson from the nutritionist, who, observing that the absence of a vitamin is regularly accompanied by the occurrence of a particular disease, concludes that there is a biological need for the vitamin. The psychotherapist, finding that the absence of love or safety, for example, is psychopathogenic—that is, that it leads to psychological "disease"—can conclude that love or safety is a biological need (1969, 124). Maslow remarks that, proceeding on this basis, neurosis can be considered a "deficiency disease" (1968, 21–23). He thus considers as basic needs those fundamental human demands that, when thwarted, either actually or by way of threat, issue in psychopathological outcomes, psychological malfunctioning, and, when adequately and properly gratified, prevent deficiency disease (1970a, 56–57, 108; 1970b, 123).

Sickness, Maslow says, consists of losing our essential—biological—nature. Unimportant desires can be thwarted without psychopathological consequences. Merely being deprived of a basic need, moreover, doesn't make us sick: an individual who has loved and been loved all his or her life is not greatly threatened by the withdrawal of love (1970a, 114). It is the *thwarting* of the basic needs, Maslow asserts, that is psychopathogenic, not their mere deprivation. Though conflict and frustration plague us, we become psychologically sick only when the conflict or the frustration "threatens or thwarts the basic needs" (1970a, 57). Maslow proposes the following list of basic human needs (1970a, 35–47):

1. Self-actualization
2. Esteem (high evaluation of self and others)
3. Belongingness and love (including not only the need *to be* loved but the need *to* love as well)
4. Safety (e.g., the need for security)
5. Physiological needs

These are said to be the fundamental goals of human life (1970a, 54). The basic needs are pregiven, hence, relatively constant and, to a degree, independent of the weight of the environment and the current situation. They are said to be, strictly speaking, biological needs (1970a, 88–95). As such, the basic needs are found in all people, a universal endowment of human nature. We develop from within, in Maslow's view, in accordance with these intrinsic laws of human nature. Maslow says that, largely unconscious, the basic needs, and especially the higher ones, tend to remain hidden and to require some digging in order to be unearthed as the essential potentialities of human life.

Only unsatisfied needs, needs properly speaking, dominate the organism and organize its behavior (1970a, 38). This means that the individual who is satisfied in the more fundamental needs—physiological and safety needs, for example—no longer has these needs.

The more fulfilled we are in the full range of our basic needs, Maslow says, the healthier we are. The higher the need, moreover, the less selfish it is found to be. In the hierarchy of needs, the higher, spiritual needs are at the top (1971, 194). Our higher, less selfish nature is said to build and rest on the foundation of our lower, more self-centered nature (1968, 172–74). The former, it is remarked, would collapse without the latter.

Basic Needs and Intrinsic Values

Ends, purposes, and goals stand in a necessary relation to needs. As already mentioned, the affirmation of basic biological needs is at the same time an affirmation of intrinsically valuable ends to be sought by the organism. Our own nature, Maslow affirms, supplies us with "a ready-made framework of ends, goals, or values" (1970a, 79). Maslow corroborates Gestalt psychologist Wolfgang Koehler's discovery of "intrinsic requiredness" (1970a, 62). There is, for example, seen to be one, and only one, genuine satisfier for a love-starved individual: "honest and satisfying affection" (1970a, 62). A loving person, a person to be loved, is exactly appropriate to the need, the one value that corresponds to the individual's longing and that can satisfy it. If we are starved for sex or for food or for respect or for water, only sex or food or respect or water will do (1970a, 62). Maslow thus holds to intrinsically correct gratifications, to an "intrinsic appropriateness" between a need and its fulfilling value, rather than to a fortuitous connection between a response and its stimulus as favored by associative learning theory. Basic need theory is a theory of the organism's ultimate values, of ends that are "intrinsically, and in themselves, valuable to the organism" (1970a, 63).

Maslow thus claims to have discovered a hierarchy of higher and lower values intrinsic to human nature corresponding to the hierarchy of higher and lower basic needs. He feels that a naturalistic value system can be worked out on the basis of these essential values. Individuals long for such a system and tell us the values that constitute it by sickening when thwarted in their attainment.

THE NEED FOR SELF-ACTUALIZATION

Maslow has given special attention to one basic human need in particular, the need for self-actualization. Self-actualization is said to be our highest need. The highest human values are accordingly said to be associated with it. Self-actualization is described as the striving for health, the search for identity and autonomy, and the yearning for excellence. Maslow began his work on self-actualization by selecting people for study who, in his judgment, were extraordinary human beings. He then sought to describe the pattern common to them all.

If someone is satisfied in the lower needs (physiological, safety, belongingness, and esteem), a new discontent arises. The individual, no longer deficient (needy), is no longer concerned with obtaining what one lacks, but in being everything that one can be, in seeking self-fulfillment, and in tending to become fully developed and actualized in one's individual talents, capacities, and potentialities. These organismic concerns for growth, excellence, identity, and upward movement express the need for self-actualization.

Self-actualization, normative, in Maslow's view, for all human beings, is the need for the development of our essential human nature: it is a pressure toward a unified personality, toward "spontaneous expressiveness," toward identity and full individuality, "toward seeing the truth rather than being blind," toward being good rather than bad, and toward creativeness (1970b, 126); "the tendency for people to become actualized in what they are potentially" (1970a, 46); and the need for the attainment of "full humanness"

(1971, 28–30). The full humanness characteristic of the self-actualized individual is Maslow's criterion of psychological health. Psychological sickness, by contrast, is any falling away from this humanness. What human beings *"can* be," Maslow says, "they *must* be" (1970a, 46).

Becoming Self-Actualized

In addition to a defining mark of character structure, self-actualization can also be thought of as an experience in which all one's energies are concentrated and one is totally absorbed, as experiencing fully and selflessly. When such a "self-actualizing moment" is in process, Maslow says, the individual is "wholly and fully human" (1971, 45). The experience of self-actualization can be had by anyone (see below, "Peak-Experiencing as Episodic Self-Actualization"). Self-actualization as a relatively constant state of personality, moreover, is something the average person can work at attaining.

Human nature, in Maslow's view, is no "blank slate" (tabula rasa) indiscriminately written upon by the environment, no lump of clay that can be molded to a desired shape. There is, to the contrary, Maslow insists, a *self* to be actualized, a self that each of us ought to be, that each of us is to become (1971, 45). And this self is what we are deep down (1971, 112).

We "become what we are," this deeper self, at once specieswide and idiosyncratic, by choosing it. Maslow remarks that self-actualization is an ongoing process that takes place—or perhaps fails to take place—in each of a multitude of single and ordinary everyday choices: being courageous and making the growth choice rather than the fear choice; being honest instead of lying; using one's intelligence instead of declining the effort; giving up illusions instead of yielding to them and the comfort afforded; deciding not to steal instead of stealing; listening to the live impulse voices within us instead of to the routinized voices of parents, the establishment, and the tradition; finding out what we like and don't like for ourselves instead of liking and not liking what "they" like and dislike; and discovering the sacred in all aspects of life instead of defensively turning away from it (1971, 45–50).

Each such behavior, Maslow remarks, is a choice of what is "constitutionally right" and a small step in the direction of self-actualization (1971, 47). We learn what is right for ourselves by a day-to-day attentive listening and obedience to our "inner voices" (1971, 124). Self-actualization, in short, is not only an "end state" but a process of actualizing potentialities to a greater or lesser extent, in accordance with the requirements of the momentary situation (1971, 47). Self-actualization, being a matter of individual small gains, is something one can attain to a greater or lesser degree (1971, 50).

Growth-Motivation and Deficiency-Motivation

There are not, in Maslow's opinion, many self-actualized people, and so, when we come across one of them, we are struck by how different such an individual is from the average. Lower needs dominate the value system of the person unfulfilled in the more basic needs, turning the world into a jungle. Once "inner deficiencies" are gratified by "outside satisfiers," on the other hand, Maslow says that self-actualization, the single problem of the development of the individual as a human being, begins (1970a, 162). The individual is then free to dedicate himself or herself to the higher satisfactions associated with the actualization of his or her unique and specieswide biological potentialities.

Self-actualized people are said not to strive in the ordinary sense of the word: they are not trying to attain a state of affairs other than the one they find themselves in. Gratified by definition in such needs as safety, belongingness, affection, respect, and self-esteem, self-actualizers are not attempting to get something they don't have (1971, 299). Basically satisfied, they are no longer lacking. No longer motivated by need, self-actualizers are "beyond Deficiency" (1971, 299–301). "Unmotivated," they *grow*. The actions of self-actualizers are thus said to spring from "Growth-motivation," instead of from "Deficiency-motivation." Not directed outward toward what they lack, they are engaged in expressing what is intrinsic to the organism. Real development of individuality, proceeding from within—"intrinsic growth"—is in process.

Self-actualization, Maslow remarks, is "Growth-motivated" rather than "Deficiency-motivated" (1970a, 134–35). What is already there unfolds. Things now come effortlessly of their own accord. The actions of self-actualizers are not for any other end but the present one, the activity presently engaged in. Work is play for them, duty pleasure, and virtue its own reward. Self-actualized persons are gratified when they give love. They act as an apple tree does when it bears fruit, as an expression of its intrinsic being, without effort or strain. Their spontaneity, naturalness, and health are not motivated—not motivated, that is, by lack. Their healthy and natural spontaneity is the "contradiction of motivation" (1970a, 233). "Motivation" for self-actualizers is simply growth, expression, maturation, and development of character, which is to say, self-actualization itself (1970a, 159).

Maslow has called growth-motivated, self-actualizing individuals "metamotivated" to distinguish them from those who are motivated in the ordinary sense of the word: that is, from Deficiency-motivated individuals. Rather than needs (lacks), self-actualizers are said to have "meta-needs." Strictly speaking, then, there is no "need" for self-actualization. Self-actualized individuals, acting out of fullness rather than Deficiency, lack nothing. Their "metamotivations" are for the metaneeds of excellence, truth, beauty, and other such higher values to be discussed below (see "Being-Values"). These metaneeds, or yearnings for the higher or spiritual life spring, in Maslow's view, from human nature itself. They have a biological character.

Maslow says that the expanded science of psychology he has called for is to be founded on the study of self-actualizing people. Because such people exist, they are said to be possible. And, indeed, Maslow maintains that self-actualization is in principle open to all (1971, 230; see above, "Becoming Self-Actualized"). It is thought that the free value-choices of self-actualizers, intrinsically (biologically) grounded as they are in the reality of human nature, could well serve as universal standards for human development, models for our young people, and, indeed, for everyone, to look up to (1968, 157–58). Self-actualized people have "a taste" for what is right, true, and beautiful and shun what is wrong, false, and ugly (1970a, 293). Self-actualizers tend to agree among themselves about what is right and what is wrong, not out of personal preference but out of a perception of "something real and extrahuman" (1971, 10). The fact that a small number of wonderful people actually exist, Maslow says, gives us faith in human possibilities and the courage and strength to keep on fighting (1970a, xxiii).

Maslow is more than aware that no perfect people exist or ever will (1970a, 174–76). Self-actualizing individuals, possessed of faults and problems, have "feet of clay." Self-actualizers, for example, are sometimes found to be ruthless. What makes these people different, Maslow says, is not their flawless perfection but the fact that, freed from the Deficiency problems of youth, they have progressed from unreal problems to real ones, to the never completely resolved existential problems of life (1968, 115). Maslow remarks that the most important difference of all may turn out to be the greater closeness of "deficit-satisfied" individuals to "the realm of Being" (1968, 39). It is to this realm, with its direct bearing on the psychology of religion, that we now turn.

THE REALM OF BEING

The central terms in Maslow's characterization of the realm of Being are Being-love, Being-cognition, and Being-values.

Being-Love

Self-actualizing people are said to have the greatest love of others and of the species as a whole. They transcend the limits of their ego and merge with others. They see the human species as a single family and identify with it. Maslow calls self-actualizing love "Being-love" (the love of Being, B-love). Being-love is pure love for the Being of the other, the complete acceptance and liking of the object just as it is, as an *end* in itself, and not as a means to one's own interests or, for that matter, to anything else. Asking for nothing, Being-love is its own end and reward, an experience with no purpose whatever beyond itself, an "end-experience." Maslow describes Being-love as involving a perspective that is noninterfering in the Taoistic sense. In such "Taoistic noninterference," the object is observed for its own sake, nonintrusively. The other is allowed to be, to rule, to speak to the hushed experiencer-listener (1971, 124).

It is a real accomplishment, Maslow remarks, to attain the total, real, self-effacing, and respectful listening that occurs in Being-love, that listening that doesn't presuppose, classify, evaluate, approve or disapprove, improve, or dispute (1969, 96). More passive than active, the Being-love experienced by healthy individuals is described as a sort of "spontaneous admiration," not unlike "receptive and undemanding awe and enjoyment" before a fine work of art (1970a, 196–99). The end-experience of admiration before a sunset wants to do nothing to the sunset. One simply loves and respects it in its proper Being, or "endness," without any intention to use or improve it (1971, 142–43). There is no self-aggrandizement on the part of the observer, no "will to power." One simply surrenders. Other instances of Being-love are the parental experience, the creative moment, the intellectual insight, and the orgasmic experience. The "letting be" of "Taoistic noninterference," Maslow points out, is nothing like indifference or an unwillingness to become involved. Being-love is a highly involved—but not highly ego-involved—experiencing that often leads to extensive activity.

Having no end beyond itself, the almost always enjoyable and deeply fulfilling love of Being is nonpossessive. This kind of love, fostering in the other a self-image that includes self-acceptance and "love-worthiness," in fact helps the other to become autonomous and grow. Being-love, Maslow says, "creates the partner" (1968, 43). Maslow points out that Being-love, in which there is no trace of self-interest, was once regarded as belonging to the gods alone. Very different from Being-love is "Deficiency-love" (D-love) (1968, 42–43). Whereas the former Being-love is disinterested love for the intrinsic "endness" or Being of another, the latter D-love is love moved by deficit—needy and selfish love.

Being-Cognition

There are, then, according to Maslow, perceptions of objects (people and things) that focus upon the nature of the object rather than upon the nature of the perceiver. Maslow calls these perceptions "cognitions of Being." Such "Being-cognition" (B-cognition), which holds the place of honor at the center of Maslow's psychology, stands in sharp contrast to "Deficiency-cognition" (D-cognition): that is, to cognition organized by an individual's Deficiency needs (1968, 73). Being-love fosters Being-cognition: that is, unselfish love for the Being of the other, for its "intrinsic nature" or "endness" ("end-in-itself"), promotes "illumination-knowledge," the perceiving of the "intrinsic nature" or "endness" or Being of the other (1971, 108, 122).

Thus, Maslow says, if you love something at the level of Being, you will leave it alone and let it be itself ("Taoistic noninterference"), which means that you will be able to see it as it is (1969, 116). Loving another as an "end-in-itself," Maslow remarks, allows the other to come out of hiding, to open up and be seen as he or she is, or at least as he or she could be (1971, 17). Maslow says he uncovered Being-cognition in Being-love (1968, 73). When speaking of Being-cognition, Maslow also uses such expressions as "love knowledge" and "Taoistic objectivity."

Maslow thus points out that, when you love the Being of the other, you are in a position to know the other's true nature. Being-love is said to be able to bring to light things in the object that are invisible to those acting out of Deficiency-motivation. Self-actualized, or healthy, individuals are found to be much more capable of Being-cognition than the average (1971, 167). It is indeed generally the case, in Maslow's view, that self-actualizers perceive reality and truth more efficiently and accurately than others. This is due to the fact that their perception, unclouded by self-interest, is centered on the Being of the other (1971, 129). Maslow points out that Being-cognition, while documented primarily in peak experiences (see below, "Peak Experiences"), may also issue from a tragic turn of events, from "desolation experiences" (1971, 252).

The following are characteristics of the cognition of the world's Being, as described by individuals participating in Maslow's research (1968, 71–96; 1971, 260–66). The whole world is seen to form a single unity and one has a place in it—compare "cosmic consciousness," the experience of the ultimate identity of all things (1971, 130). The object perceived is fully attended to, to the exclusion of everything else; there is total absorption in the concreteness, uniqueness, and richness of the object. All sides of the object are seen simultaneously and as of equal importance. The object is not compared to or seen to be in competition with anything else. The object, "human-irrelevant," is viewed on its own terms, in its own Being or "endness"; there is a nonstriving, Taoistic cognition of the object; the individual does not impose his or her own preconceptions, expectations, hopes, and fears on the object. The object is seen as complete and sufficient in itself and as though alone existing. The object is often perceived as holy, inviting awe and reverence. The object is seen as irreplaceable;

nothing else will do. The object is perceived as a unity and as though symbolic of all reality.

Being-cognizing is further described as becoming richer with repetition. The absorption in the experience is so complete that the self is transcended and everything comes to be reorganized around the object but without confusion of experiencer and experienced; there is a reciprocal "isomorphism" (likeness of form or structure, a one-to-one relation) between experiencer and object: as the world is experienced in its Being, the perceiver moves in the direction of his or her own Being, and as the perceiver approaches his or her own Being, the world is experienced in its Being. Paradoxically, as the other, in its Being, comes to rule my life, I become autonomous, and as I approach autonomy, the other comes to take over.

Being-cognition, moreover, is seen to possess intrinsic value as an end in itself; the experience justifies itself. The perceiver experiences himself or herself as outside space and time; a minute may seem like a day, and a day like a minute. The experience is absolute, beyond the particularities of locale, culture, history, and human interest. Conflicts and dichotomies are resolved; inconsistencies are seen to make sense and even to be necessary. The self and the world are often found to be amusing, poignant, playful, cute, lovable, and charming. The perceiver can love, forgive, and accept all in others; it becomes possible to accept the evil of human actions.

Being-Values

When people are asked to provide an account of reality as encountered in Being-cognition, they describe it in terms of certain values. Maslow calls these values "Being-values" (the values of Being, B-values) and regards them as his most important discovery.

The love of Being fosters the cognition of Being. When people describe the Being of the world as it presents itself in Being-cognition, they do so in terms of the values of Being. In the cognition of Being, Maslow says one has a direct perception of the values of Being, of reality as a whole. These Being-values are real in Maslow's view and constitute "ultimate reality" (1971, 331). They are spiritual values, the highest values in the hierarchy of values, and to them correspond the highest needs in the hierarchy of basic needs. Being-values are paralleled by such states of affairs as the ideally good environment. Being-values are said to have a naturalistic meaning. The following is the list Maslow provides of the irreducible, intrinsic values of Being (1968, 83): truth, goodness, beauty, wholeness, aliveness, uniqueness, perfection, completion, justice, simplicity, richness, effortlessness, playfulness, self-sufficiency, and meaningfulness. These are the described attributes of the world as experienced in B-cognition, reality as perceived (1971, 109).

Maslow insists that these values are not independent parts of Being. The Being-values are rather seen to form some kind of unity, and each individual value to be one aspect of the whole, one manifestation of some underlying general factor (1971, 194, 324). Being-values are "facets of Being," "different facets of one jewel" (1968, 84). The fact that the Being-values constitute a unity, Maslow comments, means that the scientist dedicated to the discovery of truth and the lawyer devoted to justice are committed to one and the same thing. It also means that each single Being-value brings with it all the others: in its complete definition, beauty must be good, true, perfect, alive, and so forth, and truth beautiful, good, and so forth (1971, 324). The fusion of the Being-values is said to be a fact of experience for the self-actualized person. While these values thus fully correlate with one another in the experience of our healthiest individuals, they do so only moderately for the average member of our culture (1968, 84).

Being-values, as aspects or facets of reality, are to be distinguished from the attitudes and emotions of the B-cognizer (1970c, 94; 1971, 334–35). Among the B-cognizer's psychological states are awe, love, adoration, worship, humility, approval, devotion, sense of mystery, gratitude, fusion, bliss, and ecstasy. These metamotivated feelings are experienced as entirely appropriate to the "intrinsically loveworthy" B-values: B-values are eminently worthy of such responses, even requiring or commanding them (1971, 336). It is indeed a fitting and proper reaction, in Maslow's opinion, to "celebrate" the values of Being (1971, 337).

Maslow points out that there is no mention of anything even approximating evil in the list of Being-values (1968, 81–82). Reality is described only as full of value, only as possessed of high positive "demand character," only as "to be valued," "to be accepted." Maslow says his theistic friends talk about God the way he does about the values of Being (1971, 195). The Being-values are what have been called "the eternal values, the eternal verities" (1971, 108–109). Our most inspiring values, the B-values are said to define the higher life. People have sacrificed everything for them, even their lives. We look up to these qualities in our greatest heroes and saints and in the gods. Being-values, Maslow comments, are what life is all about for people in general (1971, 44). Living in beauty rather than ugliness, for example, is said to be a necessity inherent in human nature. Maslow points out that humankind's most serious thinkers have agreed on practically the same list of ultimate, spiritual values.

Because the values of Being fulfill the highest human needs—more properly, metaneeds—in the hierarchy of basic needs, their attainment is said to bring the highest satisfactions (1971, 328–29). When, on the other hand, people are deprived of the Being-values—when they are "intrinsic-value-starved" (1971, 320)—they are found to develop "metapathologies" (1971, 22, 44, 316–22). Some of these "sicknesses of the soul" are meaninglessness, boredom, despair, and anguish. "We're dying," Maslow writes in his *Journals*, "from lack of spirituality" (1979, 876). Maslow conjectures that repression and denial, and perhaps all the Freudian defense mechanisms, are mobilized against the highest in us—against our biological tendencies toward the highest, ultimate values—just as they are against the lowest (1971, 322).

Science, Facts, and Being-Values

Maslow notes that conventional Western science has presupposed that the less ego-involved one is in observing something—that is, the more objective one is—the more remote from the domain of value that something is found to be. But he remarks that in the highly ego-detached cognition of Being, when people are asked to describe reality, the account is found to turn on the values of Being. People at their cognitive best are seen to claim to have a direct perception of values intrinsic to reality. In the most discerning perception of "facts," the "is"—facts—and the "ought"—values—are seen to merge, or fuse. "Is" and "ought" become one and the same. What "ought" to be "is"; the world "is" what we would like it to be; "ultimate reality" is a "value reality" (1971, 109, 331).

And, Maslow points out, the better we get to know anything, the more "oughtness" it is seen to acquire: Being-cognition, experiencing an object's "deeper facticity," is an experience of its "oughtness," of an "oughtness" that, intrinsic to a properly discerned facticity, is itself a perceived fact, the truth of the world (1971, 120–22). Facts thus have a "requiredness" about them, an "intrinsic requiredness." They are, as the Gestalt psychologists recognized, vectorial: possessed of a direction (of positive requiredness) that is properly their own. They don't just lie there like so many pieces of wood (1971, 118). Maslow finds the conclusion that values cannot be separated from reality accurately perceived to be the kind of insight made possible by a science expanded to include the fullness of human experience. The perception of the intrinsic nature of the object, and hence the recognition of its true value, is said to be more frequent in healthier individuals. Maslow comments that this discovery has profound ramifications for science, as for every human endeavor.

Being-Values and Self-Actualizing People

Maslow believes that self-actualizers, tending to perceive facts clearly (Being-cognition), are "better cognizers" (1971, 6). But, we have seen, when things are seen in their "deeper facticity," the perception of facts and the perception of values prove to be one and the same. Facts and values fuse (1971, 105–25). Self-actualizing individuals, accurate perceivers of facts—of what is, of reality, of Being—are consequently most adroit at perceiving the values of Being. Self-actualizing Being-cognition is a perception not only of "factness" but of "oughtness" as well, of "extrapsychic required-ness" (Being-values) (1971, 271).

Facts create "oughts." Maslow points out that self-actualizing people, eminently receptive to the facts, are able to discern what the facts demand of them: the "ought." A clear perception of the "ought" is a call for action in keeping with that perception. It leads to sureness of decision. Not to know the facts, on the other hand, leads to evil. "Fact-blindness" is said to mean "ought-blindness." Maslow's "normative biology" finds within human nature a biological affinity for the values of Being, an openness to them, an aptitude and longing for them (1971, 5). Intrinsic to outer reality, Being-values are intrinsic to inner human nature as well. An isomorphism is said to prevail between the Being-values within and these values discovered outside, a kind of "preestablished harmony," or consanguinity, between inner and outer value, "a mutually enhancing and strengthening dynamic relationship" between inner and outer requiredness (1968, 170; 1971, 301–302).

Maslow thus sees human nature as most fundamentally—at its highest and deepest—oriented to the values of Being. And he sees self-actualizers as those individuals who have been able to turn this inherent potentiality into an actual relationship. Self-actualizing individuals have incorporated Being-values into their personality. These values are now the innermost self's most essential qualities, its defining characteristics. The goodness, truth, beauty, and justice that are characteristic of outer reality have found their inner resonance in the self: the person has become good, true, beautiful, and just. Maslow says that this merging, or fusion, of inner and outer realms is possible precisely by reason of the original isomorphism or "preestablished harmony" between inner human nature and outer cosmos.

Self-actualized people, beyond Deficiency and in touch with their deeper, higher self, live in the realm of Being. They love and know reality as an "end-in-itself," in its "endness"; they love and know "ultimate reality," the Being-values. Thus, loving and knowing the ultimate values of reality, self-actualizing individuals have metaneeds for these values. They prefer and yearn for "truth, justice, goodness, beauty, order, unity, comprehensiveness" (1969, 43). Such metamotivations are theirs, in Maslow's view, because they have actualized an intrinsic biological endowment of human nature, because they have realized the values of Being in their innermost self. Value choices, Maslow says, are "built into the person in his depths." In touch with their deepest self, self-actualizers have been able to let the Being-values emerge as their principles of choice (1979, 305). They spontaneously choose truth over falsehood, good over evil, and beauty over ugliness (1971, 146). Identified with the ultimate values of reality, a self-actualized individual can be said to be wherever these values are, which is everywhere. Self-actualizers, Maslow says, transcend space (1971, 276).

Finding the Being-values with which they are personally identified to be worthwhile in themselves and metamotivated by them, self-actualizers dedicate their lives to their search and implementation. Self-actualizers, Maslow remarks, are highly ethical individuals, even when their sense of right and wrong is not that of those around them (1970a, 158). Seeking to embody the values of Being in the existing world, self-actualizers are all found to be engaged in a cause outside themselves (1971, 43–44). Self-actualizers, Maslow says, have been called to what they are working at by fate, and they love what they are doing (1971, 43).

Not out for themselves, self-actualizers are beyond self-serving attempts at self-actualization and happiness. To suppose otherwise is a serious, though unfortunately not uncommon, misreading of Maslow's psychology. Self-actualizers are dedicated not to self-actualization, per se, but to reality for itself and on its own terms, in its "endness" (Being). When reality is experienced in its Being, self-actualizers participate, isomorphically, in the perfection discovered. Thus, the unintended occurrence of self-actualization: not out for self-actualization for its own sake, self-actualization is in process. Being-values, the highest values, bring the highest satisfactions. Thus, the occurrence of happiness, precisely in its not being sought: not out for happiness, self-actualizers are happy. These are the sorts of things Maslow thinks we ought to be teaching our children.

The self-actualized person is someone who has incorporated Being-values into his or her deepest interiority. Being-values have become a personal matter. An attack upon the values of Being—the slaughter of the innocent, for example, or the plundering of the environment—is now experienced as an attack on oneself and, indeed, as a "personal insult" (1971, 312). Danger to the values of Being, Maslow comments, is "threatening to the highly matured person" (1970a, 111). A proficient cognizer of reality, who is personally identified with the Being-values, can't help but be dismayed and saddened by their rampant violation in our time: the tens of millions massacred, the deep and pervasive racism, the rampant commercialism, and the like. The self-actualizers' keen sense of the fear, blindness, and ignorance of most individuals, Maslow remarks, can only dishearten them and sharpen their tragic sense of life (1979, 851).

Were self-actualized people out for their own personal satisfaction and improvement, they would have long since disowned the Being-values, thus sparing themselves the sense of pain and personal violation visited upon them by all the injustice, falsity, greed, and ugliness in the world. The self-actualized individual would then be like everyone else, one more desperate search of happiness and a "brighter tomorrow."

Maslow suspects that self-actualizers are sadder than most people. How is this possible, if self-actualizers enjoy the highest of human satisfactions? The answer is that, paradoxically, pain and suffering are not the exclusion of happiness. Just the contrary! Maslow writes in his *Journals*, "All of my conflicts and emotions and bad dreams are not the opposite of happiness—they *are* happiness! Happiness will have to be defined as being pained and troubled in a good cause! The good life is to have good-real-worthwhile worries and anxieties" (1979, 402–403).

While the average, less sensitive person lives within a relatively narrow band of experiences, the self-actualizer is open to the full range of experience, to the very best of experiences and to the very worst, to the highest and to the lowest. The fortunes of the self-actualizer, sensitive to the values of Being and one with them, rise and fall with these values: the self-actualizer rejoices in their success and suffers in their defeat.

Self-actualizers spontaneously choose Being-values. These ultimate values are said to be real, intrinsic values of reality as a whole and at the same time to constitute the innermost potentialities of our deepest self, as reflected in that self's yearnings and preferences. The values of Being are metaneeds: people require them, on the one hand, to avoid illness (meta-pathology) and, on the other, to become fully human. They are biological—"instinctlike"—necessities (1971, 316). Maslow remarks that tendencies to the values of Being "can be seen weakly and dimly in all or most human beings" (1968, 168–69).

Maslow's characterization of self-actualizing individuals reveals them, theist and atheist alike, to be religious people. In another age, Maslow comments, self-actualizers would have been referred to as individuals "who walk in the path of God or as godly persons" (1970a, 141). The traits of self-actualizers, Maslow points out, are indeed the very ideals urged upon us by the world's major religions: forgetfulness of self, the search for spiritual existence, wisdom, focusing on ends rather than means, and the love of others. This indicates to Maslow that our deepest nature, as manifested in the healthiest of people, is not evil, no more than the larger reality of which it is an integral part.

According to Maslow, our deeper and higher nature is not something we learn: the environment does not give us our essential human potentialities (1970b, 130). Culture nourishes but is not the seed. Caring for others, spontaneity, and the like are thus seen by Maslow as natural biological features of human life, like our legs and head. This means that the organism deserves trust when it is healthy. To the responsible, self-disciplined individual—but, Maslow cautions, only to such an individual—can it be said, "Do as you will, and it will probably be all right" (1970b, 133).

The Psychology of Being

The findings that have been discussed in the preceding sections belong to what Maslow calls a "psychology of Being" (1971, 126–31). "Being-psychology" is so named because it concerns itself with ends and not means, with "end-experiences, end-values, end-cognitions, with people as ends" (1968, 73). Being-psychology studies self-actualizing people— those who live at the level of Being in the domain of ends, who have experiences that are ends in themselves, states of final goal-attainment, who experience people, objects, and the world in their "endness." Thus operating in a state of positive health rather than in a state of Deficiency, thus living at the level of Being, means attaining the "suchness" or "itselfness" of the other. All in all, Being-psychology is concerned with "transcendence," a term with a variety of meanings but one that, briefly, indicates overcoming means-experiencing and attaining the fullness of the human capacity to deal with ourselves and others as ends (1971, 269–79).

Being-psychology concerns itself with behaviors expressive of our deeper nature rather than with coping behaviors; with noninstrumental, purposeless behavior rather than with instrumental, purposeful behavior; with enjoying something rather than with getting something done; in a word, with "unmotivated behavior" (1970a, 229–39). Self-actualized thinking or perceiving is described as a spontaneous and passive receiving, "a happy expression" of the organism's nature and life, "a *letting* things happen rather than making them happen," an accomplishing as natural as an apple tree growing apples (1970a, 239). Such behavior is said to be both an expression of our deepest and truest self and a veridical cognition of reality in its ultimate and truest character. Not seeking to change the external world, perception and thinking may thus be end-experiences with an ultimate rather than an instrumental character—adventures in the psychology of Being (1970a, 236).

It may have become apparent to the reader that Maslow uses "Being" in more than one sense. In addition to using the term for end, or "endness," or proper Being, as in Being-love, Being-cognition, and Being-psychology, Maslow also uses it to refer to (1) the whole of everything, the total cosmos, "reality"—Being-values, for example, are said to be the described characteristics of all that is; (2) effortless spontaneity—"honest Being," for example, is said to result from abandoning the controls; and (3) the essential biological nature of human beings—people are said to be able, for example, to get closer to their Being (1971, 131–33).

Being-psychology, taking as its theme the unmotivated or Growth-motivated absorption in "endness"—people and things as "ends-in-themselves"—finds irrelevant to its purposes a causal-explanatory psychology, that is, a psychology that seeks to account for unmotivated behavior in terms of its antecedent conditions. Such conditions are said to tell us nothing at all about the behaviors in question, which are simply themselves.

PEAK EXPERIENCES

"Peak experiences" are experiences in the realm of Being, "transcendent states of absolute Being" (1970b, 124). Maslow began his work on this topic by asking people such questions as, "Have you ever had an experience of ecstasy?" Rather than the blank stares one might expect, many answers were forthcoming (1971, 174–75). People have apparently kept such experiences to themselves, perhaps because of fear of ridicule in a "scientific" age. Peak experiences are said to be fairly common, though not universal, in self-actualizing people (1970a, 164). It is in peak experiences, Maslow remarks, that Being-cognition is most likely to occur and that we are "perhaps most able to see into the heart of things" (1969, 137). Maslow says that peak experiences, these "transient states of absolute Being," are rewards in the unending search for "ultimate humanness" for "good Becoming" (1968, 154). Fulfilling our basic needs is said to yield many peak experiences. Maslow remarks that it was through his work on peak-experiencing that cognition of the values of Being first came to light.

Characteristics of Peak Experiences

Peak experiences are "experiences of ecstasy, rapture, bliss, the greatest joy," the best and happiest moments of human life (1971, 105). A peak experience is further described as an experience of awe, mystery, complete perfection, humility, surrender, and worship (1968, 103–14). It is a very emotional reaction to the awesome, the miraculous, the Being-values, like a passive moment on a mountaintop. Maslow also compares it to an explosion, which then comes to an end, and to visiting heaven, after which one returns to earth. Peak experiences are found to occur, for example, in love relationships, the "creative moment," insight, deep experiences of beauty, athletics, dancing, and childbirth (1971, 165).

The central characteristic of peak experiences—as experiences in the realm of Being—is a total absorption in the "endness," or proper Being, or suchness, of the matter at hand (1971, 62). There occur a transcendence of self and a fusion with the object of one's absorption, some sort of integration of self and not-self (1971, 62, 165). Where there were two, now there is one. Fused with the object, the subject becomes "an enlarged self," incorporating the world and its values into himself or herself. Such communing with the not-self to the point of merging, or fusion, with it, Maslow insists, is a biological experience (1971, 312).

Surprise and ecstatic shock are described as occurring in the peak experience. Effort and interference decrease. The experiencer participates in the "higher life." Fear, defense, restraint, and confusion disappear. The experiencer becomes more free and autonomous, more a person and less a thing, more oneself, what one really and truly is; becomes supremely individualized, strong, and secure in one's self-worth, even as one merges with the other; loses self-consciousness and transcends self and selfishness (1971, 165); and becomes more loving, more honest, and more spontaneous (1968, 103–14). Inner splits are, for the time being, resolved as the individual, accepting and embracing his or her inner self, becomes unified. There is the sense that what is happening is of the utmost importance, that a gift of grace has occurred. Conversions sometimes occur. Reality is seen as beautiful, good, valuable, and wholly worthy of acceptance (Being-values).

Being-cognition is thus found to take place in peak-experiencing, and the Being-values to be perceived (1971, 38, 105). Being-values are precisely the way the world looks during and after peak-experiencing, the world as perceived in peak experiences (1971, 106; compare above, "Being-Values"). People not only experience the values of Being as aspects or facets of reality but themselves assume many of the characteristics of these ultimate spiritual values (compare above, "Being-Values and Self-Actualizing People"). They come to identify with justice or truth or goodness, incorporating into their very selves the "ultimate reality" (Being-values) that evolved them in the first place (1971, 332–34). One's deepest self thus takes on an ultimate, even divine, quality, actualizing a superior potentiality of human nature, a sort of microcosmic "image of God" within (compare Jung in chapter 3, "The Self as an Image of God in the Psyche" and "The Microcosmic Character of the Self")—here again is an allusion to the isomorphism, or "preestablished harmony," between inner self and outer reality (see above, "Being-Cognition").

Thus, as the nature of reality and its perfection (Being-values) are perceived, people move in the direction of their inner perfection, and as people approach their inner perfection, they become more capable of perceiving the values of Being. As the world becomes integrated, so does the individual; as the individual becomes integrated, so does the individual's world. Reality and the individual thus become more similar to one another in peak-experiencing. The skin no longer dividing, what is inside and what is outside no longer oppose one another but fuse (1971, 312).

The essential person ("real self") is outside, and the essential world (Being-values) is inside—thus the actualization of our original affinity or consanguinity with the world.

Maslow points out that peak experiences are described in terms mystics have used to describe their experience of the Absolute. It is thus with some justice that a peak experience may be called a mystical experience. This parallel will be further explored below (see "The Primacy of the Peak Experience in Religion"). Because music and sex—said to be the two easiest avenues to peak-experiencing (1971, 175)—are natural occurrences, Maslow argues it is not necessary to appeal to a supernatural power or realm to account for peak or mystical experiences. Peak-experiencing is to be understood naturalistically.

Peak-Experiencing as Episodic Self-Actualization

Maslow remarks that the peak experience is self-actualization lasting for a limited period of time (1968, 97; 1971, 48; compare above, "Becoming Self-Actualized"). Average people during peak experiences become self-actualizing for a while, experiencing with complete concentration and absorption, end-experiencing, and experiencing vividly and selflessly. There thus turn out to be healthy people and healthy moments. These healthiest of moments, these moments of greatest individuation and fulfillment, are experienced as the happiest and most thrilling of our life—indeed, as peaks! Maslow is thus able to redefine self-actualization as an intensely enjoyable episode in which the individual's powers become integrated in a most efficient manner, a spurt in which the individual becomes more open, more himself or herself, more spontaneous, more creative, and the like (1968, 97).

PLATEAU EXPERIENCES

Self-actualizers have fewer and less intense peak experiences as they grow older. Something else, however, is said to take their place. Maslow gives an account of his own transition to this other form of experiencing in a conversation that took place shortly before his death: "As these poignant and emotional discharges died down in me, something else happened which has come into my consciousness which is a very precious thing. A sort of precipitation occurred of what might be called the sedimentation or the fallout from illuminations, insights, and other life experiences that were very important—tragic experiences included. The result has been a kind of unitive consciousness which has certain advantages and certain disadvantages over the peak experiences" (Krippner 1972, 113).

The "unitive consciousness" referred to in this quote is portrayed elsewhere as the simultaneous perception of the sacred or miraculous and the ordinary, of the temporal and the eternal, as the perception of "the sacred and the profane in the same object," and as the fusion and integration of the realms of Being and Deficiency (see below, "The Unitive Experience of the Sacred in the Profane"). Maslow goes on to say, "I now perceive under the aspect of eternity and become mythic, poetic, and symbolic about ordinary things. This is the Zen experience, you know" (Krippner 1972, 113). One is now said to live in a world of miracles but without the explosiveness of peak-experiencing. There is the "awe, mystery, surprise, and esthetic shock" of the peak experience, but these have a constant and serene, rather than climactic, character.

Maslow uses the metaphor of "a high plateau" for the different sort of experience he is describing (Krippner 1972, 114). The "plateau experience" is living "at a constantly high level in the sense of illumination or awakening," living "in the easy or miraculous, in the nothing special" (Krippner 1972, 114; see Maslow 1970c, xiv–xvi; see also Maslow 1971, 348–49). Plateau-experiencing is taking casually the perpetually unfolding beauty and preciousness of things. It is going about one's daily business, even though changed forever by "mystical revelations." Maslow is thus saying that the revelations or illuminations—these glimpses in the realm of Being of B-values, of "perfection, duty, B-truth, B-love, B-completion, and perfection and excellence" (1979, 1186–87)—that occasion mystical or peak reactions remain with one long after the ecstasy has faded, continuing to influence one's daily existence.

Plateau experiences are described as serene and peaceful. Being-cognition occurs in the serene plateau experience, as it does in the explosive peak experience: plateau-experiencing is "serene Being-cognition or plateau cognition," an appreciating, "a serene, cognitive blissfulness" (1970c, xiv; 1971, 276). Plateau-experiencing involves a quiet, nonclimactic sense of the miraculous, "quiet sacralizing, quiet wonder," a sort of "quiet peak experience," awe, fascination, incredulity, and gratitude (1979, 1215). The plateau experience is more cognitive than emotional. Plateau-experiencing in fact always has a cognitive dimension, while the always-emotional peak experience sometimes does not (1979, 1215). Rather than the shock of good and great things of peak-experiencing, in plateau-experiencing one has become used to wonderful things, living "casually in heaven," on "easy terms" with the infinite and the eternal, in relative calm and serenity in the company of the values of Being (1971, 275).

Plateau experiences are thus less intense than peak experiences and are experienced as "pure enjoyment and happiness." Maslow cites the example of a mother's speechless awe and sheer delight as she watches her baby play by the hour (1971, 348). The passing glimpse of the sacred gained in the peak experience is one thing. Lasting residence on the "high plateau of unitive consciousness" is said to be quite another. There one achieves a permanent state of being "turned on." One becomes, to some extent, perfect, sacred, and even divine. Maslow says plateau-experiencing is better in this sense (Krippner 1972, 114). One cannot live a constant climax, but one can live a constant experience of the sacred in the everyday.

The plateau experience is much more voluntary than the peak experience. Maslow remarks that it is indeed possible to learn unitive perception and to exercise it practically at will. One can sacralize any dimension of life one chooses. Maslow says he was personally able to transcend space and time and unitively revision reality whenever he wanted to, literally, at times, in the form of a vision, beginning perhaps in the here and now and extending into the remote past, the distant future, and the far away (Krippner 1972, 116).

One earns plateau-experiencing, according to Maslow, by long, hard work. Pointing out that the subjects in his study of self-actualization were older people, Maslow says the self-actualized life has to be earned (1979, 1180; compare above, "Becoming Self-Actualized"). One has to live and learn for oneself; one has to mature, and this takes time (1971, 349). The spontaneity of the "unitive life," paradoxically, requires practice. One has to make a conscious effort to attend to intrinsic values (B-values). One has to expose oneself to good people, to great music, to nature; one has to learn to enjoy being alone, and the like (1971, 337). Maslow says we can and ought to make the effort to attain the heights of plateau-experiencing.

Maslow rejects the "big-bang" theory of self-actualization (see above, "Becoming Self-Actualized"). Peak experiences are not a way of life ("the peak-experience interpretation of life"), not enough to build a life on (1979, 1180). Drugs, such as LSD, and specially designed weekends are not the routes recommended by Maslow. He comments that some pretty nasty people have peak experiences—through sex, for example—and that Nazi leaders had exalted musical experiences at the very time they were planning and carrying out the extermination of millions. B-illumination, we have seen, may be absent in peak-experiencing. The plateau experience, by contrast, is essentially cognitive, "a witnessing of the world" (Krippner 1972, 115). Plateau-experiencing carries with it the certain conviction that something of the real world is being seen, something transcending the concrete here and now: the symbolic, the transcendent, the miraculous, and the unbelievable (Krippner 1972, 115).

Maslow remarks that attaining the "second naivete" by which one sees the beauty of things in the very midst of life's troubles and vices is quite different from the "first naivete" of childhood. The innocence of those who have struggled with and endured the realm of Deficiency (D-realm), and yet, without leaving it, have managed to transcend it, is far removed from

the state of innocence of the child (1971, 256). Earned "self-actualizing innocence" is not the "ignorance-innocence" of children. It is anything but a
return to an undifferentiated state of mind. Consciousness has been transformed, rather, in the course of putting up with and working through reality. There is, says Maslow, no return to Eden. The realm of Deficiency is
transcended only by full adulthood, by true knowledge and growth (1971,
257). The D-realm is transcended not by being left behind but by becoming fused with the B-realm, that is, by unitive consciousness.

The knowledge of Being (Being-cognition) is thus seen to be attainable
in more sober, arduous ways than the peak experience. The passivity and
receptivity of Taoistic noninterference give us only one side of the picture.
These alternative paths are voluntary and active, requiring an effort on
our part, and lead to plateau cognition, to the permanence of serene unitive consciousness and its fusion of the realms of Being and Deficiency.
These other paths always involve cognition. Maslow remarks that these
other approaches may turn out to be more advantageous in the long run.
He thinks that seeing in this unitive way, unitive consciousness, being
earnable and learnable, is something we can teach our children (1971,
191). "You could hold classes," he comments, "in miraculousness" (Krippner 1972, 114).

HUMAN NATURE IN THE LIGHT
OF BEING-PSYCHOLOGY

The argument presented thus far in this chapter can be summed up in the
affirmation that human beings have a higher nature that is part of their biological constitution. Maslow insists that our higher aspirations—the
Growth-motivations associated with self-actualization—must be taken
into account for an adequate understanding of human life. He assumes in
almost everyone an "active will" to health, an "impulse" to grow and actualize human potentialities (1971, 25; see above, "Assumptions of
Maslow's Psychology of Health").

Integration

Maslow argues that all aspects of human life that have been torn apart—
body and mind, conscious and unconscious, and so forth—must be restored to their original unity. The healthy (self-actualizing) person has
done just this. "The high without the low," Maslow comments, isn't high
but "pseudo-high," fake (1979, 1062). The healthy individual has achieved
a working together or synergy of primary process (the unconscious) and
secondary process (consciousness), between one's deeper and one's con-

scious self. The animal and the spiritual are sufficiently developed in such a person to form a "superordinate unity," for "hierarchical integration" to win out over "dichotomous antagonism," over all "either-or's" (1969, 49). The individual has become what he or she is—"an integrated, organized whole" (1970a, 19). The healthy human being, the human who is most human of all, is "all of a piece," whole. The neurotic is the one at war with himself or herself (1970a, 271). Self-actualizers are "integrators," capable of uniting what is separated and opposed in most people. Integrating conscious and unconscious, Maslow says that such healthy, whole individuals have the most fun (1971, 89–93).

Siding with Jung (see, for example, chapter 3, "The Function of Myth") against Freud (see, for example, chapter 2, "Religion as Illusion"), Maslow rejects the notion that mythological thinking is obsolete and to be analyzed out of existence by "enlightened" reason. The symbolic, mysterious, illogical, ambiguous, and paradoxical are, to the contrary, said to be characteristic of the human species at its highest level of development.

Our Biological Spiritual Life

The higher, and thus more spiritual, the basic need, the deeper it is said to lie within us and the harder we have to work to reach it. Our deeper self is "deeper" because we have to dig for it (1971, 82). "Highest" is thus deepest. It is also weakest: least compelling, most likely to be overlooked, to be repressed, and to yield to the more pressing needs at the lower end of the spectrum of basic needs (1971, 305–306). And yet, the higher reaches of human nature, the metaneeds for the Being-values, are no less biological, in Maslow's view, than the needs for food and water. "The spiritual life," he writes, is a basic component of "our biological life" (1971, 325). Maslow indeed regards the spiritual life as constituting our most essential humanity. He remarks that because the spiritual life is "instinctlike"—part of the "real self"—it can be heard through the "impulse voices" arising from within. Maslow encourages us to listen attentively to these quiet voices.

Evil

The following must nevertheless be taken into account in order to avoid a serious misreading of Maslow's psychology. Maslow, well versed in "abnormal psychology," was fully, even painfully, aware of human shortcomings and problems. As already mentioned, he was, by his own characterization, possessed of an overwhelming "tragic sense of life and evil" and anything but "unrealistically optimistic" (1979, 200). Maslow insists that psychology give human weakness its due. Otherwise, he says, psychology develops too optimistic a reliance on the powers of reason. The trouble with many humanists and liberals, he feels, is their total confusion on the topic of evil. He says that some talk as if there were no psychopaths or mean people or paranoids or "true believers" around to louse things up (1979, 951).

Maslow finds "two sets of forces pulling at the individual—not just one": pressures toward health and self-actualization and "regressive pressures backward," in the direction of weakness and sickness (1970b, 134). Actual human beings are "good and rational," he says, but also "bad and irrational" (1979, 11). They have both good and bad impulses (1971, 148). Because of these convictions, Maslow insists that our children need education in "control, delay, limits, renunciation, frustration-tolerance, and discipline" (1970b, 133). Basic-need gratification is not enough, he says, because pathology is sometimes associated with certain forms of such gratification. The child also needs experience with "firmness, toughness, frustration, discipline, and limits" (1970a, 71). Health is always "to be attained" (see above, "Becoming Self-Actualized").

Maslow, thus keenly aware of the fact of human evil, nevertheless does not hold that human nature is inherently—biologically—evil. He rejects any version of the doctrine of original sin. "Nothing intrinsically human" is empirically evil; "empirical psychodynamic evil" is nothing more than "falling short of one's humanness" (1979, 308). Maslow assumes that evil, rather than instinctlike, is mostly *reactive*, a response to bad treatment (1979, 817; 1968, 195): "nasty aggressiveness" is effect and not cause, developed and not inborn (1970a, 274). Certain unfavorable conditions evoke the human potentialities for evil (1979, 704). The real problem, he says, is not "evil human nature" but (1) the thwarting of basic human needs and (2) human timidity, bungling, and superstition (1979, 1160). He remarks in a similar vein that the evil generated by human nature does not spring from "inborn malice" but from the likes of "ignorance, stupidity, fear, miscommunications, clumsiness" (1970a, 257). Maslow says this accounts for the fact that there's more evil in the world than evil people.

Neurosis

As for neurosis, Maslow thinks it best to consider it in its relations to "spiritual disorders": to the loss of meaning, to anger and grief over lost love, to the loss of hope or courage, to despair over the future, to awareness that one's life is being wasted, to the impossibility of joy or love, and the like (1971, 31). All these, he says, are failures to measure up to "full humanness" (1971, 31). Any failure to achieve full humanness (self-actualization), in Maslow's view, issues in psychopathology. Such an approach, which gets beyond the mere classification of illness, makes the person and his or her search for health primary. It gives Maslow the means to answer the frequent objection that his theory of spontaneity, to be consistent, ought to allow pyromaniacs and rapists the same freedom of self-expression as it does self-actualizers: neurotic behavior doesn't warrant sanctioning because it doesn't spring from the inner biological core of human nature (1979, 213).

Our Essential Nature to Be Promoted

In Maslow's view, a perfect human being is inconceivable, but human beings are open to far more improvement than generally assumed. The human organism, as seen in its best examples, has a natural tendency to choose to grow, to be healthy, and to succeed biologically (1971, 14). Our higher nature is a universal potentiality: there is a yearning within us for "truth, beauty, goodness, justice, order, humor, completion, etc."—a yearning that emerges, however, only under the best of conditions (1979, 148).

Once it is recognized that our essential biological nature is not evil but either "good or neutral" and that most psychological disorders result from the "denial or frustration or twisting" of our "essential nature" (1970a, 269), then, Maslow says, it becomes apparent that this nature is to be promoted in the face of an environment that stifles it with all too much ease. Maslow insists that transcendence of the environment, not adjustment to it, is the ideal (1968, 179–80). When human nature guides people, life is seen to gain health, happiness, and fulfillment. This, in any case, is what Maslow finds with self-actualizers.

BEING-PSYCHOLOGY AND RELIGIOUS EXPERIENCE

Maslow's psychology of Being—Being-love, Being-cognition, and Being-values—contains essential elements of a "psychology of religion." This section explores some of the connections between Being-psychology and religious psychology.

The Primacy of the Peak Experience in Religion

Maslow rejects the notion that organized religion is the source of human spiritual life. A distinction must be made, he argues, between organized, institutional religion and personal religious experience. Personal religious experience is said to be the primary element in religion: religion is first and foremost experiential religion (1970c, 19–29). Organized religion, by this view, is a secondary phenomenon deriving from the primary experience. The "peaker," directly experiencing the primacy of personal religious experience (peak experience), tends to find and develop a private religion of his or her own. Maslow points out that in our day, for the first time in history, noninstitutional religion is possible.

In terms reminiscent of William James (see chapter 1, "The Primacy of Personal Religion"), Maslow argues that the origin and core of all the world's major religions is the lonely, personal "illumination, revelation, or ecstasy of some acutely sensitive prophet or seer" (1970c, 19). Such an individual found, in isolation, the truth about "what is" and how life is to be lived. The crucial experience is described as a natural peak experience, with its Being-love and attendant Being-cognition of the values of Being. The prophet had no choice, Maslow remarks, but to couch his experience in the supernatural terms of the available conceptual framework (1970c, 72–73). Maslow says he doesn't find it at all remarkable that peak experiences were portrayed as having a supernatural origin and character: the transcendence of ego, the union of the self and the non-self, ecstasy, and the vision of a truth not known before are jolting happenings indeed, so much greater than ordinary human experience (1971, 62).

Maslow points out that, on the whole, religions believe (1) God is the embodiment of the Being-values; (2) the ideal or saintly human being is the one who has succeeded in incorporating the Being-values into his or her life; (3) rituals and creeds are the means to attain the Being-values; and (4) heaven represents the final attainment of the Being-values (1971, 140). Religions are, moreover, said to maintain that conversion and salvation consist in accepting the truth of these ideas. Maslow cites the centrality of the Being-values in religious belief everywhere as evidence of the key role of the peak experience in the origin of religion.

Maslow insists that mystical or peak experiences, with the illuminations (Being-cognition and its perception of Being-values) they bring, are natural, not supernatural, phenomena. It is now possible, Maslow comments, to construct "a completely coherent and comprehensive psychology and naturalistic theory of religion" (1979, 6). Mystics are "peakers." Just about everything that happens in the naturalistic peak experience, Maslow insists, could be categorized as a religious phenomenon (1970c, 59). Attempting to encompass the essential of religion within an expanded naturalistic science, Maslow detaches the natural peak experience from the institutional creeds secondarily arising from it.

An unavoidable problem in such an undertaking is the fact that words like "sacred," "eternity," "heaven," and the "divine" are the only ones available to describe natural religious events. Such words are said to be the language of a theory about such occurrences. This theory claims that the events in question have a supernatural origin and character. Maslow believes that such a theory is no longer necessary, and so, when he uses the words of the theory, he is not implying anything supernatural. He instead employs them the way many atheists and agnostics do when they describe their religious experiences. These words can and do "have referents in the real world" (1970c, 44). In view of the universality of religion, Maslow concludes that these real events are universal.

The Unitive Experience of the Sacred in the Profane

Maslow comments that "peakers," mystics, and nowadays the humanists teach that the sacred is in the ordinary, in people, in one's own backyard (1970c, x–xi). In Maslow's view, looking for miracles is a display of the fundamental ignorance of the fact that "everything is miraculous." The holy is not the property of some one group but belongs to everybody, and anybody can experience it. All kinds of serious people are found to be capable of discovering the sacred anywhere and everywhere in life (1970c, 31–32).

Maslow argues that if unitive consciousness, with its cognition of Being (see above, "Plateau Experiences"), is under our control to some extent, then religious experience is under our control to that extent, even apart from peak experiences. Heaven can always be visited. At least in principle, unmotivated "experiences of transcendence"—experiences organized by the object as an "end-in-itself" rather than by human interests—ought to be commonplace in healthy individuals adequately fulfilling what it means to be human (1970c, 32).

Unitive consciousness is glimpsing the sacred in and through the present. Such experiencing is an awareness of the realm of Being (B-realm) while still within the realm of Deficiency (D-realm) (1971, 115), the fusion of the sacred and the profane, of Being-values and facts (see, for example, 1970c, 103–16). Unitive perception is thus the fusion of the B-realm and the D-realm, of the mode of contemplation with that of action, of the eternal, the perfect, the infinite, the holy, and the heavenly (the psychology of Being) with the temporal, the practical, worries, bills, the local, the foolish, the stupid, the earthly (the psychology of Deficiency, "in-the-world psychology"). In unitive consciousness, one transcends the universe of space and time without leaving it.

In the unitive mode of living, the body and its appetites are experienced as holy; sexual intercourse, for example, becomes a "sacred ritual" (1971, 195). Bodily life is experienced as a miracle through and through, and it is enough to live it for what it is. The only world that is can be accessed both as a realm of Being and as a realm of Deficiency (1971, 258). Both realms, Maslow says, are equally true, equally real. Any person and any thing can be viewed under both the aspects of Being (B-cognition) and of Deficiency (D-cognition), and anyone who cannot see under both aspects is said to be blind to a basic aspect of reality (1971, 116–17). A fusion of the two realms

eliminates the dangers said to be associated with Being-cognition: the reluctance to take action, fatalism, and an overly generous and tolerant acceptance of evil people and evil actions (1968, 115–25). Perfection under
the aspect of Being is not perfection under the aspect of Deficiency.

Being-Values Are the Responsibility of All

The religious or spiritual values are not the exclusive property of any one
religion or group. Rather do they belong to everyone, in Maslow's view,
and are everyone's responsibility. Healthy individuals, actualizing the
natural human affinity for the Being-values (human life as microcosm of
the universe—macrocosm—that evolved it), incorporate these values into
their innermost self, yearn for them, and serve them. Self-actualizers thus
show themselves to be religious in their character, attitudes, and behavior
(see above, "Being-Values and Self-Actualizing People"). The human being is naturally religious, according to Maslow, biologically destined to
the service of the values of Being.

TRANSPERSONAL PSYCHOLOGY

Maslow calls humanistic psychology "Third Force Psychology" and proposes it as a viable alternative to objectivistic behaviorism and orthodox
Freudianism—psychology's first two forces (1971, 4). But Maslow does
not stop here. He finds humanistic Third Force Psychology to be transitional in character, a preparation for a "Fourth Psychology" that is higher
still. This Fourth Psychology will be transpersonal and transhuman in
character. Such a "transhumanistic psychology," maintaining its concern
with the biological essence of human nature, yet passing beyond such
themes as "humanness, identity, self-actualization, and the like," will
center in the cosmos rather than in human interests and needs (1968,
iii–iv).

God, Maslow comments, "is getting reborn, redefined" (1979, 524).
Only now the godlike is coming to be seen as an inherent possibility of
human nature, a possibility that flourishes when the conditions are right.
The transcendent or transhuman or godlike "is no longer dead" but alive
"within human beings" (1979, 524). What we crave today, he says, is
"knowledge of reality, of truth, of what is hidden from us" (1979, 679).
Our *personal* motivation is to *nonpersonal,* transhuman truth. Maslow insists that, without the transpersonal, we get "sick, violent, and nihilistic"
or else lose hope and become apathetic (1968, iv). Humans have an absolute need for something bigger and higher than themselves.

Being-psychology is a decided move in the direction of the "transpersonal psychology" Maslow glimpses on the horizon. Being, with its values (Being-values), while not constituting a supernatural realm of any shade or variety, transcends Deficiency-motivation and its preoccupation with reality as a means to needy ends. Reality is discovered, under the aspect of Being, as wondrous, beautiful, awe inspiring, and a privilege to behold (1979, 29).

Maslow eventually came to distinguish two kinds of healthy human beings, two degrees of self-actualizing people: the "transcenders" and the "merely" healthy. "Transcenders" are those who "transcend," who live more at the level of Being (Being-cognition), who are metamotivated (Being-values), who are more inclined to have had peak experiences with startling revelations and to live on the "high plateau of unitive consciousness." "Transcenders" are further described as transhuman and transpersonal, identified with and committed to transhuman, cosmic values (Being-values), transcending their ego, Taoistic, beyond the courage–fear dichotomy, manifesting Being-humility, contemplative, mystically fused with others and the cosmos, self-sacrificial, devoted to Being and engaged in Being-love, and wholeheartedly embracing their fate (1971, 284–86). "Transcenders" transcend "merely healthy" self-actualization: that is, they go beyond being strong selves and having a strong identity, beyond knowing who they are, what they want, where they're going, and what they're good for (1971, 292). They transcend to Being. Their identity, rather than the personal identity of the "merely healthy," is with the cosmos (cosmic identity).

As Maslow characterizes them in his *Journals* (1979, 848–49), "transcenders" go beyond the basic needs and love the "ultimate good things, excellence, perfection, the good job"; identify with the cosmos and belong to it by right (cosmic consciousness); sacralize life, "religionize" it; transcend the ego and are "impersonal-end motivated," "impersonally motivated"; have a "transcendent kind of objectivity," and thus "see reality better"; transcend deciding, choosing, planning, and being an agent; let the cosmos, from which they are no longer different, decide and the current take them; aren't preoccupied with their own uniqueness; are beyond healthy selfishness and extreme individualness; and see the "ought" with complete clarity: "right is right and wrong is wrong" (1979, 860).

Transcending to Being, in Maslow's view, is no less biological in character than engaging in sexual intercourse or eating—his "whole psychology," he says, is "fundamentally biological" (1979, 885). Living in the realm of Being is biological, he says, in that it accords best "with the biological prosperity of the person and of the species" (maximum happiness and growth, survival and "growth-and-prosperity" values, and the avoidance of aggression) (1979, 885).

PROBLEMS AND PROSPECTS IN CONVENTIONAL RELIGION

Maslow identifies a number of problems that tend to arise in institutional religion. He judges these problems not to be insurmountable, however, and finds many of the questions raised by the churches to be important ones.

The "Organizers"

Maslow sees organized religion as an attempt to reduce the original peak experience or revelation to a code and to pass it on, thus codified, to the masses (1970c, 21–26). But, according to Maslow, the organizers, who are seen to rise to the top in any complex bureaucracy, tend to be nonpeakers (1970c, 24). Nonpeakers, in Maslow's view, are people not who are unable to have peak experiences but who are afraid of them, who deny or suppress or turn away from or "forget" them (1970c, 22). This refusal of the peak experience is not surprising, Maslow remarks, given the universal human fear of direct experience of the divine (1971, 37)—for more on this fear, see Rudolf Otto (1977) and Jung (chapter 3, "Archetypes as Gods"). Maslow says that Deficiency-motivated individuals, in a defensive search for safety, tend to become adherents of a religion or philosophy that organizes the cosmos and human life into a "satisfactorily coherent whole" (1970a, 42).

Religions are seen to divide into two groups, the legalistic and the mystical. The legalistic group is bureaucratic, conventional, empty, dogmatic, and formalistic. The organization becomes the primary thing. Maslow affirms that many "concretize all the symbols, all of the words" and make them "functionally autonomous" of the original revelation, "the sacred things and activities" at the core of religion (1970c, 24). Objects, replacing the founding revelation, thus come to be worshiped instead of what they symbolize (the Being-values). Maslow remarks that this is idolatry. The original religious experience is forgotten, and the machinelike, the automatic, and the external are now termed "religious."

Religious experience in this way becomes its opposite, and organized religions "the major enemies" of religious experiencing (1970c, vii). Conventional religiousness may be defensively employed to resist "the shaking experiences of transcendence" (1970c, 33). The legalistic organizers—nonpeaking "organization men"—tend to be antagonistic to the mystics—"peakers"—for whom religious experience is primary and whom, therefore, Maslow would call the truly religious. The "organization man" is the loyal servant of the organization and its bureaucratic structure, as well of its official version of the original prophet's vision (1970c, 21).

Splitting the Sacred Off from the Profane

Maslow finds in conventional religion a tendency to split the sacred off from the profane—the exact opposite of unitive perceiving (1970c, 14–15). When thus split off, the sacred, no longer belonging to everyone, becomes the property of a certain few—an elite cadre, select guardians of a private "hotline" to heaven, "the elect." Rather than permeating all of life, the sacred is compartmentalized, becoming confined to a certain day, ceremony, and building (1970c, 14). The ideal (value) is separated from the actual (fact). Then, Maslow remarks, one can support actual evil with the promise of a future ideal situation—"pie in the sky." When heaven is far removed from earth, Maslow says it becomes impossible to improve human life here and now.

In conventional institutional religion, then, one part of life and reality tends to be made "religious" and the rest to be removed from the religious domain altogether. Maslow says this serves to prevent people from having religious experience: not believing that the sacred permeates all, people are less likely to look for it everywhere around them (1970c, 30–31). And when the holy is confined to one day of the week, people may feel released from the necessity of religious experience at any other time, from their everyday responsibility to the B-values.

The Closing Off of Further Knowledge

Maslow finds science to become sick when it sets values aside (see above, "The Sickness of Value-Free Science"). But he detects a parallel sickness in religion when it turns away from facts and empirical verification (1970c, 12–14). As always, in Maslow's psychology, "dichotomizing pathologizes." The moment everything "religious" was removed from further testing and knowledge, and thus from the possibility of growth and purification, Maslow remarks, "such a dichotomized religion was doomed" (1970c, 13). Institutional religion is inclined to hold that the original revelation, of which it claims to be the sole guardian and preserver, was total and final, the last word, and that it has nothing more to learn. But then, Maslow says, faith tends to become blind faith, and obedience unquestioning obedience. For the reasons cited, Maslow does not deem it wise to hand values over to any church for safekeeping.

The Positive in Conventional Religion

Maslow tempers his generally negative comments on institutional religion in the preface to his book on religion (1970c, xiii–xiv). He remarks there that organizations are not necessarily bad or bureaucratic. The mystical group in any religion—in Maslow's view, the truly religious people—is seen to be able to integrate the mystical and the institutional. In that eventuality, rituals, creeds, and the like (the institutional) remain grounded in experience (the mystical). Maslow notes, moreover, that in his day many religious groups were beginning to commit themselves once again to the values of Being in practice as well as in theory (1971, 195). Maslow also believes that the churches were trying to answer valid questions, which coincide with his own. He disagrees with their answers but thinks that such religious questions, yearnings, and needs are deeply (biologically) rooted within human nature. While he believes these matters can be adequately handled by an expanded psychological science, he takes issue with those nonbelievers who have discarded the valid questions along with the unacceptable answers (1970c, 18). He thinks that contemporary humanistic psychology would probably consider such individuals to be sick or abnormal.

Maslow believes it is possible to establish a criterion for the sort of religion congenial to human interests. Because any movement in the direction of the values of Being means increasing health, a helpful religion would be one that has incorporated the Being-values into all the dimensions of its life. Being-values, he says, define "true" and beneficial religion (1971, 140). He holds that a similar criterion can be set up for intrinsic or healthy guilt. We ought to feel bad, to hurt, he says, when we violate a Being-value or betray our inner nature in any way (1968, 194; 1971, 338–39). Intrinsic guilt—metaguilt—is "essentially justified self-disapproval" (1968, 194). Maslow indeed judges people sick when they violate the Being-values and *don't* have symptoms—thus the sickness of those who are well adjusted to a sick culture (1968, 8). Not to be troubled when one ought to be is a definite indication of sickness to Maslow. In the words of Viktor Frankl, "An abnormal reaction to an abnormal situation is normal behavior" (Frankl 1963, 30).

POSSIBLE POINTS OF AGREEMENT

Maslow believes that both the humanists and the clergy can accept certain defining characteristics of religious experience (1970c, 55). Both groups can agree, for example, that religious experience is an experience of oneness with the whole universe, one's littleness, the holy, the divine, the indescribable, and the eternal, that religious experience has the quality of exaltedness, and that religious experience makes one want to give thanks, surrender, and even kneel before the awesome mystery.

Definition of God

In addition to agreement on the basic characteristics of religious experience, Maslow thinks people may even come to agree on a definition of God. If God is defined as "Being itself," "the Gestalt quality of the totality of reality," or in some other nonpersonal way, then, according to Maslow, the atheist will have nothing to disagree with (1970c, 45, 55). The impersonal B-values tell us what an impersonal God—such as Maslow can accept—means: pure cosmic beauty, truth, and goodness, as experienced, for example, in the wonders of nature. Such an impersonal God is not above nature (supernatural), not a God that loves and watches over us and that we can pray to. But it is a God that we can properly be in awe of, identify with, and serve.

Definition of Essential Religiousness

Perhaps the most important thing Maslow hopes serious people will be able to agree about is "essential religiousness" (1970c, 20). Religions could agree to teach what is common and essential in peak or mystical experience. All originated, in Maslow's view, in just such experience. The differences among them, stemming from particularities of time and locale, could thus be considered as not touching the essential. Because peak experiences are found to occur outside the context of organized religion, moreover, Maslow remarks that there is the possibility of a working coalition of all sorts of people. All could agree on the primary importance of the basic revelation (Being-values) and on the secondary character of everything else (1970c, 47). Maslow considers belief in the supernatural to be secondary and inessential, of importance only for individual comfort.

The Grown-Ups and the Children

The crucial thing, in Maslow's opinion, is not the differences between believers and nonbelievers: a truly religious member of an organized religion and a serious agnostic are not that far apart (1970c, 56–57). The former is closer to the latter than to a conventional member of his or her own religion. These serious people are said to be the seekers, the grown-ups. The other group is described as childish, selfish, and superficial. The fundamental questions are never raised. Maslow says it's almost as if "we wind up with adults, on the one hand, and children, on the other" (1970c, 57).

EVALUATION AND CONCLUSIONS

The empirical fact, according to Maslow, is that human life is beyond itself to the cosmos. Except in sickness, no opposition or gap or difference is found to exist between ego and world (1979, 117). A search for the actualization of this our fundamental identity with the cosmos, human motivation, at its highest and deepest, is a reaching out for the ultimates of truth, beauty, goodness, justice, and the like. Such Being-values are said to form the heart of true religion: the human being is naturally religious. Being-values are the way the cosmos is. Maslow's "naturalism" is thus an invitation to savor the splendor of all things, to bear witness in this mortal flesh of ours to the extraordinary in the ordinary (unitive consciousness). Maslow's psychology, addressing the ultimately spiritual or cosmic character of human life, is a courageous and bold undertaking.

Especially promising in Maslow's psychology of religion would seem to be his notion of the plateau experience, with its unitive consciousness. Participating in Being-cognition even as firmly anchored in one's time and place, earnable and learnable plateau-experiencing perhaps best represents the model form of living that was the object of Maslow's search. Although Being-values came to be discovered—perhaps too quickly—in the study of peak-experiencing, their further theoretical development may well belong to investigations of plateau-experiencing. Indeed, considering the role Being-values are said to play in life, a systematic exploration of their character and validity, wherever they are found to occur, seems a priority.

Maslow considers essential religion to be an individual, prelinguistic experience. As suggested in other contexts in this book (see the evaluative comments on James and Alan Watts), such a viewpoint fails to take into account the sociohistorical determinants of all human experience. A noninstitutional form of religion may indeed be possible in our day, but hardly one without connection to the human community in origin, unfolding, or consequence.

Maslow realized that what psychology needed wasn't more studies but a better philosophical foundation. And, indeed, the new concepts he has given us constitute one of his major contributions. Not limiting himself to certain fixed ideas that the facts had then to match, Maslow's theory was in constant change. A theory in flux creates loose ends. But, to speak with Maslow, better an evolving psychology that captures the true flavor of experience than a neatly packaged one that doesn't. Maslow's psychology is a comprehensive one: human health, virtually identified with true religiousness, lies in the fulfillment of our biological essence and its orientation to cosmic value; neurosis, unhappiness, destructiveness, and evil, on the other hand, lie in the thwarting of this essence.

REFERENCES

Frankl, V. E. *Man's Search for Meaning: An Introduction to Logotherapy.* New York: Washington Square Press, 1963.

Goldstein, K. *The Organism.* New York: American, 1939.

Krippner, S. (ed.). "The Plateau Experience: A. H. Maslow and Others." *Journal of Transpersonal Psychology* 4 (1972): 107–20.

Maslow, A. H. *Eupsychian Management: A Journal.* Homewood, IL: Irwin-Dorsey, 1965.

——. *Toward a Psychology of Being.* New York: Van Nostrand, 1968.

——. *The Psychology of Science: A Reconnaissance.* Chicago: Regnery, 1969.

——. *Motivation and Personality.* New York: Harper and Row, 1970a.

——. "Psychological Data and Value Theory." In *New Knowledge in Human Values,* ed. A. H. Maslow, 119–36. Chicago: Regnery, 1970b.

——. *Religions, Values, and Peak-Experiences.* New York: Viking Press, 1970c.

——. *The Farther Reaches of Human Nature.* New York: Viking Press, 1971.

——. *The Journals of A. H. Maslow,* ed. R. J. Lowry, 2 vols. Monterey, CA: Brooks/Cole, 1979.

Otto, R. *The Idea of the Holy.* New York: Oxford University Press, 1977.

6

✛

Alan Watts

If someone brought up in a Christian culture says, "I am God," we think
that he is insane. But, in India, when someone declares, "I am God,"
they say, "Congratulations! At last you found out."

—Alan Watts

Alan W. Watts (1915–1973) was born and grew up in England, settling
in the United States as a young man. Raised an Anglican, Watts was
profoundly influenced from his teen years by Eastern religious philosophy and psychology. Holding particular interest for him were Hinduism,
Mahayana Buddhism, Taoism, and Zen. Watts described these alternative
approaches to reality in his many readable books, thus making them accessible to a mass Western audience. Watts is highly critical of Western
culture, believing it to stand in urgent need of an Eastern complement.

Watts's interpretations of Eastern thought are to be understood experi-
entially. Thus, when he says that whatever he is, is "also what stars and
galaxies, space and energy are" and that "every sentient being is God—
omnipotent, omniscient, infinite, and eternal," his aim is to put an experience into words, not to construct a metaphysics (1973, 4, 224). His "pantheistic" view is thus offered not as a proposition to be grasped but as a
mystical feeling to be shared (1973, 211). Watts indeed says that his whole
purpose is to convey to others the feeling that their sense of separateness
from the unified field of the universe is a conceptual artifact.

Understood psychologically and not conceptually, Watts envisions a
possible reconciliation of Hinduism, Taoism, Christianity, and Buddhism.
Indeed, it is his view that all the great spiritual traditions are ultimately

talking about the same thing: the felt unity of all in the divine (1973, 445). Having undergone "an undeniably mystical state of consciousness" through experimentation with LSD, Watts draws the further conclusion that there is no difference between the mystical experience underlying the world's great religions and drug expansion of the mind (1973, 399).

Watts thinks of God after the fashion of the Chinese Tao, "which loves and nourishes all things" but is not the creator or boss of the universe (1973, 400). The Tao expresses itself within us, Watts says, in the form of a harmonizing of opposites (yang and yin). This inner harmonizing is a kind of unconscious intelligence and may be called on for a wisdom higher than our linear Western logic can provide (1975, 28, 76). The unconscious is thus viewed as a sort of natural wisdom attuned to the Tao, the one cosmic law. Watts sees basic or mystical religion as beyond good and evil. He nevertheless remarks that individuals who live in harmony with the Tao do not engage in immoral actions.

THE PROBLEM

Watts argues that our Western style of seeing the world is a form of narrowed perception (1966, 27). We are like a bright and sharply focused flashlight, throwing its beam serially first here, then there, into the enormous vastness of the universe. We view reality bit by bit, classifying and dividing it up. We think and observe one thing at a time, and to each thing we attach a name.

Words

Watts says that, having looked at the world one bit at a time, we eventually become convinced that this is how reality actually is: a collection of bits, things, and events entirely separate from one another (1966, 27). We fail to realize that this assessment of things is an outcome of our manner of attending to reality, of our division of reality into easily thinkable things, into words that express reality one thing at a time. The world just naturally seems to correspond to our ideas about it, to our one-at-a-time words (1970, 72). Because we have separated reality into words about reality, reality now appears to be an endless series of individual and separate things. We are seen to be fascinated by words.

In doing this, according to Watts, we forget that words and thoughts are human conventions, symbols established by human beings (1951, 44–45). We confuse words with reality, what is said with what is. We think that nature is structured the way language is, that it is divided the way words are, that the logic of words is the logic of things. In this way is the universe confused with our thought and talk about it.

The universe has thus been broken apart by our symbols. Things have been conceptually isolated from their context, which is the total field of the universe (1970, 34–35). Such separations, Watts insists, exist only in a system of mental abstractions. They are only "fictions of language" (1966, 90). Distinct things exist as concepts alone (1973, 212).

We look at reality through "a net which seems to chop it up into bits" (1966, 90). We then think that these bits manage to get together somehow to constitute the whole, that "the whole is the sum of its parts." Watts thinks that this is a great confusion indeed, a veritable sickness of the mind. He says that what we call reality is constructed out of repression. We are taught to abstract things from the whole and to screen out relations. Watts points out that altogether different ways of experiencing reality exist but that our culture neglects or represses them.

The Ego

Watts sees nature as in constant change. Naming and defining things serve to isolate them from their context in the changing stream of existence, to fix them. Reality changes. Ideas and words tend to remain relatively unchanging, however. "I" is a word that defines a certain portion of reality (1951, 46). Part of our experience goes by this name, just as other parts of it go by other names, such as "tree," "water," and "dog." When a portion of our experience is called "I," it tends to be removed from the rest of reality, to be separated out and given an aura of permanence and fixity. Watts says we have hypnotized ourselves through our words into the "hoax of egocentricity" (1966, 52).

The Ego-Illusion

"I," separated from nature, is taken to be a permanent reality, a separate ego-substance (1951, 47–50). The ego seems to exist on its own as a thinker, knower, and experiencer. Watts says that this is only possible by way of an abstraction from memory (1968, 71). When we consult our memory, "I" actually seems to be there, one bit of reality that remains unchanged among all the changing bits. But Watts sees this as a great confusion. What is remembered is mistaken for what presently is (1968, 73). I can never capture what I am or am doing, for what I now am is the someone who is trying to do the catching. All I can ever capture is what I no longer am. What I know about myself, then, is always what I was and what I was doing. I only capture myself in retrospect. Our highly valued "self" is not our true self at all, only the self's echo or trace in memory, only an idea—an illusion or fabrication, at that (1968, 73–74).

Watts affirms that the ego has been separated from God and from nature. We feel like a "separate ego enclosed in a bag of skin" (1966, ix). Our skin seems to us to serve as a barrier setting the ego off from everything else (1966, 51). We feel that "I myself" is a bounded-off center of activity existing on this side of (inside) our skin (1966, 6). We feel we are lonely substances who live and act in a body that allows us to encounter, "out there"—on the other side of (outside) our skin—a stupid and essentially foreign nature. The ego feels isolated and alienated, a stranger. We think we came into the universe, as it were, from outside of it. Watts insists, to the contrary, that we don't "come into" the world at all but "out of it, as leaves do from a tree" (1966, 6).

Watts argues that the ego is in actuality one thought among many. It is one's idea of oneself. The skin divides us from everything else in thought only, not in reality. We have talked ourselves into the illusion that the ego is something apart from everything else. The ego is no substantial reality, in Watts's view, just a role we play (1969a, 96). Having been defined as Jane Smythe or John Smith, we confuse ourselves with our definition. Our own names fool us. Again, words are said to be at the heart of the problem. We confuse our names and what actually is. We think that having a separate name means being a separate reality (1966, 64). The greatest taboo of all is seen to be the one against knowing what we really are behind the ego-mask (see below, "Identity").

The Ego-Role

Watts says that society shames us into an identification with the ego (1966, 64–70). We learn, at the hands of others, to play the part of predictable actors who mistrust themselves and resist change. Society gets us to do what it wants by conning us into thinking that it is our inmost selves who are issuing the orders, when in reality it is society that is doing the commanding. The words and deeds of others, "masquerading as my inner or better self," control us (1969a, 98). Others thus control us, under the guise of our better self. Society, "thinking only of us, of course," thus gets us to identify with the ego-image and to assume the ego-role.

The Ego as Controller of Its Body

Now that we identify ourselves with the ego—with an idea about ourselves—Watts says we feel we have no alternative but to try to control things. The original spontaneous mind is no longer at the center of things, but the ego. "I" tries to restrain "me" (1968, 77). Watts thinks such a "divided mind" has created all manner of problems.

Watts thus sees us as divided against ourselves, against our own nature, which must be mastered by the violence of human law (1970, 176–77). The body, an integral part of a universe that we moderns have declared to be material and dumb (René Descartes' *res extensa*, pure spatial extension), is not to be trusted in its spontaneous actions but only to the extent it measures up to law, to some diagram to live by. The body must submit to the rule of law, under the surveillance of the ego. Our "lower" self must be controlled by our supposedly "higher" self. Order has to be imposed on what is taken to be chaos. Ours is a political universe in which the force of law must govern the body.

We are at war with nature, then, with our own body, unable to let things happen according to the wisdom of the organism that sponsored intelligence in the first place. The law that we have made, in Watts's opinion, is vastly inferior to the natural order and structure of the organism, its natural wisdom.

Because natural processes can no longer be trusted to unfold spontaneously, we must choose the course. We must take charge. We have thus gotten ourselves into the trap where the ego must figure out how to do things. But Watts says this only leads to anxiety because we are not sure what the right thing is. And it is seen to lead to guilt because we are responsible, and as soon as this separate "I" begins directing things, "something goes deeply and strangely wrong" (1964, 66–68, 81–82).

The Ego as Controller of Other Egos

Watts remarks that, from the political perspective of control dominant in our culture, other people are separate egos whose wills must be restrained by external force. "I" is no more able to trust them than it is itself. Law and order must prevail.

The Ego as Controller of Nature

Watts says that Westerners experience things as foreign and hostile to themselves. The "chaotic" universe appears as something for us to conquer. In our day, for example, we are engaged in any number of "wars on . . ." And we carry on our pledge to "conquer" space. Committed to getting "one-up on the universe" and assuming complete mastery over it, the ego valiantly takes its stand against "mindless" nature (1966, 74). Watts sees a concrete result of our separate ego-feeling in our misuse of technology and the resultant damage to our planet.

Nature, denied its inherent wisdom and order, is thus said to have been split off from the ego. The universe, made into the pure spatial extension (*res extensa*) of modern scientific investigation and control, is no longer trusted to operate spontaneously, to grow from within. We have created a political universe in which separate things, facts, and events—people and our own body included—are "governed by the force of law" (1970, 53).

The Future

The ego seeks security and protection from change. But Watts says that this amounts to a search for a divorce from life. He thinks that what makes us deeply insecure is not flux but our very ego itself, which separates us from the flow of life and isolates us. We are said to crave security because of our belief in the permanent ego.

Shying back from a changing present, we seek permanence in the future. In the present we renounce and postpone, longing for tomorrow and the fulfillment of our dreams. But Watts says that when the future finally arrives, we will be incapable of enjoying it: having only ever lived for tomorrow, we will not know what to do with the present (1969a, 190). Living for the future is said to mean missing the point of life. Tomorrow, forever a day away, never comes (1968, 131–32).

All in all, in Watts's view, feeling oneself to be a permanent and separate ego means permanent anxiety and misery. "A hoax from the beginning," the personal ego can only engage in phony actions (1966, 79).

God

When reality is separated into unrelated bits, God comes to be viewed as "the ego of the universe," the "Supreme Bit" (1970, 88). Unchanging and without flesh, he is the ideal ego, "a disincarnate ego," in perfect control (1968, 77). God is the completely good Controller of the universe.

Watts points out that we are taught that while God is all good, human beings are capable of any amount of evil (1972b, 106–13). I, the sinner, am totally separate from an infinitely removed God. A consequence of this is that we feel we must try ever harder to do the impossible and conquer ourselves, thus making ourselves worthy in God's eyes.

EXPERIENCE RATHER THAN WORDS

It's not nature that deserves mistrust, in Watts's view, but words and ideas inadequate to things as they really and truly are. Language, Watts has argued, creates many of our problems. He says we don't need new words, a new religion, a new bible, but a different experience and, in particular, a new feeling of what it means to be "I" (1966, 9).

The new experience we are said to need is a direct experience of things as they are, a reality-oriented experience. It is Watts's hope that people will come to listen to reality as they do to music, as it unfolds (1973, 4). He invites people to a mystical experience of things, that is, to a direct seeing and feeling of reality for what it is, without the mediation of words and ideas. His goal is to portray reality thus experienced, to describe it in its own terms. He knows he is attempting the impossible: using words to convey the wordless. The poet is said to find himself or herself in a similar situation. He or she, too, undertakes the task of saying what cannot be said.

Two prominent features of reality directly experienced and described are its holism and dynamism. We have heard Watts to the effect that human consciousness artificially breaks the world up into isolated parts and that, as a consequence, someone has to assume responsibility for putting the bits back together again. The task of undoing the fragmentation generated, of imposing order on an endless multiplicity of fragments, has to fall to an agent external to the fragments. This external agent is the ego, which, as we have also heard, tries to control the body, others, and the world. But, says Watts, this attempt is bound to end in failure.

Watts believes it's the very way our Western consciousness works that's the problem. Seeing parts as the primary reality out of which the whole is contrived is said to be an error. Individual people, nations, insects, plants, and animals simply "do not exist in and by themselves" (1966, 82). Watts insists instead on the primacy of the whole and its organic order. Refusing the notion of the whole externally assembled, he sees the whole as parts growing mutually from within. Gestalt theory speaks in this connection of a "dynamic self-distribution" of parts: the whole, neither the sum, nor more than the sum, of its parts, arises precisely in and as the self-governing action of its parts. Order arises spontaneously from within a whole; it isn't imposed from outside. The parts order themselves. Parts ordering themselves—that's what a whole is; that's what reality is.

A whole thus stands in no need of an external controller, be the whole my body, the immediate environment, or nature as a whole (the universe). No ego is needed to watch over and bring order to an otherwise chaotic body. No Supreme Ego—be it God or modern man—is needed to watch over and bring order to the universe. Both the body and the universe, unfolding spontaneously, are quite capable, in Watts's view, of accomplishing their own organic order. Nor are the ego and its environment found to be separate and opposed to one another. The ego is thus no longer seen as having the responsibility of managing the environment. The parts of my body naturally unfold as a unified, integrated whole. So do the constituents of nature. And so do my body and the environment. They, too, form a single unified and integrated whole. Our skin, rather than a barrier between us and the rest of reality, is a bridge uniting us with everything that is not ourselves (1966, 51). Watts thus sees the ego and the environment as forming a broader unity, a unity, as will be seen, that finally embraces all of reality.

Reality, when listened to, is a natural whole. Reality is also dynamic. Everything in the universe, says Watts, is a moving pattern. "I," moreover, is a constantly changing stream of experiences, sensations, and feelings (1973, 387). Memory, it was suggested above, accounts for the impression that the ego is still and solid. The ego, Watts says, is bondage to the past, out of which it is constructed, and to the future, for which alone it lives. Watts insists that the only way to make sense out of a changing order of things is to change with it. If reality is in truth a river ever flowing on (Heraclitus), the only sensible thing to do is to take the plunge (1951, 43). Christianity, faithful less to the Bible than to Plato and Aristotle (that is, to the notion that permanence is of a higher order than change), is seen to have made the mistake of creating fixity out of flux: an unchanging God, an immortal soul, and eternal union of this soul with the changeless God.

REALIZATION

Watts is interested in experience, in the holistic and dynamic character the universe is found to display when observed for its own sake and on its own ground, in the universe mystically—directly—experienced. It is the empirical orientation of Watts's religious views, his interest in religious experience, that justifies his inclusion in the present series of overviews of religious psychologies. Religious dogmas don't interest Watts, per se, only to the extent they can be traced back to the experiences at their origin, only as symbols of reality. Watts thus joins William James, Carl Jung, and Abraham Maslow.

Watts has said we are in need of a new kind of religious experience of reality, a direct, mystical experience not based on words and false ego-feelings. The experience Watts is thinking of is not new in the sense of never having happened before. It has indeed been named "the perennial philosophy." Since it is foreign to our culture, however, it would be new to us.

The experience in question is diametrically opposed to the egocentricity that infects the West. Watts points out that this experience tends to occur when the ego is in a state of wrongness and hopelessness and has no alternative but total surrender (1967, 29–30). Watts feels that we are presently at our wit's end in our egocentric chase after happiness, power, and righteousness, which suggests that we might be ready for the more reality-oriented, mystical perception of things Watts is speaking of.

Rightness

The new experience is one of spiritual awakening. It is an increasing realization that whereas everything seemed as wrong as possible, in actuality everything is as right as possible (1967, 15, 37–38). Obviously, such an experience is an astonishing one. It has been called cosmic consciousness. Jung refers to it as the experience of the self; Maslow calls it peak-experiencing. Watts thinks it is humankind's most impressive spiritual experience.

Watts points out that the individual undergoing this experience gains the certainty that the universe is completely right just as it is and stands in no need of further explanation or justification (1967, 19–21). Everything in its newness and individuality acquires a divine authority. The experience is seen to be perfect and beautiful. It convinces the person undergoing it that the universe is "in every respect a miracle of glory" (1967, 28). Rightness, then, the "intrinsic requiredness" of reality as a whole, is said to form the core of the different experience Watts is pointing to (compare chapter 5, "Being-Values"). Such experienced rightness wipes out anxiety and replaces it with joy. Existence loses its problematic character.

Newness

Watts remarks that the experience he is trying to describe convinces the experiencer that the present moment is the total and ultimate reason for living and the universe's existence. The universe in the newness of this moment is perceived as a glorious miracle.

This insight is accompanied by emotional ecstasy and a sense of freedom and relief. Watts insists, however, that the insight is the primary thing. Ecstasy passes. The insight, if clear enough, remains. A similar point is made by Maslow in his discussion of the unitive consciousness of plateau-experiencing (chapter 5, "Plateau Experiences").

Identity

A crucial aspect of the insight gained in the reality-oriented, mystical experience of reality is the realization of the identity, the "Supreme Identity"—the title of one of Watts's books (1972b)—of all things. Watts founds his interpretation of this insight on the mythology of the ancient Hindus, and more specifically on the philosophy of Vedanta. Vedanta is the teaching contained in the collection of stories, dialogues, and poems called the

Upanishads. The core of this teaching is that the only real self is the Brahman, the Self of the Universe, and indeed that there is no reality but Brahman (1973, 266, 288). The philosophy of the Hindus begins and ends with experience. Only secondarily is it an attempt to translate experience into words. The following paragraphs attempt to present the meaning of the experience of identity as described by Watts (1972b, 75–98).

The Identity of Atman and Brahman

The human being knows himself or herself as an object. This known object is the ego. As the knower, which is to say, as the knowing subject, however, he or she is the Self. This Self is one with the infinite or indefinable Self. The infinite is the "total Knower of the universe" (1972b, 48): infinite consciousness, omniscience. The infinite is timeless, spaceless, and sizeless (1972b, 54). Thus, the finite ego is the known, and the infinite Self is the Knower. The existence of the finite human being (ego) depends on the fact that he or she is not separate and apart from the infinite, from God—the true Self, our true Self. Rather is God in space and time as everything else (1972b, 68). In Hinduism, God is the sole experiencer, the only knower and seer (1964, 17). The human being as Self is the infinite in the process of identifying with the finite ego. The Self is infinite. The ego is not.

Mystical experience centers in the realization of identity: the identity of the finite ego-object and the infinite knowing subject, or Self. Upon the Self's realization of its true identity, however, the ego with which the Self has identified does not go away. There is no loss of individuality. But individual consciousness and existence are now experienced as a temporary point of view taken by something immeasurably greater than the individual. In the experience of the ego's identity with the infinite, the individual realizes that what he or she is has always been what everything else is. The finite retains its reality, but by comparison with the infinite, it is as nothing.

The finite personality of the individual is by no means abolished, then, by the realization of identity (1972b, 72–73). In fact, as Watts points out, religious traditions teach that the more the finite personality is related to the infinite by way of subordination, "the more intensely personal and unique it becomes" (1972b, 73). The experience of the infinite underlying our existence, far from depersonalizing us, individualizes us down to our truest selves. Watts remarks that the self-conscious attempt to develop one's personality is in fact a recent trend in Christianity. Personality doesn't prosper by dint of hard work, any more than happiness results from the search for happiness.

Watts describes consciousness as a field, an "integrated pattern of energy" (1972b, 85–86). In this field there may be any number of points of view. The field is the infinite Reality, and "my" consciousness one restricted area or viewpoint. As a Self, the individual human being is the field in the process of containing a point of view.

In the terminology of the Hindus, the infinite in its absoluteness and omnipresence is called "Brahman." Brahman is the sole possessor of knowledge, the total knowing Self, or Knower (1972b, 48). The infinite in its hereness and nowness is the "atman." As object of my knowledge, I am ego. As knowing subject, however, I am Self, atman, and as such one with the infinite, one with Brahman, "the total Knower of the universe," the Self of the Universe (1972b, 48, 72). The knowing Self, atman, by no means to be identified with the empirical ego or particular individuality as which I know myself, is Brahman (1972b, 84). The Self here and now is atman; the Self in its infinity is Brahman—atman is Brahman; the ego is an object known by Brahman, the total knowing Self. Outwardly, I am one of the apples; inwardly, I am the tree (1970, 47). Within each viewpoint, the Self identifies with the ego, which is a group of related sensations, thoughts, traits, feelings, and memories (1970, 84–85). The Self is the consciousness that knows this object, this group of sensations, the known ego. This consciousness as limited in scope, a point of view with a restricted region of experience or range of objects known, is the point of view taken by the Self. Although the Self does indeed identify with a point of view, it remains the infinite Reality, with a total viewpoint (omniscience): Brahman. Our true goal in life is said to be the realization of the "Supreme Identity of atman and Brahman, of the Self and the infinite" (1972b, 72).

Thus, our true identity, or awareness, is seen to be that of a viewpoint taken by the infinite, "a viewpoint of the eternal Self" (1972b, 88). All our experiences are known by the infinite Self, which identifies with all points of view. By a total absorption in the life of all living beings, the infinite Knower imagines itself to be every finite object (1972b, 67).

The Self is thus described as our real identity. As the knowing subject, the Self does not have the characteristics of the individual and, therefore, is never an individual known object, such as the ego. The knowing Self can never be an object of knowledge. This means that God cannot have self-consciousness, cannot know himself. God is eternally a mystery to himself and, so, is continuously surprising himself, amazing himself with his own glory (1968, 75). He doesn't even know how he manages to be God. God creates the universe, comments Watts, "and then—surprise!—sees that it is good" (1968, 75). The God Watts is talking about is not what might be called the processed and sanitized God of nailed-down dogma but the living God who spontaneously evokes a "Wow!" on our part, not "the God of the philosophers" (Blaise Pascal), not the moralizing and nagging God, but the wonderful and marvelous, mythological God of far-out and outrageous stories, "the God of Abraham, Isaac, and Jacob" (Pascal), the God in whose presence one can sing and dance, the "more godly God" (Martin Heidegger), the true God.

Identity and Myth

With a striking unanimity across cultures, Watts says myth expresses what is always true. Myth thus possesses the dignity of "timeless truth" (1968, 2). Myths are numinous stories that speak of God and his doings, a "revelation" of "the mighty acts of God" (1968, 68). Myths are not hypotheses, the way separate things are. Nor are myths untrue (1968, 7). Watts remarks that a myth is in fact a story that represents the deepest truths of life, a story widely regarded as a portrayal of the deeper meaning of the universe and the place of human life in it (1968, 7). Myth is said to be magical and wonderful because that's the way reality is (1968, 66). We cannot pin down or understand the real world. Watts says it's too fantastic for that, and so, we need myth. What is marvelous about mythological events is not that they came to pass in such and such a way at a definable moment in history but their meaning, which is inexhaustible and forever (1964, 116–17).

The first state of things, as depicted in Hindu mythology (Vedanta), is a self-abandonment by God, a forgetting of his—our—divine nature (1972b, 131–63). The supreme Self wills to give itself over to the limitations of finite life. Putting aside omniscience, the Self identifies with finite viewpoints. The illusion of individuality arises, culminating in the experience of the complete separateness and isolation of the ego, which, in Watts's view, is our present state of consciousness.

The second state is the event of realization. Here the Self wakes up to its true identity as the One behind the many (1972b, 142). The Self discovers anew that its appearance as many is "maya"—illusion (1971, 97). When the ego surrenders, the Self gives up its identification with the ego and awakens to its independence. It sees the ego as a finite object apart from itself. There is a remembering of divinity, a birth of the Godhead in human life. All in all, then, the Self gains awareness of its distinction from the ego and its unity in principle with the infinite. Realization of identity is thus the Self waking up from its dream, God remembering who he is and changing the ego (see, for example, 1973, 260). A recognition of the cosmic and eternal dimensions takes place. Watts remarks that the picture of the universe of the Hindus is a dramatic vision in which the Self plays hide-and-seek with itself (1964, 38–50, 126–30). Every time a baby is born, the Self looks at the world in astonishment, as if the world had never been seen before. Watts says we are like cells in a larger organism. Everything that is alive, that feels and perceives, is God and has God's attributes but is pretending in all sincerity that such is not the case.

In playing hide-and-seek, God is making believe he is all of us, all human beings, animals, plants, rocks, and stars (1966, 12). According to the mythic view of Hinduism, all experience is God's. Watts points out that the Hindu God is not in charge of the universe as a person; nor does he act on it by will—thus the Hindu myth of the identity of God and the universe, of God losing and finding himself again and again, as told by Watts.

The Self doesn't abandon the finite world at this point but uses it as an instrument of experience. The finite is not completely left behind but, as we have seen, retains its reality. Watts says this is because the meaning of the infinite entering the finite state is precisely the expression of the infinite in the finite. Realization lies only through the state of ego-consciousness, with all its struggles and responsibilities. The sense of extreme isolation, of total opposition to God and the universe, is said to be the necessary preparation for the consciousness of union.

The first state, as symbolized in Christian mythology, is a Fall (1964, 88–89; 1972b, 144–45). The first man, Adam, disobeys God and "falls" at once from his high state and God's favor. Watts argues that the primitive state of harmony enjoyed in the Garden of Eden, wherein object and subject are confused, had to be brought to an end by the truly necessary sin of Adam. Adam had to eat of the tree of knowledge of good and evil so as to become conscious for the first time as a human being. His guilty knowledge thus serves to render him human, which is also to say, exiled from his prehuman state of bliss in the Garden. Alone and banished from paradise, human life must now fend for itself. God no longer walks and talks with man, as he did in the Garden.

Christian mythology portrays the second state, in which this status of guilt and alienation is overcome, as salvation through the person and events of the life of Jesus Christ (1964, 91). The First Adam sinned and put himself and other human beings at a distance from God. Through Jesus, the Second Adam, sin and separation from God are overcome as human beings are brought back to God and made participants of the divine nature. Jesus is able to accomplish this for humanity because he is the very Son of God, because the divine and the human are already fully united in him. The Second Adam, entering our world and undergoing a horrible death, reunites human life in its entirety with the divine (1964, 91). God became man so man might become God (St. Athanasius).

Watts points out that the two states of the timeless myth have also been portrayed as taking place within the life of Jesus, in the two phases that characterize his life. The first state is that of God emptying himself of his divine status and taking on the likeness of a human being: God appearing as a servant (Philippians 2:5–8). God the Son comes down and partakes of all the limitations and sufferings of human life. Dying on the cross, Jesus is as far from the Father as imaginable. He is heard to cry out and ask his Father why he has abandoned him (1964, 92; 1972b, 142).

The second state quickly follows Jesus's surrender of his humanity on the cross: resurrection in direct consequence of crucifixion. Jesus's risen body, Watts says, is finite life transformed. In the events of his life, as in later Christian doctrine, Jesus is the "analogy par excellence" of God, a perfect and beautiful analogy of the eternal principles (1972b, 51).

Interpreting Jesus Christ and Christianity from the viewpoint of Vedanta, Watts says that the difference between Father and Son corresponds to that between Brahman and atman, between the infinite and the infinite "imagining itself" as the finite (1972b, 68). Incarnation is interpreted as God losing himself in humanity, entering into an identification with a finite human life, crucifixion as the infinite Self's surrender of this finite life, and resurrection as the Self's realization of identity and awakening to divinity (compare chapter 3, "Psychology and Christian Doctrines").

Christianity began to die, says Watts, when theologians started treating the story of the God-man's life literally, as "a record of facts in the historical past," when, in other words, they no longer experienced and lived this story symbolically, as a myth expressive of an "eternally now" process (1968, 67). Watts does not believe that God's incarnation is an event that happened once only, back in history. Myth is true to its nature only so long as it expresses "what is always true," not what *was* true (1968, 81). The incarnation, "the only real event," is always going on (1968, 129). All in all, then, "the tragedy of Christianity" is seen to be the way it has confused "its myth with history and fact" (1968, 84). The latter, the over and done with, is "the realm of the abstract and the dead." Watts's view is that Christianity is to be understood mystically as an instance of "the perennial philosophy" (1973, 180).

The finite universe, from the mythological point of view—which, for Watts, means from the point of view of Vedanta—is forever being created by a cosmological game of hide-and-seek or "lost and found." Every aspect of life is an image in miniature of a single cosmic drama: the self-abandonment and self-realization of infinite Reality in the finite order. In reality, the infinite is said to remain undivided. It can be at once finite and infinite, many and one (nondual) without contradiction. The theme of death and resurrection is cited as perhaps the most common variant of the mythological play in which the infinite first hides, then finds, itself in the finite realm (1972b, 132).

God and Experience

It is indeed possible, Watts says, to attain consciousness of our identity with the Self as infinite ground of the universe and to be assured of it. The

Self, however, as we have seen, cannot be made an object of knowledge. Nor, as a consequence, can the Self be adequately described in words. In the realization of the Supreme Identity, God is an experience, vividly real and indefinable, and not a conceptual object that can be caught in words (1972a, xiii). Saying anything at all about God, accordingly, requires the greatest caution. Watts remarks that all positions regarding God, atheism included, can only point to an experience. He therefore insists that notions of God be allowed to remain vague (1973, 86). When God is reduced to words, the immediate experience of God is lost.

Watts feels that some sort of pantheism is least inconsistent with direct, mystical experience of God (1972a, xviii). Pantheism means to Watts that God is the "total energy-field of the universe." Every single thing within this field is a microcosm; the whole field or macrocosm is expressed in each part. I myself reside in the total "surge of energy which ranges from the galaxies to the nuclear fields in my body" (1966, 10). Watts feels that a major strength of this pantheistic position is that it is based on experience rather than on a fixed revelation happening some time ago and on belief in that revelation—a belief said to be often enough lacking in personal involvement and conviction. The Supreme Identity is radically empirical: God is an experience and not an idea. Watts remarks that the doctrines propagated by religions can be misleading unless we are aware of the concrete experiences to which these highly refined formulas refer (1951, 23). By "realization" Watts means an actual experience of the ultimate Reality, the ground of the universe (1972b, 18). Watts says that it is implausible today to hold that God is a monarch in the manner of the pharaohs and that a spirituality based on such a belief is a political affair of self-control (1972a, xiii; see above, "The Ego"). Watts nevertheless finds the popular conception of God in the West to remain that of a reigning monarch, a cosmic ego ruling the universe. In Watts's view, there comes a time when belief and its securities—as furnished by kindly divine parents—must be discarded.

Watts thinks that traditional religious ideas can become meaningful again not as beliefs but as symbols of experience, as indications of reality. Religious doctrines are said in fact not to have to do with a future Second Coming but with present reality. The reality corresponding to "God" and "eternal life" can be experienced by anyone (1951, 23). The doctrine of "eternal life" can be understood as the awareness that the present is the only reality and that life is complete in each moment. "God!" would be an exclamation about the eternal state, expressive of wonder and love for reality as it already is (1973, 212). It is along such lines that the doctrine of eternal life, as well as other Christian doctrines, can be seen to relate to present experience and that Christianity can be understood and made meaningful today. One must go behind literal teaching and discover what the symbols mean, what they express, how they function as analogies. Without mystical experience, Watts sees religion as a futile struggle to do what cannot be done. Christianity needs mystical awareness.

We have seen that Watts takes religious doctrines to be analogies of the reality-oriented mystical experience of the Supreme Identity (1972b, 35). We have also seen that people encounter grave difficulties when they turn symbols (myths, doctrines) of the inexpressible into statements of fact (1972b, 133–36). When God is nailed down in concepts, when Jesus and his resurrection are made into objective facts of history, creative images have been transformed into "dead idols" (1968, 21). Watts feels we need to get away from the verbal descriptions that have installed themselves in reality's place and back to what is actually happening. Realization grasps the truth behind myth, religion, and metaphysics. The truth is not beliefs but realities corresponding to our ideas of God, eternity, and the like. Watts thinks that realization lies behind the world's main religious ideas, the reality behind the symbols. The problem is that all too many people, rather than going through the symbol to the reality, make the symbol into the reality. Watts comments that this is idolatry: confusing images with what they stand for. Attempts to define God may seem more spiritual than statues, but pinning God down in words (doctrines) serves to take us away from God: "lofty abstractions," Watts remarks, can represent a graver danger than idols made of bronze (1966, 141).

Watts remarks that the reality is there for everyone to see. What is needed is "faith"—an opening of the mind to what is. Preconceptions about the truth are idols that block faith. Beliefs in all ideas (concepts, words) of God must be abandoned, according to Watts, in order to see God. God, Being, and other words are seen to be names given to indicate the content of mystical experience. Watts insists that God in his infiniteness is not a speculation but an experience of realization. The Self then simply knows it is eternal and inclusive of everything.

Watts remarks that the terms used to interpret the experience are quite naturally taken from the culture of the individual undergoing it. Sometimes the language is seen to conceal the cross-cultural self-sameness of the experience. It is nevertheless possible to find the deeper meaning of symbols behind "the screen of literal dogma" (1973, 180).

Watts thinks that the various religions could get together if they came to realize their shared basis in experience. The immediate experience of God is similar everywhere, and mystics of all religions teach the same thing. This experience occurs in almost all cultures, whatever the period. This common teaching, says Watts, is the most strikingly unanimous teaching in the world (1972b, 41–42). It has remained the same down the ages. In science, by contrast, theories are seen to yield to new theories.

The Primacy of Consciousness

The intellectual and scientific establishment is still said to believe that human intelligence is a chance event in a mechanical and stupid universe (*res extensa*)—as if grapes could grow on thorns (1971, xiv). Watts thinks it makes more sense to view the total cosmic energy system as being in continuity with our consciousness. A universe that "grows" human beings is just as human—or "humaning"—a universe as a tree that grows pears is a pear tree (1964, 222). That the infinite is conscious is not a proposition to be proved, in Watts's view, but comes from the realization that our consciousness is essentially identical with ultimate Reality as a mode of it, from the mystical experience that human consciousness is a "particular mode of the ultimate Reality," that our consciousness is identical in essence with the universe's ground (1972b, 57). We come out of ultimate Reality, like fruit from a tree. The universe grows humans. According to Watts, what is at the base of a universe that grows human beings can hardly be less, but must indeed be immeasurably more, than the humans it grows, than what comes out of it.

Consciousness is the ground of the universe, then, and no mere accident of matter, and we humans are in essential continuity with it—the "material" world, Watts points out, is simply the world as measured or measurable, the universe as caught in the net of human conceptualization and measurement, the universe subjected to abstraction (1966, 55). All consciousness is an unfolding of what was contained in the total energy system from the beginning (1970, 186). Our galaxy must be viewed as intelligent. How else can we understand human intelligence as a "symptom" of it (1966, 91)?

Identity and the Ego

Watts states that whereas selfishness is identifying with the ego, self-denial is refusing the ego and realizing one's true identity in the Self. The ego is superficial, a disguise or distorted sensation of the Self.

This Self is everything there is in the universe. "That is the Self. That is the real. That art thou!" (the Upanishads). "The 'Ultimate Ground of Being' [Paul Tillich] is you" (1966, 15). When the realization of one's true Self takes place, the "I" is seen to be unreal and comes to an end (1968, 148).

The Universe as Play

Why does God assume points of view, like an actor effortlessly playing all the parts? It cannot be for any purpose, because purpose means that something is lacking and is being sought. God could not have purposes

(1972b, 92). Lacking nothing, God does not strive. The nearest human equivalent to activity that is both without effort and purpose is play. The universe, in the final analysis, is "one thing playing at being many" (1972b, 92–95).

RELATEDNESS

Watts says that the experience of realization transforms our view of the world. Things are now perceived in their essential inseparability. Realization is exactly realization of things and events in relationship. The universe is experienced as a system of "interdependent 'thing-events'" separated in name only (1966, 64). The universe is indeed differentiated into a multiplicity of "thing-events"—a differentiated unity of an immeasurably great number of changing relationships or interconnected patterns—but differentiation is not separation (1966, 73). To experience relatedness is to know that all things are in relation, that all things go together and depend on each other, that the world is a harmonious system, that organism and environment require each other, that the world is an extension of our body, that the only true indivisible reality is the universe, that the ego does not control this system, and that we are the whole energy system of the universe. It is to know that individual "things" are just glimpses of a single undivided process (1966, 82).

Taoism is cited in particular as restoring to nature its original seamless unity (1971, 9). According to Taoism, every "thing-event" determines every other "thing-event," and in such a way that each of them is itself only in relation to all the others (1971, 43). Nature is viewed as "a simultaneity of patterns" incapable of linear representation (1975, 7).

In the experience of realization, the usual distinctions are said to disappear. The individual senses himself or herself as one and the same as that which he or she is perceiving. The individual does not feel he or she is "in" an environment but an integral part of an organism-environment relationship (1973, 400). Our bodily organs have different names, but they develop simultaneously and in mutual dependence. Watts says that it is the same with individuals, who are said to differ from the universe in name only. I am this organism, but I am my environment, too (1971, 76). The world and my body form a single process, no more different from one another than the heart is from the lungs (1971, xiv). Just because the connections are less obvious does not mean they are less real. If gaps and distances are essential to the way bodily organs form an organism, why can't gaps and distances be equally essential to the formation of the organism-environment relationship in general and of the body politic in particular? The sun and the forest are thus seen by Watts to be features of the individual's bodily life, no less than his brain and the neurons that constitute it. In this sense, it can be said that air pollution is a personal disease. The human body is a "dancing pattern of energy" that only happens together with a great many other patterns: animals, plants, bacteria, and the like (1971, 22).

In this way, Watts sees our context as a relationship to the undivided unity of the whole universe. "I" is the activity of the universe in this space and time. When I thus see myself as one moment or expression of the universe, one incarnation of the Self, the only thing left to identify with, Watts says, is everything. Parts have meaning when joined to a living whole (1972b, 26). We are significant because we are seen to have our true goal in the infinite Whole. The human being, like everything else, is a microcosm, inseparably bound up with the macrocosm.

The experience of relatedness, Watts points out, erases the anxiety guaranteed by an exaggerated sense of responsibility. The sacredness of the individual remains, but the ego as a problem is overcome. The ego-fiction is no longer required for the fulfillment of individuality. Cosmic consciousness frees the individual from the idea that he or she is an absolute and separate thing or substance (in Aristotle's sense), as distinguished from a convenient unit of perception.

Watts says that the experience of relatedness conveys the impression that everything happens of itself (see below, "Spontaneity"). My individuality seems to be a function executed by everything that is not "me." Yet it seems that everything that is not "me" is a function executed by "me." Everything thus makes everything else happen. In realization the universe is not a manufactured one. It is not produced by a God who acts on it from outside, by extraneous acts of creation. The universe is experienced instead as growing from within as an organic unity. The principle of the universe is said to be one of spontaneous growth. Watts does not claim to know how the universe grows. But it is seen to grow without effort, the way an apple tree grows apples. Just as the tree is implied by the fruit, a "cosmic energy system" that "peoples" is implied by the human organism (1971, 76). The Self is the cosmic energy system that "embodies itself in all bodies" and that, consequently, each of us is (1971, 76).

The experience of relatedness is not our usual experience because we have separated things from one another and put them into discrete categories (see above, "The Problem"). We lack a simultaneous vision. Our divisions are said to be a matter of conceptual convenience, of words. But Watts remarks that the divisions we make do not divide in reality. The world is never divided in fact (1966, 53). The universe is no mere aggregate of things but a system of inseparable relationships (1970, 185). Actions are inter-actions. Our task now, it is asserted, is to find our way to

an experience of the inseparable relatedness of all those things we have
torn apart.

THE ETERNAL NOW

Realization is said to be an intensely clear attention to the "now," to things
as they are rather than as they are named (1951, 76). The now, Watts says,
is the "door of heaven" (1951, 143). "Eternity is now." Now is what is, all
there ever is. It is from attention to the now, Watts remarks, that all other
knowledge is elaborated through reflection.

Anyone who has any understanding of the eternal Reality, according to
Watts, will see life as it actually flows before him or her and, thus, will live
mostly in the present. When there is only now, Watts says that everything
is seen as infinite. In the light of the "Eternal Now," the universe of bodily things is "divinity itself" (1968, 187). Living in this way is said to mean
an expanded and deepened awareness of the moment, without preconceived judgments or ideas about reality. Living in the now means being
open and completely receptive to each moment in all its newness and
uniqueness. The present is experienced as the only reality, and the world
at this very moment is seen to be just what it should be, just right (compare above, "Rightness"). With each now thus lived completely, the individual experiences a deep sense of personal fulfillment (1951, 114). Experiencing this way means no longer being fascinated with the names given
to things—labels, it has been seen, are but interpretations based on the
past.

Having no past, the eternal Self has no memory—has no need of memory (1972b, 91). The consciousness of the Self is strictly a now-conscious-
ness, unfettered by the limitations of time—past, present, and future are
simultaneous in the eternal Self and leave no traces. Ego-consciousness,
that complex of memories (past) and anticipations (future), by contrast, is
bondage to time (1972b, 178). Living the Eternal Now is being liberated
from time and at the same time from ego-consciousness (1968, 197). The
present is sizeless. There is only room for the infinite, not for the ego. Living in eternity projects living in the present, the way Brahman projects the
atman (1972b, 179).

Watts remarks that living in the present means a more playful attitude.
Nature appears to be more playful in character than purposeful (1967, 34;
compare above, "The Universe as Play"). That nature has no future goals
is not seen as a flaw. Nature's processes are compared to music, which unfolds without an aim in the future. The point of music, according to Watts,
is not to get better as it goes along; nor is it to reach the finale. Rather its
point is found in each moment. Life is not going anywhere, Watts re-

marks, because it is already there (1969a, 210). He says that if we are always trying to improve our lives, we may forget to live them. Life is thus to be lived as play, with less emphasis on results. "This present experience of the everyday, 'this' is IT," the complete point for the universe's existence (1967, 13).

SPONTANEITY

Watts has already been seen to hold that we don't trust the spontaneous action of our nature. We have been taught to fear our body and to fight its natural inclinations. We are split, Watts has told us, into a higher controlling part and a lower controlled part (see above, "The Ego"). We look for guides to action outside, in the laws of society or of God. We then order ourselves to conform, in all spontaneity, to the instructions coming down to us. But such double binds cannot work. Spontaneity, rather than an action of the ego, is action that is not inhibited by the ego's "social control mechanism" (1969a, 172). We are seen not to have confidence in the good-and-evil of our nature (1967, 84). We try to retain the positive but to distance ourselves from the mistrusted negative. All the while, the answer is never forthcoming as to how we are to trust our mistrust.

To overcome the divisions we have created, Watts believes we must come to realize that it is the controller that must be controlled, not spontaneity (1970, 88). We have to come to the discovery that the ego never was an effective agent in the first place (1964, 126). We need to come to accept ourselves and to flow with nature rather than against it. We have to learn to trust our brains, which are immeasurably more intelligent than our minds or intellect, and not our words and rules (1971, 73; 1973, 237). The most important scientific insights are seen to come through a nonthinking and effortless form of awareness. Human actions, when left alone, simply happen of themselves, the way snow falls and water flows (1973, 190). Give the brain a chance, for example, and the person's name we couldn't recall through conscious effort suddenly makes an appearance.

Watts remarks that nature does not make mistakes. Affirmation and acceptance of nature, along with cooperation with it, are what are needed. An objective of Zen is an awakening, an escape from the crippling double bind into which the "dualistic idea of self-control" has gotten us (1967, 67).

The Tao acts by *wu-wei*, the Chinese expression for "nonstriving" or "nonmaking"—Taoism sees natural forms as grown, not produced (1970, 39). The world grows organically—and not mechanically—from within (1970, 45). The Tao which "grows the world" by *wu-wei* belongs to the world, is integral to it (1957, 16; 1970, 40). It is not an external agent.

Spontaneity, Watts says, means being completely sincere (1970, 112). It is involvement without reservation. And yet, spontaneity is effortless, without straining. Apple trees do not strain. They do not control themselves. They move according to inner spontaneity, growing from within out, and not according to external law or principle. Watts says that this spontaneity of nature goes contrary to our popular belief in the inertness of matter. Inert matter doesn't move itself and, so, requires a supreme Craftsman (Creator) outside it to shape it into separate things and account for its movement (1966, 55–56). But, with nature thought of as self-moving, the notion of an extraneous unification becomes superfluous.

Watts says that we, too, can find our inner workings, which are as spontaneous as the motion of the planets around the sun. There is said to be real wisdom in the circulation of the blood (1951, 56). Like the configuration of our nervous system, and indeed the organism as a whole, it happens of itself. This "itself" is said to be the real "myself" (1967, 89). There is here, says Watts, neither mistake nor anxiety. Whether we live or die, whether we are right or wrong, there is seen to be no problem about it.

DEATH

Watts remarks that what dies is the ego. But the ego is seen to be an abstraction from memory originating in social pressure. The ego is not of vital importance. Identifying with the ego is said to confuse the organism with its history, to find the guiding thread of one's life in the inaccurate and incomplete record of the past provided by memory. It is just this, this socially imposed abstraction from memory, that is said to be lost at death. What dies is the collection of memories, attitudes, roles, and possessions (1970, 116). Consciousness does not die. There is no death because there is no birth—in the sense of a separate individual, with an identity all its own, coming into the world—just a forgetting of our true identity (1966, 35). In order to see God, we have to pass through the "death" of our false identity, our identification with the ego. Our true identity can neither be born nor die (1964, 203).

Watts says that life resides in the total movement of energy of the universe. The comings and goings of individuals are the vibrations of the one, eternal, cosmic energy system, which grows people the way a plant grows flowers. "I" rises again and again. It is always the same, yet always new. With the birth of each baby, there is born the same experience of being at the center of a world that is "other." Each time the infinite Reality is born as a baby, it gets lost and has to seek itself anew.

It is precisely death, in Watts's view, that makes a renewal of life possible. With each new life, "I" is born again with an uncluttered memory. The wonder of life is thereby constantly restored. At birth we are seen to wake up. At death we go to sleep, returning to the unknown state in which we existed before birth.

Watts sees death as no more a sickness than birth. Death is simply the natural end of life. The corpse is "the dissolving trace" of what the Self no longer identifies with (1966, 73). We transcend death in the sense that we are identical with the processes of the universe in their totality. We do not survive as systems of memory. Memory dies. Liberation from the ego, in Watts's eyes, is the same thing as full acceptance of death. Living forever, it is asserted, would be an unbearable burden, an overload of monotony and memory. The body is said to die when it wants to, when it is worn out and exhausted (1951, 66–67).

EVIL

Because everything in the universe is in relation with everything else, opposites are relational in character. Good and evil, light and darkness, on and off, and the like, in Watts's view, are aspects of the same thing, the one harmonious energy system of the universe—God, if you will (1966, 30). Such opposites are poles within the larger field (1972a, xiv). What is separated in language is said to be one in fact.

Good exists only in relation to evil. Good and evil define each other, make each other be: without evil, there would be no possible experience of good; there would be no good. Watts points out that Westerners have been unable to believe this. But he says that accepting the relativity of evil to good makes it possible to affirm that there is no sin or suffering without a positive significance in the eternal scheme of things. "Outward human agony" is "inwardly" the divine abandoning itself (1964, 135). Watts says that there is no imperfection in the necessary polarity of good and evil because, from the viewpoint of eternity, these opposites are experienced in the exquisite harmony they form with one another (1969a, 57). Darkness makes light stand out in all its brilliance. The beauty of the vision makes the worst evil in time infinitely worthwhile, and thus acceptable.

In our eternal state, good and evil thus form parts of a single "indescribable harmony," a "superior harmony," a beautiful grand-design (1969a, 57; 1972b, 114–21). The universe is said to be thoroughly the play of love in every sense of the word (1967, 38). But, from a viewpoint within time, the harmony goes unseen. Unable to accept things as they are, Christians try their mightiest to get rid of evil and make things "more good." History indeed is viewed as nothing other than the process wherein good conquers evil once and for all. The mystical realization that everything is as it should be right now, that evil has its necessary place in the order of things, is problematic to Christianity.

The negative has no place in our Western conception of an all-good God. By this view, evil never had to be and might never have been if Adam hadn't sinned. Ultimately, evil isn't considered as part of reality (being) at all but as a sort of absence or nonbeing. This very conception has made evil into a problem (1970, 89–91). Independent life has been bestowed on the negative in the form of the devil (1969b, 134). Nor can the devil and God ever share the same ground in Christian doctrine (1969b, 33). Evil has in this way become absolutized, with a power and life of its own. When thought separates the inseparable opposites, Watts says people can then dream of a victory over death and evil, of life without death and good without evil. But what actually happens, in his view, is that death and evil become insoluble problems causing no end of misery. Siding with one side over the other only serves to confer on the other side its corrosive qualities. Eastern thought, by contrast, aims at a state where opposites cooperate with, rather than exclude, each other. There is no question in the East of ridding the universe of evil.

REALIZATION AND CONDUCT

Watts argues that most of the actions we call evil result from the divided mind (1951, 126–27; 1972b, 124). Two immediate causes of evil are said to be insecurity and pride. If we feel insecure, we grasp at pleasure while we can; we steal, cheat, lie, and evade reality. And pride has always been considered one of the greatest of sins. But, Watts says, if we know that we are one with infinite Reality, insecurity and pride disappear (1972b, 124). Finding our security in God, there is no need for a greedy snatching at life. And if every good is of God, we have no ground for pride. Realizing our basic identity with God is thus seen to undermine the very causes of evil.

As for human cruelty and aggression, Watts thinks that these result from our social institutions, not from our nature. Wars and revolutions don't result from a "release from repression" but are outlets a repressive civilization must provide for anger (1969a, 195).

Positively, realization of the Supreme Identity is said to bring discipline of life, kindness, charity, joy, peace, and unity. The life of the individual who experiences things mystically, Watts remarks, is necessarily a life of service to others, just as the life of the divided mind is necessarily a life of conflict and divisive action.

True morality is spontaneous morality, not an attempt at morality. God does not work at making himself and others good. True morality, moreover, is living not by the book but according to the demands of the moment. Rather than measuring up to external rules, it is loving God and others.

Watts says that love is the organizing principle that makes the world a unified universe and individuals a community. The universe is in its totality and in its every aspect "the playing of love" (1967, 38). Mystical experience is said to reveal that we are love. Love is said to be visible in the actions and the life of unity lived by the "undivided mind." Things are to be loved because they came into being through the self-abandonment of the infinite. Thus, loving things for what they are, as God does, and not for what we can get out of them, makes us want them to flourish, makes us want to develop them.

EVALUATION AND CONCLUSIONS

Watts has performed a real service by making Eastern philosophy and religion accessible to a larger Western audience. At the same time, his sharp criticisms of our Western psychospiritual state of mind give us pause for thought. He finds fault, among other things, with our Western tradition of atomism—the whole as the sum of its parts; our emphasis on the substantiality and permanence of the ego; our bewitchment by words and concepts; our reliance on external control—"law and order"; our distrust of nature and the body; our fascination with "progress"; and our postponing of life to a future that never arrives. Watts proposes replacing these conventional stances with an alternative mystical openness to things in their rightness at this very moment, a trust in life's organic and spontaneous patterns, readiness for change, orientation to the primacy of the whole and the interconnectedness of all things, and living experience of the divine. Watts, like Jung, encourages a renewed respect for myth: mythical awareness, he says, can help us recover the sense of magic and wonder lost through our fascination with individual things. Watts's critique of a literal, behavioral religion prone to idolatry is a provocative one.

James, Maslow, and now Watts all claim a direct, uninterpreted experience of ultimate Reality at the origin of religion. The pure experience of the divine, outside the bounds of language and the same everywhere, attracts the particularities of verbal formulation only later, only secondarily. The linguistic diversity in evidence in the myths and theologies of the world's religions is thus presumed adventitious, as many stories are declared one story. University of Chicago theologian David Tracy, among others, has challenged this notion of an ultimate mystical oneness of all religion: "Mystical experience, like all other experience, is also interpretation, and, like all other interpretation, mysticism participates in the discourse of highly particular traditions and societies. . . . There is no 'natural religion' freed from the history and discourse of the historical religions" (1987, 91–92, 108). The experience of Buddha, it was remarked in chapter 1, is not the experience of Jesus. The experience of ultimate Reality was shaped in the two cases by a certain tradition. Similarities in mystical experience, Tracy remarks, are "similarities-in-difference" (1987, 92).

A related objection may also be raised. Myth, Watts insists, is a symbolic expression of an ineffable mystery and not to be taken literally. Christians are said to have gone wrong precisely here, in turning the symbolic truth of their religion into literal fact. The symbolic truth of Christianity, Watts says, is the Supreme Identity of all in Brahman—universal divinity. Christians, by making Jesus into a special case (of divinity), are thus charged with missing the point of their own religion. But, by subordinating Christian doctrine to the doctrine of the Supreme Identity, Watts has literalized Hindu myth: the Supreme Identity is made the absolute, true myth, of which the Christian—and every other—myth is a relative and analogous approximation. The myth of the Supreme Identity, like every myth (doctrine), is an interpretation, a historically particular religious expression. No myth is the pure expression of eternal being.

A danger with preoccupying oneself with "eternal things" is the failure to come to terms with everyday value and responsibility for our actions and the future. By asserting that true and ultimate reality is an eternal Knowing (Brahman), Watts relegates things known, everyday human meanings in general, to the status of illusions. If everything is already perfect, moreover, why work for any goal, why fight tyranny and oppression? Indeed, what difference does it make what one does? Finally, Watts seems to condone actual evil and suffering, in view of the overall grand design of the universe and the possibilities of play and enlightenment.

REFERENCES

Tracy, D. *Plurality and Ambiguity: Hermeneutics, Religion, Hope.* New York: Harper and Row, 1987.
Watts, A. W. *The Wisdom of Insecurity.* New York: Random House, 1951.
———. *The Way of Zen.* New York: Random House, 1957.
———. *Beyond Theology: The Art of Godmanship.* Cleveland, OH: World, 1964.
———. *The Book: On the Taboo against Knowing Who You Are.* Toronto: Collier-Macmillan Canada, 1966.
———. *This Is It.* Toronto: Collier-Macmillan Canada Ltd., 1967.
———. *Myth and Ritual in Christianity.* Boston: Beacon Press, 1968.
———. *Psychotherapy East and West.* New York: Ballantine, 1969a.
———. *The Two Hands of God.* Toronto: Collier-Macmillan Canada, 1969b.
———. *Nature, Man, and Woman.* New York: Random House, 1970.

———. *Does It Matter? Essays on Man's Relation to Materiality.* New York: Random House, 1971.

———. *Behold the Spirit.* New York: Random House, 1972a.

———. *The Supreme Identity.* New York: Random House, 1972b.

———. *In My Own Way: An Autobiography.* New York: Random House, 1973.

———. *Tao: The Watercourse Way.* New York: Random House, 1975.

7

✛

Erich Fromm

If a person has not succeeded in integrating his energies in the direction of his higher self, he canalizes them in the direction of lower goals. He has only the choice of better or worse, higher or lower, satisfactory or destructive forms of religions and philosophies.

—Erich Fromm

Erich Fromm (1900–1980) was born, grew up, and spent his early ca-reer in Germany, relocating to the United States in 1934. Although Fromm gave up the practice of his Jewish faith in his twenties, his out-look was forever changed by the religious education he received at the hands of a number of prominent Talmudic scholars. He was particularly impressed by the compassion and the promise of human redemption found in the Bible's prophetic tradition and many of its narratives. The greed, war, and injustice surrounding him in his formative years, on the other hand, made a strong contrary impression. Fromm was deeply in-fluenced by both Sigmund Freud and Karl Marx. His attempts at seeing through illusion form part of his Freudian legacy (see, for example, 1962)—Fromm is usually classified among the neo-Freudians, those who forged a link between psychoanalysis and social psychology. His em-phasis on the revolutionary possibilities for the unfolding of human powers belongs to his legacy from Marx (see 1961), who has himself been tied to the Bible's prophetic tradition. Affinities with existential phenomenology are also in evidence in Fromm's work. Taking the view-point of a "humanistic psychoanalysis," Fromm wrote extensively on the human condition and the measures needed for human transformation.

He addressed himself specifically to religious issues in the book *Psycho-analysis and Religion* (1967).

The central theme of Fromm's work is the capacity of human beings to actualize their inherent potentialities and attain fullness of freedom and consciousness. Fromm defines himself as a "radical humanist" who finds no force in the universe superior to human life. There is, he says explicitly, "no spiritual realm outside of man," no God above human life (1956, 72). The only meaning to be found in life, he says, is the meaning people give it. While thus an avowed atheist, Fromm nevertheless finds religion to be universal in human life. People have, he says, a religious need rooted in their pressing desire to overcome their split from nature. Fromm thus sees religion as an attempt to resolve the contradiction in human life: the fact that human life belongs to nature, yet transcends it by reason of consciousness.

But not all religion is the same. Specifically, Fromm distinguishes between a humanistic and an authoritarian religion. Humanistic religion involves a commitment to the unfolding of all human powers and to a God that is a symbol of all that the human being is capable of becoming. Authoritarian religion entails submission to external might and authority and to a God that wants blind obedience above all else.

Fromm says we must break with our cherished illusions, idols, and ideologies. To this end he probes the human reality behind the thought system. In the process, he finds the same authoritarian vision underlying a variety of conceptual systems and the same humanistic vision beneath a number of others. Fromm would undoubtedly agree with Abbé Pire: "What matters is not the difference between believers and unbelievers, but between those who care and those who do not care."

THE CONTEMPORARY HUMAN SITUATION

Fromm discovers a remarkable agreement among the great religions of the world on the goals of life and the standards for living: truth, the decrease of suffering, autonomy, responsibility, the unfolding of the human powers of love and reason, and the development of our higher nature (the "soul") in general (1967, 18–19). But Fromm remarks that these goals and standards are not those of people in our day. Ours is rather an age of spiritual disorder and confusion (1967, 2). We are not content, do not love one another, and are not happy. And we are no longer seen to place our confidence in human reason's ability to establish the validity of standards by which to live or to penetrate reality and uncover truth. Intellect has instead been given the task of serving as an instrument for the manipulation of others and nature (instrumental reason). Psychology, for its part, is seen to have become a science without its "main subject matter, the soul," which is to say, without love, reason, conscience, and values, and to busy itself instead with defense mechanisms, habits, instincts, and the like (1967, 6).

Fromm is of the belief that psychological disturbances are to be understood in terms of moral problems. The patient is said to be as he or she is because he or she has neglected the demands of the soul (1967, 7). And, so, Fromm says that as a psychotherapist he finds himself dealing with the same problems that theology and philosophy have concerned themselves with, the human soul and its cure. He insists that it is not necessary to believe in God—Fromm, as we have seen, does not believe in God, at least as conventionally defined in the West—in order to be concerned with the human soul. Nor does the soul have to be considered a supernatural substance. It can be studied in purely experiential terms as a natural human reality. Fromm argues that the psychoanalyst is able to investigate the human reality behind systems of symbols (thought-concepts), the symbol-systems of religion included (compare below, "Thought-Concepts and Religious Experience"). If a person lives a life of love and thinks truth, according to Fromm, the system of symbols (beliefs) is secondary. If a person does not live this way, then his or her symbols are said to be worthless (1967, 9).

Fromm's nontheistic "radical humanism" is a global philosophy emphasizing the oneness of humanity and the capacity of human beings to develop their own powers, to arrive at inner harmony, and to establish a peaceful world (1966, 10, 14–15). This humanism considers the goal of human life to be total freedom and independence. This goal requires that people penetrate the fictions and illusions ever so tenaciously clung to and achieve a full consciousness of reality.

THE BIRTH OF THE HUMAN BEING

Fromm has interpreted the biblical story of humanity's Fall and expulsion from the Garden of Eden in terms of his general views on human nature. Human life is seen as having been secure in every way in the Garden. Adam and Eve were "one with nature," in the manner of animals. They lacked discriminative knowledge of good and evil. They were blind. They were "incestuously bound to blood and soil" (1966, 57). Human history begins with an act of disobedience. Adam challenges God and eats of the tree of the knowledge of good and evil. This is said to mark the beginning of human freedom and discrimination. By disobeying, human life cuts its ties with nature and inaugurates its process of individuation.

The significance of this break with nature and emergence of consciousness is comparable, in Fromm's eyes, "to the first emergence of matter, to the first emergence of life, and to the first emergence of animal existence" (1965, 29–30). This is not the story of the "Fall" of the human being, says Fromm, but of humanity's first awakening and of the initiation of its upward journey (1966, 57). When the animal goes beyond nature, the human being, the most helpless of animals, is born (1965, 30). Life has become, with this event, aware of itself.

But, with the severance of our original ties with nature, our original harmony with nature is said to be lost (1966, 57). Conflict and suffering thus come to replace a peaceful and untroubled state of existence. Humans are now alone, separated from nature, but also, Fromm says, from other human beings and from their very selves (1966, 70). The Fall is said to mark the beginning of human "alienation." Following G. W. F. Hegel and Marx, Fromm takes alienation (estrangement) to mean (1) that nature, things, others, and their very selves have become alien to human beings, and (2) that human beings do not experience themselves as subjects of their own acts but only in the things they have created, that humans are in touch with themselves only to the extent they surrender to their externalized creations, which is to say, to the externalized manifestations of their own powers (1962, 44).

Fromm finds the most passionate human desire to be to return to nature, to the tranquil and comfortable home we were forced to give up because of our disobedience and the corresponding increase in consciousness. We want most of all, Fromm says, to give up reason, self-awareness, and choice. We want to return to the womb, to mother earth. We want to escape the burden of conscience and responsibility. We want to escape from our newfound freedom and be rid of the very awareness that makes us human. We want to run away from our very essence as human beings. Fromm says that this most central passion of human life manifests itself in the many forms of idolatry we engage in from day to day: submission to the state, to production and consumption; craving for possessions, power, and fame. Fromm indeed believes that human history is principally the story of the worship of idols (1966, 37). He insists, however, that there is no turning back (1966, 70–71). Self-consciousness and the knowledge of good and evil cannot be reversed. Human nature cannot be undone.

Human beings are thus seen to make themselves in history (1966, 97). This history begins with an act of disobedience, our first free act, the act that first defines our humanity. Human destiny is now to go through alienation in order to overcome it. Fromm remarks that Hegel and Marx saw this—that the alienating break had to occur and must be endured (1962, 57). We must experience our present state as strangers to ourselves, others, and nature (1966, 71). We must take the responsibility for and work toward the new harmony between ourselves and nature, which is our future goal. We are, Fromm says, left to ourselves in this. Nobody can do for us what we will not do for ourselves. Human life creates its own history. We are free to choose our own course and must accept the consequences of the decisions we make. Fromm remarks that in this way we will become what we potentially are, like God himself, which is precisely what the tempting serpent promised in the garden of Eden: "You shall be as gods" (1966, 97).

Fromm thus pictures the beginning of human history as a leaving of home (Eden). The original harmony with nature is broken and a split occurs. Fromm sees this as the cutting of the "primary ties" that bind human beings to land and to father and mother. Primary ties are those that exist before the full emergence of the individual (individuation): ties that bind child to mother, medieval believer to church, and "primitive" to tribe (1941, 25). Primary ties provide security but exclude freedom. Their dissolution spells freedom: "freedom from" primary ties, and especially freedom from the instinctual determination of human actions (1941, 32). Liberated from primary ties, one leaves the comforts of home. Having become individuated, we stand alone in a threatening and overpowering world (1941, 29). We become anxious, plagued by doubts about the meaning of it all, terrified by our aloneness and isolation, insecure. Freedom—freedom from primary ties, negative freedom—is a burden.

Thus it is that arise impulses within ourselves to give up our individuality, to submerge ourselves in the world in order to be rid of feelings of powerlessness and aloneness, to "escape from freedom" (1941). These impulses, our strongest passion, are what Fromm calls impulses to "secondary ties." Secondary bonds function as substitutes for lost primary ties (1941, 141). The essence of secondary ties lies in submission—submission to anything whatsoever (1941, 30). One submerges oneself in some power bigger than oneself—"a person, an institution, God, the nation, conscience, or psychic compulsion" (1941, 155). To gain a measure of security and comfort, one sacrifices one's humanity.

The single productive solution to the surrender of our humanity to secondary ties, in Fromm's view, is "active solidarity" with all human beings and spontaneous love and work (1941, 36). Spontaneous activity reunites us with the world, but now as autonomous individuals and not by primary ties (1941, 36). The alternatives Fromm proposes as available to us are thus: an escape from "freedom from" primary ties and submission to secondary ties ("freedom from": negative freedom) or a productive becoming "free to" the human destiny of full consciousness and responsibility ("freedom to": positive freedom); becoming ensnared in secondary ties and thereby inviting self-destruction or achieving a productive orientation and moving forward to the promise of a new harmony (1962, 174–82).

One of our options, then, is to move forward to a new future, to the harmony of a human being completely aware of itself, capable of knowing

right from wrong, freed from delusion and semislumber. Fromm is saying, in other words, that it is open to us to become what we now are potentially. Then it is, he says further, that we will have become like God.
Then it is that we will have awakened from the dream we are presently
dreaming (Marx) and become fully born. We will have then found our
home again, in the world. This will not be the end of history, Fromm comments, but a new achievement in history.

THE RELIGIOUS NEED

Fromm comments that to Westerners the word "religion" implies a God
who rules the universe. But there are religions—Buddhism, for example—
that do not hold to such a God. "Religion" must thus be given a broad
enough definition to include these other religions. With this in mind,
Fromm defines religion as a shared system of thought and action that
gives its adherents "a frame of orientation and an object of devotion"
(1967, 22). Fromm says that by this definition all cultures have a religion.
The religious need, in his view, is deeply rooted in human existence itself,
being a direct consequence of the Fall, which is to say, of the emergence of
human consciousness and freedom (see above, "The Birth of the Human
Being").

   Human existence, according to Fromm, is characterized by a split: we
are in nature, yet transcend it by reason of consciousness (see, for example, 1947, 48–58). Human self-consciousness, reason, and imagination
have broken the original harmonious state, in which animals still exist
(1967, 22–23). We are part of nature, weak and subject to inevitable death.
Yet we transcend the rest of nature. Human reason, while a great blessing,
is thus also seen to be a curse (1965, 30). Having achieved consciousness,
human beings find that they have lost their balance. How to live is a problem for us alone among the life-forms on earth. We have no instincts to
guide us, and so, existence remains a problem to be solved. Because, in
Fromm's view, there is no going back, the solution to the problem of existence can only lie in going forward, with the help of reason, until the new
harmony is found.

   Fromm sees the split in human existence as the very motive behind our
ongoing search for a solution in which we will be at peace with ourselves,
our fellow human beings, and nature (1965, 31). Now is a state of separation. The split creates conflict and suffering, and so, we are driven to find
ever new ways to resolve it. Finding we have not discovered the solution,
we remain bothered and puzzled and are motivated, for this very reason,
to continue looking for the solution. Fromm thus argues that it is the very
contradiction in human existence that keeps us on the move (1967, 29).

Now that paradise has been lost to them, human beings are seen to be on a journey. The only possible course now is forward. Human beings must chart the unknown, in Fromm's view, and find the meaning of their existence in the future that lies ahead of them.

Humans must thus overcome the split they find within themselves and become fully human. They must achieve unity and harmony on a higher level, not the harmony with nature that was theirs in the merely animal state (primary ties) but the harmony of a creature that has become fully conscious and free. Fromm thus insists that our split from nature creates needs in us not found in animals, needs that generate an "imperative drive" to reestablish our lost unity and balance (1967, 24). Fromm sees our life as a search for unity.

It is in the context of the human search for renewed unity and balance that Fromm locates religion. Seeking an object of devotion beyond ourselves, such as an idea or a God, is an expression, in Fromm's view, of our need for equilibrium, for a new completeness. Having lost our instincts, we need something to be devoted to with our whole heart, an object able to provide a focus for all our strivings and values. We need such "an object of devotion" to "integrate our energies," to "transcend our isolated existence," and to attain a meaning in life (1981, 124). The need for religion, for a "frame of orientation and object of devotion," is thus viewed as inherent in our present state of unbalanced existence. Fromm thinks there is nothing else in human life that is as powerful a source of energy, and thus of movement, as the religious need. We are consequently said to have no choice but to have ideals. It is up to us, however, to choose the ideal we will have, between devotion to "the worship of power and destruction" and devotion to "reason and love" (1967, 25).

Fromm thus insists that we are all idealists, necessarily requiring more than food and shelter. Having an ideal is inevitable. And so, it's not whether or not we have an ideal but the truth-value of the ideal we have, whether or not it is a worthwhile one. The best and worst of human action are seen to arise from "idealism." Ideals must all be tested, according to Fromm, and this includes the truth-value of secular ideologies, which are also expressions of the need in question. We must search into every ideal in order to determine whether it hinders or fosters human development, to see whether it is a true or a false solution to the problem of the split in human existence.

Every human being is an idealist, then, in Fromm's view, and every human being has a religious need (1967, 25). The question is not whether one has or doesn't have a religion but its actual quality (1967, 26). Is it a tree, money, nature, or God that is worshiped? Does our religion lead to love or to destructiveness? Does it help us advance in our quest for the new harmony, or does it cripple our powers? These, to Fromm, are the real questions. It is said to be irrelevant what people think their religion is, only what their religion actually is; it is irrelevant that people think they are worshiping God, when they are in fact worshiping possessions or power. Fromm is interested in the value of the religion actually practiced by people, whether that religion is for them or against them.

Fromm points out that the fact of the universality of religion attests to the reality of a need inherent in human existence to have a frame of orientation and an object of devotion: that is, to the reality of the religious need. Fromm finds additional evidence for this need in the practice of psychotherapy. The psychoanalyst discovers his or her explorations of neurosis to be, in fact, explorations of religion (1967, 27). Fromm says Freud saw the connection: neurosis can indeed be regarded as a private religion, a regression to primitive religiousness. The fundamental aims of life, according to Fromm, are independence, love, truth, and a productive existence. A neurotic has failed in these aims. Anyone who misses life's goals is seen to develop a neurosis. People do not just live. If higher goals are not achieved, energies are said to be channeled into lower ones. We only have the choice of "better or worse, higher or lower, satisfactory or destructive forms of religions and philosophies" (1967, 28). If people do not have an approximately correct vision of the world, Fromm says they develop a picture based on illusion to which they cling with all their might.

SOME CONTEMPORARY FORMS OF RELIGIOUSNESS

Fromm remarks that much of Christianity in our day and many atheistic and agnostic philosophies are a thin veneer over the older, primitive religions (1967, 28). There is said to be a great deal of idolatry in the West today, even in religions claiming to be monotheistic. Fromm points to the worship of power, success, and the marketplace as widespread and influential forms of idolatry currently in evidence. There are, in addition to these collective forms of idolatrous religion, a great number of individual varieties of primitive religion. Many go by the name of neurosis, but Fromm argues that we may as well call them by their religious names: ancestor worship, totemism, ritualism, fetishism, the cult of cleanliness, and so on.

Ancestor worship, for example, is said to be a widespread form of contemporary religion. Fromm cites the case of a gifted woman to whom, aside from her painting, nothing was of any interest except her father (1967, 29). When her father died, she committed suicide, asking only to be buried by his side. Her whole life revolved around an ancestor, who was "an object of devotion" and provided "a frame of orientation." This is religion by Fromm's definition. For this woman to have achieved a higher form of religion, Fromm says a profound personality change would have been necessary. Before one can be freed from a religious form of devotion to a parent, one must become free to think and to love.

Totemism is cited by Fromm as a very powerful and popular religion in our culture. Anyone who dedicates himself or herself exclusively to the state or to a party, who passes judgment on things on the basis of this dedication, and who worships the flag of his or her group is seen to have a totemistic religion (1967, 31). Fromm cites Nazism and Stalinism as examples of such religion. Millions were ready to sacrifice everything to the principle that their country could do no wrong. Fromm remarks that nationalism is "our form of incest," "our idolatry," and that "'patriotism' is its cult" (1965, 60). Fromm similarly singles out a religion of cleanliness. Some individuals are seen to use cleanliness and neatness as their standards for judging people. He also points to compulsive individuals as displaying many of the symptoms (rituals) of a private religion. Fromm, like Freud, cites isolation as an added disadvantage of the neurotic form of religion. Belonging to a group gives comfort, no matter how evil or irrational the beliefs and actions of that group.

Many contemporary instances of regression to primitive religiousness are thus uncovered through Fromm's hermeneutical approach. He states that monotheism would have helped ward off such regression if it had only succeeded in achieving its ideals (1967, 33). But it is pointed out that history reveals time and again how religion has yielded to, and joined forces with, secular power, frequently against the good of the people. Religion has all too often collaborated with "the powers that be." Organized religion has in the past, moreover, tended to put more emphasis on doctrinal orthodoxy than on the practice of love.

AUTHORITARIAN RELIGION

Fromm insists that we cannot talk about religion in general but have to distinguish between two forms of religion, the authoritarian and the humanistic. This distinction is said to cut across both theistic and nontheistic religions. Humanistic and authoritarian forms of religion can be seen to exist, moreover, within the same religion (1967, 41). Fromm says one can see the two trends in the history of both Judaism and Christianity.

Description of Authoritarian Religion

Authoritarian religion is seen to center around obedience to and worship of some "higher" power that controls people (1967, 34–36). Surrender is the keynote in authoritarian religion. The chief virtue is obedience, the key sin disobedience (1967, 35). People believe things simply because the authorities tell them to. In authoritarian religion, God is everything—a symbol of power, force, and domination, and the human being nothing—poor, powerless, and insignificant, able to gain power only through total surrender to the all-powerful God. Such submission (secondary ties), allowing an escape from loneliness and finitude and affording protection and a kind of security, brings a measure of relief from the human predicament and some comfort. By submitting, however, autonomy and integrity are surrendered. One "escapes from freedom" (1941). The mood of authoritarian religion is sorrow and guilt. Fromm remarks that the ideals of authoritarian religion are often abstract and far off in the future. For "life after death" or "the future of humanity," people are denied happiness in the present and even murdered.

Fromm says that the Protestant reformer Martin Luther, while talking all the while of the loving and voluntary nature of his relationship to God, in fact submitted to his God: his relations to God are said to have been characterized by overriding feelings of powerlessness and wickedness (1941, 68). Luther is said to have viewed human nature as helpless, vicious, and rotten and to have sought certainty as to his salvation through unqualified submission to God, conceived of as an overwhelmingly strong, extrinsic power (1941, 74–75, 78, 81). Luther, in love of, and in awe before, authority, emphasized his own insignificance and humiliated himself. His faith is said to have been "the conviction of being loved upon the condition of surrender" (1941, 81). Fromm also describes secular authoritarian religion (1941, 207–39). He cites, for example, the Nazi religion. While Hitler was an object of worship (a god), individuals were worthless except as they denied the intrinsic value of their lives. Submission to a dictator, as in Nazism, is said to parallel Luther's surrender to God.

Dynamics of Authoritarian Religion

Fromm views projection as the principal factor in authoritarian religion (1967, 49–50). While he sees the powers of love, truth, and justice as properly characterizing the human sphere, in authoritarian religion they are said to be found in God alone. What is originally ours—the human capacity for reason and love—is thus projected onto God. With everything of value, the very best, in human life viewed as God's own, virtually nothing is left to the human (1967, 49). God thus grows in stature in direct proportion to human impoverishment: the stronger God becomes, the weaker becomes the human. God is an idol, a thing of our making into which we project all our powers and to which we then submit (1981, 30). By thus submitting to this thing, Fromm says, we ourselves become a thing, estranged from the human powers of freedom and reason. The projection of our powers onto this thing thus impoverishes us, while submission to it puts us "in touch with ourselves in an alienated form" (1981, 30).

Fromm asserts that the same process of projection occurs in secular authoritarian religion. Only then, it is the political leader, rather than God, who is exclusively endowed with all the best qualities. Fromm characterizes the projection at work in authoritarian religion as an alienating factor. The best in ourselves is now seen outside in God or in a leader. We are thus away from ourselves, far from our own life. We feel as nothing. In order to get in touch with ourselves and all that actually is our own, we are said to have to go through our projected God (1967, 49). We try to get in contact with our split-off and projected parts by a total surrender to God. We pray to God to give us some of what is, after all, our own. We are at God's mercy. We see ourselves as incapable of love because our loving capacities are projected onto God, alone endowed with the capacity to love. In order to gain love from God, we have now to prove to God how loveless we are. We thus become, in an authoritarian type of religion, totally dependent on an infinitely superior God.

Fromm says such alienation from ourselves makes us bad. We have no faith in our own powers or in those of others. We have no experience of our own capacity to love and to think. The final outcome of all of this is said to be a separation of the sacred from the profane. In this world (the profane), we act without love. This makes us feel like sinners, which, Fromm points out, is the exact truth of the matter. To find our lost powers, we must turn to God. To gain forgiveness, we proclaim how worthless we are. But this only aggravates the problem because our absence of love, our sin, and our utter worthlessness are the direct consequence of our incorrect perceptions of ourselves as worthless sinners incapable of love.

Thus, the higher God is elevated, the lower the human being becomes and the greater the sinner. Use is here made by Fromm of the thesis of Ludwig Feuerbach (1804–1872) on the transferring of human powers to God: the stronger and richer God is, the weaker and poorer becomes the human being (1962, 44). The more we exalt God, the lower we descend; the lower we descend, the more of a sinner we become and the more we feel the need to praise and exalt God; and the lower we descend and become a sinner, the more . . . We thus become ever more alienated from ourselves and ever less able to find ourselves.

Fromm argues that when a small group subjugates the masses, those subjugated become incapable of feeling autonomous and powerful. Their religion will consequently be authoritarian in character, whether it is God or another human being who is worshiped. The kind of religious experience people have is thus said to depend on social structure. Religion is said to become authoritarian, moreover, when it aligns itself with secular power. Hatred and intolerance of others are seen to compensate for the submission that is found at the heart of authoritarian religion. Fromm believes that human beings have historically turned away from themselves and submitted to higher powers (secondary ties) in the manner outlined above. To worship any superior force—any force superior to human life—in his view is masochistic, self-destructive, and self-humiliating.

HUMANISTIC RELIGION

Humanistic religion, in sharp contrast to authoritarian religion, centers on human life and its inherent strength and capabilities (1967, 36). We are seen to be able to grow in our powers of reason and our ability to grasp the meaning of our existence, our potentialities, and our limitations (1967, 36–37). We can grow in our capacities for love for ourselves, for others, and for humanity as a whole. We are seen to be able to find the standards by which to live. The goal, in humanistic religion, is to become as strong as possible. The chief virtue is self-realization. Religious experience in humanistic religion, according to Fromm, is an experience of unity with the All, grounded on our relatedness to the world. Humanistic religion is seen to prosper when individuals are free and responsible for themselves (1967, 51). When humanistic religion takes theistic form, Fromm says, God is a symbol of human powers, of all that we could be but are not (1967, 37). God is an ideal we approach as we grow in these powers. Just as secular religion can be authoritarian, so, too, can it be humanistic.

BEING VERSUS HAVING

Fromm draws a sharp contrast between "being" and "having" in a late work (1981). An orientation toward being centers on persons; an orientation toward having centers on things. The latter orientation, in the form of "greed for money, fame, and power," is seen to dominate our Western industrial civilization (1981, 7). The being mode of existence means "aliveness and authentic relatedness to the world" (1981, 12). The having mode means possessing and owning, wanting to turn everything and everybody, oneself included, into one's property. Greed is the natural outcome of the "having orientation" (1981, 99).

Happiness, in the having mode, lies in being superior to others, in a capacity to "conquer, rob, kill" (1981, 68). In the being mode, happiness lies in "loving, sharing, giving." The mode of being presupposes autonomy and critical thinking, and its fundamental characteristic is "the productive use of our human powers" (1981, 76). The being mode means renewal, growth, transcendence of ego, and being interested in the surrounding world. The "dead word" rules in the mode of having, the "alive and inexpressible experience" in the mode of being. According to Fromm, human beings have a deeply rooted desire to be: to express themselves, to relate, to escape the prison of selfishness (1981, 88).

The having orientation is constituted by a certain attitude toward objects, not by the objects themselves (1981, 52). Anything can become an object of craving, even God. The having mode transforms everything it comes into contact with into something dead and subject to the exercise of power (1981, 64). "I have it" nevertheless, at one and the same time, means "it has me." Both "I" and "it" have thus become things. If "I am what I have," the loss of my possessions will wipe me out (1981, 65). If "I am who I am," on the other hand, nothing can destroy me (1981, 97). If life is a possession, it is something we have to hang onto. Living, in the having mode, necessarily means fear of dying (1981, 112).

Faith, in the having mode, is possessing an answer that affords complete certainty (1981, 30). We get such an answer from others, who formulate it and then pass it along for our consumption. Faith, in the having mode, is submitting to these others and their answer. The price we pay for this unquestioning, yet unshakable, certainty is our independence. We believe because of the power the promulgators of the articles of faith have managed to accrue to themselves—their prestige. Faith, in the being mode, is not so much believing in a certain set of ideas as an "inner orientation," a certainty based on experience (1981, 31). Such faith is an active and creative relating to self, to God, and to others. Faith in God, in the being mode, is "a continuous and active process of self-creation." Such a God cannot be put in one's pocket and manipulated for reasons of personal whim or gain. Love, in the having mode, involves controlling or confining the object of one's "love" (1981, 33). In the mode of being, love is the gift of oneself to the other in view of the other's growth and enrichment.

Fromm remarks that a major theme of the Old Testament is that human beings have to leave what they have behind, become liberated, and "be" (1981, 37). The New Testament, he says, is even more radically opposed to the having structure than the earlier Judaism (1981, 42). In the story of the temptation of Jesus, for example, Jesus and Satan are said to represent fundamentally opposed principles. Satan stands for "material consumption, power over nature and Man" (1981, 45). Jesus stands for being, for the "idea that not-having is the premise of being" (1981, 46). Jesus was "the hero of love," "a hero of being, of giving," a hero "who did not want to have anything," a hero who did not want power and who did not use force (1981, 127).

Fromm cites other prophetic leaders to the same effect. The Buddha, he says, discovered that having, wanting, and consuming are what make human beings unhappy (1981, 91). And Meister Eckhart urged that we not tie ourselves to what we own and what we have, not even to God himself; Fromm says Eckhart even prayed to God "to quit him of god" (1981, 51). Finally, Marx wrote, "Private property has made us so stupid and partial that an object is only ours when we have it," and "The less you 'are' and the less you express your life, the more you 'have' and the greater is your alienated life" (*Economic and Philosophical Manuscripts*, translated in Fromm 1961).

FAITH

Fromm sees faith more as a character trait than as faith in something (1947, 200–12). Fromm distinguishes two sorts of faith: rational and irrational. Rational faith is defined as a basic attitude that pervades one's whole life, enabling one to face reality positively and without illusion (1947, 201). Rational—humanistic—faith is a strong conviction "based on productive intellectual and emotional activity": "certainty of conviction" based on personal experience (1947, 207; 1967, 37; see above, "Being Versus Having"). Science, for instance, is seen to proceed by way of a vision, and not blindly. Science's history is filled with examples of faith in reason, joined to a vision of truth (1947, 207). Fromm indeed views (rational) faith in the other as indispensable in all truly significant human relationships (1947, 208). Nor can we succeed in fruitful relations with others without faith in ourselves. And there is the important "faith in humanity" (1947, 209). The basis of rational faith is productiveness, the experience of our own active strength and abilities (1947, 210).

Irrational faith, by contrast, is said to be a belief in something, be it "a person, idea, or symbol," that arises not through personal experience but through an "emotional submission to irrational authority" (1947, 204). Such faith is a fanatic conviction rooted in submission. An example of irrational faith was faith in the dictator Hitler. Fromm remarks that power—in the sense of "power over"—and rational faith are mutually exclusive. A religion, even when first born on the basis of rational faith, disintegrates when it comes to rely on power (1947, 211). Fromm says people cannot live without faith. The question is whether the faith in question is of the rational or the irrational variety (1947, 212).

LOVE

Love is seen to be an art, requiring knowledge and effort, rather than "a pleasant sensation," a state that one has had the mere "good fortune" to "fall into" (1956, 1). Love is active, primarily a giving rather than a receiving (1956, 22). As a giving, love expresses our aliveness and, so, fills one with joy (1956, 25). Love is the ability to experience concern and respect for another person—"active concern" for the other's life and growth (1962, 26; 1967, 84). It is the capacity to understand the other (1967, 84). In order to become a master at "the art of loving," Fromm says one must devote oneself to it. This requires disciplined effort throughout one's life (1962, 110). Love is seen to proceed from strength and not from weakness.

What counts in systems of thought is not so much the stated concepts, in Fromm's view, but the underlying attitude, the underlying human reality (1967, 37). The human capacity for productive love, which is to say, for a love without greed and submission, for a love that arises out of human fullness, is "the human reality behind the concept" of love for God in humanistic religion (1967, 84). Fromm says that the love of others— "Love thy neighbor as thyself" (Christianity), "compassion for all sentient beings" (Buddhism)—is the essence of the teachings of all humanistic religions (1967, 83). He remarks that psychoanalysis confirms this teaching (1967, 83–84). Dealing with neurotics, says Fromm, reveals that love is the most important of life's rules and that violation of this rule is the fundamental reason for unhappiness and psychological disturbance.

Neurotic complaints are thus said to be grounded in an incapacity to love. Psychotherapy is seen by Fromm as basically an attempt to overcome this incapacity, an attempt to help the patient "gain or regain his capacity to love" (1967, 84). Love, Fromm says, is the answer to the split that plagues human existence to its core. Our deepest need is to overcome the aloneness in which we are imprisoned (1956, 9). The desire for fusion with others is our deepest striving, our most basic passion, *the* unifying force (1956, 18).

RITUAL

Fromm points out that psychoanalysis has seen that compulsions are rooted in the unconscious. But, when psychoanalysis looked at religion, it was struck by the similarity between religious rituals and compulsions. Investigators suspected that the same unconscious mechanisms were behind both (compare chapter 2, "Religion as 'Universal Compulsive Neurosis'"). Overly preoccupied with the psychopathological, these researchers failed to take note of the fact that rituals don't always display neurotic compulsiveness (1967, 104). Fromm sees irrational rituals as indeed based on repression and its return but argues that rational rituals also exist and that these have nothing to do with repression.

Fromm thinks that rituals are an extremely important element in every religion (1967, 103). We humans have a need, according to Fromm, to express our religious devotion in actions shared with others. Rituals are defined as shared actions that express strivings rooted in shared values (1967, 105): symbolic expressions of thoughts and feelings by actions. Fromm argues that rational rituals are not defense mechanisms protecting against repressed desires but serve to express valuable strivings. The absence in them of a compulsive character is further evidenced by the fact that the omission of a rational ritual is not followed by anxiety.

Fasting is singled out as an example of a religious rational ritual (1967, 106). Our manner of greeting one another, applause, and reverence before the dead are cited as examples of secular rational rituals. Fromm points out that nowadays we have relatively few occasions to share actions of devotion with each other (1967, 106–108). Any such ritual is consequently seen to have a tremendous appeal. On the one hand, we don't have many meaningful rituals. On the other, we have a need for shared symbolic actions. According to Fromm, this need is vastly underrated. Rituals nevertheless cannot be manufactured at will. Before meaningful rational rituals can develop, shared values must exist.

PSYCHOLOGY AND ETHICS

Fromm affirms that there is no way to divorce psychology from philosophy (1947, vii). His experience as a practicing psychoanalyst has convinced him in particular that the study of personality is inseparable from problems of ethics (1947, v). Mental health depends on our actions, which in turn depend on our ethical judgments. Humanistic ethics judges the failure to achieve a mature and integrated personality a moral failure (1947, 226). Neurosis, Fromm says, is a "symptom of moral failure" (compare above, "Love").

Objective Ethics

It is Fromm's view that there are right solutions to the problems of human life and that there are wrong ones. Fromm proposes a normative humanism on the basis of this assumption (1965, 22–23). Psychology, he thinks, can be the "basis for building objective and valid" standards for conduct. Such standards are said to be within the reach of reason to formulate and, indeed, should be formulated on no other basis (1947, 16). Fromm points out that, by "objective" standards, he does not mean "absolute" ones—that there is nothing absolute in the ethical realm (1947, 25–26).

The source from which objective and valid ethical standards are to be drawn, in Fromm's view, is human nature itself. A human being is not a tabula rasa. Needs for happiness, love, belonging, and freedom are said to be inherent in human nature (1962, 81). Violation of these intrinsic needs, which are at once norms, leads to "mental and emotional disintegration" (1962, 17; compare chapter 5, "The Basic Needs"). If human beings develop into full maturity in accordance with the laws of human nature, Fromm says they achieve mental health; if not, he says mental health is denied them (1965, 23). Such a criterion of mental health is seen to be valid for all human beings. Fromm thus sides with those who hold there are moral laws that have inevitable consequences when violated. The aim of human life is seen to be "the unfolding of [our] powers according to the laws of [our] nature" (1947, 29). Fromm in this way takes a stand against ethical relativism.

Humanistic and Authoritarian Ethics

Fromm, in a contrast akin to that between authoritarian and humanistic religion, distinguishes authoritarian from humanistic ethics. In authoritarian ethics, some agency "above" the human being lays down the rules for conduct. An irrational power presides over people in such ethics—some "power over" (1947, 19). No criticism of this "superior" agency is permitted. Authoritarian ethics relies on repression as the safest avenue to virtue (1947, 228–29). "Power over" implies the inequality of some "under"—someone who is subjugated. Authoritarian ethics denies that people are able to discover for themselves what is good or bad (1947, 20). The authority alone, rather, determines good and evil. Fromm says the authority takes this power upon itself in its own interests, rather than in the interests of the people being dictated to. The authority exploits the people. This it accomplishes by excluding the use of reason (conscience), invoking awe, and inducing submissiveness. "That's the way it is, we are in a position to know, it's for your own good, trust us," they say in their way. The main sin in this sort of ethics is rebellion (1947, 22). Idolatry is said to be always involved in alienated, authoritarian ethics (1966, 46).

In humanistic ethics, by contrast, the human being is both the source and the subject matter of ethical rules. Humanistic ethics is based on the notion that the criterion for virtue and sin can only be determined by people themselves (1947, 22). "Good" is what is good for human beings and their development, and "evil" is what is harmful—the welfare of human life is the sole criterion. Values being rooted in human existence, Fromm sees no need to refer ethical behavior to a transcendent power. Value judgments are properly to be based on human beings and not on "higher" norms. Love of neighbor, for example, is seen to belong to the human being, to radiate from human life as a basic necessity and route to fulfillment. Love is thus not thought to originate in some higher sphere, only then to make its descent upon human life. Once again, in a humanistic ethics, the knowledge of human existence is to serve as the foundation of values (1947, 34). Virtue, in this sort of ethics, is responsibility to our existence and its laws; vice is irresponsibility. Virtue, fulfilling our inherent needs, is in our interest—our true, unselfish self-interest (1947, 138–45)—while vice is not.

Fromm points out that a humanistic ethics does not assume that the human being is the center of the universe. Humanism is nevertheless seen to hold that there is "nothing higher and nothing more dignified than human existence" (1947, 23). Nor, in opposing the repression so widespread in authoritarian ethics, is Fromm advocating indulgence—which is also viewed as bondage—but productiveness (1947, 230). The "productive orientation" is seen to be the basis of "freedom, virtue, and happiness" (1947, 231). Humanistic ethics is neither alienated nor idolatrous in its attitude (1966, 46).

CONSCIENCE

"Humanistic conscience," independent of external contingencies, is "our own voice," not that of swallowed (introjected) authority (1947, 162). Fromm views humanistic conscience as the voice of the total personality expressing the demands of growth and life (1967, 85). Conscience is the reaction of our total self to our proper or improper functioning as human beings. Fromm says that conscience reminds us when we are close to violating our ideals. Sin is, accordingly, not viewed as in the first instance against God but against ourselves, against our true self-interest and integrity.

Humanistic conscience is knowledge, Fromm says, knowledge with an affective quality (1947, 162). Behaviors of ours that foster our overall well-being lead to feelings of inner approbation (1947, 162). Behaviors that are harmful to ourselves, by contrast, produce uncomfortable feelings. Conscience is thus a "re-action" of ourselves upon ourselves. It calls us back to ourselves, to become what we potentially are (1947, 163). Fromm points to happiness as a sign indicating that we are on the right track in the discovery of the answer to the "problem of human existence" (1947, 192). Happiness, Fromm says, is to be our "criterion of excellence in the art of living." Depression, on the other hand, the opposite of happiness, results from "inner sterility and unproductiveness."

It may be difficult and take some practice, but we have to learn to listen to ourselves in order to understand the communications of our conscience (1947, 164–65). Fromm does not think that it is possible to learn how to live from a book. We have to learn, rather, to hear the voice of our own conscience, to listen to and follow it (1967, 89–90). Failure to live up to one's standards is viewed with understanding in humanistic religion, not with disgust. Guilt is experienced not as an invitation to self-hatred but as a prod to future improvement. Humanistic religion is permeated with love, Fromm says, not only for our neighbor but also for ourselves (1947, 163). It is possible to shut ourselves off from the voice of our conscience, Fromm says, except in sleep. Dreams communicate messages about our threatened or violated integrity that might otherwise pass unheard (1947, 168–69). Fromm remarks that our better self may also speak in symptoms: in dizzy spells, for example (1947, 226).

"Authoritarian conscience" is the internalized voice of an external authority (1947, 148). Authoritarian conscience, Fromm points out, is what Freud called the superego. When authoritarian conscience rules the day, the prescriptions and proscriptions issue from authorities above us and have nothing to do with what the Gestalt psychologists called "intrinsic requiredness" (1947, 149). The "validity" of the demands of an authoritarian conscience depends completely on the authorities, having nothing to do with personal judgment.

Someone governed by an authoritarian conscience is thus bound to outside authorities and their "internalized echo," symbiotically one with an authority that is greater and stronger than oneself (1947, 149, 151). Fear and admiration of the authority prevail. The authority, demanding unquestioning submission, exploits the subject, who must remain in a subordinate position (1947, 152–53). The individual ruled by an authoritarian conscience can be counted on. He or she feels it a duty to obey, no matter what the authority orders. This becomes a serious problem, of course, when the authorities command evil. There is no crime, Fromm says, that has not been committed in the name of duty and conscience.

"Good" conscience, the sense that one is pleasing the authority, makes one feel secure and good (1947, 150). The authoritarian "bad" or "guilty" conscience, the awareness of displeasing the authority, results, by contrast, from the person's assertion of his or her proper individuality (1947, 150, 154). "Sin," the violation of the prescripts of powerful authorities, requires expiation. The "sinner" fears punishment. One feels one has disobeyed and must now make up for one's failure by further acts of submission. One hates oneself for one's "disgusting" conduct. One is morally weakened and, after one's masochism has had its day, is likely to sin again. The authority controls all the means of forgiveness and, thus, increases its hold over the subject (1947, 159).

RELIGIOUS EXPERIENCE

Fromm finds the mystics to have experienced the reality of human strength and the basic identity of the human being and God. Mystical experience thus leads to the affirmation of human powers, of which God is a symbol. Mystics have seen, moreover, that God needs us as much as we need God. Fromm sees mysticism not as an experience in contradiction to reason but as the highest development of rationality in religious thinking. Fromm sees religious experience as a human and not a supernatural experience and to underlie and be common to certain thought-systems, whether these are theistic, atheistic, or antitheistic (1966, 46–47). While the experiential core of the thought-systems in question is said to be the same everywhere, its expression in words and concepts is found to differ. Fromm notes in particular an essential identity between Eastern and Western mystical attitudes. He points out that it is necessary to distinguish between a false religious experience, rooted in mental illness, and the healthy religious experience of union and love.

Common Characteristics of Religious Experience

Fromm indicates several common features of mystical experience (1967, 91–92). One of these is awe before reality. Another is "ultimate concern" (Paul Tillich) with life's meaning and the task life has set for us. A further common element is the experience of a definite hierarchy of values, the highest value being the optimal development of our human powers of reason, love, compassion, and courage. Worldly achievement is subordinated in the hierarchy to these spiritual values. Human life is experienced only as an end and not as a means to anything else. Everything is viewed from the perspective of whether or not it leads in the direction of our becoming stronger, more sensitive, more human. The mystic realizes that we are not in the world to transform it but for our constant self-transformation. The world is not experienced as an opposing object but as the medium in which we are to discover our own reality and that of the world.

Another characteristic of mystical or religious experience is a letting go of one's "ego" and greed and, with that, of one's fears (1966, 48–49). The ego is no longer clung to as an indestructible separate entity or "substance." One opens oneself to the world, rather, becomes filled with it and loves it. The mystic, thus transcending the ego, leaves the prison of selfishness and separateness behind. A final common element is an inner "attitude of oneness" that embraces all human beings, all life, and finally the whole universe (1967, 92). Individuality, however, does not get lost. There is, at one and the same time, a complete sense of one's individual existence and a sense of the All. Fromm views religious experience as springing precisely from the polarity between individuality and the All. The experience is one of both pride and humility.

Mystical experience, Fromm says, points away from all ties that stand between us and human freedom and growth. The individual finds himself or herself moved to give up all destructiveness and love of death. The aim of life, in the experience of the mystic, is that it be lived: the aim of life is life, not death, as Freud had it. Life is experienced as something to be loved. Fromm thinks that a highly developed psychological science will in the future confirm the essential correctness of mystical experience (1966, 50).

Psychotherapy and Religious Experience

Fromm points to the parallels between psychotherapy and religious experience. In psychotherapy, the task is to bring the individual ego in touch with the split-off part of himself or herself in the unconscious (1967, 93). The aim is something like the All of religious experience. Fromm sees the unconscious as that which is excluded from the organized ego. Split-off and outside the ego are said to be "all human potentialities, in fact, the whole of humanity" (1967, 94). When the individual gets in touch with the unconscious, the ego comes to be experienced as but one of an unlimited number of life's versions. Repression, Fromm says, is a matter of force, of "law and order," that cuts off the link between the ego and the life from which it springs. Repression brings growth to an end. When repression is broken up, on the other hand, we are said to get back in touch with life and to come to believe in it rather than in order. Integration and permeation then replace repression. Fromm cautions that the unconscious contains both the best and the worst (1967, 93). We must approach this other part of ourselves humbly as it is, with neither horror nor awe.

THOUGHT-CONCEPTS AND RELIGIOUS EXPERIENCE

The psychoanalyst, Fromm says, is equipped to study the human reality behind religion and symbol-systems in general (1967, 9, 60). Psychoanalysis tries to discover what the thoughts actually express—whether the attitude they portray accurately expresses one's true inner state or is a rationalization hiding an opposite attitude.

Fromm believes that the Western concept of God is a historically conditioned expression of religious experience (1966, 18). In the Near East, God is said to have been pictured as a being like those who had supreme power in society. Religious experience was accordingly expressed in the concept of a supreme tribal chief or king. "God"—God as ruler—thus became the supreme concept of Judaism, Christianity, and Islam, all of which were rooted in the social structures of the region. In India, Buddhism could express the experience in other forms, with the result that no concept of God as a supreme ruler was necessary (1966, 178).

The battle against idolatry is seen to be the principal religious theme running though the Old Testament from Genesis to Isaiah and Jeremiah (1966, 36). An idol is defined by Fromm as the object of the central human passion: namely the desire to return to the "soil-mother," the craving for such things as power and possessions (1966, 36). Humans transfer their passions to the idol, Fromm says, which thus comes to represent them (1966, 37). The idol is a thing, a partial aspect of human life that has been externalized. Idols have no life. God, on the other hand, is living. The contrast, in the final analysis, is said to be between "the love of death and the love of life" (1966, 37).

The God of the Old Testament, Fromm says, represents the supreme value and goal for human life: union with the world through the full development of the specifically human capacities of love and reason (1966, 20–21). We have seen that Fromm is not a theist: he does not view God as a reality in itself. But he says there is an advantage in speaking of "God" in that the word points to an experience that many in history have shared (compare above, "Religious Experience"). A disadvantage is said to lie, however, in the fact that the concept of God can be separated from the experience it refers to and be made into a being subsisting in itself, a Supreme Being outside the natural order and above it.

When the harmony that can be attained by the development of the human powers of love and reason was first experienced, Fromm says, the experience was given a name: Brahman, Tao, Nirvana, or God. This experience is said to have occurred all over the world between 1500 BC and 500 BC (1966, 20). The named experience of human possibilities was soon turned into an absolute standing on its own, however. The common vision all but disappeared because of all the nonessentials that came to be tacked on, all the "fictitious additions." Ideologies developed—an "ideology" is defined by Fromm as a system of thought without reference to experience and concrete reality (1966, 17–18). As soon as a system of thought becomes the nucleus of an organization, Fromm says, bureaucrats rush in. In order to keep power and control, the bureaucrats emphasize the fictitious additions rather than the similarities between their own and other organizations. The nonessential differences thus end up as important as the original experience, and sometimes more so. Fromm thus sees the experience at the core of all "high" religions—what he calls the "religious orientation"—to have largely been perverted in the course of their development (1981, 124).

"God," to Fromm, is a poetic expression of the highest value in humanism. His own position he calls "nontheistic mysticism" (1966, 18). Fromm believes that the next logical step for the Jewish religion of biblical times would have been "to give up 'God'" altogether and develop a concept of the human being as "alone in this world," but with the capacity to attain peace through proper relationships to his or her fellow human beings and nature (1966, 178). Fromm thus views the God-concept not as indicating something outside of ourselves but as a pointer to human reality itself, to the human reality behind the words: what we call the religious attitude is the experience that we humans can find harmony by progressing in the development of human love and reason (1966, 178). To the extent that believers and unbelievers share the same aim, namely the liberation and awakening of human life, Fromm says they can join forces in a common fight against idolatry (1966, 41). Individuals who worship God in an unalienated fashion and those who strive for the same goal in purely human terms recognize that thought-concepts are secondary to the human reality behind them.

Fromm sees religions as inclined to violate their ideals of freedom when they become large, organized, and bureaucratic. They then tend to keep people in bondage. The group is worshiped rather than God. Many believers, moreover, are said to practice idolatry: their belief is in an omniscient and omnipotent power allied with those who wield power on this earth. Then again, many unbelievers are idolaters, too, worshiping success, material possessions, sex, and the flag. It is Fromm's view that the fact of the matter is that most people in industrialized society are not striving for authentic human goals. They are anxious, empty, and isolated. Bored with life, they compensate for their depression by a compulsive pursuit of things. Gadgets are more attractive and fascinating to them than life. They seek to have and use much, not be much.

The psychoanalyst is said to find the same attitude animating different religions (1967, 62). Love, truth, and justice are the human realities behind Socrates, Jesus, the Buddha, and Isaiah. Submission to power and a lack of love and respect for human life are said to be the human reality behind the theology of John Calvin, for example, and behind authoritarian governments. The results produced by the various religions offer one test of the reality behind their words and beliefs. When the teachings of a religion lead to autonomy, happiness, and freedom on the part of the believer, Fromm says, it may be concluded that these teachings flow from an underlying love. If the religion's teachings lead to weakness, slavery, and discontent, on the other hand, it is to be concluded that these teachings do not proceed from love—however much talk there is of love.

HUMANISTIC GOALS

Fromm points out that many religions and philosophies agree that we can become fully human by developing our powers of reason in the pursuit of truth. They teach that we can achieve the freedom and independence that are inseparably bound up with truth. They propose that human life is not a means to anything else but an end in itself. Human beings are viewed as capable of attaining love of self and others. We are seen as being able to know right and wrong, to hear the messages of our conscience, and to have the freedom to follow them. Both humanism and psychoanalysis have, according to Fromm, these same goals. The aim of psychotherapy is to help the patient develop a religious attitude in the humanistic, but not the authoritarian, sense (1967, 90).

Fromm thinks that Freud's great discovery of the incest theme was clouded by the fact that he cast it in the terminology of literal sexuality. Fromm sees incest not as a sexual craving for the actual mother but as the more fundamental craving to remain a child protected by certain figures, of which the mother is the first and, for a long time, the most prominent (1967, 77–79). Incest, for Fromm, thus refers to affective ties to mother and nature, "blood and soil." The great necessity and challenge in life, as Fromm sees it, is for people to detach themselves psychologically from primary ties to the family. The nation, the race, and the class "become home and family" for most (1967, 78). People become incestuously attached to them, bound to them by secondary ties. This leads, of necessity, to nationalism and racism. These secondary ties must also be severed, like the primary ties to family.

Fromm thinks that most people are well adjusted because they have given up on the struggle to become fully human. Annexing themselves to the majority, they have avoided anxiety. It is Fromm's view that, in terms of the actualization of their aims as human beings, the well-adjusted majority is sicker than neurotics (1967, 80). The neurotic, Fromm says, has not given up. In short, all incestuous ties must be broken in order for us to flourish as human beings. Fromm affirms that the real history of humanity, the real story of human progress, is its development from "incest to freedom" (1967, 78–79).

THREATS TO RELIGION

Fromm does not see the natural sciences as a threat to religious feeling (1967, 97). But he does see a threat to humanistic religion in the contemporary human being's everyday manner of acting (1967, 97). People are seen to have stopped looking for life's purposes in themselves and to have made themselves into cogs in the economic machine, a commodity for sale to the highest bidder. Fromm says that when success becomes a supreme value, people may continue to profess the Christian ideals of love, truth, and justice, and they may think they are worshiping God, but they are in actuality worshiping an idol. The real goals are in the marketplace. Professing a religion doesn't make one religious.

THE EXISTENCE OF GOD

Fromm thinks it unfortunate that so much time has been spent on the existence of God rather than on the more fundamental attitudes of people (1967, 109–15). Discussions of God's existence typically turn into mere arguments over words, arguments that only end up dividing people. The reality of experience is never brought up. Fromm remarks that focusing on God's existence can actually interfere with the development of a humanistic religious attitude. The time has come, he thinks, to stop arguing about God and to unite instead in the "unmasking of contemporary forms of idolatry" (1967, 115).

We have heard Fromm to the effect that many people who say they believe in God are actually idolatrous in their "human attitude" (1967, 110). Many atheists, on the other hand, are seen to devote their lives to people, thus revealing a deeply religious attitude. The real conflict, Fromm says, is not between atheism and theism but between a humanistic and an idolatrous attitude (1967, 111). Idolatry is still idolatry, no matter in what form it is disguised, no matter how glorious the words. Idolatry is an attitude in which things and parts of reality are made into gods to which people submit. Anything can be made into an idol: science, statues, the opinion of others, the state, the flag, or mother (1966, 40). God himself, bestowing his blessings upon his favorite nations and their armaments, has at times been turned into one of the idols (1962, 155–56). Fromm says that because God is the official object of worship, idols, the actual objects of human worship, often go undetected.

IS GOD DEAD?

Fromm remarks that for the contemporary world, dominated neither by the idea of kingship nor the thinking of Aristotle, the traditional God-concept has lost its social and philosophical underpinnings. For many, then, a certain conception of God has indeed died. As for religious experience, if it is dead, Fromm says that we should then ask not whether God is dead but whether the human being is (1966, 180). To Fromm, this is the central problem. We humans are in danger of becoming mere things, of becoming increasingly alienated, and of losing sight of the real problems of human existence. If we continue in this direction, Fromm thinks that we actually will be dead. Then the whole problem of God will no longer bother anyone. The main issue today, in Fromm's view, is to recognize these dangers and to strive for conditions that will bring the human being back to life again. We need the rebirth of a humanism that focuses on the reality of experienced values. The concept of God may be dead, Fromm says, but the experiential reality behind the concept must live (1966, 180).

EVALUATION AND CONCLUSIONS

Fromm's psychology raises broad and general questions and offers broad and general answers. This has both advantages and disadvantages. His questions concern the very well-being and survival of the human species. His answers are love, reason, truth, freedom, independence, productivity, courage, community, justice, and peace. These are wonderful solutions, to be sure, but Fromm remains vague on the means to achieve them. Fromm is better at generalizing about ideal human fulfillment than at detailing the specifics of its attainment. Fromm's definition of religion is likewise vague: by it, everyone is religious.

It's precisely here, however, in speaking in general terms about religion—and life in general—that Fromm may be seen to make his contribution. For Fromm distinguishes. Applying, on the one hand, a "hermeneutics of suspicion" (Ricoeur 1970, 32) to forms of religion—and life in general—that are demeaning to human life and that diminish it and, on the other, a "hermeneutics of recollection" (Ricoeur 1970, 28) to forms of religion—and life in general—that add dignity to human life and that further it, Fromm comes up with a system of alternatives between which we are to choose: being versus having, rational versus irrational ritual, freedom versus incest, reason versus rationalization, truth versus illusion, rational versus irrational faith, humanistic versus authoritarian religion, objective versus subjective ethics, active versus passive love, humanistic versus authoritarian conscience, productive orientation versus secondary ties, love of life versus love of death, God as model of human powers versus God as authority figure, and peace versus violence. Much of the success of Fromm's bold psychological venture would indeed seem to depend on the correctness of the twofold hermeneutic explication of human existence engaged in by Fromm the philosopher, the psychotherapist, and the psychologist.

Fromm's nontheistic "radical humanism" admits of no being higher than the human. The human being striving for the best in human nature can say, in Fromm's words, "God is I, inasmuch as I am human" (1956,

70). Fromm's position in this regard, defining as it does the whole of reality, is a metaphysical one and, although metaphysical positions abound in psychology—for example, a widespread objectivism (the physical-causal = the real)—metaphysics is out of place there.

REFERENCES

Fromm, E. *Escape from Freedom.* New York: Holt, Rinehart, and Winston, 1941.
———. *Man for Himself.* Greenwich, CT: Fawcett, 1947.
———. *The Art of Loving.* New York: Harper and Row, 1956.
———. *Marx's Concept of Man.* New York: Ungar, 1961.
———. *Beyond the Chains of Illusion.* New York: Simon and Schuster, 1962.
———. *The Sane Society.* Greenwich, CT: Fawcett, 1965.
———. *You Shall Be as Gods.* Greenwich, CT: Fawcett, 1966.
———. *Psychoanalysis and Religion.* New York: Bantam, 1967.
———. *To Have or to Be.* New York: Bantam, 1981.
Ricoeur, P. *Freud and Philosophy: An Essay on Interpretation.* New Haven, CT: Yale University Press, 1970.
Suzuki, D. T., E. Fromm, and R. DeMartino. *Zen Buddhism and Psychoanalysis.* New York: Harper and Row, 1960.

8

✛

Viktor Frankl

If there is a reason for happiness, *happiness ensues*, automatically and spontaneously.

—Viktor Frankl

Viennese psychiatrist Viktor E. Frankl (1905–1997) was decisively influenced by the phenomenological philosophy flourishing in Europe at the time of his young adulthood. Especially influential were Max Scheler and his views on values, the secondary character of pleasure, and the specifically human character of human life.

That Frankl spent several years as an inmate in concentration camps during World War II is widely known through his book on his experiences, *Man's Search for Meaning* (1963). In it he comments that the completed manuscript of *The Doctor and the Soul* (1962), his major exposition of his views, was confiscated when he arrived at Auschwitz and that, while imprisoned, he reconstructed parts of the lost manuscript on scraps of paper (1963, 165). It is thus the case that Frankl's concentration camp experiences authenticated and deepened a singular psychological viewpoint already in a mature stage of development.

Frankl's psychiatric approach, to which he has given the name "logotherapy," is an attempt to help people recover the meaning in their lives, their reason for being on earth. According to Frankl, every last human life is irreducibly meaningful: meaning is always there for the discovery. Indeed, if meaning can be found even amid the horrors of a Nazi concentration camp, where can it not be found? There is always meaning, in Frankl's view, then, and the human being is forever responsible to meaning and, in the final analysis, to the ultimate being (God) and ultimate meaning. Of the psychologists of religion surveyed in this book, Frankl is the most explicitly committed to the existence of a personal—or, better, superpersonal—God.

All the while admiring and adopting a number of Freudian notions—the harmful effects of repression, for example—and techniques—dream analysis, for example—Frankl challenges Sigmund Freud's reductionistic mechanism, and in particular the belief that the higher, spiritual dimension of human life is nothing but the sublimation of animal instinct. Similarly, while praising Carl Jung for uncovering unconscious religiousness, Frankl criticizes Jung for his psychologism. Frankl challenges, on phenomenological grounds, both Freud and Jung—and indeed psychology in general—for their conception of human life as playing itself out inside the psyche (compare "Evaluation and Conclusions," in chapters 2 and 3). For Frankl, meaning—what life is all about—is precisely beyond any and all psychological processes.

THE ESSENCE OF EXISTENCE

Frankl, as already suggested, is an advocate of the phenomenological approach in psychology. Phenomenology is a method that, setting aside, or "bracketing," preconceived patterns of interpretation, turns to "the things themselves" (Edmund Husserl): "the immediate data of actual life experience," the "prereflective self-understanding" of human beings in their active engagement in everyday living (1967, 2n, 14). Phenomenology aims to describe—to survey and give a faithful portrayal of—the self-presenting phenomena of human life in rigorous and systematic terms. A principal feature of phenomenology is its focus on the specific and original humanness of human existence (1967, 73).

Thus committed to phenomenological methodology, Frankl rejects any psychological approach that presumes to explain the range of human behavior in instinctual terms. He is especially critical in this regard of the approach of Freud, who, he says, "never took a human phenomenon at its face value" (1967, 7). Frankl insists that a preconceived pattern of explanation such as Freud's must yield a distorted picture of human existence. The Freudian account is cited as a form of "reductionism," a procedure that "explains" human behavior through processes found in beings below the human (1975, 115). Rather than taking the rich and varied phenomena of human existence at their face value, rather than finding conceptions adequate to the phenomena on their own level of occurrence, reductionism tailors the phenomena to fit its preconceptions, takes the phenomena down—reduces them—to a lowest common denominator. Reductionism, Frankl comments, is "subhumanism" (1978, 17).

Phenomenology, reductionism's exact opposite, is the search for those phenomena of human existence that cannot be reduced to lower dimensions without their betrayal. Through a description of human life exactly as it presents itself, phenomenology hopes to discover the "irreducible," the "specifically human," the "essence of human existence," that which neither exists in animals nor can be traced back to them. The phenomenological method that Frankl would like psychology to adopt is thus an attempt to preserve what is human in human beings. Frankl envisions a psychology and a psychotherapy "in terms of the mind" (1962, 12).

The Noological Dimension of Human Life

Through the use of phenomenological methodology, Frankl discovers a sharp line of demarcation in the constitution of human existence between the regions of the instinctual and the specifically human (1975, 26). On the one side, Frankl says, are bodily and instinctual facts, and on the other, characteristically human openness to the world. Frankl's aim is to supplement the important discoveries of Freud with the specifically human dimension of existence, to complete his vision with a vision that doesn't limit itself to a single plane of human life but extends to the whole human being. This distinctively human dimension is said to transcend, but also to embrace, the instinctual and bodily dimensions of human life. This higher dimension Frankl calls the "noological dimension" or "dimension of the noetic" (1967, 3; 1978, 47). The terms "noetic" and "noological" serve to indicate the realm of the mind.

Intentionality and Self-Transcendence

Frankl says that the principal characteristic of human existence when examined descriptively—phenomenologically—on its own ground is its "self-transcendence." Such self-transcendence is the directedness of human life to a realm of meanings everywhere surrounding it. The noological dimension of the mind is no inner realm of private mental states but an orientation of all such states beyond themselves to a network of self-presenting values, to a world of meanings. Human self-transcendence, Frankl writes, refers to human life as a "relating to something or someone, other than oneself, be it a meaning to fulfill, or human beings to encounter" (1978, 47). The "meaning of life," by this view, is the realization of as many positive values or meanings as possible.

Frankl's notion of "self-transcendence" is a restatement of phenomenology's fundamental theory of the "intentionality" of human behavior (compare chapter 4, "Intentionality and Religious Behavior"). According to the theory of intentionality, human behavior transcends itself in every case to meaning, to intentional objects; the mental is forever beyond itself and in direct contact with the nonmental. The intentionality of behavior is thus its directedness beyond itself to the other of its concern, be that other a thing, an idea, a memory, a person, a goal, or whatever. A basic tenet of phenomenology, then, is that human life never concerns itself with inner mental states, with "subjective modifications of the mind": "Perceiving is always perceiving *of* something, remembering is in every case remembering *of* something, lifting is a lifting *of* something" (Fuller 1990, 37–38).

By thus maintaining that human life is not confined to its own states of mind, that human life is instead involved in every case with something beyond itself in the "lifeworld" (Husserl), phenomenology's theory of intentionality challenges prevailing psychological and philosophical views. When a subject's cognitive processes reach an object, Frankl insists, the object does not become part of the subject, a mental image or representation, but remains precisely other—nonmental (1967, 48). Human existence is an openness to others in their intrinsic otherness or objectivity (see below, "The Objectivity of Meaning").

In his notion of intentional self-transcendence, Frankl offers a distinctive psychological approach to human life in general and to psychotherapeutic practice in particular (1969, 25, 30). This approach centers on human life as a search for meaning and on the human capacity to find and live a meaningful life, regardless of inner and outer circumstances. Frankl insists that intentional self-transcendence is to be found only on the noological level of life.

In accordance with the noological self-transcendence of human existence, Frankl, unlike Freud and Jung, finds neither that human life is in bondage to the unconscious nor that it possesses an essentially intrapsychic character. Of central importance is no longer what originates and operates behind our back *within* the mind but what has an authority and integrity of its own *beyond* the mind. Meanings could never challenge us, Frankl insists; nor could we ever commit to a cause or a person for its own sake, if meaning were not beyond us, if meaning were not something other than the product of an instinctual or archetypal activity of the psyche (1967, 64). Self-transcendence, Frankl remarks, is the most essential human phenomenon of all, the very act of existing itself.

Conventional psychologies are seen to remain bound to this day to an antique monadological philosophy according to which human beings are self-contained unities, or "monads" (Gottfried Leibniz), closed in upon themselves and without direct access to a surrounding world of meaning (1978, 67; compare Fuller 1990, ch. 1). Frankl rebukes these psychologies for failing to envision human behavior as a response to a world that addresses and challenges it from beyond. Rather than understanding hu-man behavior as due to *reasons* in the world beyond it, conventional psy-chologies, modeling themselves on nineteenth-century physics, are said to see it as determined by *causes* within a universal domain of pure spa-tial extension—the *res extensa* of René Descartes. These psychologies fail to come to grips with the noological dimension of human life, where ac-tions have reasons ahead of themselves in the form of lifeworld meaning, rather than causes behind them in the body or psyche (1978, 69).

Freedom of the Will

Freedom of the will is found to be a unique feature of human life and, so, to be a further characteristic of the noological dimension. There are ad-mittedly conditions—sociological, biological, and psychological—that limit human life and freedom. But the human being, Frankl says, is not a fully conditioned and predictable thing among things. Conditions are not causes. While mere things determine one another causally, human beings determine themselves in freedom (1963, 213). People are always able, in Frankl's view, to take a stand toward the various conditions that limit and destine their lives (1962, 85–108; 1969, 16–17). It is up to us, he remarks, whether we surrender to conditions—detrimental hereditary or environ-mental factors—or bring the human dimension to bear and defy condi-tions and, thus, rise above them in noological space (1978, 47).

The important thing about conditions, then, as Frankl sees it, is the at-titude we adopt toward them. Conditions are but the raw material we have to work with in continuously deciding who we are going to be (1967, 110). Thus, as regards emotions, for example, what is crucial is not our anger or fear or hate, per se, but how we deal with and live our anger or fear or hate. All in all, then, human beings, determining themselves in noetic space, are not fully conditioned by forces and facts, either in the en-vironment or arising from the instinctual or bodily dimensions of their life (1967, 59). Frankl sees no way for human beings to avoid decisions and, thus, to avoid deciding on themselves (1967, 35). Humans are responsible for what they are and what they become.

Conditions, we have seen, are not causes. A residue of freedom is left even in the most abysmal of situations. Frankl comments, for example, that the "innermost core of the patient's personality is not even touched by a psychosis" (1963, 211). While there are psychotics who, besieged by delusional ideas of persecution, kill their presumed adversaries, there are other similarly besieged psychotics who, summoning up their human-ness, manage to take a stance toward their illness and to forgive their "en-emies." While some depressed people commit suicide, others find a way to overcome their suicidal impulses through a commitment to a cause or a person (1978, 49). Freedom, Frankl remarks, is freedom only in the face of destiny: freedom is "free conduct toward destiny" (1962, 86).

Everything, Frankl says, can be taken from the human being except one thing: the choice of one's own way in any situation whatsoever. "Existing," human beings always have the freedom to decide their own being (1962, 88). All in all, Frankl insists that people are able to decide what shall become of them, both "mentally and spiritually," even under the most terrible of circumstances (1963, 105).

Freedom is taken by some to mean freedom to do as they please. But Frankl views freedom without responsibleness as arbitrariness. Being freed "from" a necessary chain of behavior—"freedom from," or "negative freedom"—does not yet tell what people are freed "to"—"freedom to," or "positive freedom" (1962, 265–66). Negative freedom does not yet specify a positive decision for a task in life. As Frankl sees it, such a life task is not itself set by freedom, either positive or negative, for that would make that task relative to human life and deciding, and hence arbitrary in content. Frankl insists that our life task is instead given to us from beyond. What we are to live for—meaning—precedes our freedom to choose or refuse it. Our life task is grounded in intentional self-transcendence.

The Will to Meaning

Human existence as self-transcendence is "open to the world"—"a being reaching out beyond itself" (1969, 8, 31). So long as it has not been "neurotically distorted," Frankl insists that human existence is forever directed to something that is not itself, a meaning to be fulfilled or "another human being to encounter lovingly" (1975, 78). Meaning, no human construction or decision, no constituent of the mind, is beyond us in the world (1963, 175).

"Meaning is what is meant," Frankl remarks, when someone asks us a question or when a situation implies a question calling for an answer from us (1969, 62). Frankl thinks that life asks questions of everyone: life is always expecting something (1975, 23–24). And he thinks that we can only answer by being responsible to life for our own life. There is said to be only one correct answer to each question life directs at us, exactly one valid meaning in each of life's various situations (1962, 47–48). We all have particular "value-potentialities" assigned to us that it is our task to fulfill. The actualization of these value-potentialities, Frankl says, is "what life is all about": the meaning of life (1962, 10). Each and every situation of our life, Frankl says, is "a call, first to listen, and then to respond," to the meaning that is waiting for us (1978, 60).

All in all, Frankl regards the "search for meaning" as the most fundamental and most representative, "the most human phenomenon of all"

(1962, x). A "will to meaning," the striving "to find and fulfill meaning and purpose," is what motivates human life (1969, 35). This is to say that the basic human motivation is to bring as much meaning to life as possible, to actualize as many positive values as circumstances allow (1962, x). Being directed beyond oneself to meaning—self-transcendence—is said to be most strikingly seen in the phenomena of love and conscience (see below, "Conscience"). Noologically speaking, the human being is someone who encounters others and who reaches out for meanings to fulfill. This, according to Frankl, is the central fact of human life that the phenomenological method can analyze: human existence *is* a will to meaning. Human existence is directed to meaning as its "intentional referent" (1978, 66). What we ought to be centers on the fulfillment of meaning. Frankl speaks of a tension between human existence as a will to meaning and meaning fulfillment, between what *is* and what *ought* to be (1969, 51). The real and the ideal—human being (will to meaning) and the meaning that ought to be (fulfillment of meaning)—never coincide.

We have seen that human behavior is due to "reasons out there in the world" and not—as a "psychology without Logos (meaning)" maintains even to this day—to psychological or bodily causes (1978, 69). Aggression, for example, is not, as Freud proposes, a negative psychic energy springing up from the sum total of bodily cells and compelling us to engage in behaviors injurious now to ourselves, now to our father, now to "them" (1978, 70). In keeping with his notion of human self-transcendence, Frankl argues that aggression is not properly understood without a consideration of its object: aggression is in every case aggression *against* someone or something (compare above, "Intentionality and Self-Transcendence"). Psychology, respecting actual human life, must not limit itself to the intrapsychic.

Reasons, ahead of our life, belong to the future—to meaning fulfillment. Causes, behind us, belong to the past. Reasons pull. Causes push. Tender sexual intimacy, for example, embodies a love that has its reasons in the partner himself or herself. Frankl remarks that sexuality, as an integral part of the noological dimension, as *human* sexuality, is always different from a mere instinctual or bodily fact, for it now serves to express love (1975, 86).

There is, according to Frankl, always an ideal ahead of us, a meaning we are being called on to fulfill. We can, of course, choose not to respond to life's call, not to answer the question directed at us. We always have the freedom to accept or refuse the value we are invited to actualize in a given situation (1969, 57). Refusal is one of freedom's options. It is always a matter of choice whether or not we fulfill the meaning addressed to us by life as a question, whether or not we give the appropriate answer. The fulfillment of meaning always implies a decision on our part.

The Objectivity of Meaning

Frankl insists that the meanings to which our life is directed exist beyond the arbitrariness of mere self-expression and self-assertion. Despite its obvious and growing appeal, Frankl rejects the notion that meanings are the free creations of human subjectivity. He is convinced, rather, that meanings are there for the discovery (1969, 60–61; 1975, 113). This is the same as saying that a situation's "demand characteristics" (Kurt Lewin) or "requirements" are "objective qualities" (Max Wertheimer). Frankl thus joins classical Gestalt psychology in the belief that objectivity intrinsically belongs to meanings. Citing the work of James C. Crumbaugh, Frankl remarks that the discovery of meaning has something to do with the Gestalt laws of organization, which represent an unlearned striving to form meaningful and unified configurations or gestalts (*Gestalten*) (1975, 114–15).

Frankl thus underscores the otherness or objectivity of the other. Only if such objectivity is retained, he maintains, can meaning display that "intrinsic requiredness" (Wolfgang Koehler) that renders it something "to be accepted" (positive demand characteristic). Only a meaning that is not simply an expression of our own being is said to be able to challenge us. Meaning (the ideal) must not be the same as human existence (the actual) but has to be ahead, setting the pace for human life (1967, 12). A certain tension, arising from the otherness of the other, must be in play between object and subject, between transcendent meaning and human existence as will to meaning (1969, 51).

Human existence is oriented to the world, then, and the world—the network of all our meanings—has objective meaning. The real meaning of life lies in such a world. Our acts, to the extent they are adequate, transcend to the objects these acts objectively bring to light (1962, 46–47). It is thus that Frankl argues that the objectivity or otherness of the object must never be lost sight of when discussing human life and its motivation. Every true cognitive act means attaining such objectivity, for what else could *knowing something* possibly mean but reaching the other in what it is "from itself" on its own ground (1967, 48–49)?

Self-transcendence is going *beyond* ourselves *to* objective reality. Values and ideals confront us from and on their own ground of otherness. Objective meanings are what we live by, what make life meaningful (1962, 49). The meaning we ought to fulfill can only effectively challenge us, we have heard, if it is something we discover rather than something we create. Self-discovery is not accomplished by turning inward. Frankl agrees with Johann Goethe: "Try to do your duty and you will soon find out what you are." Our duty lies beyond, and with it our fulfillment.

Frankl admits that it is obvious that we all perceive the world subjectively from our own vantage point. The fact of perspective places certain limitations on everything we see or can see. Human "subjectiveness," however, in Frankl's view, does not diminish the "objectiveness" of reality (1969, 59). "What is seen through the perspective," Frankl writes, "is the objective world" (1969, 60). We are always selecting among alternative possibilities, but we are making "a subjective selection from the objective world" (1967, 49). Objectivity is through the subjective lens; nor could it be otherwise: humans have no access to objective reality except through an inherently selective subjectivity (compare chapter 1, "Human Selectivity").

For human beings to be a subjective perspective on the world and its meanings is for each of us to discover properly individual objectivities: different objectivities arise for different individuals. Objective meanings are "concrete duties" that correspond to the daily actualities of the individual (1962, 47). Each of us has a life task of our own, and this life task consists of particular meanings to be fulfilled in each of life's manifold situations (see above, "The Will to Meaning"). Meaning is always particular—our life task in each case unique. The objectivity attained through subjectivity nevertheless is, and always remains, objectivity. Meaning is forever beyond, for the discovery. Frankl rebukes the subjectivism and relativism prevalent in contemporary theories of meaning and value and, indeed, of life in general. We have thus heard Frankl challenge both the objectivism of a mechanistic and reductionistic science and the subjectivism of our culture and social-scientific value theory. Frankl rejects both "plagues" of modernity.

The Meaning of Life

Frankl points to freedom of the will, the will to meaning, and the meaningfulness of life as the three fundamental assumptions of his psychology. The first two have been considered above. We turn now to the third. "Life," Frankl writes, "never ceases to hold or retain a meaning" (1967, 14). Life is said to be meaningful in three ways: (1) through what we create and give to life, principally through our life's work; (2) through the values life presents us with, through the good, the true, and the beautiful; and (3) through the stance we are able to take when faced with an unchangeable fate, in particular through our attitude toward suffering.

Life is always meaningful, Frankl maintains, because every one of us has a unique vocation or life task to fulfill, a certain meaning to actualize in each of the manifold situations of life (see below, "Responsibleness as the Essence of Existence"). The fact, moreover, that we are able to find a meaning in life even when we are no longer capable of working and creating or of appreciating life's goodness—even when we have nothing more to give to life or take from it—is said to bear eloquent testimony to the constancy of life's meaningfulness. No matter how intense the suffering, even if we be at death's door, we can always take a stance and find meaning.

Frankl calls suffering, guilt, and death "the tragic triad of human existence" (1967, 24). It is not in spite of the finiteness of life revealed by these three, Frankl says, that life takes on meaning. Life is meaningful, rather, precisely through the weaknesses and limitations inherent in it, through our acceptance of suffering, failure, and death. Frankl, contrary to popular wisdom, locates life's deepest meaning in suffering (1962, 121–33). Suffering's hidden meaning is said to be accessible through a commitment arising from the depth and center of human life. Frankl characterizes despair, on the other hand, as "suffering without meaning" (1975, 137).

As to failure and guilt, Frankl remarks, it is the recognition of the fact that we have missed the mark and gone astray that makes us want to do better (1967, 30). And, finally, as regards death, it is in the realization of our limited stay on earth that taking action assumes an urgency: if we were never to die, everything could be postponed (1962, 72–79). Frankl is thus able to conclude that the meaning of life is without condition. Life is meaningful even in failure and guilt, even for the helpless victim in a hopeless situation, and even to our dying breath (1962, xii; 1978, 39). We are responsible for a meaningful life as long as we remain conscious (1967, 50).

Pleasure and Power

Frankl views Freud's "will to pleasure" and Alfred Adler's "will to power" as derivatives of the real concern of human life—substitutes for a frustrated "will to meaning" (1967, 6; 1969, 35–36, 96). One becomes pre-occupied with oneself, with pleasure and power, Frankl remarks, only after failing to find a meaning in life. Frankl points out that pleasure, self-actualization, happiness, peak experiences, and the like are all byproducts of meaning fulfillment (1975, 85). Experiences refer to objects (the intentional self-transcendence of human life). Satisfying states of fulfillment are thus to be understood and evaluated in terms of the objects that occasion them, in terms of their reasons (1969, 40). In straightforward, prereflective living, according to Frankl, we do not seek or relish satisfying states of mind for their own sake. Directly sought, rather, are the people and other meanings that bring these subjective states about. People are thus interested in the "intrinsic value" of what they are involved in, not satisfaction, per se. People, at least when they are adequately living the meaning of their existence, simply want the values that constitute a "transcendent realm of objective things" (1962, 46).

The Will to Pleasure

States of mind belong to the subject and thus, in Frankl's view, are not, properly speaking, values, which by definition transcend all subjective acts and states. Pleasure, a subjective state resulting from the fulfillment of objective meaning (Scheler), is simply not something to pursue. Freud is held to have mistakenly adopted a motivational theory in which human activity is essentially a search for pleasure (tension reduction). Frankl views such a search, wherein one takes an effect for an end, pleasure for the goal of life, as a neurotic and self-destructive one. Freud, it may be noted, took the pleasure principle to its logical conclusion in the death instinct, which is to say, in the organism's presumed search for the reduction of the sum total of all bodily tensions. There is no pleasure principle in people, says Frankl, unless their lives are already neuroticized as a result of a frustrated relation to meaning: the pleasure principle is a motivational theory invented by psychology after the model of the striving of neurotic individuals (1969, 36). People don't want pleasure, in Frankl's view; they simply want what they want (1962, 41).

If people pursue meaning, it has been suggested, pleasure, happiness, and similar states of mind spontaneously follow. There is happiness, Frankl says, when there is a reason for happiness: when one lives forward one's self-transcendence, one's service of a cause or love of someone (1969, 34; 1978, 83). Pleasure occurs automatically whenever a meaning is fulfilled (1967, 40). Happiness and pleasure sneak up on you when you're least expecting. The active pursuit of such states of mind, on the other hand, tends to keep them at arm's length. Paradoxically, then, the way to fulfillment and happiness is through forsaking fulfillment and happiness, through looking away from them and pursuing what's worth pursuing: a person, a work of art, nature, a cause, and the like. Living in such a manner, Frankl says, brings with it encouraging and fulfilling states of mind.

Self-actualization, according to Frankl, accompanies the successful execution of the self-transcending intentionality of human existence (1969, 38). One becomes self-actualized, Frankl says, not by seeking to actualize oneself, but by forgetting about oneself and directing oneself outward toward value (1978, 34). Self-actualization is thus seen as the by-product of a certain style of acting, the unintended concomitant of a life dedicated to meaning fulfillment (1969, 38–39). The essential of human life is forever a search for meaning, not a search for oneself; a meaningful life is never found within (1969, 50–79). All in all, it is "ruinous and self-defeating," in Frankl's view, to make self-actualization a life goal (1978, 35).

As to the worth of peak experiences induced by chemical *causes* (such as LSD), Frankl comments that there is literally no *reason* for such experiences

(1969, 40). Chemically induced highs, moreover, can occasion all sorts of problems.

The Will to Power

As for the will to power (Friedrich Nietzsche, Adler), Frankl points out that power is a means to an end (1967, 6). A certain amount of power is generally necessary before meaning can be fulfilled. While the will to pleasure mistakes an effect for an end, the will to power mistakes the means to an end for the end itself. The will to pleasure and the will to power are thus viewed as fundamentally misdirected intentions. Both aim at the attainment of states of mind rather than at transcendent meaning. Both aim at ourselves rather than at a world of meaning ahead of human life and setting the pace for it. Both are a will to self rather than a will to meaning.

The Existential Vacuum

Frankl calls the meaninglessness and emptiness characteristic of our age "the existential vacuum" (1969, 83–98). This frustration of our specific humanness, of the human search for meaning, is called a "noogenic neurosis" (1967, 43). A noogenic neurosis is one that owes its origin to conflicts, problems, and crises on the specifically human level of existence. The existential vacuum is said to be today's "mass neurosis," bringing with it depersonalization and dehumanization, as well as the "mass neurotic triad" of depression, aggression, and addiction (1963, 204; 1978, 15, 26). Frankl says that people kill one another when their lives become meaningless, not when a pool of intrapsychic aggressive energies takes over and takes aim at others (1978, 97–98).

Logotherapy

"Logotherapy," we've seen, is Frankl's name for his psychotherapeutic approach, which he developed in the 1930s to deal with noogenic neuroses. Logotherapy is an analysis of existence in terms of responsibleness—an analysis, in other words, that deals with the "intentional objects" beyond human existence that are the reasons or motives for human behavior (1978, 53). Thus concerned with meaning, or "Logos," logotherapy is literally "therapy through meaning" (1967, 66; 1978, 19). The aim of logotherapy, Frankl says, is "to unlock the will to meaning," to help the patient discover a meaning in his or her life, something he or she ought to be fulfilling (1975, 131). Meaning-centered logotherapy focuses on the future, on the future meanings the patient is to actualize (1963, 153). Frankl remarks that it was those inmates who were oriented to the future, who lived for a task they were attempting to fulfill or for a person who was waiting for them, that survived the Nazi concentration camps (1978, 20). Meaning for Frankl, we have seen, is unconditional: life can never be devoid of meaning (1962, 50). Not even death can detract from life's meaningfulness. What we are said to need is faith without conditions in meaning without conditions.

It is characteristically neurotic, in Frankl's view, to regard one's life's situation as a fate about which nothing can be done. Such "neurotic fatalism" is a tactic by which one seeks an escape from the full awareness of one's life task—a disguised "escape from responsibility" (1962, 99). The logotherapist tries to marshal what is specifically human, the "existential," against the "fated." The logotherapist's purpose, in other words, is to bring the person into an awareness of freedom and responsibleness. The awareness of one's essential humanness is thus opposed to "neurotic fatalism" (1975, 28). Frankl's logotherapy contests the psychoanalytic interpretation of life according to which a tragic ego is torn between a merciless id and superego (1978, 60).

By focusing on meaning, logotherapy seeks to break up the neurotic's characteristic self-centeredness (1963, 153). What people are said to need is not a tensionless state but the struggle for a goal worthy of them (1963, 166). Logotherapy, in the final analysis, is "education toward responsibility" (1962, xv; see also p. 29). People need always to demand more and more of themselves. Frankl believes the idealism characteristic of logotherapy to be the true realism (1975, 83). He agrees with Goethe that treating people as they ought to be helps them become what they can be.

Logotherapy concerns itself with uncovering "the distress of the human spirit" and with alleviating this distress (1962, 12). Confusion over the meaning and value of life, at its extreme reaching the point of despair, is indeed, in Frankl's view, "a spiritual distress" (1963, 163). It is Frankl's belief that the unbiased individual, through the prereflective understanding of his or her own life, knows that human existence means responsibleness for fulfilling the meanings inherent in life's various situations (1975, 125–31). The task of phenomenology, Frankl says, is to translate this wisdom of the heart into the rigorous and systematic language of science (1975, 129). Frankl thinks that the average person can, on the basis of his or her everyday experience, become the true teacher of morals.

The "real business" of logotherapy, Frankl says, is to purge psychotherapy of "psychologism," "the pseudo-scientific procedure," which analyzes and judges mental activity solely in terms of the psychological conditions at its origin (1962, 17–22). Frankl says that Freud's genius lay in bringing hidden motivations to light. Frankl respects this genius for unmasking the neurotic but insists that psychoanalytic debunking must come to an end when the genuinely human (noological) is reached: the search for meaning, the desire for as meaningful a life as possible (1963, 156; 1978, 14). Unmasking beyond this point, comments Frankl, serves but to reveal the therapist's own lurking motivation, the unconscious wish to devalue the authentically human (1978, 14).

"Nihilism" is defined as the doctrine that being has no meaning (1967, 121). In the final analysis, Frankl thinks that the Nazi Holocaust was prepared in the ideas and lectures of "nihilistic scientists and philosophers" (1962, xxi), that the gas chambers were the logical outcome of the belief that a human being is "nothing but" the product of environment and heredity.

Responsibleness as the Essence of Existence

Responsibleness, "willing what I ought to will," is said to be the objective aspect that completes freedom, the subjective aspect (1967, 63–64). Frankl sees the subjectivity of human existence and the objectivity of meaning as together forming a single total phenomenon. Subjective freedom and objective responsibleness to meaning—more precisely, human responsibleness to objective meaning—are indissolubly bound. We are responsible for giving the right answer to each of the questions life's unique situations direct at us (1969, 62). Meanings, "in the world," challenge and obligate us. Responsibleness is a decision in favor of the meaning of life. We are responsible as well as free, free to be responsible: freedom is destined to become "freedom to" objective meaning.

Logotherapy is "existential analysis"—analysis of human existence (1975, 23). It strives not to make the ego conscious of the id but to bring the unified whole that is the self into consciousness of itself, to bring the personal core to itself. The noological dimension, considered by Freud an epiphenomenon of "instincts and their vicissitudes," is thus made into the cornerstone. Through the existential-analytic discovery of the essence of human actuality as a directedness to the ideal (meaning), responsibleness is brought to light as "the very essence of human existence" (1967, 13). To be human, Frankl says, is to be conscious and to be responsible, to live the tension between the real or actual (human existence: consciousness, freedom) and the ideal (essence of human existence: responsibleness to the meaning that ought to be), between (human) being and meaning (1962, 5; 1967, 10). The specific aim of existential analysis is to help the patient become conscious of his or her responsibility (1962, 268). Responsibleness forms the very core of intentional self-transcending to the world.

The concreteness both of an individual human life and of a given situation is necessarily implicated, in Frankl's view, in the response we are called to give to meaning. Meaning is always relative to context. The question life is addressing to us doesn't concern the meaning of our life as a whole, which is beyond our grasp, but "the unique meanings of the individual situation" (1969, 55). Frankl says that tasks come to us one at a time; each of life's situations, we have heard, contains exactly one right question and a single right answer. It is for this reason, Frankl points out, that each life task is absolute.

Life is thus described as a "chain of questions" to each of which we bear the responsibility of discovering the proper answer (1967, 17). "A single and unique course," Frankl says, has been marked out for each of us (1962, 63). Discovering and following this course leads to the "realization of our most personal potentialities" (1962, 63). We each have our own goal in life, then, and there is only one path to that goal. Frankl says that it is this very uniqueness of our vocation in life, of our life task, that makes human existence meaningful. When asked where to make a beginning with meaning, Frankl answers that one can only begin with the requirements of today's situations.

Our responsibility in life is to make values actual. Opportunities for such value-actualization are said to be continually changing. Every hour brings with it a concrete demand, a personal invitation.

PHENOMENOLOGY AND RELIGION

Religion is a specifically human (noological) phenomenon, in Frankl's view, and thus to be taken at its face value rather than reduced to something else. Phenomenology is held to be the proper approach to religion's irreducibly human character. It has been seen that the search for meaning is the most human phenomenon of all in Frankl's psychology. In view of this, religion is defined as the "search for ultimate meaning"—the human search for the final reason for the unconditioned meaningfulness of life (1975, 13). Faith, based on trust in the ultimate being (God), is said to be trust in ultimate meaning. Frankl holds that psychology, though unable to grasp the object of religious belief, is able to investigate the human aspects of religious phenomena. By Frankl's definition of religion as the search for ultimate meaning, the human being is basically religious. Frankl discovers the existence of a "religious sense" deeply rooted in people's "unconscious depths" (1975, 10). Neither psychosis nor imprisonment is able to annul this sense, for it has been found to break through unexpectedly in both conditions (1975, 11–12).

The Specifically Human Unconscious

Frankl holds that any human phenomenon, be it bodily, instinctual, or personal in character, can occur on an unconscious, preconscious, or conscious level (1975, 25–32). This means, among other things, the existence not only of an instinctual unconscious but of a specifically human one as well. The final criterion of a truly human act, in Frankl's view, is not its consciousness or unconsciousness, which is largely irrelevant, but its noo-logical, as opposed to its merely instinctual, character. Again, to be human is to decide what one is going to be.

Inaccessibility of Human Existence to Reflection

The depth of any human phenomenon, Frankl says, is unconscious. This means that what is specifically human, the person, is unconscious in its depth. The person as executor of specifically human acts is so absorbed in their execution that he is unable to reflect "on what he basically is" (1975, 30). We exist in action, in other words, not in reflection. Because re-flection engages the personal center where actions originate only in in-trospection or retrospection, this center of action is held to be inaccessible to reflection.

The specifically human foundation of human existence is thus uncon-scious: the specifically human in its origin is a specifically human uncon-scious, unable to observe itself. There is a "blind spot" precisely where the noological is "original" and fully itself (1975, 31). Frankl agrees with the saying of India's Vedanta: "That which does the seeing, cannot be seen." Existence, unconscious in its depth and origin and unable to catch itself in reflection, is never fully conscious of itself (1975, 26).

The authentic person is said to form responsible decisions prereflec-tively out of his or her very substance (1975, 31). Deciding and discerning (discrimination) are specifically human acts. They are unconscious in the sense already indicated: that is, their essence cannot be captured by re-flection. Frankl points out that even that which decides whether some-thing will become conscious is itself unconscious. A mother sleeps right through the loud street noises but wakes at the first signs of her child's troubled breathing. In order for "the guard" to decide whether an expe-rience will become conscious or remain unconscious, it must be able to discriminate, something generally attributed to consciousness alone. The unconscious depths that ground human life thus have a consciousness of their own. Unconscious deciding takes place in a characteristically hu-man way.

Frankl thus discovers the grounding of the human orientation to mean-ing in specifically human unconscious depths. It is in these depths, out of the very substance of human life, that the great human decisions are said to be made. Human responsibleness is similarly said to reach down into a specifically human unconscious foundation. There is unconscious, as well as conscious, responsibleness. To the extent that existence cannot be fully reflected upon, it cannot be fully analyzed. Logotherapy, Frankl comments, can only be "analysis toward existence" and its essential characteristics, consciousness and responsibleness. A psychoanalysis that claims to render an exhaustive account of human existence in terms of prehuman instinct is rooted not in the self-presenting phenomena of human life, in Frankl's view, but in scientistic presupposition.

Human Existence Grounded in Neither Instinct nor Reason

The immediately preceding paragraphs indicate why Frankl considers the Freudian concept of the id inadequate to the reality of the unconscious: the unconscious by far exceeds instinct. A one-sided and overconfident rationalism, on the other hand, is likewise said to be too narrow in scope to account for human existence in its totality. Just as the unconscious exceeds the id, human life exceeds reason. Logotherapy rejects any position which idolizes either instinct or reason.

Conscience

Frankl's psychology attributes an important role in human life to conscience: to bring meaning to light (1969, 63–67; 1975, 115–19). Conscience leads and guides in the search for meaning, intuiting (directly grasping) the unique patterns of meaning latent in each of life's unique situations, the requirements of the given situation (1969, 63). Conscience is irreducible in human life: there is no psychological mechanism (such as identification) behind it that causes it to rise and to which it can be traced back. Conscience is simply itself, belonging to the noological dimension of human life and performing a role that it alone can. Frankl remarks that conscience has not yet had its say so long as human motivation remains extrinsically grounded in either the fear of punishment or the hope of reward.

Conscience and the Specifically Human Unconscious

Conscience, reaching down in its origin into the prereflective depths of human existence, stems from an unconscious ground. The unconsciousness of conscience is that of the specifically human—eminently personal rather than prepersonal or impersonal—unconscious. Conscience is unconscious in that it belongs, in what is most itself, to the inaccessible depth and activity of the person. Frankl sees the important, authentically human decisions as taking place entirely on the level of lived experience: conscience is the person exercising moral judgment unconsciously, at a level inaccessible to reflection. Conscience precedes all logic and conceptual argumentation; its operations can never be rationally explained or justified (1975, 33). Frankl takes conscience as a model of the specifically human unconscious for the light it is able to shed on the subject (1975, 33–39).

The Intuitive Character of Conscience

Conscience is the intuitive capacity of human existence to discover the meaning inherent in a given situation. Frankl points out that what is revealed to *consciousness* is something that *is* but that what becomes manifest to *conscience* is what *ought* to be. What ought to be is not anything real, not an existing actuality, but a possibility. What ought to be, while belonging to the realm of the possible, is nevertheless viewed as necessary—an ethical necessity. In anticipating something not yet actual, conscience is an intuiting that anticipates something to be made real—something that ought to be realized (1975, 34). The task of conscience is to bring to light the "unique and necessary meaning" ahead of us in the world (1969, 19; 1975, 35). Conscience discovers what we are to be responsible to, that which we are to answer to in each of life's situations, the unique meaning to be fulfilled. Frankl remarks that what conscience unearths as "ought to be realized" is prior to responsibleness. The "ought" revealed by conscience is that *to* which we are now free (freedom to).

Because meanings are particular and unique for each situated individual, Frankl says we cannot look to any universal law for answers. Conscience alone can serve to discover what is to be done in a given situation and how it is to be done. In an age such as ours, characterized by meaninglessness and the eclipse of conventional values, Frankl thinks that education must do more than convey bits of information. It must help our young people develop their individual consciences, which is to say, help them grow in the capacity to discover for themselves objectively valid meanings worth living for (1975, 120).

Conscience and Love

Frankl draws an analogy between conscience and love (1975, 34). The meaning of love is seen to lie in living the uniqueness of another person's experience (1962, 149–83; 1978, 67). Love is no mere emotion or intrapsychic condition, in Frankl's view, but an intentional act in and by which, transcending ourselves, we reach the other's essence as a human being. Love is a timeless and imperishable act whose essence not even death can touch (1962, 154). In an envisioning of something not yet real, love, like conscience, intuits its object. What love is said to refer to (its "intentional referent"), however, is not an ethical necessity but a personal possibility. Love reveals possibilities of existence in the other yet to be made real.

Both conscience and love are said to have to do with an absolutely unique object (1975, 36). Conscience enables us to grasp a situation's unique meaning, to discover the one and only thing required of us in a situation. Love, on the other hand, enables the discovery of the unique potentialities inherent in the person loved, the uniqueness of the loved one. Meaning, for Frankl, is always both ideal—ahead of us, not yet real—and unique. Love, like conscience, is an irreducibly human phenomenon rooted in the intuitive depths of the specifically human unconscious. Both love and conscience are held to belong to that essential self-transcendence of human existence where the meaning of life is located.

While imagining and clinging to his wife's image in a Nazi concentration camp—he says his wife was "there" with him—Frankl first discovered for himself the truth that love is the ultimate and highest goal to which one can aspire (1963, 58–59, 63). Our salvation, he writes, is "through love and in love" (1963, 59). Frankl points out that the inspiration of the artist parallels the intuition characteristic of both conscience and love (1975, 37). All specifically human activity necessarily stems from an unconscious source. Where the specifically human self immerses itself in its unconscious depths, there, Frankl comments, occur conscience, love, and art (1975, 39).

The Transcendent Quality of Conscience

Phenomenological analysis also reveals a further quality of conscience. If it is agreed that we are called upon to engage in the active exercise of our conscience and serve it, Frankl says we may well ask whom we are serving, who it is that is doing the calling. This "who," Frankl comments, may be someone other and higher than ourselves. Frankl argues that we cannot truly be the servant of conscience unless conscience is a phenomenon that transcends our lives, unless conscience is an intermediary for some other reality (1975, 52–59). The human being, Frankl writes, "cannot be its own lawmaker" (1975, 57). In the phenomena of conscience, rather, a transhuman agent is said to be "sounding through" (1975, 53). On the farther side of conscience, in Frankl's view, "stands an extra-human authority" (1962, xx).

Frankl thus insists that we are not responsible to ourselves alone. Responsibleness instead depends on a being higher than ourselves for the validity of the demands made upon our lives. Not only our being free, but our being responsible as well, must have something *to which* it is referred. Just as freedom only makes sense as freedom *to* something, *to* meaning, so, too, it is argued, is responsibleness only completely understood as responsibleness *to* something, *to* "transcendence." Just as freedom requires the "to what" of a meaning that precedes it, so, too, responsibleness requires the "to what" of transcendence preceding it.

Because his concern with the origin of conscience is centered on the human being and not God—because his discipline is psychology and not theology—Frankl has little more to say about the transhuman agent that sounds through conscience and to which we humans are ultimately responsible. But he does say that this agent is necessarily personal, or, more accurately, "superpersonal" in nature, and that the human person is an image of sorts of this superpersonal agent (1975, 53–54). The "to what" of conscience and responsibleness must be a "to whom." In this way, conscience, which Frankl chose as a model of the specifically human unconscious, discloses the essential transcendence of our specifically human unconscious depths to a superpersonal dimension. The fact of conscience reveals the human being as directed beyond itself to a higher dimension.

Not only does human existence *transcend* itself to meaning (see above, "Intentionality and Self-Transcendence"), then, but to a higher, superpersonal dimension as well—to *transcendence*. Transcendence speaks through conscience. As the voice of transcendence, Frankl says, conscience must be recognized as itself *transcendent* (1975, 54–55). Since it is not easy to recognize the transcendent character of the voice that speaks through conscience, Frankl does not find it surprising that some take this voice to have a merely human character. Frankl points out that such individuals nevertheless do have a conscience and do respond to it. Preferring to stay on solid ground and not to venture into the uncertainty beyond, however, these people stop at responsibleness to conscience.

Frankl comments that it takes the religious individual to "hazard the hidden summit" (1975, 56). Such an individual, said to be possessed of a keener sensitivity, recognizes both the task and the taskmaster, hears the speaker as well as what is spoken (1962, xiv). All in all, it is Frankl's view that an adequate theory of the specifically human or noological dimension needs to recognize the openness of human existence to a higher dimension. Frankl remarks that some who admit transcendence do not feel it necessary to call this dimension "God" but that others see no reason not to use this age-old name.

Conscience is not only directed to a higher dimension of transcendence, in Frankl's view, but originates in it as well (1975, 56). This is said to account for conscience's irreducible quality. Frankl argues that any attempt to reduce conscience to an introjected father-image—superego—is in vain. He points out, for example, that it is not uncommon for conscience to challenge the conventional standards of the superego: conscience often enough takes the individual down paths where it becomes his or her duty to violate merely tribal codes (1969, 63). Attempts to reduce conscience to a lower dimension are able neither to account for it nor to dispense with it. Frankl thus finds conscience to be an irreducibly human phenomenon indicative of a transhuman origin.

The Hidden God

Frankl comments that the human and the divine (transcendence) belong to different dimensions, as do the animal and the human (1969, 142–57). The ways of God are said to be as much above the ways of human beings as the heavens are above the earth. We humans can nevertheless trust in God, the ultimate *being,* and on that basis reach out in faith for the ultimate *meaning*—trust in God, for Frankl, comes before faith in the ultimate meaning.

Humans in a way can understand animals, Frankl remarks, but animals cannot understand humans (1969, 144–45). Nor can animals understand their own suffering, which is only comprehensible in the human dimension. In the higher transhuman dimension—the dimension of transcendence (see above, "The Transcendent Quality of Conscience")—Frankl says the question of the ultimate meaning of human existence might find an answer—one not accessible on its own noological level. The higher dimension being referred to is the theological, the space of the ultimate being, the divine.

Some people insist that God be visible. But Frankl points out that when one is standing on a stage, the audience is invisible (1969, 152–53). We are said to be standing on the stage of life and to be unable to see before whom we are playing our part and to whom we bear responsibility for its proper execution. In the glare of the foreground of daily life, Frankl says, we sometimes forget we are being observed. Referring to ultimate meaning, Frankl remarks that the more comprehensive meaning is, the less comprehensible it becomes (1978, 59). A finite being is in no position to grasp infinite meaning.

The difference of dimensions between the human and the divine keeps us from really being able to speak *of* God. Frankl says to talk about God is to turn being itself, that which is beyond all beings, into a being (1969, 146)—compare the words of French philosopher Gabriel Marcel: "When we speak of God, it is not of God that we speak" (1964, 36). Frankl says, however, that we may pray, that we may speak *to* God.

Frankl asserts that, in our day, God is not dead but silent and hidden, as always (1969, 154).

Unconscious Religiousness

All in all, Frankl claims to have uncovered, through phenomenological analysis, a latent relation to transcendence inherent in human nature: an "unconscious religiousness" (1975, 60–70). One approach to such religiousness, we have seen, is through the phenomenon of conscience (see above, "The Transcendent Quality of Conscience"). Frankl says that unconscious religiousness can be thought of as a relationship between the human self and divine transcendence, between the human "I" and "the Thou beyond human nature." Frankl indeed says we couldn't lift a single finger if not saturated in the depths of our being with a basic trust in the ultimate meaning (1969, 150–51). Without such trust, breathing would cease. One cannot live, says Frankl, without trust in meaning.

Frankl comments that human existence has always stood in a relation to something beyond itself. We are directed to transcendence, even if only unconsciously. Frankl thinks that people are often much more religious than they think (1962, xx). If the object of such an unconscious relation is called "God," Frankl says we can speak of an "unconscious God" (1975, 61–62). He is quick to point out, however, that this is not to say that God is unconscious, only that human beings may be unconscious of the divine and of their relation to it. The phrase "unconscious God" refers, then, to our "hidden relation to a hidden God."

In addition to rejecting the idea that God is unconscious, Frankl also rejects the pantheistic notion that the unconscious is God or that it has any of God's attributes. Frankl thus denies that our unconscious relation to the divine is to a God "within us" (1975, 63). Profoundly personal in character, the "unconscious God" is no "impersonal force" at work within human nature—no instinct (1975, 63). While Frankl credits Jung with discovering distinctly religious aspects in the unconscious, he is said to have missed the eminently personal character of the "unconscious God." Jung places God among the instincts, among the archetypes, explicitly defined by him as "instincts capable of representation." God is thus conceived of as an autonomous "power" *in* the psyche.

Jung is thus found to hold to an unconscious religiousness beyond personal deciding, a religious drive in the collective unconscious impelling the ego to the divine. But, Frankl insists, human religiousness is a deeply individual decision, one that cannot be derived from a collective psyche, from an impersonal drive, from "archetypes of the collective unconscious" (1975, 64). Frankl indeed insists that the human being's relation to the divine is not something that takes place within the psyche at all, as Jung claims. The human relation to the divine is rather *to* transcendence, to that which is radically beyond human life and all lower dimensions, to the "other."

Religiousness, for Frankl, then, is a question of personal "decidingness," not of impersonal "driven-ness" (1975, 64). For Jung (and Freud), the unconscious, outside of the ego, by and large determines the ego. For Frankl, the self, deeply personal right down to its unconscious roots, is a deciding self. For Jung (and even more so for Freud), religiousness is an affair of psychological conditions. For Frankl, religiousness properly belongs to the noological dimension. Specifically, human unconscious religiousness, Frankl writes, is an "existential agent rather than an unconscious factor" (1975, 65).

Unconscious religiousness for Frankl, then, rather than stemming from "autonomous powers," from "an impersonal pool of images shared by humankind," stems from a personal center (1975, 65). Religion is thus seen as involving the most personal of human decisions, even if made on an unconscious level. The specifically human unconscious, and, even more, its religious aspects, the religious unconscious, decides. Relation to the divine springs from the depths of the personal core of human existence. Frankl points out that personal religiousness is shaped by preexisting cultural forms. We enter at birth into a world of symbols, which we both adopt and adapt (1975, 66). No one has to invent God.

Frankl comments that the religiousness inherent in human life may never become conscious in the first place (1975, 67–70). Then again, having become conscious, it may be forced back out of awareness. Human religiousness can be repressed. Indeed, what is said to be repressed nowadays is not instinct (sexuality) but noological meaning, not *Eros* but *Logos* (1967, 87; 1975, 130). Even buried in the unconscious, however, repressed transcendence is found to make its appearance as an "unrest of the heart." Frankl says that it is a task of therapy to bring repressed religiousness back to mind.

Frankl says that what Freud discovered in the realm of sexuality holds for the religious domain as well, and indeed for human life in general: repression winds up in neurosis. The basis of neurotic existence thus sometimes lies in the repression of transcendence. Frankl cites clinical evidence that suggests that compulsive neurosis may well be religiousness in a diseased state (1975, 69; compare Freud's view, chapter 2, "Religion as 'Universal Compulsive Neurosis'"). When the angel in us is repressed, Frankl comments, it turns into a devil. Repressed religion often enough makes its return ("return of the repressed") in the form of superstition. Frankl remarks that religion in our day has been sacrificed to "the repressive structures of reason" made into God and to technology characterized by delusions of grandeur (1975, 70). This sacrifice of transcendence is said to explain much of our present situation, which indeed does resemble a "universal compulsive neurosis of humankind." Frankl says that God is a vengeful God: neurosis is sometimes the price we pay for a "crippled relation to transcendence" (1975, 70).

At times in therapy, Frankl says he comes across an unconscious belief, an "invisible religiousness," even in the "visibly irreligious person." It is just that the patient has not yet become conscious of the "unconscious God." In any case, it is pointed out that true religiousness cannot be forced but must develop in its own time and be freely chosen; therapy must leave the door open to individual spontaneity (1975, 71–72). Frankl is of the opinion that people will stop believing that religion is the sublimation of unruly instincts, that they are "sublimated animals," once they come to realize that there is within them a repressed relation to transcendence, a "repressed angel" (1975, 59). Frankl relates that many prisoners in Nazi concentration camps went through a religious conversion, their repressed relation to the divine breaking through in even these most trying of circumstances: "and the light shineth in the darkness" (1963, 63–64; 1967, 99). Unconscious religiousness is also found to break through unexpectedly in the lives of psychotics.

The ultimate meaning is not attainable by rational thought (1969, 145–46). Human intellect is simply too limited, in Frankl's view, to encompass transcendence and come to grips with the ultimate meaning. The ultimate meaning can only be grasped, Frankl says, "out of our whole being, which is to say, through faith" (1969, 145). The ultimate meaning of reality yields not to rational thought, then, but to existential commitment. We are called upon to decide between the alternatives of ultimate absurdity and ultimate meaning through the life we lead (1967, 33). Frankl says that we decide, decision by decision, upon ourselves. Once again, what we become depends on what we choose to do.

Dreams and the Specifically Human Unconscious

Dreams are said to be the true creations of the unconscious. Psychoanalysis analyzes dreams in order to render unconscious instinctual processes conscious. Frankl extends such efforts to the specifically human unconscious (1975, 40–51). He reports success in this application of Freudian methodology to noological space: elements of the specifically human unconscious have indeed been found to come forward for integration into consciousness and responsibleness.

Some dreams spontaneously reveal repressed religiousness. One occasionally finds, Frankl says, "flagrantly religious motifs" in the dreams of "manifestly irreligious" individuals (1975, 48). A dormant religiosity is thus seen to be released in psychotherapy, and the patient's life to take a decided turn for the better (1967, 166). Frankl remarks that some religious dreams are striking in the ecstatic bliss they bring, a bliss unknown in waking life. One unbeliever, encountering in her dream a great light and coming once again to belong to God, experienced "a wonderful feeling of joy, humility, love, shelteredness" (1967, 178). Through the analysis of dreams, Frankl thus finds not only repressed instinct but repressed religiousness as well.

The Future of Religion

Frankl does not see religion as dying or God as dead, even after the Holocaust. Belief in God has to be unconditional, in his view, or it is not worthy of the name (1975, 15). We may not set a threshold of human tragedy beyond which we will abandon belief. Frankl says that the truth of the matter is that far more of those who suffered the terrors of Auschwitz grew in their religiousness than gave it up. Catastrophe is seen to weaken weak faith but to strengthen strong faith (1975, 15). Frankl remarks that religion apparently cannot be wiped out, not even by psychosis. Freudian psychoanalysis sees God as a projected father (1975, 58). Frankl counters that some people have a bad father-image, out of which projection could never have constructed a good God. In point of fact, he remarks, a deep religious life can provide just the means needed to overcome a bad father-image and hatred of one's father (1963, 210).

Frankl takes "religion" in its broadest possible sense. Thus conceived, religion goes beyond the limited concept of God proclaimed by certain ecclesiastical institutions (1975, 13). Frankl isn't interested in an infantile God who throws temper tantrums—such a God is indeed a projection. Frankl thinks God must *not* be portrayed the way many representatives of institutional religion in fact portray him, as someone who wants most of all to be believed in and who requires people to become members of the institution being represented. Frankl does not find the trend away from religion as such, but from those denominations that are preoccupied with attacking each other and proving they are always right. The trend, Frankl thinks, is away from emphasizing the differences between churches.

A manipulative attempt is seen to underlie any attempt to render faith, hope, and charity capable of being ordered into existence (1975, 14). Faith, hope, and charity are intentional acts, with proper intentional objects of their own. When they are turned into things at our disposal, however, both their character as acts and the objects to which they are directed are said to be lost sight of. Faith, for example, is a trusting relation to transcendence, not something we can seize hold of. We cannot "get faith," no matter how determinedly we are told we must "have faith" or how hard we try. If you want to cheer someone up, Frankl says, you don't order him or her to laugh; you tell a joke. It is said to be the same with religion (1975, 14–15). If you want people to believe, you don't preach at them but point in the direction of the object of faith by portraying your God believably and by being believable yourself.

Religions, like languages, are systems of symbols. Just as it cannot properly be claimed that one language is superior to another, so, too, Frankl argues, it cannot be claimed that one religion is better than another (1969, 153). Frankl does not see the trend as toward a universal religion but toward a profoundly personalized one. Each individual, Frankl says, is to find his own words "when addressing himself to the ultimate being" (1969, 154). Genuine religiousness is said to conceal itself from public view (1975, 47).

Frankl thinks that, in the final analysis, religion may be said to be an experience of our fragmentariness and relativity in relation to the nonfragmentary and the nonrelative. This experience of fragmentariness and relativity is said to be the religious individual's sense of being sheltered and safe. What the seeker has sought is said to be always there and to be given to the seeker not in its "whatness" but in its pure "thatness." We are always directed beyond ourselves; we are always being taken beyond. Frankl states that the religious person is always directed to God, but God is always beyond. God is called upon by the religious person, but God remains silent.

EVALUATION AND CONCLUSIONS

Psychology has yet to address Frankl's (phenomenology's) critical distinction between psychological act and nonpsychological meaning. True to its Cartesian heritage, mainstream psychology continues to regard meanings as images populating an inner, closed, and private domain of consciousness—the Cartesian *res cogitans*—and the world, including the human body and brain, as a realm of pure spatial extension—the Cartesian *res extensa*. Viewing consciousness as a relationship to the world constituted—as indeed we find it—as a network of meanings, Frankl has made a definitive break with the notions both of the mind as situated inside itself and of the world as "an army of molecules" (William James).

With consciousness no longer an inner realm of mind, no longer either is the unconscious a mind beneath or below such an inner mind, a "mind behind the mind." So engaged in lifeworld meaning is human life that it has no access to its own origin—thus Frankl's important redefinition of the unconscious as the inaccessible depth of the human relation to meaning, the hidden depth of the human being's "beyondness" to its other. Essentially personal in character, the unconscious is no impersonal force of nature.

Mainstream psychology, in its attempts at a "scientific" account of human behavior, has invoked any number of mechanisms. Human life, Frankl counters, is not mechanistically governed by forces of whatever sort—biological, psychological, or environmental. Frankl calls for a personal, not a mechanistic-causal, rendering of behavior. Particularly worthy of note is his critique of the tension-reduction model of motivation. Needs are not expressions of an objective organism (*res extensa*), he argues, but intensely personal relations to meaning. It is not some "it" that wants, not a quantum of impersonal energy seeking to cancel itself out, but someone, profoundly invested in its world.

Frankl, with phenomenology in general, rejects the philosophical presupposition of "psychologism." Psychologism, the belief that the laws governing meaning belong to the psyche—and not to meaning itself—is an essential feature of mainstream psychology: beauty, truth, goodness, and the like are defined as constructions of the brain/mind. Rejecting this nihilism, Frankl insists that meanings, possessed of intrinsic laws—an "intrinsic requiredness" or value—of their own, challenge us from beyond, from their place in the lifeworld.

Religion, Frankl says, is the "search for ultimate meaning," for the final reason for the unconditional meaningfulness of life. Frankl says that everyone has, at least in his or her unconscious depths, a relation to the ultimate being. Frankl's notions of a spiritual unconscious and a personal relation to an unconscious God are provocative ones, as are his reports of the clinical discovery of unconscious religiousness.

Frankl sees one and only one meaning as laid out in advance, there for the discovery and the choosing, in any given situation. This position is open to challenge on a number of fronts. Existential phenomenologists, such as Martin Heidegger and Maurice Merleau-Ponty, for example, have recognized that meanings come into being, in part, through the activities of a historically and communally situated human being. Meanings are thus seen not as pregiven, as Frankl argues, but as emerging in time and as codefining, in their emergence, an emerging human life. The tendency today, on the other hand, is the utter subjectivization of meaning and, so, Frankl's insistence on the objectivity of meaning—properly understood and stripped of any sort of predestinationism—may appear to many as a breath of fresh air.

REFERENCES

Frankl, V. E. *The Doctor and the Soul: An Introduction to Logotherapy*. New York: Alfred A. Knopf, 1962.
———. *Man's Search for Meaning: An Introduction to Logotherapy*. New York: Washington Square Press, 1963.
———. *Psychotherapy and Existentialism: Selected Papers on Logotherapy*. New York: Simon and Schuster, 1967.
———. *The Will to Meaning: Foundations and Applications of Logotherapy*. New York: World, 1969.
———. *The Unconscious God: Psychotherapy and Theology*. New York: Simon and Schuster, 1975.
———. *The Unheard Cry for Meaning: Psychotherapy and Humanism*. New York: Simon and Schuster, 1978.
Fuller, A. R. *Insight into Value: An Exploration of the Premises of a Phenomenological Psychology*. Albany: State University of New York Press, 1990.
Marcel, G. *Creative Fidelity*. New York: Farrar, Straus, 1964.

9

✝

Developments

Isn't it obvious that there is a Biblical truth *and* a Darwinian truth (and many others as well), each of which functions within a particular perspective and a particular language game?

—Paul Pruyser

This chapter reviews a number of developments in the psychology of religion for the most part subsequent to the work surveyed in the first eight chapters. Authors discussed are Donald W. Winnicott, Paul W. Pruyser, Ana-Maria Rizzuto, and Antoine Vergote on object relations and God-images; Bernard Spilka and C. Daniel Batson on the scaling of religiousness; and Stanislov Grof on modern consciousness research and experiential—"holotropic"—psychotherapy.

DONALD WINNICOTT

According to Freud, human life runs its course essentially inside the psyche in pursuit of tension reduction. Environmental objects, by this view, stand in a fundamentally accidental relation to the tension to be reduced. It was not long, however, before a number of psychoanalytic theorists challenged the Freudian view, arguing for an intrinsic, rather than an adventitious, relation between drive and satisfying object. Thus did a mechanistic account of an internal economy of energies yield to an interpersonal account of the child's relations to significant others. Thus did "object relations" arise in the psychoanalytic tradition.

British psychoanalyst and pediatrician Donald W. Winnicott is well known for his pioneering work in object relations theory. Winnicott points out that the child, in his or her development as a separate person, has the troublesome task of coming to recognize the external reality of objects. In order for this acceptance of the object as an entity in its own right to take place, says Winnicott, the child has to place the object outside his or her omnipotent control, a development that is seen as the "most difficult thing" and "the most irksome of all the early failures" (1971, 89). Winnicott's originality lies in his notion of "an intermediate area of experience" in human development between the infant's "primary creativity," with its omnipotent control of the object, and "objective perception based on reality-testing," between the subjective or conceptual world the infant lives in and objective perception (1971, 2, 11). The terms "transitional phenomena" and "transitional object" refer to this intermediate area of experiencing.

The transitional object, such as a teddy bear or cuddly blanket, eases the child's passage from inner independence, in the form of a hallucinating of satisfying objects, to an actual dealing with outer objects. The transitional object arises neither from within nor from without. It is not an internal object, not a concept under the child's control, but a possession—in Winnicott's phrase, the "original not-me possession" (1971, 4). Neither is it an external object. The transitional object, rather, occupies a place midway between inner and outer experience, inner and outer reality. With both inner and outer realms making their contribution to it, the transitional object is thus able to help in the crucial transition from the former to the latter: in other words, in the child's acceptance of hard reality. This assistance is through the consolation the transitional object offers. Winnicott points out that the transitional object is very important to the child. The parents recognize this and, so, for example, take it along on vacations.

Winnicott says the transitional object typically stands for the mother's breast. The teddy bear or piece of blanket is a symbol for the infant of its union with the mother (mother's breast). The symbol is said to arise precisely when and where the transition is taking place from the infant's being merged with the mother to its perceiving of her as a separate being. The transitional object thus symbolizes the *union* of now *separate* infant and mother (1971, 96–97).

Winnicott remarks that the infant is at first under the illusion that the mother's breast is part of its body and under its magical—omnipotent—control—that it creates the breast time and again out of need. The mother, Winnicott says, gives rise to this illusion: she offers the breast just when and where the infant is ready to create it. The infant creates the breast, but it wouldn't have been created if it weren't already there. The breast is, in Winnicott's words, a "subjective phenomenon," a "subjective object." On the one hand, this object is the object of the infant's first relationship. Yet, on the other, it is experienced as part of itself and not outer reality. The mother's breast thus differs from the transitional object to which it yields: the subjective object is not yet "a not-me phenomenon" (1971, 80–81).

Not fully objective, the subjective object, through the mother's fostering of illusion, comes to be "gradually related to objects that are objectively perceived" (1971, 71). The illusion the mother produces in the infant that it creates the breast is crucial, Winnicott says, for the development of a relationship to externally real objects (1971, 1). The transitional object, it has been said, is a symbol of the union of mother and infant. The teddy bear or piece of blanket unites what has been separated and does so in the manner of illusion. The transitional object represents the "mother's ability to present the world in such a way that the infant does not at first have to know that the object is not created by the infant" (1971, 81). The transitional object, like the mother's breast, which the infant creates even as it is presented, is a matter of illusion. Illusion is the intermediate state between the infant's "inability and his growing ability to recognize and accept reality" (1971, 3). The transitional object, the first "not-me possession," smoothes the way over to hard reality. Unlike the inner concept, the transitional object is never under the child's omnipotent control but represents the child's passing from magical control to control by using.

It is precisely the illusory character of the transitional object that softens the blow of the infant's loss of omnipotent control over the object. The teddy bear is the child's very own, a soothing illusion that no one will challenge: no one will ever ask of the child, "Did you conceive of this or was it presented to you from without?" (1971, 12). Belonging to the intermediate area of experience that, in Winnicott's words, is a "resting-place for the individual engaged in the perpetual task of keeping inner and outer reality separate yet interrelated," the child will not be disillusioned in its regard (1971, 2). The infant is thus not challenged as to the difference between the subjective and the objective precisely where the transitional object is concerned. All in all, transitional phenomena—the subjective object (mother's breast), transitional object (teddy bear or cuddly blanket)— make it possible to "cope with the immense shock of loss of omnipotence" (1971, 71).

Winnicott characterizes the intermediate area between inner psychic reality and the actual world where transitional phenomena originate as one of play: the transitional object represents the first instance of play (1971, 96). Both joining and separating infant and mother, the intermediate area of experience eventually expands out into "creative living" and our entire cultural life (1971, 102). Creativity and culture thus belong, in Winnicott's view, to the third area intermediate between inner and outer reality, the same "potential space" that prevailed between mother and child at the time of their separation and the child's acceptance of objective reality

(1971, 107). The "infinite area of separation," Winnicott says, is now filled with playing, with symbols, and with shared cultural life (1971, 108). Thus does intermediate experiencing negate the separation of mother and infant.

And so, Winnicott sees culture as originating in the potential space where creative activity first manifests itself as play. We are said never to be finished with the task of accepting objective reality. The unchallenged intermediate area of experiencing—culture in general—provides relief from the strain of having forever to relate inner and outer reality (1971, 13).

Winnicott cites art and religion as resulting from the expanding out of transitional phenomena from the child's transitional object to culture in general. We have seen that no one challenges the infant on the transitional object: no one asks whether the teddy bear is subjectively conceived or objectively presented. This unchallenged character is retained in the intense experiencing in evidence in art and religion—and creative cultural living in general. The illusion allowed in infancy is thus continued into adult life. All in all, then, religion, in Winnicott's view, is a transitional phenomenon, an illusion functioning in the intermediate space between inner and outer reality.

Others have elaborated on Winnicott's provocative suggestions on religious psychology (see below, "Paul Pruyser" and "Ana-Maria Rizzuto"; the sections on Winnicott, Pruyser, and Rizzuto illuminate each other and are best studied in light of one another—the section on Pruyser is particularly helpful, for example, in coming to grips with Winnicott's difficult notion of illusion). Given Winnicott's view of the pivotal role of the mother in the origin of illusion, on the one hand, and his definition of religion in terms of illusion, on the other, Winnicott may be seen as marking a significant departure from Freud's view of the exclusive role of relations to the father in the origin of religion.

PAUL PRUYSER

Paul W. Pruyser, deeply influenced by William James, Freud, and Winnicott, has been an important figure in the psychoanalytic approach to religion in recent decades. Psychology, Pruyser insists, must be interested in human object relations with God, in our concepts and images of God and their development. Pruyser's reflections on object relations with God are here considered in terms of his three books, *A Dynamic Psychology of Religion* (1968), *Between Belief and Unbelief* (1974), and *The Play of the Imagination: Toward a Psychoanalysis of Culture* (1983). The latter two works are especially concerned with Winnicott's intermediate sphere of play and illusion.

Pruyser points out that a new affinity between God and humans has been brought to light by psychoanalysis (1968). The awareness that family relations shape our image of God and the names we give him has shortened the psychological distance between the divine and the human. Pruyser points out in a general way, moreover, that "our psychic organization, our perceptions, our thoughts, our wishes, our moods participate in the shaping of our beliefs" (1968, 8). Religion does not descend upon us from above, then, but is interwoven with our experience of ourselves, our parents, and our world. Religious ideas are, accordingly, necessarily distorted and approximate.

Pruyser agrees with Gordon Allport's dictum that "all of human life revolves around desire" (1968, 201). He points out that an important function of religion is to come to terms with human desires. Religion, he comments, sometimes helps fulfill desire, sometimes modifies desire, sometimes allows the expression of some desires and forbids the expression of others, and sometimes is suspicious of desire quite in general. Considering object relations in terms of desire, Pruyser remarks that objects aren't "sought for their own sake, but as satisfiers of desires" (1968, 222). An individual's relations to objects, say, to another human being, originate in, and are maintained by, desires actively seeking expression. The object, Pruyser remarks, has no inner power to compel an otherwise passive human being. He says this applies to our relations to the object God as well. Needs, wishes, and longing are involved in all human relations to the divine. People do not irresistibly move toward God by reason of an invincible "drawing power" on God's part (1968, 223). Both subject and object are described, rather, as "dynamic partners in any bond." Pruyser says we gain in maturity by realizing the contribution of our drives and needs to the power of the object over us, reducing that power and gaining in flexibility in our choice of objects.

Maturity involves decreased relations of dependence on other human beings. Pruyser points out that adult dependence on God is nevertheless not only allowed but at times encouraged (1968, 224). A continuing, even increasing, dependence on God might be accounted for as a compensation for renounced infantile dependence on other human beings. Pruyser nevertheless points out that some individuals, wanting to get on with their life, are happy to grow up and come to stand on their own two feet (1968, 225). A parallelism is thus sometimes found between relations to others and relations to God: dependence on God is at times outgrown at the same rate as dependence on others.

Reference has been made to the shortening of the psychological distance brought about by psychoanalysis between the human and the divine. Pruyser points out, however, that not only similarities, but differences, exist between our relations to others and to God. First, as regards

differences in the nature of the object, relations to a parent are not relations to a creator. "Creators and creatures are of incomparable dimensions," Pruyser writes, "whether the former are fictitious or not" (1968,
225). Next, as regards differences in aim, while the aim in human relations
to humans has been portrayed in sexual terms, the aim in human relations
to the divine is "far more cognitive, ethical, and esthetic" (1968, 227). Finally, as regards differences in satisfaction, satisfactions derived from relations to the divine are far more disclosive than those derived from relations to others. The "blissful state of being nurtured, cuddled, smiled
upon, wanted, and put at ease" by others is not the "tense and daring situation of encountering the novel, the awesome, of having one's power of
comprehension stretched to the limit" (1968, 227).

The above is but a fraction of what Pruyser has to say in *A Dynamic Psychology of Religion*, which also considers perceptual, intellectual, linguistic,
and emotional processes in religion; organization of thought in religion; religion and the motor system; and relations to things and ideas, and to the
self. Pruyser has expanded on illusion and the illusionistic sphere as defined by Winnicott in the other two works cited (1974, 1983). Illusion formation, Pruyser says, is a "unique process" deriving from the imagination
(1983, 165). The illusionistic products of the imagination, when successful,
are "linked with, but formally different from, the realities of the outer
world and the *common* human stratum of the inner world" (1983, 166).
While doing so with "seriousness and utter dedication," the intermediate
illusionistic sphere opts for "fun, zest, and venturesomeness" (1974, 240).
Illusion—a term Pruyser reserves for the phenomena of culture—enriches
us with such goods as literature, music, painting, drama, religious ideas,
and ethical propositions (1974, 166). All in all, Pruyser speaks of the illusionistic sphere as the "matrix of growth and culture and the beginning of
the human spirit" (1974, 240).

Religion's two key terms, Pruyser remarks, are mystery and transcendence, and he finds a promising approach to these, as well as to the holy,
in Winnicott's notions of the illusionistic sphere (1974, 108). The child
stands in a special relation to the transitional object (teddy bear, cuddly
blanket), which is "his property, his cherished symbol" (1974, 111). In
Pruyser's words, "The transitional object is the transcendent": it transcends
the division between "the mental image produced by the mind itself and
the objective perceptual image produced by the real world impinging upon
the sensory system" (1974, 111). Illusion is not only transcendent, Pruyser
points out, but involves mystery as well: the transitional object has a number of "surplus values" one does not question (1974, 111). Finally, illusion
involves the holy: the transitional object is special and, indeed, regarded as
sacred (1974, 111). Neither outer objects nor inner fictions, the holy, the
transcendent, and mystery, Pruyser remarks, arise precisely in the interme-

diate transitional sphere of reality. According to Winnicott, the transitional sphere marks the beginnings of play—in Pruyser's words, of "an infinite playful relation between mind and world" (1974, 112)—and, among other things, of religion.

Pruyser says that religion deals with beings neither given in the external world nor of an inexpressible, inner, and private character. On the one hand, religion, directed not to the tangible but the ultimately real world, "revels in the 'reality of the unseen,'" while, on the other, religion is a "visible public affair" that has "changed the face of the earth" (1983, 152–53). Religion has indeed been characterized as "the illusionistic enterprise par excellence" (1983, 152).

Pruyser joins Paul Tillich in finding symbols to be "dynamic representations" that participate in what they point to (1983, 154). Revealing and concealing at the same time, symbols "mediate between the seen and the unseen." "With one leg in the concrete world," symbols potentially disclose "a truth not yet fully grasped." Symbols, seen as exercising their proper function in the illusionistic sphere, bring the primary process under cultural norms. Certain fantasies, according to Pruyser, thus attain a measure of objectivity within a culture. Religious symbols, such as "God," "nirvana," and "human dignity," elaborating the transitional sphere, come to wrap up shared cultural ideals. Freud, in Pruyser's view, identified illusion too narrowly with pleasure-oriented wish fulfillment. Insofar as an illusion is an ideal, Pruyser points out, it is not a mere wish fulfillment but imposes the demand of achieving a certain goal. There is a "common value of excellence or completeness" in the living symbols of a culture (1974, 201).

Religion "transforms human experience into an imaginative, illusionistic conception sui generis" (1983, 165). Individuals, confronted with death, guilt, and evil, and thus their essential limitations, are often rendered speechless. Through the symbols of religion, Pruyser writes, people are better able to come to terms with such experiences than through reason. Only the "finely tutored imagination," he comments, seems up to the task of fashioning an "illusionistic product" adequate to the range of the experience under discussion (1983, 178).

Belief arises, according to Pruyser, out of a play that brings inner and outer reality together—the greatest gift, he says, is "to play and make beliefs" (1974, 269). In the third illusionistic sphere, "one comes to the thought of a Ground of Being, or of a God behind the gods, or of the Holy which is no longer confined to burning bushes, altars, amulets, and fatherly caretakers," but found "in star and cells, in evolution" and the beauty of certain scientific formulations (1974, 241).

Pruyser sees illusion's validation as lying in one's encounter with the transitional object itself, and not from somewhere else. Religion, like art, comes from itself, is itself, and gives rise to itself (1974, 229). The "playful, inventive, and insightful" mode of thought characteristic of the illusion-istic sphere, Pruyser says, has its own "consensual validation" (1974, 217–18). There are, moreover, poor and good fantasies, childish and so-phisticated religion, bad and good art. These are to be judged on their own ground: "Fantasy, myths, the imagination, symbols, art, and religion will have to be evaluated not by comparison with something else, but by standards that evolve from within each of these activities" (1974, 194).

Pruyser points out that the illusionistic sphere of religion, with its sym-bols, is susceptible to perversion both in the autistic and the realistic di-rection. The realistic danger consists in treating "religious illusionistic ideas or entities" as belonging to external reality (1983, 166). The autistic danger consists in the religious imagination running wild, concocting vampires, demons, and gods sitting on clouds keeping tabs on human be-havior. Many believers are "exceedingly childish, drive-determined, and self-seeking" (1974, 227). Pruyser views an orientation to reality as needed in order to keep "the boundless and dangerous impulsivity of the autistic world" in check (1983, 176). A positivist realism, on the other hand, fail-ing to take into account the proper functioning of the third illusionistic sphere, thus considering illusions to be errors, distortions, and mistakes, tends to smother the imagination and, hence, to truncate human poten-tialities (1983, 176).

ANA-MARIA RIZZUTO

Ana-Maria Rizzuto, a psychoanalyst born and educated in Argentina, re-marks that her book *The Birth of the Living God* (1979) is on object relations and, in particular, on that special object, God. Primarily through the use of case material, the book studies, in her words, "the epigenetic and de-velopmental formation, transformation, and use of the God representa-tion during the course of human life" (1979, 182). Rizzuto says that by the term "God representation" she is referring to "the totality of experiential levels obtained from the life of an individual, which under the aegis of the human capacity to symbolize *are gathered by a person under the name God.* The representation always includes visceral, proprioceptive, sensorimo-tor, perceptual, eidetic, and conceptual components" (1980, 122–23). She proposes that the God representation, however widely shared culturally, inevitably goes back to the individual child's early relations with parents or other primary objects. God originates, she says, as a "special type of ob-ject representation" in what Winnicott calls "transitional space," the space of illusion (1979, 177). God, psychologically, is "an illusory transitional ob-ject." Our illusions, among which figures prominently our God, illumine "the transitional space each of us has created between his objects and himself to find a 'resting place' to live in" (1979, 209).

Rizzuto says the child actively uses his or her God representation in order to maintain relations to parents and a "minimum of relatedness and hope" (1979, 202). In this use of the God representation, the child sometimes rejects the existence of God—this is not the same as the representation of God, which is a psychic image—and sometimes draws nearer to God (1979, 202). As a "transitional object representation," God is forever there "for further acceptance or further rejection" (1979, 179). It is this ability to protect one's minimum relationships with primary objects, as well as one's self-respect, according to Rizzuto, that gives the God representation its "psychic usefulness." The God representation remains with us all our life, moreover, serving us in our dealings with ourselves, others, and life itself: it is reelaborated time and again out of our need to adjust these dealings. God may be essentially ignored for years, Rizzuto remarks, only to be brought back during a crisis for further acceptance or rejection. The God representation, whether active or dormant, thus remains forever available "for the continuous process of psychic integration" (1979, 180).

Rizzuto points out that children sometimes use the God representation to soften parental shortcomings in their regard. Failing to meet their parents' unrealistic expectations, for example, children may develop a deep sense of wrongness about themselves. They may accordingly develop the representation of a God that hates them, in this way preserving intact idealized parental images. Such children are deprived of their space for play, of their chance to relax with their fantasies (Winnicott). Instead, their parents "imprison" them "in the narrowness of the only path open to them" (1979, 190). Fortunately, Rizzuto finds such children to be the exception. Most are able to "populate their transitional space generously with fascinating creatures—God among others" (1979, 190).

A variety of factors—social class, peers, and institutional religion, among others—affect the meaning, shape, and potential use both child and adult confer on their God representation. While the God representation thus originates out of many sources, its primary sources are the parents. The child indeed creates his or her God "in silent exchanges" with his or her parents (1979, 210): "God's representational characteristics can be traced to experiences in reality, wish, or fantasy with primary caretakers in the course of development" (1980, 123). Thus, unlike other transitional objects, such as the teddy bear, God is created primarily from parental "representational materials" (1979, 178). The young child, for example, hearing from adults how formidable God is, can find but one representation approximating the object being referred to, that of the formidable parent. The child, moreover, takes both from what the parents say and from what they do in shaping and reshaping "his God according to his needs" (1979, 210). All in all, according to Rizzuto, the God representation carries many parental traits, its fortunes varying with those of parental relations. Rizzuto comments that, unlike other transitional objects, God does not lose meaning for the child but, instead, becomes increasingly important, reaching His most appealing at the height of the Oedipal experience. The God representation, while not originating at the time of the Oedipal crisis, is said to undergo change at this important time, as are parental representations and one's self-representation.

Nor is this the last development the God representation is destined to undergo. Given the never-ending "strain of relating inner and outer reality" (Winnicott), the "psychic process of creating and finding God" extends over the life cycle in its entirety (1979, 179). Rizzuto thus finds the God representation to evolve in the course of the individual's life, often in complex ways, retaining, and even gaining in, its usefulness as an "illusory transitional object" (Winnicott). Indeed, if one's God representation is not updated, it becomes outmoded and maladaptive and is "experienced as ridiculous or irrelevant or . . . threatening or dangerous" (1979, 200). Rizzuto says every major life crisis, every significant change in self-representation, furnishes an opportunity for revision of the God representation.

At the conclusion of the Oedipal stage, Rizzuto finds the God representation to be useful in softening the blows of separation: "God is always there" for the lonely. The child, moreover, discovers in God a "better and more powerful ally" than his or her parents, someone who can answer prayers (1979, 199). Adolescence is singled out as testing "the elasticity of the God representation to the extreme" (1979, 202). During this period, many reject their God. Some of those who maintain their belief are said to hold on to an anachronistic God representation. Others manage to support a representation adequate to their needs, "thus keeping belief compatible with development" (1979, 203). If God is to remain believable, Rizzuto says, the God representation must be recreated with each developmental crisis. As life continues to unfold, the God representation, ideally, changes to keep pace with a self-representation that has changed in response to revised relationships with others. Finally, at the point of death, the God representation makes its return, in Rizzuto's words, "either to obtain the grace of belief or to be thrown out for the last time" (1979, 201).

It has already been suggested that one does not always believe in the God representation possessed. Belief or disbelief in God indicates the inner and outer balance actually achieved in adapting to life. Both belief and disbelief, in Rizzuto's view, express loyalty to one's images of oneself and of parents, with disbelief giving expression to this loyalty in opposition to the God representation in question. In Rizzuto's words, "To believe or not to believe is always an act of fidelity to oneself and to our mental representations of those to whom we owe our past and present existence" (1980, 117).

Rizzuto says her psychoanalytic study shows that Freud was right in locating the origin of God in parental representations. She parts company with Freud, however, in finding that the father is not alone in determining the character of the God representation. Mother also makes her contribution, as do grandparents and siblings. Furthermore, while agreeing on the pivotal role of the Oedipal crisis in the formation of the God representation, Rizzuto does not find the Oedipal stage of development to be its sole determinant. In the interest of mature object relations, the individual is called upon, time and again throughout life, to develop a more adequate image of God. Finally, Rizzuto does not agree with Freud that God is simply a wish-fulfilling illusion that mature adults will outgrow: "Psychic reality . . . cannot occur without that specifically human transitional space for play and illusion. . . . After the Oedipal resolution God is a potentially suitable object, and if updated during each crisis of development, may remain so through maturity and the rest of life" (1979, 209).

Rizzuto's thoroughly researched book on Freud's own religious beliefs, *Why Did Freud Reject God? A Psychodynamic Interpretation*, appeared in 1998. In it, Rizzuto traces Freud's religious development from a young boy with rather conventional beliefs to adult atheism. She provides a wealth of information on Freud's family's background and his parents and shows how his relations with his father and mother shaped his religious development and his self-proclaimed atheism. Applying his own psychodynamic theory to him, namely that the individual's representation of God largely derives from the child's relationships with its parents and is shaped in their image, Rizzuto arrives at the conclusion that Freud's early life ruled out the psychic possibility of his believing in a provident and caring divine being.

ANTOINE VERGOTE

Belgian psychologist of religion Antoine Vergote has undertaken a project, which dates back to 1962, on parental figures and their relation to the representation of God. This project entails a series of studies conducted by Vergote and his colleague, A. Tamayo, and are reported in *The Parental Figures and the Representation of God: A Psychological and Cross-Cultural Study* (1981). In order to study the correspondence between each of the parental figures and the representation of God, the Semantic Differential Parental Scale, consisting of a list of eighteen stereotypically maternal and eighteen stereotypically paternal characteristics, was devised. In the administration of this instrument, subjects are asked to associate, on a seven-point scale, each of the thirty-six qualities to father and mother figures, as well as to their representation of God.

The various studies of Vergote and Tamayo yield the following findings (1981, 185–225). Both father and mother possess, in different degrees and on different levels, the qualities of the other figure. The fundamental factor of the "maternal symbolic figure" is "availability, receptivity, or tenderness"— "mother" represents "unconditional love" (1981, 186). The sample of schizophrenics and delinquents alone fails to characterize the mother as available. Authority, the specific quality of the father figure, is almost always attributed to the mother but never in a primary manner.

Most important among the components of the "paternal symbolic figure" is the "law and authority factor"—"father" is the "representative and custodian of the law" (1981, 191–92). The schizophrenics, delinquents, and Hindus, however, don't characterize the father in this way. The authority generally attributed to the father is not of an authoritarian character. Availability, the specific quality of the mother figure, is secondary in the father figure. The "symbolic parental functions," it is pointed out, are the same for both sexes (1981, 193). Vergote draws the general conclusion that the differential attribution of items to father and mother would seem to indicate that the two "parents fulfill complementary functions with respect to the child" (1981, 185).

Virtually all the maternal items are variations on the fundamental maternal theme of "affective availability." The fact that the "maternal structure" is found to be the same in the representation of God and in the paternal figures also reveals "the structural simplicity of the maternal dimension" (1981, 200). The paternal items, on the other hand, indicate the existence of three dimensions: "authority, dynamic power, and knowledge" (1981, 201).

To what degree do the parental figures mediate the representation of God? Except in the religious, the pathological, and the Hindu groups, Vergote reports "a remarkable universality in the representation of God. The representation of God integrates to a high degree the two parental dimensions"; it is a "complex unity holding the two parental dimensions in tension" (1981, 205–207). Of the two factors forming the representation of God, the maternal factor of availability is found to account "for a very high percentage of variance in all the groups," while the paternal factor of law and authority is found to account for a very low percentage (1981, 206). The representation of God, stressing (except in one group) "more the maternal qualities than the paternal," may thus be said to be "more maternal than paternal" (1981, 206). This result is directly contrary to the Freudian view of God as nothing but an "exalted father."

Despite the factor-analytic finding that the most significant factor in the representation of God is the maternal factor of availability, Vergote cautions against the hasty conclusion that "the mother figure is the privileged symbol in the representation of God" (1981, 217). Within the context of the studies conducted, Vergote says no final decision can be made as to "a privileged capacity for symbolization by one or the other parental figure." In one way, the God representation, being characterized more by availability, is more maternal; in another way, however, "law and authority pertain to it directly as they do to the father figure," and so, the representation of God is more paternal. All in all, with regard to this question, Vergote concludes that "more refined methods are necessary to explain adequately the complex signification of the representation of God as it is constituted by the transposition of the parental qualities" (1981, 217).

BERNARD SPILKA

Bernard Spilka has long been a leader in the empirical investigation of religious behavior in the United States. First, as regards God-images, L. Benson and Spilka, in the belief that the kind of "God" whom believers select is consistent with self-esteem, predicted that "self-esteem will be positively related to loving God-images" and "negatively related to rejecting or nonloving images" (1977, 210). Subjects were 128 male Catholic high school subjects. Both hypotheses were confirmed. The authors conclude that the data "provide some support for the explanation that self-esteem is a major determinant of God-images" (1977, 220). The results of this study, together with the finding of Rizzuto (1979) that self-representations as they develop over the course of the life cycle in its entirety affect representations of God, suggest that factors other than early experiences with parents must also be taken into consideration in accounting for God-images.

Reference was made in chapter 4 to the Allport-Ross Religious Orientation Scale and its contrast between intrinsic and extrinsic religiousness, as measured by Intrinsic and Extrinsic scales. R. O. Allen and Spilka (1967) make a similar contrast between consensual and committed religiousness, as measured by Consensual and Committed scales. Consensual religion refers to socially accepted forms of religiousness, committed religion to personal forms. Conversion, Allen and Spilka say, can be of either sort: consensual conversion is mere change of ecclesiastical affiliation; committed conversion is an internal attitudinal shift. The authors' research confirms the earlier findings of a link between type of religiousness and prejudice: consensual religiousness is associated with increased prejudice, and committed religiousness with decreased prejudice (see chapter 4, "Religion and Prejudice"). Spilka and P. H. Werme (1971) suggest, moreover, that those who score high on consensual religiousness score high on measures

of inadequacy and anxiety and those who score high on committed religiousness do not. Rather than linking psychopathology to religion in general, the authors conclude it wiser to relate types of pathology to forms of
religion.

Batson, P. Schoenrade, and W. L. Ventis maintain that the Allport-Ross
Intrinsic scale misses out on much of the emphasis in Allport's original
notion of mature religion on "flexibility, skepticism, and resistance to ab-
solutistic thinking" (1993, 161). The authors indeed suggest that intrinsic
religiousness "may have as much in common with Erik Hoffer's (1951)
concept of the 'true believer' as with Allport's concept of mature religion"
(1993, 163). The probability is, accordingly, that the Intrinsic scale measures "intense, perhaps even rigid, devotion to orthodox beliefs and practices" (Batson, Schoenrade, and Ventis 1993, 163). The authors argue further that something similar happened, in the course of the development
of the Spilka Religious Viewpoints Scale, with committed religiousness:
"Much of the emphasis in the initial concept of committed religion on
complexity, flexibility, and self-criticism was lost" (1993, 165).

A high positive correlation has indeed been found between scores on Allport and Ross's Intrinsic scale and those on Spilka's Committed scale. Batson and his associates point out that this correlation is not surprising given
the fact that seven of the nine items on the Intrinsic scale are included in the
fifteen-item Committed scale (1993, 165). They conclude that the Intrinsic
and Committed scales are apparently measuring the same thing and that it
is therefore appropriate to refer to the Intrinsic-Committed orientation, as
Spilka himself has. Given the difficulties associated with the Intrinsic scale,
Batson and his colleagues consider this a less-than-favorable development:
"The Committed scale," they comment, "like the Intrinsic scale, seems to
be primarily a measure of intense devotion to orthodox religious beliefs"
(1993, 165–66).

DANIEL BATSON

In view of the problems cited in connection with the Allport-Ross Reli-
gious Orientation Scale and the Spilka Religious Viewpoints Scale, C.
Daniel Batson has developed a further set of questionnaire scales (Batson,
Schoenrade, and Ventis 1993, 166–88). Two of these scales are based on
Allport's distinction between extrinsic and intrinsic religion. The first, the
External scale, is intended to measure religion as "a means to other self-
serving ends" (1993, 168). The second, the Internal scale, is designed to
measure religion as "an ultimate end in itself." The third new scale, the
Quest scale, is meant to measure something new, religion as an open-
ended struggle with life's existential questions (1993, 169). The Quest

scale is designed to include aspects of Allport's "mature religion" considered missing from the Allport-Ross Intrinsic and the Spilka Committed scales: a readiness to confront the contradictions and tragedies of life in all their complexity, an "openness to change," and a positive acceptance of religious doubt and self-criticism. The fourth new scale, the Orthodoxy scale, is meant to measure the degree of "belief in traditional religious doctrines."

The fact that a positive correlation was found between the Intrinsic and Orthodoxy scales, but not between the Intrinsic and Quest scales, is taken as confirmation of Batson's belief that "the Intrinsic scale measures devout—perhaps even rigid—adherence to orthodox beliefs" (1993, 172). Further analysis of responses to the six scales (the Allport-Ross Extrinsic and Intrinsic scales, and Batson's new External, Internal, Orthodoxy, and Quest scales) revealed three underlying, independent dimensions: (1) religion-as-means, primarily defined by the Extrinsic scale (but not by the External scale; contrary to expectation, a higher positive correlation was found between External and Intrinsic scales than between External and Extrinsic scales); (2) religion-as-quest, primarily defined by the Quest scale; and (3) religion-as-end, primarily defined by the four remaining scales (Intrinsic, External, Internal, and Orthodoxy scales).

The following empirical findings have been reported in connection with the Quest scale. As predicted, Batson and L. Raynor-Prince (1983), in a study of thirty-five undergraduates interested in religion, found a significant positive correlation between complexity of cognitive structures and the quest dimension. G. L. Sapp and L. Jones (1986) found a significant positive correlation between level of moral judgment and the quest dimension. Batson, Schoenrade, and Ventis remark that a positive correlation is generally found between mental health and the quest dimension (1993, 289). They comment further that studies attempting to eliminate the problem of self-presentation—answering questions so as to appear free of prejudice—suggest that the quest dimension is associated with decreased prejudice (1993, 329). Finally, the authors draw the summary conclusion that "the quest dimension is associated with increased tolerance and sensitivity to the needs of others," pointing out in particular that the help offered others by those high on the quest dimension seems more in the interest of the welfare of the other than of looking good oneself—the latter self-concern is said to be more characteristic of those scoring high on intrinsic, end religion (1993, 363–64).

Does the Quest scale measure what it is supposed to? Batson and his colleagues argue that the evidence is "surprisingly supportive of the possibility that this scale is actually measuring something close to what it was designed to measure" (1993, 180). Opinion, however, is divided. D. M. Wulff points out that one factor analysis of the Quest scale revealed two factors: an identity factor, found to be positively correlated with the Intrinsic scale and measures of psychological adjustment, and a doubt factor, found to be negatively correlated with the Intrinsic scale and measures of maladjustment (1991, 237–41). "Given the accent on doubt and identity," Wulff comments, "the Quest scale may represent reasonably well the views of the college students whom Batson employed in most of his studies. There is no question that in operationalizing their outlook, he has made a genuine and lasting contribution to the field" (1991, 238).

J. Watson and colleagues (1988) found, on the one hand, that scores on the Quest scale tend to decrease with age and that, on the other, scores on the Intrinsic scale tend to increase with age. This is interpreted as supporting the suggestion of R. W. Hood and R. J. Morris (1985) that the intrinsic orientation (of those who have made peace with life's existential questions) and the quest orientation (of those who are still struggling with such questions) represent two stages in religious development. The quest orientation may thus be a phase through which individuals pass on the way to something else.

Pointing out that the Quest scale has yet to correlate with any other measure of religiousness, M. J. Donahue (1985) remarks that this scale may not be measuring religiousness at all but perhaps agnosticism or sophomoric doubt. Batson and his colleagues respond, in part, by pointing out that were the Quest scale in fact a measure of agnosticism, there should be a strong negative correlation between it and the Orthodoxy scale, which there is not (1993, 179). Spilka, B. A. Kojetin, and D. McIntosh (1985) have suggested that, rather than measuring the intended open-ended confrontation with life's existential questions, the Quest scale may actually be measuring religious conflict accompanied by anxiety. Batson and his colleagues comment that religious conflict and the quest dimension, while connected, are not the same, which indicates to them that the connection is consistent with the scale's original purpose (1993, 180).

STANISLOV GROF AND
MODERN CONSCIOUSNESS RESEARCH

Psychiatrist and consciousness researcher Stanislav Grof remarks that his personal experience with LSD induced a profound experience of cosmic consciousness in him, awakening him to a deep interest in nonordinary states of consciousness. Since that experience, his clinical work and research have centered on systematically exploring the potential—"therapeutic, transformative, and evolutionary"—of these states (2000, ix). He calls them "holotropic" states of consciousness and has worked with them for many years as a therapist. He has also written and spoken extensively on the subject.

Holotropic States of Consciousness

Holotropic states are extraordinary states of consciousness. Grof explains that "holotropic" means "oriented toward or moving in the direction of wholeness," "aiming at the totality of existence" (2000, 2–3). Holotropic states are described as a deepening of consciousness. Feelings of ecstasy and profound bliss and, alternately, of terror and profound suffering may prevail in these states. Individuals may attain deep insights about themselves, nature, and the cosmos and about philosophical and spiritual matters. There may be an experience of psychological death and rebirth. Archetypal, otherworldly figures and realms may appear (see chapter 3, "Archetypes and Myth" and "Archetypes as Gods"). In short, other—spiritual—dimensions of reality confront the individual, often strikingly, in holotropic states of consciousness.

Grof remarks that holotropic states are the key to an understanding of "the ritual and spiritual life of humanity from shamanism and sacred ceremonies of aboriginal tribes to the great religions of the world" (2000, 3–4). Grof believes that holotropic states mediate direct experiential contact with archetypal realms, the gods, the mythological, and nature's mysterious forces and are the main origin of "cosmologies, mythologies, philosophies, and religious systems describing the spiritual nature of the cosmos and of existence" (2000, 3–4). Grof remarks that ancient and indigenous cultures have held these conscious states in the highest regard and have gone to great lengths to develop safe and effective "technologies of the sacred" to produce them. These "mind-altering" technologies use a combination of drumming, chanting, and rhythmic dancing. The great religions of the world have also developed "technologies of the sacred" for inducing holotropic states (2003). Especially noteworthy in this regard are the various techniques of Yoga and Zen and Tibetan Buddhist forms of meditation (2000, 12). Particularly effective for altering consciousness holotropically, Grof remarks, has been the "ritual use of psychedelic plants and substances," such as peyote. The production of holotropic states is the chief characteristic of shamanism, which Grof characterizes as "the oldest spiritual system and healing art of humanity" (2000, 7). A further sort of "psychospiritual transformation" is found in rites of passage, the widespread practice of transforming the initiate into a different individual (2000, 4–5).

Holotropic states of consciousness also occur spontaneously (1988, xiii). These spontaneous states are among what Grof and his wife, Christina, have termed "spiritual emergencies" (1989). Spiritual emergencies are described as "psychospiritual crises" or "crises of transformation," which, when respectfully treated and properly supported, can lead to radical personality transformation, self-discovery, healing, and an enhancement of everyday functioning (1988, 2–3; 2000, 177). Grof believes that difficult and trying spiritual emergencies are real and are proper to the psyche, and he encourages people to give in to these experiences and to support fully the unconscious material that emerges through them (2000, 19, 137). A combination of biographical, perinatal (surrounding or associated with birth), and transpersonal (beyond the personal) experiences occurs in spiritual emergencies (2000, 142–43).

Grof considers spiritual emergencies to be integral to a spiritual journey of transformation. Mainstream psychiatry, however, diagnoses them as psychotic and seeks to suppress them through medication (2000, 215). Grof points out that modern materialistic science, as the paradigmatic worldview of our day, dominates mainstream psychological and psychiatric theory. According to this view, observable "matter" alone is "real," consciousness is an insignificant byproduct or epiphenomenon of "material" brain processes, holotropic states are mere fantasy or hallucination, and, so, spirituality and the spiritual life do not really exist (1984, 3–23). Grof firmly rejects the materialistic assumption, remarking that mainstream psychiatry is seriously misguided in disregarding the abundant evidence that experience and research have provided for the reality and positive transformative power and effect of holotropic states of consciousness. Grof readily admits that there are nonordinary experiences that are pathological in origin and character and that require medical intervention. He argues, however, that spontaneously occurring spiritual emergencies are not psychotic states but are to be respected for their spiritual and transformative character (2000, 140).

The Revelatory Power of Holotropic States

We have seen that Grof finds holotropic experience to be produced ritually, that it can occur spontaneously and can be induced chemically through psychedelic drugs. And it can be induced therapeutically, for example, through holotropic breathwork (see below, "Holotropic Breathwork"). Using both drug and nondrug techniques, Grof has extensively investigated the therapeutic induction of holotropic states for self-exploration and psychospiritual healing. Through this research, Grof claims to have marshaled ample evidence to the effect that consciousness is "a primary attribute of existence" (1988, 238–49, 265–73; 1998; 2000, 300). Grof cites the following transpersonal experiences occurring in holotropic states in support of this claim of this primacy of conscious experience: identification with God, with other people and the whole of humanity, with other forms of life and all life, and even with inorganic processes and the entire planet; visits to mythical realms and fantastic landscapes; and encounters with the deities of various cultures, demons, legendary heroes, and spirit guides (2000, 57, 62–63, 231). Holotropic states, he says, provide a vision of the universe as "an infinitely complex virtual reality," which "superior cosmic intelligence, Absolute Consciousness, or the Universal Mind" created and permeates (2000, 270). The Absolute, Grof comments, is an immense and ineffable field of consciousness (2000, 274; see chapter 6, "Realization"). In short, deep holotropic experiencing reveals the profound truth of ancient cosmic images, which Grof insists are based on "authentic experiences of alternate realities" and don't derive from hallucinations, magical thinking, or superstition (2000, 271).

Grof writes, "The spectrum of transpersonal experiences is not only extremely rich, ramified, and variegated, but includes levels of reality governed by laws and principles that are different from those that rule ordinary reality" (1988, 40). He says that ordinary states of consciousness can attain only a certain range of reality. Holotropic states of consciousness, on the other hand, can reach its remaining aspects and present us with contents from other dimensions of existence (1988, 38–39). We are said usually to think of ourselves as separate persons "inside our skin," tied to a body with set boundaries in space and time, and bound through our senses to a physical world "out there" (1984, 18; see chapter 6, "The Ego"). Transpersonal experiences, Grof says, render all these limitations relative: to experience on the transpersonal level is to transcend our body and our ego and the spatial and temporal limitations of ordinary consciousness (1988, 38). Grof sees us as thus capable in holotropic states of loosening our identification with our narrow body-ego and reclaiming "our full identity"—"the Divine Within" (2000, 2, 209, 270, 290–91). Transpersonal psychology teaches that consciousness is not simply an individual possession *personally* but that the individual *transpersonally* belongs to consciousness. Thus belonging to a consciousness transcending space, time, and ordinary causality, Grof says, the individual has the potential of gaining access to the whole universe and, in a sense, *is* the whole universe (2000, 69). In deep self-exploration, we are thus able to realize that there are no separate selves and that our true identity lies in an identification with the "cosmic source," with the Absolute, with our divine nature. The culmination of the revelatory power of holotropic states lies, in Grof's reckoning, in experiencing and living this cosmic relation, this "Cosmic Consciousness."

Cartography of the Human Psyche

Grof comments that academic psychiatry has restricted the individual's significant life history to individual biographical events following birth and the Freudian individual unconscious (2000, 20). To account for experiences in holotropic states and related observations, however, as already suggested, Grof thinks we are in need of a much more expansive view of the human psyche, along with a radically revised understanding of consciousness. To this end, he has devised a "cartography of the human psyche," which "maps" not only the psyche's postnatal biographical level but also two transbiographical domains: "the perinatal domain," or the domain related to birth and its severe trauma, and "the transpersonal domain," or the domain that accounts for the individual's various experiential identifications with nature and that is the source both of memories reaching beyond the individual's lifetime and of "visions of archetypal beings and mythological regions" (1988, 1–167; 2000, 20–69).

The Postnatal Biographical Level of the Psyche

The postnatal biographical domain of the psyche, to which traditional psychiatry is exclusively committed, consists of life memories after birth and is closely matched by the forgotten or actively repressed life material constituting the individual unconscious (2000, 21–22). Grof's research with holotropic states, however, has in his view made it necessary to broaden this biographical level to include aspects of one's personal biography typically overlooked by investigators using verbal psychotherapy, namely the experiencing anew of the original emotions, sensations, and even perceptions involved in significant life events, including the reexperiencing of physical traumas, such as near drowning.

The Perinatal Level of the Psyche

Chiefly constituting the perinatal level of the psyche are the "twin phenomena of birth and death" (1988, 6). Grof remarks that "experiential psychotherapies," which involve the induction of holotropic states, show that biological birth is preserved in detail in memory and that it constitutes "the most profound trauma of our life," a psychospiritual event of such importance that it profoundly affects our whole psychological development (2000, 31–32). Experiencing this traumatic event anew and integrating it into our lives are accordingly seen to be of major importance in experiential psychotherapy and the adventure of self-discovery. Such reliving, Grof says, is not a mere mental reviewing of a past event but an actual psychospiritual event of death and rebirth of the moment. This event is described as involving intense emotions and physical sensations— "the anxiety, biological fury, physical pain, and suffocation" that accompany biological birth, the pain and threat to life occurring in the struggle of actually being born (2000, 29–32, 52).

The ego is found to die in this psychospiritual sequencing of dying and being born (2000, 52–54). Grof says that the old notion of our self's identity and of the world's character, our "old programs," the old "matrix" of our lives, dies. Grof remarks that "our old ego," under the pretense of being "our true self," in reality is a false ego. The death of this ego, of everything we know and have ever been, is frightening but also profoundly healing. After psychospiritual death, Grof remarks, we are reborn, undergo "spiritual opening" and "ecstatic rapture," and have the sense of gaining anew "our divine nature" and our "cosmic status" (2000, 33, 54).

Grof remarks that the symptoms of emotional, psychosomatic, and psychotic disorders have deep roots in the perinatal domain, in "complicated interplay" with the postnatal biographical and transpersonal domains—among the emotional and psychosomatic disorders cited are phobias, conversion hysteria, obsessive-compulsive neurosis, depression, and sexual disorders (2000, 73–136). The complex roots of these symptoms in the perinatal domain, as well as in the transpersonal domain, account for their content and great power. Grof further remarks that modern consciousness research has shown that both "malignant aggression" and insatiable greed not only go back to the traumas and frustrations of early life but also have significant relations to the perinatal level of the psyche (2001, 92, 94).

The Transpersonal Level of the Psyche

Grof sees, beyond the perinatal, another major domain of the psyche that calls for inclusion in the map of the human psyche when holotropic states are given serious consideration, a domain beyond the biographical that he says is best called "transpersonal" (1988, 37; see chapter 3, "The Collective Unconscious"). A transpersonal psychology not only acknowledges the reality of certain spiritual experiences on their own terms but holds that they are extraordinarily significant in our lives and that we have a fundamental need for them (1988, 237; 2000, 217). Transpersonal states are characterized by greatly enhanced perception and emotion, insights of a philosophical and spiritual nature, and clarity of thought (2000, 110–11). Grof remarks that these nonordinary states occur under the influence of psychedelics, in experiential psychotherapy, in near-death experiences, in spiritual emergencies, and in meditation (2000, 68). By definition, transpersonal experiencing stands in contrast to ordinary, "normal" experiencing as defined by cultural convention and contemporary psychiatry. The gist of what this experiencing reveals, both about ourselves and about reality as a whole, has been described above ("The Revelatory Power of Holotropic States").

Grof points out that the transpersonal level of the psyche is not always associated with favorable outcomes. It has been found, for example, to underlie psychosomatic disorders and has been implicated in psychotic states in which gods, demons, and extraterrestrials encounter individuals (2000, 135–36). Grof adds the further comment that the difference between the mystic and the psychotic lies not in the nature and content of the transpersonal experience but in the individual's personality and attitude toward the experience. The experience represents a challenge on a spiritual journey for the mystic but terror for the psychotic.

The Healing Potential of Holotropic States

Holotropic states of consciousness, as we have seen, reveal for Grof that the spiritual is real and an essential feature both of the human psyche and of the universe at large. These insights, he says, have far-reaching implications for the theory and practice of psychiatry and warrant wide application (1988, 249–65). Indeed, Grof sees the main contribution of holotropic therapy to consist in "the recognition of the healing, transformative, and evolutionary potential of nonordinary states of consciousness" (1988, 267). To the extent that psychological disorders have origins deep in the perinatal and transpersonal domains, Grof remarks that healing, both individual and collective, also involves the depths of these domains, where therapeutic mechanisms are seen to be in operation (2000, 130).

In view of the great healing potential of holotropic work, Grof remarks that a number of effective experiential psychotherapies have been developed (1988, 250; 2000, 178–83, 231). He sees the induction of holotropic states through such therapies as a modern version of ancient and aboriginal forms of spiritual healing (2000, 18). He argues that verbal psychotherapies, by limiting themselves to the individual's personal biography and individual unconscious, are simply incapable of reaching "the deeper roots of the conditions" they seek to remedy (2000, 178). Experiential therapies, rather than focusing on verbal exchange and intellectual analysis, are described as emphasizing the direct experience and expression of emotion. The techniques employed aim first at activating the unconscious and liberating the energy "bound in emotional and psychosomatic symptoms," and then converting the energy thus released into flowing experience (1988, 166).

A basic tenet of holotropic therapy, Grof remarks, is that people are naturally oriented toward wholeness—that is, are naturally holotropically oriented, but that our culture promotes the actualization of only a fragment of their true potential (2000, 181–82). Holotropic therapy, thus envisioning the organism as naturally seeking to become whole, regards emotional and psychosomatic symptoms as attempts on the part of the organism to heal itself (2000, 179). Grof comments that the general strategy of holotropic work, then, is to place confidence in the body's inherent wisdom and "follow the inner clues," to nurture respect "for the autonomy and spontaneity of the healing process" (2000, 185, 188). Experiential therapies thus seek to activate the healer within. The therapist's role is essentially that of a "facilitator," who supports and is accepting of a spontaneously occurring process, someone who relies on the client's "inner radar" to select the appropriate content (2000, 28). Grof writes, "The nature of holotropic therapy . . . is such that the process itself automatically selects in each session the material that is most emotionally relevant at the time" (1988, 206). It is precisely this automatic choice of material, he remarks, that led to the uncovering of the perinatal and transpersonal levels of the psyche.

Holotropic therapy has been seen to be widely effective and to produce significant changes in just a few hours. The following highlights some of the major therapeutic effects Grof reports as occurring in experiential psychotherapies. Holotropic therapy has been found to bring improvement in many psychotic conditions (2000, 181). Experiential psychotherapies have led to "dramatic and lasting improvements of various psychosomatic disorders" (2000, 130). Reexperiencing physical traumas, and the trauma of birth in particular, has shown itself an especially effective healing mechanism. The psychospiritual event of death and rebirth has brought about dramatic improvement in various emotional, psychosomatic, and interpersonal problems, problems said to have resisted all psychotherapeutic attempts concentrating on individual postnatal biography (1988, 234). Deep inner self-exploration at the perinatal and transpersonal levels has reduced both aggressive and self-destructive impulses greatly (2003, 104). Holotropic therapy has fostered compassion and tolerance, reverence for life, and sensitivity to the environment.

Holotropic Breathwork

"Holotropic breathwork" is a form of experiential psychotherapy developed by Grof and his wife (1988, 165–219; 2000, 183–205). Kylea Taylor, a therapist active in treating addictions and conversant with nonordinary states of consciousness, writes, "*Breathwork* is the modern term for a system using the breath combined with a variety of supportive techniques to mobilize our bodies, minds, and spirits for spontaneous healing" (1994, 3). Grof describes holotropic breathwork as inducing powerful holotropic states through a combination of extended accelerated breathing, evocative music, and, if required, bodywork to bring the session to its completion (2000, 183).

Grof says that it has long been known that consciousness can be influenced by certain breathing techniques, such as are found in Yoga and Buddhist meditation. Faster, more effective breathing induces nonordinary states of consciousness, Grof remarks, and these states have been found to effectively reduce stress and to promote emotional and psychosomatic healing (see above, "The Healing Potential of Holotropic States"). Holotropic breathwork is said to work by loosening defenses, thus resulting in the release of blocked energies and the surfacing of unconscious and superconscious material (1988, 170–84; 2000, 188–203). Appropriate music during breathwork serves to stimulate emotions associated with repressed memories, thus helping to bring them out into the open. One is encouraged to give in to the music "in a spontaneous and elemental fashion," "to give full expression to what the music brings out," to "surrender to the flow of the music, to the breathing rhythm, and to any experiences that might emerge, without analyzing them or attempting to change them, and with full trust in the process" (1988, 186, 208). Grof remarks that combining music and accelerated breaking is remarkable in its ability to alter the mind and to heal. Holotropic breathwork, it should be noted, is not to be undertaken without a trained therapist.

REFERENCES

Allen, R. O., and B. Spilka. "Committed and Consensual Religion: A Specification of Religion-Prejudice Relationships." *Journal for the Scientific Study of Religion* 6 (1967): 191–206.

Batson, C. D., and L. Raynor-Prince. "Religious Orientation and Complexity of Thought about Existential Concerns." *Journal for the Scientific Study of Religion* 22 (1983): 38–50.

Batson, C. D., P. Schoenrade, and W. L. Ventis. *The Religious Experience: A Social-Psychological Perspective*. New York: Oxford University Press, 1993.

Benson, L., and B. P. Spilka. "God-Image as a Function of Self-Esteem and Locus of Control." In *Current Perspectives in the Psychology of Religion*, ed. H. N. Malony, 209–24. Grand Rapids, MI: Eerdmans, 1977.

Donahue, M. J. "Intrinsic and Extrinsic Religiousness: Review and Meta-Analysis." *Journal of Personality and Social Psychology* 48 (1985): 400–19.

Grof, S. (ed.). *Ancient Wisdom and Modern Science*. Albany: State University of New York Press, 1984.

———. *The Adventure of Self-Discovery*. Albany: State University of New York Press, 1988.

———. *The Cosmic Game: Explorations of the Frontiers of Human Consciousness*. Albany: State University of New York Press, 1998.

———. *Psychology of the Future: Lessons from Modern Consciousness Research*. Albany: State University of New York Press, 2000.

———. "Consciousness Evolution and Planetary Survival: Psychological Roots of Human Violence and Greed." *International Journal of Humanities and Peace* 17 (2001): 89–99.

———. "Technologies of the Sacred, Part Three." *International Journal of Humanities and Peace* 19 (2003): 104–106.

Grof, S., and C. Grof (eds.). *Spiritual Emergency: When Personal Transformation Becomes a Crisis*. Los Angeles: J. P. Tarcher, 1989.

Hoffer, E. *The True Believer*. New York: Harper and Row, 1951.

Hood, R. W., Jr., and R. J. Morris. "Conceptualization of Quest: A Critical Rejoinder to Batson." *Review of Religious Research* 26 (1985): 391–97.

Pruyser, W. *A Dynamic Psychology of Religion*. New York: Harper and Row, 1968.

———. *Between Belief and Unbelief*. New York: Harper and Row, 1974.

———. *The Play of the Imagination: Toward a Psychoanalysis of Culture*. New York: International Universities Press, 1983.

Rizzuto, A.-M. *The Birth of the Living God: A Psychoanalytic Study*. Chicago: University of Chicago Press, 1979.

———. "The Psychological Foundations of Belief in God." In *Toward Moral and Religious Maturity*, ed. C. Brusselmans, 115–35. Morristown, NJ: Silver Burdett, 1980.

———. *Why Did Freud Reject God? A Psychodynamic Interpretation*. New Haven, CT: Yale University Press, 1998.

Sapp, G. L., and L. Jones. "Religious Orientation and Moral Judgment." *Journal for the Scientific Study of Religion* 25 (1986): 208–14.

Spilka, B., B. A. Kojetin, and D. McIntosh. "Forms and Measures of Personal Faith: Question, Correlates and Distinctions." *Journal for the Scientific Study of Religion* 24 (1985): 437–42.

Spilka, B., and P. H. Werme. "Religion and Mental Disorder: A Research Perspective." In *Research on Religious Development: A Comprehensive Handbook*, ed. M. P. Strommen, 461–81. New York: Hawthorne, 1971.

Taylor, K. *The Breathwork Experience: Exploration and Healing in Nonordinary States of Consciousness*. Santa Cruz, CA: Hanford Mead Publishers, 1994.

Vergote, A. "The Dynamics of the Family and Its Significance for Moral and Religious Development." In *Toward Moral and Religious Maturity*, ed. C. Brusselmans, 90–114. Morristown, NJ: Silver Burdett, 1980.

Vergote, A., and A. Tamayo (eds.). *The Parental Figures and the Representation of God: A Psychological and Cross-Cultural Study*. New York: Mouton, 1981.

Watson, J., R. Howard, R. W. Hood Jr., and R. J. Morris. "Age and Religious Orientation." *Review of Religious Research* 29 (1988): 271–80.

Winnicott, D. W. *Playing and Reality*. New York: Basic Books, 1971.

Wulff, D. M. *Psychology and Religion: Classic and Contemporary Views*. New York: Wiley, 1991.

10

✛

Feminist Psychology of Religion

This chapter surveys a broad range of feminist approaches in the psychology of religion. Some key themes to look out for are the critique of the androcentric/misogynistic biases of certain psychologies and religions, the importance of hearing the feminine voice, Erik Erikson's preference for the "feminine sexual mode," the role of Sigmund Freud's physicalism in advancing feminism, the goddess movement, and the high regard in which certain feminists hold object relations theory.

DIANE JONTE-PACE: FEMINIST CRITICS, INCLUSIVISTS, AND ANALYSTS

In her review of feminist research in the psychology of religion, Diane Jonte-Pace, professor in the Department of Religious Studies at Santa Clara University, comments that feminist theory and methodology in the psychology of religion have flourished in recent decades and have come to be broadly accepted (2001, 141). Her article distinguishes three sorts of feminist projects in the psychology of religion: feminist *critics*, feminist *analysts*, and feminist *inclusivists* (2001, 129). She sees feminist critics as having uncovered and challenged androcentric (male-centered) theories and methodologies. Feminist analysts have shown how culture and religion have constructed gender, on the one hand, and how gender is constructed in religion and culture, on the other. And feminist inclusivists have initiated theories and methods for studying the religious lives and experiences

of women. Jonte-Pace examines how each of these three projects has re-
sponded to important topics in the psychology of religion: Freud's study
of the psychological origins of *morality*, Carl Jung's reformulation of *God-
imagery*, and object relations studies of the psychodynamics of *ritual*.
Jonte-Pace concludes her essay by considering how poststructuralist Julia
Kristeva's analytic and inclusive projects of a feminist psychology of religion have contributed to an investigation of these three topics. Jonte-
Pace's overall judgment is that the three kinds of feminist projects she surveys have made a dramatic contribution to the psychological study of
religion (2001, 141).

Feminist Responses to Freud's View on the
Psychological Origins of Morality

Carol Gilligan, called a "paradigmatic feminist critic" by Jonte-Pace, rejects Freud's view that women are incapable of "true morality," that men
alone can achieve "full moral development" (2001, 130–31). Gilligan
traces Freud's error to his androcentric Oedipal theory, according to
which the phallus is crucial to moral and cultural development. She says
that, on the basis of this theoretical preconception, Freud can only see
women, who are lacking in the male genital and its history, as doomed to
developmental failure and as incomprehensible. Gilligan's approach is
considered in a separate section below.

Judith van Herik, cited as a prominent feminine analyst, examines
Freud's treatment of the masculine and the feminine, essentially his
misogynistic views, in the broad context of his theory of culture and religion (2001, 131–32). Van Herik notes that, on the one hand, Freud associated wish fulfillment (illusion) with Christianity and both wish fulfillment and Christianity with femininity; on the other, he associated the
renunciation of wish fulfillment with Jewish morality and both the renunciation of wish fulfillment and Jewish morality with masculinity.
Freud further located a "higher" masculinity in "a post-religious, morally
renunciatory, scientific rationality" (2001, 132). A "broad cultural pattern"
is thus discerned: on one side is the inferior, feminine pair of wish fulfillment and Christianity and, on the other, the superior, masculine trinity of
the renunciation of wish fulfillment, Jewish morality, and scientific rationality. Jonte-Pace remarks that where Gilligan critically judges Freud to
have simply failed to understand women, van Herik interprets the same
facts analytically, showing that "an analysis of the masculinity of ideal
morality in Freud's writings exposes the gendering of Freud's entire theory of religion and culture" (2001, 132). Jonte-Pace classes Jay Geller as another important feminist analyst, who provides a cultural and psychological context for understanding van Herik's thesis of Freud's feminization

of Christianity and masculinization of Jewish morality. Geller comments that Freud was a Jewish male living in a world that was both anti-Semitic and misogynistic and that "feminized Jewish males" (2001, 132). Freud, in her view, reverses all this by pointing to the "psychological femininity" of wish-fulfilling Christianity and the "psychological masculinity of renunciatory Jewish morality and intellect" (2001, 132).

Feminist Responses to Jung's View of the Reformulation of God-Imagery

Jonte-Pace points out that Jung advocated a major reformulation of the Christian God-image to include "the archetypal feminine": that is, the "relational, 'Eros' side" of the unconscious (2001, 133–34). Before the late 1980s, she goes on to say, Jung's psychology was seen as compatible with feminist approaches. Numerous feminist inclusivists, she comments, seeking to incorporate women into the scholarship of the time, endorsed Jung's views on feminine symbols. His critique of the one-sided masculine character of culture and religion is said to have been in tune with "feminist critiques of patriarchal (father/male dominated) culture and male God-imagery" (2001, 135). Jonte-Pace says this approach came to be challenged by many feminist critics, however, upon the realization that seemingly "inclusivist" female images and symbols in fact harbor dualistic, misogynistic, and sexist viewpoints—that in actuality the notion of the "archetypal feminine" assumes and perpetuates female inferiority.

Jonte-Pace describes Naomi Goldenberg as having lived out both these waves of feminist interest in Jung's psychology: first committed to Jungian inclusivity—returning the feminine to the God-image—she later became a severe critic of Jung's archetypal theory (2001, 135–36; see also, below, "Naomi Goldenberg"). Goldenberg points out that, while Jung placed a high value on the feminine, he did not value women, holding that "Eros" was women's proper domain, and that's where they should stay.

Feminist Responses to the Object Relations Theory of the Psychological Origins of Ritual

Object relations theory, Jonte-Pace remarks, is concerned with the centrality in human development of human interrelatedness and the significance of "objects"—other human beings and images of them—and in particular with the relationship between mother and child during the earliest years of life, considerably before the onset of the Oedipus complex (2001, 136; see chapter 9, "Donald Winnicott"). Whereas Freud traced God, ritual, and morality back to the father and the Oedipus complex, object relations theorists find "a mother, often loving and benevolent, behind religious ideas and practices" (2001, 136–37). The earliest object relations feminists in the psychology of religion are said to have been inclusivist, the later ones analytic. A number of object relations studies of religion have featured rituals such as the Christian Eucharist or Mass.

In sharp contrast to the antireligious tenor of orthodox Freudian psychoanalysis, the inclusivist object relations approach typically finds religion, in Jonte-Pace's words, to be "valuable, adaptive, and benign, and that a loving relationship with a good or 'good enough' mother . . . provides the psychological foundations of faith, mysticism, and God representation" (2001, 137). Mary Ellen Ross and Cheryl Lynn Ross engage in this positive inclusive project, finding "benign" relations with the mother behind "benign religious experience" (2001, 138). They uncover in the Eucharist, for example, expressions of such pre-Oedipal themes as nourishment and unification.

The analytic object relations approach, by contrast, assumes that anxiety over relations with the mother generates religious fantasies and fears of "destructive and vengeful women" (2001, 137). Asceticism and ritual sacrifice, for example, manifest either fear of the mother, anxiety regarding her body, or discomfort regarding separation from her or one's identity. Analyst William Beers, for example, finds misogyny to underlie the Eucharist (2001, 137–38). He focuses on the Eucharist as sacrifice and views sacrifice as serving the interests of male power and hold over women. He points out that it is primarily men who perform sacrifice and that this primacy protects the male line of descent (patrilineal descent). He further argues that male anxiety generated in the earliest interaction with the mother finds its socially structured and controlled expression in the ritual bloodshed that takes place in the Eucharist. Ritual violence, moreover, furthers male bonding and distances men from women.

Jonte-Pace finds that Kelley Raab exemplifies an object relations feminism at once analytic and inclusive (2001, 138). Raab finds a "gender reversal" enacted in the Eucharist. In it men are said to identify with women by assuming feminine functions and at the same time to forbid women from exercising these functions. Raab locates the source of this reversal in male envy and fear of women's capacity to bear and nurse children. She goes on to make a case for women's ordination as priests and their officiating at the Eucharist.

Julia Kristeva on Ethics, God-Image, and Ritual

Under the heading "Ethics, Ritual, and God-Image Re-examined: A Kristevan Approach," Jonte-Pace sketches aspects of the psychology of religion of French psychoanalyst Julia Kristeva, which is described as encompassing both analytic and inclusive projects (2001, 139). Jonte-Pace remarks that the poststructuralist movement of recent decades rejects all claims to universal and absolute truth, placing in the foreground, instead, the enormous role of language in shaping culture, gender, and thought. She sees Kristeva as having been especially influential in the poststructuralist feminist study of religion, as well as in feminist theory in general, raising new questions about the roles that culture, gender, the unconscious, and religion play in the above topics—namely morality, ritual, and God-image (2001, 141). Jonte-Pace sees Kristeva as more interested in religion's functions and its effects on individual and society than on one or another presumed absolute origin of religion. Regarding ritual, like analytic object relations theory, Jonte-Pace says, Kristeva finds that, by warding off the fear of irretrievably losing one's whole identity in the mother, ritual serves to repress "a primal (and terrifying) abhorrence of the mother" (2001, 139–40). As to God-imagery, like inclusivist object relations feminism, Kristeva "seeks the raw material of religious faith and psychoanalytic healing in the earliest human experiences of love 'close to the maternal container'" (2001, 140). She discovers a "maternal core," for example, in the imagery of God the Father. Finally, with regard to morality, Kristeva, again echoing inclusivist object relations theory feminism, is said to investigate the sense of the "other" undergirding human morality and interrelatedness. The self itself is seen to originate in the two-in-one relationship of child and mother.

MARY DALY: *BEYOND GOD THE FATHER*

The Divine Masculine—The Inferior Feminine

In her 1973 book *Beyond God the Father: Toward a Philosophy of Women's Liberation*, radical feminist theologian Mary Daly focuses on the exclusively masculine character of traditional Western symbolism for God: God is a father, a male, and his only begotten is a son, a male. God the Son "become man" was anatomically a male, and she points out that women have been, and still are, barred from the priesthood because they don't share the Son's male anatomy. Powerful symbols everywhere, Daly remarks, proclaim "that to be human is to be male is to be the Son of God" (1973, 138). She argues that males have crafted the entire religious tradition, the "conceptual systems of theology and ethics," in its entirety, "under the conditions of patriarchy (father/male domination)" (1973, 22). These male-created and male-dominated conceptual and symbolic systems serve and protect patriarchical social purposes, ensure sexist—male—interests, and reinforce the conventional "sexual hierarchy": men above, women below (1973, 4).

Daly says that the dominating image of God the Father, a "great patriarch in heaven," has served to sanction the oppression of women as the "right and proper" thing to do (1973, 13). Like God the Father ruling his docile servants in heaven, males govern human society on earth, a governance seen to be in the "nature" of things, in full accordance with divine plan and will. The husband is thus "naturally" to rule his submissive wife, as the male God rules his dependent creation. Culture-bound religious doctrines based on patriarchical rule in heaven thus justify patriarchical social structures down below, patriarchical rule on earth. Human qualities, Daly says, become artificially polarized into traditional sexual stereotypes supportive of patriarchical roles and structures. The "eternal masculine stereotype" implies "hyper-rationality . . . 'objectivity,' aggressivity, the possession of dominating and manipulative attitudes toward persons and the environment," a caricature dependent upon the opposed stereotypical caricature of "the eternal feminine": shallow-minded, weak-willed, hyperemotional, passive, self-abnegating, and so on, inferior qualities all (1973, 15, 76). In sum, Daly sees women as deemed of a lesser nature than the male God's male representatives. Daly says that theologians have assumed for centuries that it would have been below God's dignity for "him" to have "become flesh" in the body of a member of the "inferior" sex, and, of course, the fact that "he" did not serves to confirm what they always knew, that the male gender is inherently superior (1973, 72).

The Victimization of Women

Daly points out that women have traditionally been identified with matter, evil, and Eve and labeled as "temptress," "nature-bound," "depraved," and "vicious" (1973, 76). These designations, Daly says, have served to victimize women (1973, 76). The notion that there is a "base element" in being female has led to a social brutalization of women that has "shortened and crushed the lives of women" (1973, 92, 95). Not only has the myth of feminine evil served to legitimate the projection upon women of male self-hatred, but it has also led to women hating themselves (1973, 48). Women have all too often accepted male characterizations of themselves, not even noticing their own degradation (1973, 133). Having only ever mirrored men and knowing only to mirror men, women mirror in themselves "the sickness of their masters" (1973, 197). Daly comments that feminist scholars continue to find evidence of the "fear, dread, and loathing" of women underlying this assignment of evil to the feminine. She points out that even the positive qualities attributed to women are those of a victim: passive, obedient, humble, meek, sacrificial, long-suffering, submissive, self-abnegating (1973, 77).

Overcoming Victimization

Patriarchical religion, Daly argues, exercises its privilege through language, the patriarchical language of the masculine God and the base and inferior feminine. But, she says, the liberation of sexist religious language requires the liberation of women (1973, 102). This liberation, this "becoming of women in sisterhood," represents, in Daly's view, "the countercultural phenomenon *par excellence* which can indicate the future course of human spiritual evolution" (1973, 11). Daly says that the patriarchical oppressor internalized by women has to be ejected and, with that, women's "feelings of guilt, inferiority, and self-hatred" (1973, 50). Women must come to recognize the demonic power that possesses them from within and objectifies them as deviations "from the male norm of humanity" (1973, 64). Women will have to renounce the passive ethic, will have to say "no" to "the morality of victimization" and summon up the existential courage "to affirm their unique being" (1973, 75, 104). Challenging their victimization and affirming their full humanity will amount to no less, in Daly's view, than a religious affirmation of being over nonbeing, a creation, a bringing forth of "New Being" (1973, 139).

Androgynous Becoming

Daly insists that the human psyche is itself divided when socialization divides human beings into sex roles (1973, 127). She comments that half of human beings have been denied humanity in anyone who has undergone "sexual definition": that is, the "artificial polarization of human characteristics into sex-role identification" (1973, 15, 35). Daly says that this half must be reclaimed. It has to be allowed to become. Women, along with men, have to be given the freedom to become complete human beings. Radical feminists, Daly says, are for the "total elimination of sex roles" (1973, 124). For the healing to proceed, she remarks, both men and women have to overcome their inner division and move toward "androgynous being" (1973, 50). The liberation of males and females thus means putting an end to human objectification by "sex role socialization" (1973, 172, 191). Should an ethic beyond the stereotypical masculine/feminine be achieved, Daly comments, being judged "masculine" would mean having been "masculinized"—that is, socialized out of half of oneself—and being considered "feminine" would mean having been "feminized"—socialized out of half of oneself (1973, 104). In short, women need to get beyond sex stereotyping and the divided self and to move toward "being integrated, androgynous personalities" (1973, 133, 158).

MAJELLA FRANZMANN: *WOMEN AND RELIGION*

The Marginalization of Women's Religious Experience in Texts

In her book *Women and Religion*, Majella Franzmann remarks that traditionally women and their religious experience have been looked at from the outside as *objects* of study (2000, 2). Not allowed, much less invited, to speak, women have been denied their voice. Men, rather, have spoken for them. Women have been what men have said they are. Franzmann points out that it is male religious professionals within the religious traditions who have generally done the describing, categorizing, and interpreting of women's religious experience (2000, 69). Male religious experience, taken as the norm in the language of religion, has not recognized women "as people who have valid or important religious experiences" (2000, 70). Women, Franzmann comments, have simply not been considered as having anything worth saying about themselves and their religious experience. This being so, the language women have available to them is often inadequate to their actual religious experience as women.

Franzmann remarks that it is generally male religious professionals who do the writing on religious experience not only within the religious traditions but also "within the academic areas of theology or studies in religion" (2000, 72). A normatively male language and perspective are consequently said to dominate both religious traditions and the academic arena. Scholars who are not religious professionals in such fields as sociology or history or anthropology, moreover, have in the past generally gotten their information on religious experience from male religious believers. Furthermore, academics generally and principally see "authority and orthodoxy" as belonging to those who either actually or presumably wield power "within the hierarchical structures of the tradition"—typically, male religious professionals (2000, 72). Franzmann continues by saying that textbooks on Christianity concentrate on male clergy and their doings, either marginalizing women or ignoring them altogether (2000, 73). When males control the texts, thus maintaining and shaping the religious tradition, she says, women tend to be excluded. And when they do make an appearance in texts, they are generally "problematical figures, immoral characters, the victims of men's violence, or silent characters" (2000, 74). Often women are mentioned just "to highlight men's self-perceptions."

In general, then, Franzmann comments, the official texts and presentations of both religions and the academy render the religious experience of women essentially invisible. When women's religious experience is spoken of, it is in view of the norm of male experience and is often categorized "as marginal, frightening, or dangerous or as superstition rather than real religion" (2000, 73). Women's marginalization in authoritative religious texts, moreover, often serves as a basis for their marginalization in religious practice as well. Thus are women excluded from, or relegated to the edge of, "sacred space, ritual action, knowledge of texts or stories associated with ritual, and the role of the professional in the religious tradition" (2000, 76).

Religious Representation of Women

Franzmann remarks that religions generally distinguish between men and women in approximately the same way that society at large does (2000, 80). Women's religious identity and portraits thus match their basic social identity and portraits (2000, 58, 82). For women, this means that social margins = religious margins and marginalization in society = marginalization in religion. Both the social and religious functions of women, Franzmann says, center on domestic affairs, marriage, family, and home. Women's positive identity consists in belonging to men: father, husband, sons. Religious traditions, moreover, are seen to judge domestic space to be of decidedly lesser significance than the sacred space occupied by religious professionals. At best, Franzmann comments, women's identity is as "object of benevolent paternalism"; at worst, it is as "thing, possession, and chattel" (2000, 82).

Religious discourse about women is, in Franzmann's view, virtually entirely about gender and sexual function (2000, 84–85). The "ideal woman" is one whose definition involves *not* being sexually active, a virgin or a widow, or being sexually under control, a wife or a mother. In contrast to this ideal is the sexually active woman outside the reach of familial control—the prostitute. The virgin or saintly woman and the prostitute, Franzmann remarks, are the images of woman that have figured most prominently in Christianity.

Religions have portrayed women as possessing dangerous characteristics in a multitude of ways. Franzmann says this is especially true in regard to their sexuality and its ability "to give life or bring death or sickness" (2000, 86). In order to minimize the damage they can do, dangerous women have been marginalized (2000, 88–89). Franzmann suspects that women's exclusion "from ritual and sacred space" is due to their presumed unworthiness and impurity. Women's impurity is equated with evil and immorality, and so, she comments, it is not a big step to make the connection between women and the devil or some other malevolent power; nor is it surprising that religions and societies, even to this day, speak of shame in relation to female sexuality and such bodily processes as menstruation. Women's bodies are even now still being represented as mysteriously powerful (2000, 85).

Taking Center Stage

We have seen Franzmann's critical views of the marginalized place of women in religious discourse and practice. But her book also has positive, "inclusivist" dimensions. She sketches, for example, "techniques for inviting or drawing women out of the margins to speak from center stage" and a number of strategies contemporary women are using to make such a move (2000, 134). Franzmann also points to the promise of goddess spirituality, which envisions all things, animals and humans, plant life and bacteria, and minerals as forming one "great living breathing body" (2000, 130). "Gaia," the ancient Greek earth goddess, has been at times invoked to symbolize this all-embracing and wholly sacred living body. For some sharing this vision, called "ecofeminists," feminism is said to seek the liberation from an oppressive patriarchy not only of human beings but also of everything living that suffers under it as well. Franzmann writes, "Many looking for a new spiritual identity are rediscovering old streams of spirituality within traditions and finding new possibilities that offer an integrated vision of body and spirit, of spirit and the natural world" (2000, 130).

CAROL GILLIGAN: *IN A DIFFERENT VOICE*

Women's Moral Development and the Male Norm

In her landmark book *In a Different Voice: Psychological Theory and Women's Development*, psychologist Carol Gilligan criticizes psychologists who, assuming that men constitute the norm for moral development and that there is something wrong with women if they don't follow the male "normative path," have treated women as if they were men (1982). This approach finds the "very traits that traditionally have defined the 'goodness' of women, their care for and sensitivity to the needs of others," to be characteristic of their deficient moral development (1982, 18). Women's typical concern with relationship is thus treated as a human weakness rather than as a human strength (1982, 17). The influential theory of Lawrence Kohlberg, for example, sees women as exemplifying the third of six developmental stages. In this third stage, "morality is conceived in interpersonal terms and goodness is equated with helping and pleasing others," whereas men are seen as progressing "toward higher stages where relationships are subordinated to rules (stage four) and rules to universal principles of justice (stages five and six)" (1982, 18). Compassion, care, and loyalty are thus ranked well below concern for individual rights and justice. Gilligan considers Kohlberg's low estimation of women's moral sensitivity to be one more instance of intellectual bias on the part of males. She points out that the categories traditionally employed for assessing moral development are derived from research samples that are "disproportionally male and adolescent" and that, as long as this remains the case, deviating from the male norm can only be judged a developmental failure (1982, 69–70). The omission of criteria applicable to the development of women, she says, shows the clear limitations of the conventional approach represented by Kohlberg.

Gender Differences in Identity and Moral Judgment

Gilligan believes that there are real gender differences in identity and moral reasoning (1982, 33). She believes that women tend to speak in a different, but not inferior, voice. She draws a contrast between a feminine ethic of *care* and a masculine ethic of *justice*. Justice is impersonal; ties to others don't enter into the equation. Care, by contrast, is personal; an ethic of care is focused on relationships with others.

Gilligan, rejecting biological explanations for a given moral voice, finds self-image—the view individuals have of themselves and their identity—to determine whether justice or care is the foundation of the individual's moral judging (1982, 24–25; see Griffin 1991, 81–90). Girls grow up identifying with their mothers. Like them, girls come to sacrifice themselves and their self-expression for the sake of protecting others and nurturing relationships. Women are likely to identify themselves as daughter, mother, friend, and wife. Gilligan thus sees a distinct feminine identity being gained early in life and finds this identity to be the reason for women's greater need for relationship. It is this need, arising from self-image, that underlies an ethic of care. Boys, unlike their mothers, relinquish relationships in favor of personal freedom and self-expression. Men are prone to refer to themselves in individualistic terms, in terms of their singular accomplishments. Where women are interested in keeping the group together, men just want to get the job done. The net result of the differential development of self-image and identity in females and males is seen to be men who view themselves in their separation from others and women who see life in its connectedness. Separation defines the male "I"; relationship defines the female "I."

Feminine Ethic of Care

The female approach to morality, then, in Gilligan's view, is based on the existence of the responsibility to care for others. In her research on the decision to have an abortion, she found that women, when free to choose and allowed to speak "in their own voice" about an actual moral decision, discussed their decision within a framework of care rather than of justice (1982, 73). To describe their decision, women were found, for example, to repeatedly use such words as "responsible" and "selfish."

Gilligan further describes women's ethic of care as follows: Care is a sensitivity to the needs of others, a need to respond, and "an overriding concern with relationships and responsibilities" (1982, 16–17). Women define who they are (their identity) in terms of this need to respond to others and judge themselves in terms of it, in terms of taking care. They see causing hurt as "selfish and immoral," while expressing care is viewed as morally responsible (1982, 73). This greater orientation of women to connectedness, moreover, is seen to imply "a more contextual mode of judgment" (1982, 59). Women tend to see the complexities of relationships and, so, are reluctant to pass judgment on others. They are inclined to "reconstruct hypothetical dilemmas in terms of the real," of actual people and concrete situations, and tend to shy away from judgment based on "the hierarchical ordering of principles and the formal procedures of decision making" (1982, 100–101).

Ethic of Care and Ethic of Justice: Contrasts and Complementarity

For Kohlberg, justice as a universal principle is the highest moral claim. This male approach to morality sees people as having certain basic rights, and we have an obligation to respect these rights. Morality thus has a "justice orientation." There are rules that have to be followed, rules restrictive of our behavior. Whereas "the logic underlying an ethic of care is a psychological logic of relationship," informing the logic of justice is a "formal logic of fairness" (1982, 73). Whereas "the moral imperative" for men is seen as "an injunction to respect the rights of others," rights to life and self-fulfillment, for women the imperative is found to be "a responsibility to discern and alleviate the 'real and recognizable trouble' of this world" (1982, 100). Whereas male morality is a matter of "competing rights" and is formal and abstract, the moral problem for women arises from "conflicting responsibilities" and requires contextual thinking (1982, 19–22). The morality of rights emphasizes separation over connection and considers the individual rather than the relationship primary. For an ethic of justice, independence of judgment and action is the hallmark of maturity, while for an ethic of care, concern for others defines maturity (1982, 70).

In spite of these manifest differences between the two ethics, Gilligan argues that neither care nor justice is limited to one gender and that the moral development of both males and females would "seem to entail an integration of rights and responsibilities through the discovery of the complementarity of these disparate views" (1982, 100). In the final analysis, men and women are deemed equally capable of dealing with moral issues on the basis of either justice or care.

Developmental Levels within an Orientation of Care

Kohlberg specifies three levels of moral maturity: preconventional morality, conventional morality, and postconventional morality. Gilligan finds a parallel developmental sequence within an orientation of care (1982, 73–74).

1. Orientation to individual survival/preconventional feminine morality: At this first level, women considering an abortion were focused on their own self-interest.
2. Goodness as self-sacrifice/conventional feminine morality: In contrast to the selfishness evidenced at level 1, this second level is characterized by its selflessness. Women on this level defined their moral worth by the care they were capable of exercising towards others and sought to resolve their abortion dilemma so that no one would get hurt. They made their decision on the basis of the advice others had given them or the choice others had made.
3. Responsibility for consequences and choice/postconventional feminine morality: Women at this third stage realized that serious hurt simply could not be avoided in the abortion decision facing them and that easy answers simply did not exist. They realized the seriousness of their situation and sought to take all of their conflicting responsibilities into consideration. At this level, care as a principle of judgment remains a psychological concern with relationships but is now universalized in its rejection of hurt to include oneself.

Whereas women on level 1 were concerned only for themselves, and women on level 2 located virtue in responding to others, women on level 3 realized that they had to be responsible to themselves as well as to others (1982, 82). Again, now on level 3, morality is seen to hinge on self-image: the self is now conceived as including a responsibility to care for itself, not just for others. This new sense of responsibility to and for oneself is seen as requiring "a new kind of judgment, whose first demand is honesty" (1982, 82–83). Honestly acknowledging what one is doing is said to be a precondition for taking responsibility for oneself. Gilligan comments that, when an action's morality is determined in view "of the realities of its intention and consequence," rather than on how it appears to others, "the criterion for judgment thus shifts from goodness to truth" (1982, 83). All in all, then, in postconventional feminine morality, the essence of moral decision lies in assuming personal responsibility for one's free choice and its consequences.

The Abortion Decision Research

Gilligan concludes that the abortion study shows (1) "the centrality of the concepts of responsibility and care in women's constructions of the moral domain," (2) "the close tie in women's thinking between conceptions of the self and of morality," and (3) "ultimately the need for an expanded developmental theory that includes, rather than rules out from consideration, the differences in the feminine voice" (1982, 101, 105).

There has been a great deal of criticism, as well as acclaim, for Gilligan's book. Some critics think that the notion of "a different but equal voice" only serves to strengthen the traditional stereotyped sex roles: men base their actions on reason, women on feeling. Others find Gilligan's research to offer thin support for her theory. Her account strikes many, on the other hand, as true to reality.

NAOMI GOLDENBERG: *RESURRECTING THE BODY*

Critique of the Dualistic Image of Human Life

In *Resurrecting the Body: Feminism, Religion, and Psychoanalysis*, Naomi Goldenberg, professor of Religious Studies at the University of Ottawa, mounts a forceful challenge to the traditional Western dualism of body and soul (or mind or psyche), according to which the material body, the lesser or worse part, serves as a mere temporary vehicle for the soul, the higher or better part (1993, 75, 176). This view, which, she points out, has dominated Western thought and religion since Plato, further holds that the superior soul opens upon something outside of, and superior to, itself. Goldenberg remarks that this higher transcendent something has been given various names: God, forms (Plato), archetypes (Jung). The soul, then, by this theory, is "better, nobler, cleaner, and ultimately of a different character or substance than the body" and is somehow joined with the "divine" something transcendent to everything of a physical, material character (1993, 177). While all the "truly good things" derive from the "essentially disembodied" soul, which has obtained these good things from the transcendent something, Goldenberg comments, the body is considered of little, and even negative, significance—"stained, expendable, and the vehicle of death" (1993, 75–76, 164). Christianity, Islam, and Judaism, religious philosophies such as Plato's, and religious psychologies such as that of Jung are all said to hold to a dualistic scheme of the sort described: physical body or nature or matter, on one side, and disembodied soul or mind or psyche and transcendent something, on the other.

But there's more. Goldenberg points out that the Western dualistic tradition has gone on to identify women with the body, with nature, with matter. Women have thus been identified with the supposedly "lesser, worse" part. Classified with the "lesser" and "worse," thus as "lesser" and "worse," women have been depicted "as materialistic, tempting, voracious, trivial, and lusty," as leading men astray by arousing sexual desire (1993, 169–70). So goes the story of the oppression and damaging of women. Goldenberg insists that, given this identification of women with the body, in order to stop hating women, we have to stop hating human flesh, and she urges feminists to expose and challenge "loathing of the flesh wherever it occurs." Positively stated, Goldenberg's program is "resurrecting the body," "returning words to flesh"—a program that will be further described below ("Return to the Embodied: Returning Words to Flesh").

Dualistic Thinking in the Psychology of Carl Jung

Goldenberg remarks that she "once lived and worked within" Jungian psychology, which she now considers, however, "a form of patriarchical religion" (1993, 5). She locates the real problem with this psychology in the theory of archetypes, which she sees as a dualistic form of thought (1993, 71). This theory holds that powerful, unseen, and inscrutable godlike beings—archetypes of the self and anima, for example—transcend yet govern the "physical, human world" (1993, 74, 97). The role and influence of the body are thus downgraded, and archetypes, disembodied forces devoid of social and cultural context, control what humans think, imagine, and desire (1993, 75). Goldenberg remarks that anytime we think that we are somehow under the control or direction of beings external to ourselves, be they forms, gods, or archetypes, our world is distorted, and we become dehumanized (1993, 111). She considers any thought of a transcendent realm governing human life to be "both anti-woman and anti-life" (1993, 116). All in all, she finds in Jung's psychology the kind of disembodied thinking that must be seen through and disowned (1993, 71).

Return to the Embodied: Returning Words to Flesh

Goldenberg comments that "archetypal thinking," as seen in all systems claiming "to pronounce eternal and universal truths," deflects our attention from present—biological, political, economic, child-rearing—practices that shape psychological processes; archetypal thinking shifts us away from searching for the material and human complexities that generate our actions, our ideas, and our visions (1993, 97, 105). In order to transform ourselves, Goldenberg argues that we need to explore how our world is constructed, not by transcendent entities but through human agency, both conscious and unconscious (1993, 104). What exist are not transcendent and timeless archetypes or entities of any sort but only historically and culturally situated, embodied individuals (1993, 106).

Feminists argue that improving the plight of women requires that we elevate our estimation of human physicality, human bodily life (1993, 156). Goldenberg says we must make sure that our theories enhance and support life, and we must "not cling to disembodied ways of thinking that lead us to disparage women in particular and physical life in general" (1993, 82). We need a way of thinking that reveals precisely how thought is born of physical life and, so, is supportive of that life (1993, 83). We need a way of thinking that sees our bodily life as creating psychological structures, our images, and our mythic realms. We need a way of thinking that recognizes the body as the place of connection of all human experience (1993, 83). The best feminine writing, Goldenberg comments, is returning rationality to its foundations in our bodily and emotional life (1993, 187).

Feminism can help transform human society by communicating the extent to which our lives connect to, and are implicated in, one another (1993, 66). We all begin our life, Goldenberg remarks, "in the context of a woman's body," as "beings of flesh" (1993, 6, 36). Men are inclined to think they are no longer the "bodies-in-matrix" as which they began life and to feature themselves and act, instead, as though they were "autonomous bodies." Women, by contrast, are found to be generally more aware of the "social matrix" in which they, and men, too, still exist. We all, men and women alike, Goldenberg asserts, "always exist in matrices." The body Goldenberg wants to see resurrected is not the idealized, self-enclosed, and self-sufficient male body, which, of course, never did or could exist, but the immanent "maternal body." "Our bodies," she writes, "should be understood as the sum of all our particular situations as created by a complex web of physical, social, emotional, and historical contingencies" (1993, 4, 213). She wants to return words to flesh, to restore thoughts to concrete existence, where they originated, however far from bodily flesh they may have migrated in the course of time. Her aim is to let words express desirous flesh, rather than to continue to let some male-imagined transcendent realm dominate our discourse and our lives. Goldenberg's aim is to resurrect concrete fleshly existence. She sees both feminism and Freudian psychoanalysis as paths to this goal.

The Contribution of Freudian Physicalism

Goldenberg, leaving Jungian and post-Jungian religious psychologies behind, turns to classical Freudian and post-Freudian psychoanalysis for assistance in her pursuit of a restored body (1993, 108). She says that Freud views humans as having an essentially physical nature, which means that the mind is wholly dependent on the body and its instincts (1993, 74, 83). All thought, all imagination, and all value—that is, human intellect, human aesthetic sensibility, and human morality—have somatic sources (1993, 87,

177). As Goldenberg succinctly states, "The body becomes the complex context of all experience" (1993, 179). Psychoanalysis, in locating in the body the higher qualities traditionally reserved for the mind, is not putting the mind down, in her view, but raising the body up (1993, 178).

By taking us back to infancy and childhood, Freudian theory deepens experience and grounds it in the embodied and historical reality of the living individual (1993, 86). Such thought can never escape what is real and human. Goldenberg believes, for this reason, that psychoanalytic theory can help counter the dehumanization taking place in our day (1993, 108). She finds the modern contempt for human life to be increased whenever a nonhuman origin is attributed to "any rules or laws, any propensity toward good or evil, any knowledge or wisdom" (1993, 173). Goldenberg remarks that we are no longer in a position to afford a transcendent deity. In the final analysis, she finds the physicalistic Freudian view of the mind to be more true to human life, to be less mechanical (1993, 113). She sees Freud as leading us toward deciphering our ideas, our motives, and our images—that is, our psyche—so that more of what is human can come into view (1993, 114). When we stop seeing through the psyche to its foundations in the physical and social body, Goldenberg says, we move away from what is truly human. All in all then, a humanizing psychology, a psychology that is wholly human, declares that psyche depends on the experience of human beings in their physical and social contexts. Goldenberg thus sees in Freudian physicalism a valuable ally. She is fully aware, on the other hand, of the problematic aspects of Freud's theorizing, particularly his misogyny.

Post-Freudian object relations theorist Donald Winnicott's definition of the psyche as "the imaginative elaboration of somatic parts, feelings, and functions," as "body visualized," has made a deep impression on Goldenberg (1993, 89, 112). Everything we think or imagine or feel or dream is seen as an elaboration of the body, in Winnicott's words, of "physical aliveness" (1993, 182). Seen from this perspective, Goldenberg says, encountering psyche, for example, in works of art, is in fact to encounter "imaginative renderings" of bodily experience, expressions of embodied desires, feelings, and drives (1993, 90). And regarding myths, Goldenberg comments that the world's great myths are expressions of broadly shared and deeply experienced "physical visions," which explains their lasting power (1993, 90). Winnicott's clarification of psyche thus helps us grasp the power of such spheres as art and myth without resorting, in Goldenberg's words, to "the magical machinations" of bodiless powers, such as transcendent gods or archetypes (1993, 91).

Goldenberg indicates the following points of contact between feminist and psychoanalytic theory. Both take us back to the paramount importance of the body (1993, 185). Both emphasize the importance and complexity of human sexuality. Both seek the transformation of self and world (1993, 147). Both seek "to expand the human sense of subjectivity" (1993, 153). Both seek to liberate the repressed and to bring it into the public domain. Both seek the furtherance of "a particular kind of talk," a "talk that first explores and then heals"; both use the "talking cure" (1993, 149, 153). Both engage, in the intimacy of a conversation, in the search of the "thought of the living" presently held captive by our mainstream culture (1993, 153).

The Return of the Goddess

Goldenberg sees promise for feminism in the goddess movement. She writes about goddess religion and goddess logic in an earlier book, *Changing of the Gods: Feminism and the End of Traditional Religion* (1979, 85–114). In the book presently under consideration, she cites object relations theory as the branch of psychoanalysis with the greatest relevance to the goddess movement (1993, 192). Object relations theory emphasizes human interconnectedness and the idea that people are always seeking relationships with other people ("objects"). Goldenberg comments that both goddess religion and object relations theory emphasize the distant past; the former emphasizes the distant past of our shared history, and the latter, the distant past of our earliest childhood. Goddess religion, she says, looks to the myths of the distant past in order to show how complex the experience of women is and "to dignify that experience by revealing its ancient roots," to make the experience of contemporary women real and to legitimize it (1993, 193). She sees goddess religion, moreover, as featuring powerful female figures, which had their place in our shared religious history but have been disregarded or actively suppressed in the meantime, and thus as challenging the male-dominated patriarchical version of history (1993, 195). Both the goddess movement and object relations theory find a woman at the beginning, the former in the beginning of the whole universe, the latter in the beginning of the individual life. Both thus promote a move away from male symbols to female ones.

The goddess movement joins object relations theory in holding that relationships by and large create people (1993, 200). Goddess religion, agreeing with ancient pagan belief, sees humans as forming part of "a larger web of life which includes all of nature" (1993, 201). The whole earth is said to be the body of the goddess and, as such, to be deemed sacred. Goldenberg, echoing her thought of the "maternal body," asserts the following: "Woman" means life's beginning in connectedness (1993, 202). "Woman" embraces the entire planet (1993, 203). "Woman" means the interconnection of everything with everything as "the body of the world." "Woman" means the human connection to the planet. "'Woman' is the stuff out of which all people are made" (1993, 202).

The Advantage of Taking Women Seriously

Goldenberg remarks that a way of thinking that takes women seriously diminishes the hold of transcendent entities over human beings, on the one hand, and leads to an increased consideration of the significance of the physical body and the body politic, of immanence and connection, on the other (1993, 206–207). Excluding women from our scholarship, by contrast, has given rise to belief in "an abstract presence" that creates and rules over the world. Whereas traditional doctrines of transcendent realities are far removed from the body and life's particular contexts, the inclusion of women in our scholarship spells the recognition that all creation and all thought are thoroughly dependent on the physical (1993, 207, 211).

HETTY ZOCK: ERIK ERIKSON'S FEMININE-ORIENTED PSYCHOLOGY OF RELIGION

Erik Erikson's Masculine and Feminine Modes of Organizing Space

In her 1997 article on the predominance of the feminine mode in Erik Erikson's psychology of religion, Hetty Zock, a member of the Theology and Religion Studies Department at the University of Groningen, the Netherlands, points out that while Erikson considers individual development as always psychosocial, he also stresses the importance of given potentialities of the body for psychosocial development. Among these biological potentialities, Zock says, Erikson distinguishes between feminine and masculine modes of activity, which he links "with the function of male and female procreative organs" (1997, 188–89). Zock comments that through research on his child patients, Erikson discovered distinguishable patterns in the way they constructed play, finding boys and girls to differ in the way they organize space "[b]ased on their beginning awareness of sexual organs" (1997, 189). The overall masculine way of constructing space is seen to center on the *outer space* and is described as *intrusive*. Boys "intrude" the world physically, for example, by building high towers and by yelling and running, and "intrude" the world mentally, for example, through curiosity. The masculine mode is active: "willful-striving." The overall feminine mode, by contrast, centers on the *inner space* and is *inclusive*. It is based, Zock writes, "on the awareness of having a productive inner space and an inner potential" (1997, 190). Female sexual identity, for Erikson, then, is not constituted by the lack of an external sexual organ but by possessing an internal one. Zock comments that Erikson found that girls "include" physically "by having and holding," "holding in" and "holding on," and "mentally by perceptiveness and sensory discrimination" (1997, 190). Girls "include" in play by building low, enclosed structures, interiors. The feminine mode is said to be passive: "passive-receptive." Erikson does not construe this feminine passivity as "impotence and powerlessness," however, but as having its own way of being in the world, as "perceiving and receiving," as "being open and taking in" (1997, 190).

Zock proceeds to say that Erikson views the basic bodily sexual differentiation into distinct masculine and feminine modes as representing "different ways of approaching the Divine, the Ultimate—God . . . [leading] to different experiences and images of God" (1997, 191). The masculine mode tends to locate God in the "transcendent sphere," beyond space and time, beyond man's domain, beyond what is humanly possible. This transcendent God is seen to be omnipotent, omniscient, infinite, and eternal. Zock points out that Erikson's feminine mode, by contrast, tends to locate God "in the inner space, in the here-and-now, in the material bodily world—in short, in the immanent sphere," in "the immediate" (1997, 191). For Erikson, the masculine mode has its role in the institutional dimensions of religion. He is principally interested, however, in the feminine mode and its role in establishing a relationship with the divine, and, Zock says, he apparently placed a higher value on it than on the masculine mode (1997, 196).

The Feminine Mode's
Fundamental Role in Religious Experience

Erikson is said to see the feminine mode as lying at the basis of religious experience. It is only through this mode, "the passive way," that he sees the individual to be capable of establishing "a relationship with the Divine" (1997, 192). The feminine mode thus plays a primary role in the origin of religious experience. Erikson is shown as clarifying this primacy by relating it to his account of psychosocial development. In life's first stage of development (birth to one year), the child is to gain a sense of trust, a "basic trust." Through its immediate experience of the world, in Zock's words, "the child learns that it is carried and supported by a trustworthy, benevolent universe, that it is part of a greater whole" (1997, 193). This basic experience, Erikson says, is the first religious experience. And Zock points out that, for Erikson, it is a "maternal person" who initiates this "basic numinous experience of trust" (1997, 193). The feminine mode is thus responsible, in Erikson's view, for passing on "religious presence," for transferring "a communion with the unseen and silent," for first bringing about a religious relationship with the divine (1997, 193). All in all, religious (maternal) individuals "radiate a religious, numinous presence," which allows them to bring others into contact with the sphere of the divine. While this numinous presence, derived from the basic trust experience, has a feminine, maternal character, this presence need *not* be a woman.

Erikson's "Theory of I" and Religious Experience

Zock says that critics of Erikson's "masculine psychology" often overlook the pivotal role attributed to the feminine mode in his work. Also frequently disregarded by critics, she says, is Erikson's closely related and extremely important "theory of I," which Zock discusses at greater length in *A Psychology of Ultimate Concern: Erik H. Erikson's Contribution to the Psychology of Religion* (1990, 72–77, 100–103). We've seen that Erikson links religion closely with the feminine mode, but, significantly, he also brings the "I" into the connection. Zock comments in the article under discussion, "The I is closely linked with both the feminine and religion" (1997, 195–96). Erikson describes the "I" as "the core" of a person's identity, referring to it as the ego's "existential counterpart." The "I" is said to be established and to develop "in constant interaction with Others" and to have been originally formed in the newborn infant through interaction with the "maternal Other" (1997, 195). The "I," moreover, is seen to be the core of religious development, a "numinous phenomenon." Erikson thus once again uses religious terms for the first interaction between infant and maternal Other in the first psychosocial stage, this time in the context of his theory of I. The transcendent divine is experienced in the "immediacy" of human relationship. Zock points out that, in Erikson's view, an "Ultimate Other" is basically what is experienced in and through the Other, and in the final analysis, "it is this Ultimate Other that establishes the sense of I" (1997, 195–96). Thus, Zock points out that Erikson links the origin of our core identity with the experience of the divine through interaction with the maternal Other. With his theory of I, Zock remarks, Erikson provides theoretical grounds for "the predominance of the feminine mode in psychosocial and religious development" (1997, 196).

The Two Modes Available to Both Men and Women

Zock asserts that, for Erikson, both masculine and feminine modes are present and available in both men and women (1997, 190). The feminine mode is thus strongly developed, for example, in both male and female philosophers, artists, and religious geniuses. Both modes are necessary, moreover, for the individual and society to enjoy a healthy development. Erikson accordingly argues that there is a need to develop and balance both (1997, 190, 196). Citing the arms race and environmental pollution as outcomes of a one-sided male development, Erikson is said to argue that the "preserving, caring, nursing, and nourishing" characteristic of the feminine mode "must be reintroduced in the political sphere" (1997, 190).

Both modes are thus necessary for the overall health of both the individual and society, and in Erikson's view, both "are necessary for healthy religiosity" (1997, 192). According to Zock, he thinks that "the feminine, the immanent, the immediate" are needed to correct a one-sided masculine development in evidence in religious life and theology. While he sees "masculine action" and "paternal power" as needed in order to actualize "spiritual insights" in the social and political spheres, Zock says that for Erikson the feminine mode is nevertheless undoubtedly of greater importance. "Paternal power rests on maternal care" (1997, 194).

Erikson's Contribution to the Psychology of Religion

Zock remarks that feminists have criticized Erikson's feminine sexual mode as perpetuating the traditional view of women as "passive, receptive, caring, and so forth," thus as sanctioning the relegation of women to such traditional feminine roles as childcare and housecleaning (1997, 194). Whatever the merits of this critique, Zock sees Erikson's theory of sexual modes as valuable and as contributing in a significant way to the psychology of religion. She says that modern psychology tends to overlook the role of the body in religious experience and behavior and that Erikson's theory of masculine and feminine modes is helpful here through its account of this role (1997, 197). Moreover, with his theory of modes and his theory of I, Zock remarks, Erikson has helped us understand how individuals first become religious.

REFERENCES

Daly, M. *Beyond God the Father: Toward a Philosophy of Women's Liberation*. Boston: Beacon Press, 1973.
Franzmann, M. *Women and Religion*. New York: Oxford University Press, 2000.
Gilligan, C. *In a Different Voice: Psychological Theory and Women's Development*. Cambridge: Harvard University Press, 1982.
Goldenberg, N. R. *Changing of the Gods: Feminism and the End of Traditional Religion*. Boston: Beacon Press, 1979.
———. *Resurrecting the Body: Feminism, Religion, and Psychoanalysis*. New York: Crossroad, 1993.
Griffin, E. *A First Look at Communication Theory*. New York: McGraw-Hill, 1991.
Jonte-Pace, D. "Analysts, Critics, and Inclusivists: Feminist Voices in the Psychology of Religion." In *Religion and Psychology: Mapping the Terrain*, ed. D. Jonte-Pace and W. B. Parsons, 129–46. London: Routledge, 2001.

Zock, H. *A Psychology of Ultimate Concern: Erik H. Erikson's Contribution to the Psychology of Religion.* Atlanta: Editions Rodopi, 1990.

———. "The Predominance of the Feminine Sexual Mode in Religion: Erikson's Contribution to the Sex and Gender Debate in the Psychology of Religion." *The International Journal for the Psychology of Religion* 7 (1997): 187–98.

11

✝

Neuroscience and Religion

Neuroscience is one of the most exciting fields of research today, and an exciting development within neuroscience, at least to the psychologist of religion, is its investigation of topics touching on religion. This chapter considers such investigation under four headings: "Roger Sperry," "Neurophenomenology," "Affective Neuroscience and Tibetan Buddhist Meditation," and "James H. Austin: Zen Buddhism and Neuroscience."

1. Renowned neuroscientist Roger Sperry sees consciousness as playing a determining role in brain processes, planetary evolution, and the universe at large and finds subjective human values to be "the key to world change."
2. Neurophenomenology uses reports of the conscious experience that accompanies objective measures of brain processes in order to detect and interpret the brain processes that realize such experience.
3. Richard Davidson investigates the neuroscience of positive affect and its induction, for example, in Tibetan Buddhist monks through "love and compassion" meditation.
4. James Austin explores in personal terms and in great detail the interpenetration of Zen Buddhism and neuroscience.

These four approaches represent a challenge to paradigmatic neuroscience and thus to the professional neuroscientist. The conceptual difficulty of these approaches, on the other hand, represents a challenge to the average layperson; it is thought, however, that their importance and the promise they offer of an "expanded science" (Abraham Maslow; see chapter five, "Plea for an Expanded Science") outweigh the demands they may make on the understanding.

ROGER SPERRY

Interpreting the cognitive revolution, neuroscientist and Nobel laureate Roger W. Sperry, well known for his work on the brain's two hemispheres and, in particular, on the distinctive role of the right hemisphere, has opened a promising avenue in the psychology of religion. Sperry views the cognitive revolution, which he judges to have arisen out of science itself as a whole, as the "most radical turnaround—the most revisionary and transformative" in psychology's first hundred years (1993, 878). Asserting that "reductive physicalism," the traditional explanatory model of science—behaviorism included—is no longer tenable, Sperry says that psychology is now leading the way among the sciences in shedding its traditional paradigm.

Looked at one way, the cognitive revolution is seen to mean the refutation of the traditional view that brain function can be completely accounted for in purely objective "neuronal-biophysical terms," as well as of the more general belief that materialism (objectivism) can render a coherent explanation of the universe in its entirety (Sperry 1993, 879). Looked at another way, the cognitive revolution is seen as meaning the comeback of consciousness: subjective mental states are now judged to play a causal role and, thus, to be necessary in any comprehensive explanation of conscious behavior. Sperry comments that there is not only an "upward determinism" of the neuronal on the mental (bottom-up causal determinism) but a "downward determinism" of the mental on the neuronal (bottom-down causal determinism). Not only does the brain control consciousness, but consciousness is an emergent irreducible whole that controls the brain. There is in the new view, Sperry says, above and beyond "microdeterminism," an "emergent control by holistic properties," an "emergent determinism" or "emergent causation." Thus is atomism seen as being replaced by "a more holistic, top-down view." A train of thought, for example, is held to be as determinative of the brain's neural net as the other way round.

In answers provided for an article in the *APA Monitor* (DeAngelis 1993), Sperry says he developed "the concept of emergent interaction with downward causation, the idea that overall irreducible emergent properties of a whole determine both its own interactions with other wholes and also, downwardly, the behavior and fate of embedded parts" in order to get around the idea that we "normally have two distinct minds," corresponding to the brain's two hemispheres (DeAngelis 1993, 6). Thus, in Sperry's view, left and right mind can be understood to form, in the normal brain, a "single, higher-level whole" acting as a "unified single conscious mind." Reductionism, Sperry remarks, simply does not provide an account for the "all-important causal effects exerted by . . . pattern factors in different micromacro structures—essentially causal factors that underlie Gestalt principles" (DeAngelis 1993, 7).

Sperry insists that the new mentalism is not a return to dualism. While, by the new view, mental states indeed govern behavior, such states are seen as "dynamic emergent properties of brain activity," as "inseparably interfused with and tied to the brain activity of which they are an emergent property" (Sperry 1993, 879). While "mind controls matter," in Sperry's view, "mind emerges from matter," "mind is born of matter and dies with it" (Erdmann and Stover 1991, 43; Stover and Erdman 2000, 92). In short, in Sperry's view, subjective states of consciousness cannot exist apart from the brain generating them. And yet, Sperry remarks, mental states and brain states are not the same: emergent properties are new and frequently very different from their constituents (1993, 880). Such emergent properties belong not to the components, per se, as if the whole were "the sum of its parts" (atomism), but to the spatiotemporal patterning, or Gestalt, of components; what is crucial is the way the parts "are arranged in space and time and give rise to new properties that could not be predicted from knowledge of their parts" (Stover and Erdmann 2000, 84).

According to Sperry, the new cognitivism reconciles determinism and free will. Volition, while indeed causally determined from below, is not totally "subject to the inexorable physiochemical laws of neurocellular activation" (Sperry 1993, 879). Such "lower level laws" are embedded in, and thus determined by, "higher level controls of the subjective conscious self." "Subjective agency" is said to be a "special case of emergent causality in the reciprocal up-down (bidirectional) paradigm for causal control" (Sperry 1993, 882).

Sperry points out, moreover, that the cognitive revolution might be called a "values revolution": through it "the old, value-free, strictly objective, mindless, quantitative, atomistic descriptions" yield to accounts recognizing "the rich, irreducible, varied and valued emergent macro and holistic properties and qualities in human nature and nonhuman nature" (1993, 879). The world is not driven solely by "mindless physical forces"; subjective human values are indeed taken to be the most crucial forces shaping the world today—"the key to world change" (Sperry 1991; 1993, 883). Integrating value and fact, mind and matter, and religion and science, Sperry sees the cognitive revolution as providing a moral basis for measures that would enhance, rather than destroy, our world. No longer riding roughshod over values and denying meaning and purpose in life, but giving mental states—such as values and a commitment to meaning—causal status, Sperry thinks science can now lead the way to "a universal value-belief system, a much-needed naturalistic global ethic. . . . More than any other causal system with which science now concerns itself, it is variables in human value systems that will determine the future" (DeAngelis 1993, 7).

While human values evolve, emerging in their living context, Sperry says we have put the world in jeopardy by absolutizing values (1993, 883). Today, to avoid catastrophe, we need a new outlook, "a rapid conversion of all humankind to a changed sense of the sacred, a changed sense of ultimate value and the highest good" (Sperry 1993, 884). He sees the highest good, that which is most sacred, the supreme value, to consist of "an ever-evolving quality of existence" (1993, 884). E. Erdmann and D. Stover comment, "In Sperry's view, God is not denied but equated with the creative forces of the universe" (1991, 158). Human evolution, by Sperry's "reciprocal up-down (bidirectional) paradigm for causal control," is governed not only by biophysical forces acting upward but by consciousness acting downward: evolution, by reason of the causal dynamics of consciousness, "becomes a gradual emergence of increased directedness, purpose, and meaning among the forces that move and govern living things" (1993, 884). "A new system of beliefs," Sperry writes, "when worked out and supported through religion and science combined, offers spiritual guidelines that would preserve and enhance the long-term, evolving quality of the entire ecosphere" (DeAngelis 1993, 7).

NEUROPHENOMENOLOGY

Toward an Inclusive Cognitive Neuroscience

Personal, subjective experience clearly matters enormously to people. Does such experience have within itself the potential to become meaningful for science as well? The relatively young discipline of neurophenomenology thinks that it indeed does. In the belief that personal experience can detect and interpret patterns of brain activity, this science unites neuroscience and a rigorous investigation of subjective experience. Neurophenomenological researchers hold high hopes in this regard, and some progress has been made in the realization of these hopes. It has been found, for example, that the course, depth, and intensity of meditation engaged in by long-term Tibetan Buddhist meditators correlate with objectively measured changes in the brain, such as synchronized gamma-band firing (see below, "Inducing Human Well-Being through Meditation"). Had the meditators' experience not been taken into account, the neurophenomenologist points out, information about differential change in the brain would have gone undetected and uninterpreted. Thus, experience—and indeed religious experience—can teach science something. A pilot study of depth perception (2002), undertaken by University of Wisconsin, Madison, cognitive scientist Antoine Lutz and his colleagues to test the fruitfulness and validity of the neurophenomenological approach, will serve as a guiding thread through much of the presentation of the field that follows (2002). Neuroscientific research findings and interpretations are italicized throughout the remainder of the present chapter.

First-Person and Third-Person Accounts of Consciousness

"Third-person" accounts of phenomena are accounts given by external observers, as found, for example, in the sciences of physics, biology, and chemistry. Such accounts are objective and impersonal reports of natural phenomena as externally witnessed, "reports from the outside," in contrast to accounts that are subjective and personal reports of consciousness as experienced "from within," "reports from within" (Varela and Shear 1999, 1). Third-person accounts from the outside generally aim to eliminate, to the extent possible, all subjective and personal elements, both those of the investigator and, when humans are studied, as in psychology, those of the investigated as well, and to proceed in an entirely objective manner. Third-person neuroscientific accounts of the relation between the brain and human consciousness involve the use of such technologies as the electroencephalogram (EEG) and magnetic resonance imaging (MRI). Such studies typically pursue an entirely external, objective account of internal, subjective experience in an attempt to explain consciousness on the basis of the physical workings of the brain. Conventional neuroscience, in attempting to "reduce" subjective experience to third-person, objective foundations, has been called a form of "scientific reductionism" or "scientific materialism" (Varela and Shear 1999, 9). Consciousness researcher and Tibetan Buddhist monk B. Alan Wallace remarks that there is indeed a broad consensus among cognitive scientists that "the physical world is the only reality" and "that all mental processes are nothing more than functions or properties of the brain" (2007, 11, 29). So sure are scientific reductionists "that the mind is nothing more than a biological phenomenon" that Wallace says they "confuse this belief with scientific knowledge," the only remaining question being "how the brain produces conscious states" (2007, 24, 62).

Beginning in the 1990s, a number of neuroscientists began to challenge this materialistic assumption pervasive among neuroscientific investigators. These scientists make the argument that, after all, subjective consciousness or mind is the very thing cognitive science wants to give an account of and, so, ought not be excluded from serious consideration. They contend that "lived experience" is "irreducible"—that is, that it cannot and should not be "reduced" to the physical brain and, indeed, that the only access anyone has to consciousness, or to anything else for that matter, is consciousness itself. They hold that the data of personal experience must be approached on their own personal, subjective level and are to be given a full and fair hearing. Personal data, then, in this view, are not to be simply traced back, with no voice of their own, to a purely physical origin, where all subjective elements have been peremptorily ruled out in advance. Neuroscientific accounts, they argue, must not overlook the fact that consciousness is personal, that it belongs and matters to a "subject" or "self." In short, "first-person" accounts, accounts that the subject or self gives of his or her own experiences, firsthand accounts of personal subjective consciousness, are needed, then, for a complete scientific understanding of consciousness (Varela and Shear 1999, 1). This is not to say that first-person accounts "from within" are meant to replace third-person accounts "from the outside." Rather, they supplement and complement them.

Uniting Phenomenology and Neuroscience: Neurophenomenology

"Phenomenology" is a twentieth-century philosophy dedicated to providing an adequate understanding of human life through a rigorous account of human consciousness. It was founded by Edmund Husserl and developed in an existential direction by such philosophers as Martin Heidegger and Maurice Merleau-Ponty. Phenomenology is the study of phenomena, which are defined as things just as they appear in experience, "the things themselves," conscious events "lived" by someone (Varela and Shear 1999, 3). At first glance, a phenomenological and a neuroscientific approach couldn't seem to be farther apart. The typical neuroscientist, we have seen, relegates consciousness to the status of an outcome, a side effect or epiphenomenon, and the typical phenomenologist keeps at a healthy distance from an external or objective examination of things. The distance that separates the phenomenological, the subjective domain of consciousness, and the neurobiological, the objective domain of brain, body, and behavior, has been called the "explanatory gap." Oriented to the observable and physical, cognitive scientists as a rule do not put the phenomenological and the neurobiological on an equal footing but are inclined to ask instead how "patterns of neural activity either produce or are equivalent to subjective mental processes" (Wallace 2007, 14). It is this very materialistic presumption that critics like Wallace say creates and perpetuates the explanatory gap, and so, its advocates are hardly in a position to close it.

A productive dialogue between phenomenology and neuroscience is advocated as an alternative to the presumption of materialism and is intended to help close the explanatory gap as a neurophenomenology that would join the two. To enter into such a dialogue, however, phenomenology will have to overcome its reluctance to entertain objective points of view and come to terms with them. Phenomenology will have to become, so to speak, "naturalized." And, from its side, neuroscience will have to set aside the materialistic presupposition that reduces everything to physical processes.

Phenomenology holds that "mental events *can* be observed directly" (Wallace 2007, 15). Approaching conscious experience systematically, phenomenology seeks to illuminate it by determining its categorical features— that is, those features that a proper examination would find belong to any experience whatever or to any experience of a certain kind: say, any perception (Lutz and Thompson 2003, 38). It is precisely phenomenology's systematic character, its search for categorical features of conscious experience, that is seen to allow for its rapprochement with neuroscience—that is, that permits the joint consideration of its subjective reports and neuroscience's objective data.

"Neurophenomenology" was introduced and given its name in 1996 by the remarkable cognitive neuroscientist Francisco Varela. Combining the disciplines of phenomenological philosophy and cognitive science, neurophenomenology joins subjective data, "first-person descriptive reports" of conscious experience and its categorical or structurally constant features, with third-person objective data, considered as the neurophysiological realization of these phenomena of conscious experience (Thompson, Lutz, and Cosmelli 2005, 2; Varela 1996). As we shall see, a neurophenomenology uses first-person reports, so to speak, to "go back" and detect and interpret the third-person data that realize them and, in this way, to gain access to new data. Varela saw in neurophenomenology a research methodology that would serve as a foundation for future consciousness research (Zajonc 2006, 220).

Training in First-Person Methods

Neurophenomenology uses disciplined first-person methods developed in phenomenology to get suitable reports of consciousness. Subjects serving in neuroscientific experiments are systematically trained in these phenomenological methods in order to enhance their ability to observe carefully and describe accurately their experience (Lutz and Thompson 2003, 32–33). The hope is that the subjects' newly attained "attentive self-awareness" will allow them to "gain access to aspects of their experience that otherwise would remain unnoticed and unavailable for verbal report" (Lutz and

Thompson 2003, 33, 37). Such reflection upon one's straightforward experience is said to represent "a rich and largely unexplored source of information and data with dramatic consequences" (Varela and Shear 1999, 4).

People are generally not *reflectively self-aware* of their experience as they go about their matter-of-fact, everyday lives. Unnoticed aspects of experience, rather, are simply "lived through" "without a second thought." But we have the capability of becoming consciously aware of ourselves, are able to become "attentively self-aware," "reflectively attentive" (Lutz and Thompson 2003, 37–38). It is this ability to become reflectively self-aware, "to stop and think," that can be systematically taught and used in neurophenomenological experiments. Subjects can be trained to pay attention methodically to their actual experience in an experimental situation and to what they find is consciously going on in it, then to classify—categorically characterize—it. They can be trained to open themselves to new insights into their experience and various aspects of it, giving rise in this way to new experiences, new first-person data (Rudrauf et al. 2002, 43; Varela 1996). And they can be trained to report their findings accurately to an investigator. That subjects can be trained in neurophenomenological first-person methods is seen to pave the way for the collection of first-person data for integration with third-person data.

It has already been pointed out that Lutz and his colleagues undertook a pilot study to investigate the fruitfulness and validity of the neurophenomenological approach of joining first-person and third-person methods (Lutz et al. 2002; Lutz and Thompson 2003, 42–46). The experimental task in this study was looking at a two-dimensional pattern of dots in which an illusory three-dimensional figure was designed to emerge through perceptual fusion. Prior to engaging in this task, subjects underwent intensive training in first-person methods relating to their performance of the experimental task. They were trained in particular to attend carefully to their immediate mental processes and to variations in these processes during the performance of the experimental task (Lutz and Thompson 2003, 43). The aim was to bring about a reflective self-awareness of the experiencing process involved in attaining the three-dimensional figure. Another aim of the training session was to improve the accuracy of the verbal report (Lutz et al. 2002, 1586). Subjects "defined their own stable experiential categories (structural constants) . . . to describe the main elements of the subjective context in which they perceived the three-dimensional shapes" (Lutz and Thompson 2003, 44). These experiential categories discovered in the training session were thus derived from the subjects' self-descriptions and were consequently grouped in terms of the common "factor of the degree of preparation (e.g., 'prepared,' 'non-prepared') felt by the subject" to perceive the three-dimensional figure—that is, in terms of the subject's felt readiness or unreadiness to engage in the experimental task (Lutz and Thompson 2003, 44). On the basis of these categories, individual trials of the experimental session were divided into corresponding "phenomenological clusters" represent-

ing varying degrees of preparedness: for example, a "prepared" cluster of trials (trials in which subjects described themselves as "prepared" to perceive the three-dimensional figure) and a "nonprepared" cluster (in which subjects described themselves as "not prepared") (Lutz and Thompson 2003, 44–45). Thus, when the experiment was conducted, the subjects, shortly after first seeing the three-dimensional figure, were to give the verbal report, for example, of "prepared" or "not-prepared."

Using First-Person Data to Uncover New First-Person Data

Methodologically, "the phenomenological rationale for using first-person methods is to generate new data, both first-person and third-person, for the science of consciousness" (Lutz and Thompson 2003, 33). *By reflecting, during training, on the "how" of experiencing the pattern of dots, the investigators comment, new conscious content came into view in the pilot study: namely the felt awareness of varying degrees of preparation to perceive the three-dimensional figure. Degree of preparation had thus been discovered through attentive self-awareness as a categorical feature or structural constant of experience. These newly discovered first-person data—experiential data rendered reflectively conscious—were later used in connection with the experiment proper "to uncover new third-person data about the physiological processes crucial for consciousness" (Lutz and Thompson 2003, 32). Two third-person measures, for integration with the first-person verbal report of degree of preparation, were used in the pilot study: (1) EEG signals were recorded throughout the trials, and (2) Reaction-time for pressing a button upon the complete emergence of the three-dimensional figure was measured. Subjects reported their degree of preparedness after pressing the button, that is, shortly after the complete emergence of the three-dimensional figure. The study thus involved the simultaneous collection of first-person data (verbal reports of degree of preparation) and third-person data (EEGs and reaction time) (Lutz and Thompson 2003, 43). Again, the new first-person data are the experienced degree of preparation as verbally reported—"prepared" or "not-prepared," for example. Results and discussion are presented further on in this section.*

Relating Brain Complexity to Conscious Experience

Neurophenomenology sees the nervous system as a self-governing system that generates its own patterns of interacting neurons (Thompson, Lutz, and Cosmelli 2005). This self-generated, internally arising activity of the brain is the point from which neurophenomenological analysis begins. The idea is to look at the brain's large-scale dynamic networks in order to discover how conscious processes emerge or are realized through them. But, to do that, precise (reliable and accurate) conscious (first-person) data are needed. Neurophenomenology's originality lies in its rigorous and explicit incorporation of such experiential data into neuroscientific investigations and in its aim of integrating the actual and relevant phenomenal structure of these first-person data into the third-person investigation of large-scale, self-organizing neural operations (Lutz and Thompson 2003, 42). Towards these ends, as we've seen, experimental subjects are trained to engage actively in identifying, descriptively categorizing, and verbally reporting their conscious processes while coping with experimental tasks. These reports are then to be used to identify *patterns of large-scale neural activity*. In this way, by the joint analysis of first-person verbal reports and third-person patterns of neural activity, "a rigorous relationship between brain complexity and subjective experience" can be established: "original phenomenal categories (degree of preparedness in the pilot study being followed here) are explicitly used to detect otherwise undetected original neurodynamical patterns" (Lutz and Thompson 2003, 42). Neurophenomenology's "working hypothesis," in brief, is that precise first-person data can significantly contribute to "the analysis and interpretation of the physiological processes relevant to consciousness" (Lutz and Thompson 2003, 33; Rudrauf et al. 2002, 45; Varela 1996). But before proceeding further, it will be profitable to examine first the question of the patterning of large-scale neural activity.

Large-Scale Neural Integration: Synchronized Gamma-Band Neural Firing

The process of visual perception is described as beginning with the breaking up of a given visual scene into isolated fragments detected by many widely distributed individual neurons. Yet, visual perception is found somehow to reassemble these fragments into complete objects—integrated, coherent wholes, or gestalts—which, of course, are what appear in vision. The "large-scale integration problem" or "binding problem" is how the brain activity of widely spread out individual neurons comes to be selected and coordinated in such a way as to produce unified cognition—a coherent visual whole, for example (Lutz et al. 2002). The dynamic "links" among the components of the nervous system are seen as the important thing for understanding large-scale integration, and not the components themselves. Integrated, coherent consciousness of wholes (or gestalts) requires many different parts of the brain working together in concert, requires coherence in underlying brain processes. In the early 1990s, an attractive, though controversial, theoretical solution to the large-scale integration problem emerged from the work of Wolf Singer, director of the Frankfurt's Max Planck Institute for Brain Research, and a number of others, who found a "synchronized firing" of neurons responding to portions of the same object. A synchronized firing of neurons is neurons firing together, "correlated firing," "regular, rhythmic patterns of firing activity" (Austin 1998, 710). Singer (2001) suggested that such synchronized firing might be responsible for the binding together of responses from multiple, widely dispersed individual neurons and that such binding together might underlie high-level cognitive processes. The attainment in experience, then, of coherent, integrated wholes, by this theory, would be mediated by the cooperative interacting or coherence of neurons brought about by the synchronized firing of neurons. Varela is quoted as supporting this view: "It is the precise coincidence of the firing of the cells that brings about unity in mental-cognitive experience" (Rudrauf et al. 2002, 47–48). Synchronized firing, he says, best indicates the moment of conscious integration.

But that's not all. Experimental studies have further found that it is the firing of neurons *in the high-frequency gamma range,* thirty to eighty cycles per second, that effectively serves to synchronize neural firing. The theory now becomes that gamma firing is the medium though which neurons fire together by becoming synchronized. Gamma-wave neural firing, facilitating the establishment of precise synchronized firing of neurons, may thus be the large-scale integrative mechanism sought (Rodriguez et al. 1999, 430–33; Lutz et al. 2002). This theory of gamma synchronization is seen to accord with the fundamental assumption of neurophenomenology to the effect "that large-scale, coherent neural activities constitute a fundamental self-organizing pole of integration in the brain" (Lutz and Thompson 2003, 40–41). The theory suggests that neurophenomenological research does well to look for ties between coherent and integrated personal experience (wholes/gestalts and states) and coherent and integrated neural patterns (gamma synchronization).

Evidence for the integrative role of synchronized firing of neurons in the gamma range is found in a study by E. Rodriguez and his colleagues (1999). These investigators had subjects press a button to indicate if they had or had not perceived a face upon the presentation of a picture in which a face was either discernible ("perception" condition) or not ("nonperception" condition) (Rodriguez et al. 1999, 430–33). In the "perception" condition, upon seeing the face, large-scale synchronized neural firing was found to occur, mainly in the gamma band (thirty to eighty cycles per second); the perception of an integrated, coherent whole, a face, was thus matched by integrated, coherent brain activity. In the "nonperception" condition, by contrast, where no face could be made out, no significant synchronized firing was found to occur upon the presentation of the picture.

The pilot study we have been following analyzed the EEG signals for each cluster of trials (each cluster reflecting reported degree of preparation for the dot pattern) to determine patterns of synchronized neurons (Lutz and Thompson 2003, 45). The clusters derived from first-person data (verbal reports) were thus used to detect and interpret third-person data (neural processes). The investigators hypothesized that each cluster ("prepared," "not prepared" for the presentation of

*the dot pattern) would show a distinct neural response (EEG) and a distinct be-
havioral response (reaction time) (Lutz and Thompson 2003, 45–46). The results
support the hypothesis. The average reaction time for the emergence of the three-
dimensional image for the "prepared" group of trials was shorter than for the
"unprepared" cluster. This difference between the clusters was significant. As for
the EEG measures, in the "prepared" cluster, synchronized neural firing was seen
early and continued (on average) throughout the trial. In the "unprepared" cluster, on the other hand, no stable synchronous firing was observed before the presentation of the stimulus (dot pattern); upon its presentation, a complex pattern
of weak synchronized firing and massive desynchronized firing occurred. In the
"prepared" cluster, gamma-band firing (thirty to seventy cycles per second) was
found to increase during the period leading up to the presentation of the stimulus. No such increase was found to occur in the "unprepared" cluster. This result
suggests that being prepared for the stimulus was characterized by an enhancement of gamma-band synchronization, that a particular first-person experience
was characterized by a particular third-person neural pattern.*

Using Original First-Person Data to
Uncover New Third-Person Data

*It is concluded that joining first-person, subjective data on degree of preparedness
(phenomenological clusters) with third-person, objective analyses of neural
processes (EEG) rendered brain responses less opaque (Lutz and Thompson 2003,
45). Regarding this reduction in opaqueness, the large amount of variability in
evidence in the response of different subjects to an identical stimulus (dot pattern) would have been treated as unintelligible noise if the verbally reported degree of preparedness had not been taken into account and related to measures of
neural activity; actual differences would have gone undetected. However, since
degree of preparedness was in fact considered in relation to neural activity in this
experiment, some of the variability in evidence is accounted for (Lutz and Thompson 2003, 42–46). This is an important consideration. By relating consciousness
(degree of preparedness) to "the complexity of brain activity" (EEGs), first-
person accounts detect and interpret the brain's ongoing activity (synchronized
gamma-band neural firing), activity that would have simply remained undetected and closed to interpretation if only approaches "from the outside" had been
employed (Thompson, Lutz, and Cosmelli 2005). Original first-person reports
thus served to disclose new third-person data: distinct neural, as well as behavioral, responses for "prepared" or "unprepared" clusters. Increased synchronized
gamma-band neural firing was found in subjects who described themselves as
"prepared" but not in those who described themselves as "unprepared." Thus, coherent and integrated third-person data were seen to accompany coherent and integrated first-person data, suggesting that the former may realize the latter. The
overall conclusion is that this study, in thus helping bridge the explanatory gap,*

shows the neurophenomenological approach to be both valid and fruitful (Lutz and Thompson 2003, 42–46).

Neurophenomenology and Meditation

The above introduction to neurophenomenology pointed out that first-person verbal reports of meditation experiences have been found to correlate with third-person neurophysiological data. *Thus, for example, the emergence over time of high-amplitude (amplitude = power) synchronized gamma activity of long-term meditators correlated with verbal reports of the intensity of the meditation (Lutz, Rawlings, and Davidson 2005; see below, "Inducing Human Well-Being through Meditation").* It has been hypothesized that experienced meditators, such as those used in this study, are better equipped to give accurate and reliable first-person reports than inexperienced ones, thus are in a position to provide the neuroscientific investigator with better data for determining the integrative neural processes that underlie the meditation experience (Lutz et al., 2007). Meditation, therefore, offers a promising field of research for the neuroscientist—one that, through the joint consideration of first- and third-person data, can illuminate consciousness through detecting and interpreting the neurophyisological processes that realize it.

AFFECTIVE NEUROSCIENCE AND TIBETAN BUDDHIST MEDITATION

The Encounter between Tibetan Buddhism and Western Science

Tibetan Buddhism aims at a radical transformation of consciousness: the transformation of the very *process* of consciousness itself. Meditation serves as its principal instrument for achieving this goal. Meditation is an exercise in retraining attentional habits; it develops the skill of paying attention (Goleman 1991b, 95). Tibetan Buddhist monk and president of the Santa Barbara Institute for Consciousness Studies B. Alan Wallace comments that, over its long history, "Buddhism has developed rigorous methods for refining the attention, and then applying it to explore the origins, nature, and role of consciousness in the natural world" (2007, 58). Or, as journalist Katherine Ellison puts it, Buddhist meditators have twenty-five hundred years of mental "technology" to draw on, "techniques for paying careful attention to the workings of their minds," for taking control of their minds, for fostering "awareness, calm, compassion and joy" (2006, 72). His Holiness the Fourteenth Dalai Lama, Nobel laureate and spiritual leader of Tibetan Buddhism, points out that Buddhism has long made the case for the tremendous potential for transformation inherent in the human mind and that attentional skill is "a matter of volition and focused effort" (2005b, 156). Indeed, he remarks that Buddhist psychology takes it as a psychological law that the mind can be enhanced and further developed.

The Dalai Lama has called, time and again, for active collaboration between modern science and Tibetan Buddhism on a broad range of issues pertaining to the human mind. While noting neuroscience's rapid progress in recent years, he remains convinced that it needs to supplement its objective approach with rigorous investigation of conscious experience. The Dalai Lama believes that science stands to benefit enormously from such a proposed expansion and that it is precisely here that Tibetan Buddhism has a great deal to offer. The dialogue advocated by the Dalai Lama between neuroscience and Tibetan Buddhism is well underway. The present section reviews some of the progress that has been made in this undertaking. Cognitive neuroscientist Francisco Varela is quoted as commenting, "The natural meeting ground between science and Buddhism is . . . one of the most active research frontiers today. What is involved is learning how to put together the data from the inner examination of human experience with the empirical basis that modern cognitive and affective neuroscience can provide. Such first-person accounts are not a mere 'confirmation' of what science can find anyway. . . . [They are] a necessary complement" (Harrington 2006, 7). And Wallace remarks that scientists are "beginning to join the Buddhist tradition in its pursuit of the understanding of the nature, origins, and potentials of consciousness," that science has "begun to focus on mental well-being," on "human flourishing" (2007, 5, 63).

Meditation and Neuroplasticity

Neuroplasticity refers to changes in the brain, both structural and functional, resulting from experience and training. Research on neuroplasticity has burgeoned in recent years, coming to the invariable conclusion that the brain does indeed dynamically change and does so throughout life. University of California, Los Angeles, psychiatrist Daniel Siegel is quoted as remarking, "We now know that neural firing can lead to changes in neural connections, and experience leads to changes in neural firing" (Ellison 2006, 74). The Mind and Life Institute, which was established to promote links between modern science and Buddhism, has published an article on its website based on a talk the Dalai Lama gave at the Thirty-fifth Annual Meeting of the Society for Neuroscience on November 12, 2005, in Washington, D.C. He is quoted there as remarking, "Recent discoveries in neuroscience have demonstrated the innate plasticity of the brain, both in terms of synaptic connections and the birth of new neurons, as a result of exposure to external stimuli. . . . The Buddhist tradition implies . . . that mental practice can effect observable synaptic and neural changes in the brain" (2005a). *Richard Davidson, professor of psychology at the University of Wisconsin, Madison, comments that, on the basis of animal research, "the prefrontal cortex, amygdala, and hippocampus are all sites where plasticity is known to occur"* (2002, 122).

Tibetan Buddhism, we have seen, is committed to the transformative power of meditation. Neuroscientific studies have found that this power extends to the brain: meditation has been shown to change the brain. It has been reported, for example, that long-term meditation can, on the one hand, change neural networks and, on the other, induce brain coherence by increasing the synchronized gamma-band firing of neurons—and thus improve cognitive performance (see above, "Large-Scale Neural Integration: Synchronized Gamma-Band Neural Firing").

Visions of Compassion

The Dalai Lama writes, "I believe that at the most fundamental level our nature is compassionate, and that cooperation, not conflict, lies at the heart of the basic principles that govern our human existence" (2002, 68). The Dalai Lama similarly finds happiness to be natural to human life. And he sees an intimate link between compassion and happiness, finding that compassion makes us happy (2002, 109). Compassion, and thus happiness, he says, can be cultivated through meditation. In their preface to the 2002 book *Visions of Compassion: Western Scientists and Tibetan Buddhists Examine Human Nature*, Davidson and A. Harrington comment, "Tibetan Buddhism has long celebrated the human potential for compassion, is dedicated to studying the scope, expression, and training of compassionate feeling and action, and sees compassion as a key to enduring happiness and, even more fundamentally, spiritual transformation" (2002, v). Compassion is defined as an emotional and cognitive response to another feeling (sentient) being (Harrington 2002, 21–22). By putting us directly in contact with the suffering of others, compassion is seen as challenging our sense of separate individual existence. Harrington comments that, whereas we Westerners, with our belief in original sin and more recently the id, are pessimistic about human possibilities, Buddhism discovers within human nature the resources "to purify and transform" itself. "The cultivation of compassion," Wallace comments, "is like a silken thread that runs through and connects all the pearls of Buddhist meditative practices" (2007, 113). In short, Tibetan Buddhism sees compassion—in indissoluble unity with insight-wisdom (*prajna*)—as the key to human transformation and happiness and meditation as the pathway to compassion.

Richard Davidson and Affective Neuroscience

Tibetan Buddhism has developed specific meditative exercises to culti-
vate compassion and positive affect—such emotions as happiness, sym-
pathy, affection, and good cheer—and to extinguish self-centered behaviors (Houshmand et al. 2002, 9). Very little scientific research has been
undertaken, however, on the human ability to regulate positive affect.
Largely through Richard Davidson's work in affective neuroscience, that
picture is now changing. A meditator since 1974, Davidson has been a
central figure in the neuroscientific study of positive affect and compassion in relation to Tibetan Buddhist meditators.

Davidson says he became convinced while still in graduate school "that
the contemplative traditions of the East had something meaningful to offer us in the West" and that the West could enter into fruitful dialogue with
the East without the sacrifice of scientific rigor (2002, 108). He goes on to
point out the great significance for science in our day of cultivating happiness and compassion and states his goal as the rigorous investigation of
the construct of compassion, from the perspective of affective neuroscience. In his studies, Davidson has correlated affective states with observed patterns of neural activity. By thus linking internal, subjective states
and external, objective observation, he has made a beginning in the scientific understanding of such spiritual experiences as a meditative state of
"love and compassion," previously thought to have a purely subjective
character and to be closed to scientific investigation. He has shown, moreover, that happiness, rather than a nebulous and indescribable feeling, is a
physical state of the brain and can be experimentally induced.

The Asymmetric Role of the Prefrontal Cortex in Emotion

*Davidson generalizes, on the basis of a great number of studies conducted both by
his team and by others, that when emotions are experimentally elicited, several of
the prefrontal cortex regions are activated. This activation, moreover, shows an
asymmetric pattern: "greater relative left-sided prefrontal activation is observed
during the elicitation of certain positive emotions, while greater relative right-
sided prefrontal cortex activation is observed during the elicitation of certain negative emotions" (Davidson 2002, 110–11). Davidson remarks that EEG studies,
for example, have found that positive affect is associated with increased relative
left prefrontal activation and that negative affect is associated with increased relative right prefrontal activity (2002, 113; 2004, 1397). He points out, moreover,
that "a resilient affective style is associated with a high level of left prefrontal activation," while "greater degrees of right prefrontal predominant activity were
correlated with tendencies toward such distressing emotions as sadness, anxiety
and worry" (2004, 1395). Finally, Davidson reports that positive affect experi-*

mentally induced by a movie was found to increase relative left-sided prefrontal activation, whereas induced negative affect was found to elicit "an opposite pattern of asymmetric activation" (2004, 1397–98).

Inducing Human Well-Being through Meditation

Ellison comments that "Buddhism asserts that lasting happiness is your birthright" (2006, 77). The Dalai Lama asserts that the need for happiness lies at the heart of human nature and further remarks, "The systematic training of the mind—the cultivation of happiness, the genuine inner transformation by deliberately selecting and focusing on positive mental states and challenging negative mental states—is possible because of the very structure and function of the brain" (1988, 44–45). The following paragraphs summarize studies on the induction of positive affect, mostly through "love and compassion" meditation as studied by Davidson and his colleagues. "Love and compassion" meditation does not focus on any particular object or person but aims rather at producing an intense and pervasive feeling of "loving-kindness."

Davidson makes the general remark that experimental findings underscore the fact that there is pronounced plasticity in the central circuitry of emotion (2002, 119). Davidson's brain scans of Tibetan Buddhist monks are said to demonstrate, moreover, that "emotions like love and compassion are in fact skills—and can be trained to a dramatic degree," that "meditation can radically transform emotion" (Ellison 2006, 74, 75). One particular Tibetan Buddhist monk with thirty years meditation experience in the Himalayas was the subject of a series of significant studies undertaken by Davidson. This monk was able to hold stable mental states for some time and to precisely report on them (Goleman 2003, 446–49). The monk repeatedly strove in one EEG study to attain a state of love and compassion, a task he was familiar with. Davidson found that gamma waves in the left prefrontal cortex, which has been linked to reported happiness, dramatically increased during these exercises (Ellison 2006, 77). Thus, on the one hand, as clinical neurologist James Austin concludes, a highly trained person was found capable of intentionally increasing the capacity of his brain for compassion through repeated love and compassion meditation (2006, 270), and, on the other, this increased brain capacity for compassion was seen to be strongly linked with positive affect, with happiness. This supports previous remarks about the link between meditation and compassion, on the one hand, and between compassion and happiness, on the other. On this latter connection between compassion and happiness, the Dalai Lama has said that the person who meditates on compassion for others is the first to benefit; Davidson has stated that compassion is itself "a form of positive emotion" (2002, 109); finally, it is generally remarked that the cultivation of compassion brings about an overall feeling of well-being.

Austin summarizes another EEG study conducted by Davidson's team, headed by University of Wisconsin, Madison, cognitive scientist Antoine Lutz (Lutz et al. 2004), in which a group of long-term (fifteen to forty years) Tibetan Buddhist meditators and a control group of untrained student volunteers engaged in "a state of loving kindness and compassion" (2006, 48–50). At baseline the monks showed a great deal more gamma-band activity (twenty-five to forty-two cycles per second) than the controls, this EEG activity being especially pronounced in the medial frontoparietal electrodes (see above, "Large-Scale Neural Integration: Synchronized Gamma-Band Neural Firing"). The investigators report that this difference was found to increase sharply during meditation. They summarize, "Here we find that long-term Buddhist practitioners self-induce sustained elec-troencephalographic high-amplitude (amplitude = power) gamma-band oscilla-tions and phase-synchrony during meditation" (Lutz et al. 2004, 16369). Austin comments that the monks "gradually developed a robust and extraordinarily high degree of synchronized gamma activity; moreover, the more hours each meditator had practiced over the years, the higher was their absolute gamma activity" (2006, 48–50). The likely reasons for the difference between the findings of this study—increased gamma-band activity—and those of other studies—an increase in slow alpha or theta rhythms (see below, "Meditation's Psychophysiological Effects")—during meditation were discussed by the investigators: different mea-sures were employed, and, more importantly, different styles of meditation were involved (Lutz et al. 2004, 16372). A. Lutz, N. B. Rawlings, and R. J. Davidson (2005) report that a follow-up study found that the emergence over time of high-amplitude synchronized gamma activity of long-term meditators correlated with first-person verbal reports of the intensity of the meditation.

Studies on meditation and human well-being have also been conducted using nonmonk subjects and other forms of meditation. Subjects in a recent study who underwent an eight-week mindfulness training program, followed by an in-fluenza vaccination, developed a relatively rapid rise in their influenza antibody titers, showing a significantly greater antibody response to the vaccination than the controls (Austin 2006, 56–57). A pilot study found that subjects meditating for less than a half-hour per day using Buddhist techniques underwent an im-provement of mood as great as that produced by antidepressants (Ellison 2006, 74). It has further been found that meditation, by acting on the prefrontal cortex, is able to calm emotional arousal in situations of fear or anger. An MRI study conducted by S. W. Lazar and her colleagues (2005) used typical U. S. practi-tioners of Buddhist insight ("mindfulness") meditation and a control group of nonpractitioners. The researchers found that cortical regions (parts of the cerebral cortex involved in attention and sensory processing) activated in this form of meditation were thicker in the meditators than the controls. This is the first evi-dence linking meditation with changes in brain structure (cortical thickening). Results suggest, moreover, that age-related thinning of the cortex may be lessened through meditation.

Neuroplasticity and Human Well-Being

Davidson concludes on the connection between neural plasticity and the promotion of emotional well-being, "Research on plasticity has given us new information about the realistic hope for ways to shape the circuitry of emotion to promote increased well-being and positive affect. . . . The field of affective neuroscience offers great promise for achieving significant new insights about these qualities of human experience that appear to be essential for optimal functioning" (2002, 124–25). The research of Davidson and his team has demonstrated the great potential, in particular, of Tibetan Buddhist techniques for such "optimal functioning." Their studies of long-term Buddhist meditators have shown that people have a measure of control over their emotions and can increase their cognitive functioning (Ellison 2006, 72, 77). Jon Kabat-Zinn, founder of the Stress Reduction Clinic at the University of Massachusetts Medical Center, comments broadly, "Buddhist meditation is leading to an expansion of the science of what it is to be human" (Ellison 2006, 73).

JAMES H. AUSTIN: ZEN BUDDHISM AND NEUROSCIENCE

The Interrelations of Zen and Neuroscience

James H. Austin, clinical neurologist and Zen practitioner, has written two richly informative books on the interrelations of Zen Buddhism and brain research, *Zen and the Brain: Toward an Understanding of Meditation and Consciousness* (1998) and *Zen-Brain Reflections: Reviewing Recent Developments in Meditation and States of Consciousness* (2006). Austin gives an account in these works of his own gradual transformation in the course of long-term meditative training, as well as of his experiences of alternate states of consciousness. He carefully considers his own practice and knowledge of Zen in relation to the brain sciences, on the one hand, and the relevance of the latest neuroscientific findings to Zen, on the other (2006, xxiv). Austin's basic claim is that the two fields, both of which are described as hard-nosed and skeptical in approach, complement and illuminate one another (2006, 23–24). Austin comments in his earlier book that it is "a story of one neurologist's personal quest and professional search. These two paths converge in ways that lead to one straightforward thesis: awakening, enlightenment, occurs only because the human brain undergoes substantial changes," its workings coming to be at once enhanced and simplified (1998, xix). On the one hand, then, Zen enlightenment "must come from the brain, because the brain is the organ of the mind" (Austin 1998, 18); on the other, Zen training is said to be one of the brain's "agencies of transformation," to change the psychophysiology of the human brain (Austin 2006, 138). The changed brain gives rise to Zen enlightenment, then, but Zen training changes the brain. The present overview of Austin's work is structured around two central Zen topics— "kensho" and meditation.

Kensho

Kensho as Experience of Insight-Wisdom

Rare, spontaneous awakenings, Austin says, emerge from the depths of the human brain (1998, xix). These peaks of direct experience are said to be almost impossible to put into words. "Even so," Austin comments, "these fragile events inspired our major religions in ways that still shape our cultural development" (1998, xix). He says that these awakenings, which Zen refers to as "insight-wisdom" (*prajna*), bring deep and direct experiential insight into reality. Initial extraordinary experiences of insight-wisdom are called "kensho": "seeing into one's true nature" (Austin 1998, 387, 530–622; 2006, 9–10). "Satori," on the other hand, is the name for deeper and more transformative awakenings. The brief experiences of kensho and satori are said to realize "a full grasp of reality," "things as they really are," without the intrusion of our self-preoccupied self, without the brain's "subjective veils of *self*-consciousness" (Austin 2006, xxv, 7, 9–10). Zen, Austin comments, is nothing other than an inquiry into what the world "is *really* like" in "pure, objective consciousness" (2006, xxv). Zen Buddhism finds in insight-wisdom the single lasting cure for the fundamental "ignorance" that plagues human existence (Austin 2006, 9, 157, 240). Zen is thus seen to emphasize the transformative role of insight-wisdom as an awakening that shatters our ignorance, the "deep delusion" that we are a separate and enduring self at the center of things (Austin 2006, 240, 448). Austin remarks that long periods of meditative practice often precede kensho and satori (2006, 9–10). "These two states of 'enlightenment,'" moreover, though momentary openings, "stimulate the spiritual quest" and tend to transform personality in positive and lasting ways (Austin 2006, 9–10). Indeed, Zen considers crucial the transformation of the individual that continues to unfold after these experiences as a consequence of persistent and disciplined "daily-life practice" (Austin 2006, 10–11).

On the basis of his own experience, Austin describes kensho as a "momentary state" that "starts abruptly, peaks, has a diminuendo, then sponsors various thoughtful probings after the fact" (1998, 536–39; 2006, 366–67). The sense of the insight Austin gained in kensho was that his "former, entirely self-referent way of looking intrusively at the world" was the basic illusion (2006, 367). In sharp contrast to this illusion, he says, was "that brief, penetrating view of the world through the open eyes of kensho" (2006, 367). It seemed to him that this view was "more *real.*" Both in the course of the experience itself and his reflections afterwards over several days, Austin says he found kensho's "total perspective" to be "a genuine glimpse into the immanent perfection investing *everyday things as they really are*" (2006, 366). This newly attained consciousness of "the way things really are" was found to be "utterly empirical," a "clear and objective vision" (Austin 1999, 214). Austin describes "the first wave" of his experience of kensho: "Instantly, the entire scene acquires three qualities: Absolute Reality, Intrinsic Rightness, Ultimate Perfection" (1998, 537). No viewer was anywhere on the scene, which was "utterly empty," stripped of every last hint of the "psychic self," characterized as the unified essence of the "I-Me-Mine" (see below, "The Overconditioned Psychic Self"). Kensho's "second wave" revealed to Austin "three more indivisible themes": this existing state is "the eternal state of affairs," "there is nothing further to do," and "there is nothing whatsoever to fear" (1998, 537–38).

Kensho, Austin writes, is "the prime example of a brain uncovering its latent, insightful qualities and heightening them" (1998, 366). Kensho's newly gained perspectives, seen as inborn capacities of every brain, are said to foreshadow the teachings of the Buddha, Jesus, indeed all religious teachings (Austin 1998, 600).

Kensho's "rapid onset, scope, and total impact" are described as a profound transfiguration of consciousness and represent the occurrence of "a major state change in the brain" (Austin 2006, 417). Austin surmises that "an array of net excitatory processes" converging in unaccustomed ways and degrees gives rise to the enormous shift in one's everyday consciousness in kensho, to "seeing things as they really are" (2006, 416–17).

Austin remarks that central phenomenal features of enlightenment can be correlated with changes in frontal lobe functions (2006, 162). He notes further that, while only certain cortical functions are found to be in play in the early phases of kensho, these functions are "integrally linked with their counterparts down in the subcortex and brain stem" (1998, 614). Indeed, the wordlessness of the experience of kensho and some of its subtler characteristics are said to support the notion that new configurations are taking place in "deeper subcortical circuits" (Austin 2006, 366, 417). Much of the immediate character of Zen experience, Austin comments, may arise in the back of the brain "in networks closer to our earlier percepts"—insight-wisdom may be plausibly thought to arise from a "precognitive physiological core" (2006, 230–31).

The Overconditioned Psychic Self

The infant has "minimal consciousness" but, Austin remarks, soon "starts to chase after things," soon begins to form all kinds of images, ideas, and attachments, soon becomes "cluttered" (2006, 12, 24–25). The developing individual comes to assess some things as highly desirable and endlessly longs for them, while he sees others as disgusting and utterly worthless and loathes them. Zen Buddhism sees such "unfruitful loathings and longings" as so many "subjective veils" that prevent us from seeing the world objectively and from developing our "true self" or "original nature" (Austin 2006, 21). Our loathings and longings are said to constitute our "overconditioned" or "inflated, subjective SELF" (Austin 2006, 22, 383–84). Zen locates the roots of this "overconditioned psychic self" in the "ignorance" into which the growing individual falls as certain properties of the self unite to form the impression of being a separate, unique, and independent identity. Austin calls these unified properties of the psychic self "the I-Me-Mine." The "I" has physical existence, assumes several roles, is conscious, feels, thinks, and knows, and can do no wrong (Austin 2006, 13). The "Me" is said to be the subject undergoing mental and physical occurrences (Austin 2006, 13). The "Me" "is fearful, easily threatened, and suffers accordingly" (Austin 1999, 314). "Mine" are all my thoughts, viewpoints, and bodily organs. The whole world revolves around "My" self and "My" self alone. "My" "'own' greedy longings" for position, things, and other people are said to capture the essence of the "Mine" (Austin 2006, 14). The "Mine" grasps after attractive things and, once they are in "My" grasp, refuses to let go (Austin 1999, 314; 2006, 251).

Our psychic self, Austin comments, is a higher-level process of interpreting, linking many brain networks (2006, 21). Some of the positive messages produced by these networks give rise to attractions to things and longings for them. Some negative messages, on the other hand, make us fearful, moving us perhaps to pull away in disgust and loathing or perhaps to fume with anger and go on the attack. Austin says that each of us has been pushed and pulled by these "network biases" all our lives. These biases produce our aggressive behaviors, our unfruitful loathings and longings, and our fears and anxieties in myriad "overconditioned" ways beyond our reckoning.

Kensho as Deconditioning of the Psychic Self

Zen's "real work," Austin remarks, is "abdicating the sovereign *I*, abandoning all the ramparts defending the *Me*, and abolishing each enslavement by the *Mine*" (1998, 46). Zen aims, in other words, at transforming the "maladaptive self" (Austin 1998, 34–35). Kensho's "flash of deep insight" is seen to bring an awareness freed from past conditionings, as all the longings and loathings and ignorance of the I-Me-Mine drop off (Austin 2006, 9, 110–12). Former implicit assumptions and fixed notions, "old maladaptive memory associations," all our old notions of the self, the unfruitful layers of the overconditioned self, are discarded, "let go" (Austin 2006, 102–103, 394). Austin refers to these key "deconditionings" as "subtractions" of the psychic self (2006, 263). Thus reduced, thus deconditioned and "subtracted from," the self is said to dread nothing and to desire nothing (Austin 2006, 250, 365).

The self drops off (Austin 1998, 295–96). In milliseconds, Austin remarks, the world has been completely reinterpreted "into a new realm of absolute reality" (1998, 295–96). Gone are all the old dualities (Austin 1998, 298, 533). "I" and "it" no longer stand over against one another. No "I" is engaged in grasping, and no object is being grasped. Everything, rather, is now found to coexist, to interpenetrate. All of the old pairs of "opposites" have instantly been reconciled (Austin 1998, 602).

"Letting go," Austin remarks, is trusting one's brain and its "highly competent automatic pilot" to do the correct thing (1998, 359).

Austin says that many brain functions are suspended in kensho, that many "inhibitory 'subtractions'" take place (2006, 453). In an instant, implicit assumptions represented in the brain are discarded (Austin 2006, 274). "Egocentric subtractions," seen to underlie many of kensho's early phenomena, are probably due to gamma aminobutyric acid (GABA), "the brain's major fast inhibitory transmitter" (Austin 2006, 417). Austin comments further that the sequence of phenomena that occurred in his own experience of kensho apparently represented processes of excitation, inhibition, and disinhibition in certain brain regions (2006, 166). He believes that understanding kensho's resulting overall pattern of the heightening of some faculties and the dropping of others can help us get a better grasp of Zen (1998, 367). He offers the following testable hypothesis: regions of the brain's right hemisphere are mainly responsible for the egocentric subtractions evidenced in kensho and satori (2006, 250).

Egocentric and Allocentric Frames of Reference

Austin makes an important distinction between egocentric, or self-centered, and allocentric, or other-centered, frames of reference. The egocentric frame of reference is directed inwards, back to the physical and psychic self (Austin 1998, 491–92; 2006, 324). It thus refers to a style of behavior with one's personal self at the center. The allocentric frame of reference, by contrast, is directed outwards, beyond and away from the personal self. It refers to a style of behavior externally directed to things "out there." In the egocentric frame of reference, data are referred back to such internal spatial coordinates as the position of the head. In the allocentric frame of reference, by contrast, things outside are considered objectively in terms of their own spatial coordinates (Austin 2006, 324–25). Austin remarks that, whereas implicitly self-referent constructs are said to emerge out of the egocentric system, the allocentric system is prepared to represent a simpler and wholly objective view devoid of a self (2006, 370).

Research with animals, Austin states, shows that egocentric and allocentric orientations represent two basically different ways in which the brain is prepared to process incoming sensory data (2006, 370). Austin states that regions of the frontal lobes have been connected to our more inward, "self-knowing"—egocentric—awareness (2006, 162). Positron-emission tomography (PET) data, on the other hand, are said to suggest that the back of the brain underlies allocentric frames of reference (Austin 2006, 325). If there is damage to the brain's allocentric circuits, "overactive egocentric modes of perception" seem to predominate (Austin 2006, 325). In shifting toward externalized tasks, by contrast, the four brain regions that have been identified as potentially having self-referent functions (egocentric frame of reference) "become deactivated" (Austin 2006, 197).

Kensho's Allocentric Frame of Reference

In kensho, the brain is suddenly released from the sum total of its former overcon-ditioning (Austin 2006, 370). The self's thick veils thus drawn aside, consciousness is now said to function in a mode that is impersonal and remarkably clear (Austin 2006, 370). When consciousness is thus in an allocentric mode, the "Mine" no longer butts in everywhere. The usual sovereign self peeking out at a world of independent objects dissolves, and the perceptual field takes on a tone that is "inherently objective" (Austin 2006, 16–17, 19, 200). "The awesome, impossible simplicity of Zen insight" is this: "an apple is an apple—in itself," without the self's intrusion into the picture (Austin 1998, 5). "ITS 'absolute value'" now enters into full awareness (Austin 2006, 370). In short, when the old overconditioned egocentric self, with its delusions, is set side, things are freed to reveal themselves as they really and truly are—impersonally, objectively, allocentrically (Austin 2006, 446). There results the fresh impression of "things as THEY are" and as not what they had always appeared to be to an overconditioned imagination (Austin 2006, 21–22). In kensho, it is no longer "I'm seeing" and "I'm grasping the apple" but "awareness is" and "apple grasped" (Austin 1998, 503). For the moment, only an allocentric world is seen to exist (Austin 2006, 338). We now find ourselves to be just one small wave in the immensity of the ocean, a single cell in "the Great Self" (Austin 1998, 52; 2006, 21–22, 354). Here, self is but "one other expression of OTHER" (Austin 2006, 22).

In kensho "major deep physiological shifts occur" that liberate allocentric net-works from the egocentric self's firm hold (Austin 2006, 371); kensho disconnects for the moment all of the self-centered networks that were previously overcondi-tioning the psychic self (Austin 2006, 387). The brain enters its allocentric mode, and things are now free to appear in consciousness "as THEY are out there."

Kensho as "Oneness"

Austin says that in kensho we realize that all things, ourselves included, literally interpenetrate as a single "eternal oneness" (1998, 11–12; 2006,

329–30). In kensho, the many exist as one; true reality is selfless unity (Austin 1998, 533; 2006, 239, 335, 340). *Austin comments that the "coherent function"—the acting in concert—of many regions on both sides of the brain is apparently involved in a higher-order act of integration of this sort (2006, 342, 387).*

Fearlessness and Bliss in Kensho

With the total disappearance of the self in kensho, Austin says there arises a sense of complete fearlessness (2006, 89). *He hypothesizes that an inhibition of the amygdala and its connections occurs during the moments in kensho when fear totally extinguishes (2006, 93–94). He suggests that kensho's profoundly blissful experiences may also be due to such an inhibition of the amygdala and its circuits (2006, 89).*

Meditation

Austin comments that Zen aims, through a restrained, moral, and disciplined life in the world, at character change: the decrease of self and an enhancement of awareness (1998, 7; 2006, xxv, 229). In addition to the sudden flash of insight-wisdom that occurs in kensho, Austin points out that there exists, on the path of Zen, a process of gradual enlightenment, a slow maturation process that unfolds in the course of disciplined "daily-life practice" (2006, 446–47). Zen's thrust toward the advancement of one's inborn potential thus has a twofold character: slow character development and "the rare later brief states of insight" (Austin 2006, 9). The "lightning flash" of insight-wisdom, Austin remarks, *by itself* can never constitute "enlightenment," and so, both types of enlightenment, the gradual and the sudden, are seen to be essential (2006, 446–47).

The practice of meditation is, in his view, the basic instrument of gradual enlightenment in Zen Buddhism. Long-term meditative practice is seen to transform the individual's traits cumulatively through a great number of small steps (Austin 2006, 262). The results are found to be mostly subtle and may take many years to achieve (Austin 2006, 214). Austin cites a number of character changes brought about by long-term meditation. It expands the mind, helps one to "let go" of loathings and longings, cultivates compassion, and fosters personal insight (Austin 2006, 296, 401). Putting it succinctly, Austin comments that one is instructed in Zen in Zen meditation (1998, 13, 57–145).

Mindfulness Meditation

Austin writes, "In calmness and clarity, [Zen meditation] begins to retrain the adult aspirant's brain in the refined arts of paying more mindful attention"

(2006, 387). Zen's basic point is fully living this life, this very moment, right here and now (Austin 1998, 452). Indeed, Austin gives as a short definition of Zen meditation: "living in the present moment" (1998, 72). "Mindfulness," then, is a basic Zen meditative approach, "a calm, silent, no-thought style of attending to the present moment," a relaxed and passive attentiveness free of "thought congestion" (Austin 1998, 57, 465; 2006, 29). By focusing attention on a single thing at a time, by thus concentrating on the matter at hand, Austin says meditation quiets the mind. An excellent place to start, he remarks, is becoming fully aware of something fairly simple, such as "now breathing in," "now breathing out" (Austin 2006, 29). Following this advice, so easily stated, demands a persistent disciplining of oneself.

Austin says mindful attention is a clear awareness into which any number of small insights can make their way (1998, 465). *"Undistracted awareness," he comments, may facilitate some of the brain's "intuitive functions"* (1998, 462). Mindfulness allows us to take pause and get a fresh look at who we really are, to attend actively to what is happening at this very moment and, later, on the basis of the firsthand information gained, to simplify our lives creatively (Austin 2006, 31, 275). The idea, Austin says, is to carry Zen meditation—mindful "not thinking"—over, from present moment to present moment, into everyday life (1998, 57, 76). The ultimate goal of mindfulness meditation is a state of "no-I," selflessness, the dissolution of the I-Me-Mine (Austin 1998, 141). As meditation progresses, Austin comments, one finds that, though still clearly aware, thoughts do fall away, and the sense of the bodily self does diminish (1998, 143). He remarks that this experience stands in sharp contrast to our ordinary lives, which are described as swarming with distractions and hyperactive thoughts and behaviors (1998, 462). Zen meditation slows everything down. *Austin comments that it may well be the case that a number of the brain's systems work more effectively at a slower speed (1998, 462).*

Meditation's Psychophysiological Effects

Meditation and Complex Physiological Change: *Austin comments that long-range commitment to meditative practices gradually causes complex physiological transformations in the brain (2006, xxv).*

Meditation and the I-Me-Mine: *Austin hypothesizes that, to the extent specific self-referent (egocentric) areas of the brain are involved in the maladaptive aspects of the I-Me-Mine, long-term Zen meditators would be expected to show a gradual decrease in the baseline activity of these specific areas and, at the same time, a gradual dissolving of the self's malfunctions (1998, 141–45; 2006, 203).*

Meditation and the Frontal Lobes: *The exercise of our will—intending to do something—is an "executive function" linked by research to the frontal lobes*

(Austin 1998, 274; 2006, 217). Austin reports further that, during those stages of "relaxation meditation" when subjects reported that their "willful self-control" had dropped out, PET data revealed no significant role of the frontal lobes (2006, 217). Highly trained monks being monitored by functional magnetic resonance imaging (fMRI) when in an undistracted meditative state have shown reduced signals in the orbitofrontal region, a region named for its position in the frontal lobes, just above the orbits of the eye (Austin 2006, 159).

Meditation and the Amygdala: *The amygdala is "a gateway to our fears" (Austin 1998, 175–79; 2006, 85). Austin remarks that the amygdala's relevance to Zen has to do with such important issues as the extinction of maladaptive emotions and nonattachment (2006, 94). Knowing how the amygdala functions, says Austin, can help us understand a number of functions of Zen meditation (2006, 86).*

Meditation and Stress Reduction: *Converging research indicates that regular meditation is associated with more appropriate responses to stress (Austin 2006, 54). Subjects who underwent an eight-week mindfulness training program, followed by an influenza vaccination, developed a relatively rapid rise in their influenza antibody titers. This increase is one of a considerable number of physiological and biochemical changes reported in conjunction with mindfulness meditation (Austin 2006, 56–57). Austin remarks that greater GABA inhibition may make an important contribution to the calming influence of meditation (2006, 118–19).*

Meditation and EEG Results: *Austin reports that EEGs have been shown to differentiate between receptive and concentrative forms of meditation, as well as between these forms and ordinary calm relaxation (2006, 30). One EEG study found that, during an intensive one-week retreat, theta rhythms (four to seven cycles per second) of long-term Zen Buddhist meditators increased with the deepening of meditation (Austin 2006, 106). In a study of twenty experienced meditators in the Sahaja Yoga tradition, EEG power was found to increase in the following frequency bands: theta-1 (four to six cycles per second), theta-2 (six to eight cycles per second), and alpha-1 (eight to ten cycles per second) (Austin 2006, 53). The relations between gamma-band firing (thirty to eighty cycles per second) and (Tibetan Buddhist) meditation are explored in other sections of this chapter (see above, "Large-Scale Neural Integration: Synchronized Gamma-Band Neural Firing" and "Inducing Human Well-Being through Meditation").*

Meditation and the "Monkey Mind": *Research suggests that regular Zen meditation helps temper the customary "leaps" of the "monkey mind" (2006, 104).*

Conclusion: *Austin's wide-ranging and path-breaking contribution to the investigation of the interpenetration of Zen and neuroscience is a major achievement. His neuroscientific interpretations of Zen experience remain largely hypothetical, however, and, as he readily admits, much remains to be done. He comments that we do not fully understand the psychophysiological processes involved in Zen meditation and the related alternate states of consciousness, as well as that advance in both regards depends on discovering how various brain regions "interact physiologically within widely distributed networks" (Austin 2006, 224; see above, "Large-Scale Neural Integration: Synchronized Gamma-Band Neural Firing").*

REFERENCES

Austin, J. H. *Zen and the Brain: Toward an Understanding of Meditation and Consciousness.* Cambridge, MA: MIT Press, 1998.

———. "Six Points to Ponder." In *The View from Within: First-Person Approaches to the Study of Consciousness*, ed. F. J. Varela and J. Shear, 213–16. Bowling Green, OH: Imprint Academic, 1999.

———. *Zen-Brain Reflections: Reviewing Recent Developments in Meditation and States of Consciousness.* Cambridge, MA: MIT Press, 2006.

Cosmelli, D., D. Olivier, J.-P. Lachaux, J. Martinerie, L. Garnero, B. Renault, and F. J. Varela. "Waves of Consciousness: Ongoing Cortical Patterns during Binocular Rivalry." *Neuroimage* 23 (2004): 128–40.

His Holiness the Fourteenth Dalai Lama. *The Art of Happiness: A Handbook for Living.* New York: Riverhead Books, 1988.

———. "Understanding our Fundamental Nature." *Visions of Compassion: Western Scientists and Tibetan Buddhists Examine Human Nature* ed. In R. J. Davidson and A. Harrington, 66–80. New York: Oxford University Press, 2002.

———. "Science at the Crossroads." *Annual Meeting of the Society for Neuroscience*, 2005a (available online at www.mindandlife.org/dalai.lama.sfndc.html).

———. *The Universe in a Single Atom: The Convergence of Science and Spirituality.* New York: Random House, 2005b.

Davidson, R. J. "Toward a Biology of Positive Affect and Compassion." In *Visions of Compassion: Western Scientists and Tibetan Buddhists Examine Human Nature*, ed. R. J. Davidson and A. Harrington, 107–30. New York: Oxford University Press, 2002.

———. "Well-being and Affective Style: Neural Substrates and Biobehavioral Correlates." *Philosophical Transactions of the Royal Society (London)* 359 (2004): 1395–1411.

Davidson, R. J., and A. Harrington. "Preface." In *Visions of Compassion: Western Scientists and Tibetan Buddhists Examine Human Nature*, ed. R. J. Davidson and A. Harrington, v–viii. New York: Oxford University Press, 2002.

DeAngelis, Tori. "Sperry Plumbs Science for Values and Solutions." *The APA Monitor* (August 1993): 6–7.

Ellison, K. "Mastering Your Own Mind." *Psychology Today*, October 2006, 70–77.

Erdmann, E., and D. Stover. *Beyond a World Divided: Human Values in the Brain-Mind Science of Roger Sperry.* Boston: Shambhala, 1991.

Goleman, D. "A Western Perspective." In *MindScience: An East-West Dialogue*, ed. D. Goleman and R. A. F. Thurman, 3–6. Boston: Wisdom Publications, 1991a.

———. "Tibetan and Western Models of Mental Health." In *MindScience: An East-West Dialogue*, ed. D. Goleman and R. A. F. Thurman, 89–102. Boston: Wisdom Publications, 1991b.

———. *Destructive Emotions: A Scientific Dialogue with the Dalai Lama*. New York: Bantam Books, 2003.

Harrington, A. "A Science of Compassion or a Compassionate Science?" In *Visions of Compassion: Western Scientists and Tibetan Buddhists Examine Human Nature*, ed. R. J. Davidson and A. Harrington, 18–30. New York: Oxford University Press, 2002.

———. "Introduction." In *The Dalai Lama at MIT*, ed. A. Harrington and A. Zajonc, 3–17. Cambridge: Harvard University Press, 2006.

Houshmand, Z., A. Harrington, C. Saron, and R. J. Davidson. "Training the Mind: First Steps in a Cross-Cultural Collaboration in Neuroscientific Research." In *Visions of Compassion: Western Scientists and Tibetan Buddhists Examine Human Nature*, ed. R. J. Davidson and A. Harrington, 3–17. New York: Oxford University Press, 2002.

Lazar, S. W., C. Kerr, R. Wasserman, J. R. Gray, M. McGarvey, B. T. Quinn, J. A. Dusek, H. Benson, S. L. Rauch, C. I. Moore, and B. Fischl. "Meditation Experience Is Associated with Increased Cortical Thickness." Program No. 355.10. *2005. Abstract Viewer/Itinerary Planner*. Washington, DC: Society for Neuroscience. 2005 (available online at www.sfn.scholarone.com).

Lutz, A., D. D. Dunne, and R. J. Davidson. "Meditation and the Neuroscience of Consciousness." In *The Cambridge Handbook of Consciousness*, ed. P. Zelaso, M. Moscovitch, and E. Thompson. New York: Cambridge University Press, 2007.

Lutz, A., L. L. Greischar, N. B. Rawlings, M. Ricard, and R. J. Davidson. "Long-term Meditators Self-Induce High Amplitude Gamma Synchrony during Mental Practice." *Proceedings of the National Academy of Sciences* 101 (2004): 16369–73.

Lutz, A., J.-P. Lachaux, J. Martinerie, and F. J. Varela. "Guiding the Study of Brain Dynamics by Using First-Person Data: Synchrony Patterns Correlate with Ongoing Conscious States during a Simple Visual Task." *Proceedings of the National Academy of Sciences* 99 (2002): 1586–91.

Lutz, A., N. B. Rawlings, and R. J. Davidson. "Changes in the Tonic High-Amplitude Gamma Oscillations during Meditation Correlates with Long-Term Practitioners' Verbal Reports." Program No. 536.9. *2005 Abstract Viewer/Itinerary Planner*. Washington, DC: Society for Neuroscience, 2005 (available online at www.sfn .scholarone.com).

Lutz, A., and E. Thompson. "Neurophenomenology: Integrating Subjective Experience and Brain Dynamics in the Neuroscience of Consciousness." *Journal of Consciousness Studies* 10 (2003): 31–52.

Rodriguez, E., N. George, J.-P. Lachaux, J. Martinerie, B. Renault, and F. J. Varela. "Perception's Shadow: Long-Distance Synchronization of Human Brain Activity." *Nature* 397 (1999): 430–33.

Rudrauf, D., A. Lutz, D. Cosmelli, J.-P. Lachaux, and M. Le Van Quyen. "From Autopoiesis to Neurophenomenology." *Biological Research* 36 (2002): 27–66.

Singer, W. "Consciousness and the Binding Problem." *Annals of the New York Academy of Science* 929 (2001): 123–46.

Sperry, R. W. "Search for Beliefs to Live by Consistent with Science." *Zygon: Journal of Religion and Science* 26 (1991): 237–58.

———. "The Impact and Promise of the Cognitive Revolution." *American Psychologist* (August 1993): 878–85.

Stover, D., and E. Erdmann. *A Mind for Tomorrow: Facts, Values, and the Future.* Westport, CT: Praeger, 2000.

Thompson, E., A. Lutz, and D. Cosmelli. "Neurophenomenology: An Introduction for Neurophilosophers." In *Cognition and the Brain: The Philosophy and Neuroscience Movement,* ed. A. Brook and K. Akin, 40–97. New York: Cambridge University Press, 2005.

Varela, F. J. "Neurophenomenology: A Methodological Remedy for the Hard Problem." *Journal of Consciousness Studies* 3 (1996): 330–49.

Varela, F. J., and J. Shear. "First-Person Accounts: Why, What, and How?" In *The View from Within: First-Person Approaches to the Study of Consciousness,* ed. F. J. Varela and J. Shear, 1–14. Bowling Green, OH: Imprint Academic, 1999.

Wallace, B. A. *Contemplative Science: Where Buddhism and Neuroscience Converge.* New York: Columbia University Press, 2007.

Zajonc, A. "Reflections on 'Investigating the Mind.'" In *The Dalai Lama at MIT,* ed. A. Harrington and A. Zajonc, 219–41. Cambridge, MA: Harvard University Press, 2006.

12

✛

The Evolutionary Psychology of Religion

Scholars are increasingly applying evolutionary principles to the investigation of religion. Both psychological and cultural factors are cited as crucial determinants of the cultural evolution thought by many to explain the origin and transmission of religious concepts. This chapter considers two proponents of the explanatory power of the cultural evolution of religion: Pascal Boyer and Daniel Dennett. Boyer points to psychological factors, "cognitive inference systems," as the key factors in the cultural selection—acquisition and transmission—of concepts or representations of supernatural beings and events. Dennett, while incorporating Boyer's psychological approach in his theory, emphasizes the role of the cultural units themselves, called "memes," and the power they—the religious representations themselves—acquire and wield over the human mind and human behavior. Boyer thus focuses on the psychological factors in the cultural evolution of religious concepts, and Dennett on the cultural factors in that cultural evolution. Both limit themselves to a certain kind of religion: a social enterprise featuring supernatural beings that intervene in human affairs.

PASCAL BOYER: *RELIGION EXPLAINED*

Why People Believe: Genetic and Cultural Selection

Pascal Boyer, a cognitive anthropologist and evolutionary theorist, claims that science now understands how concepts of supernatural beings and occurrences are acquired and organized in the human mind/brain, that science can now explain why people believe in gods and spirits in the absence of any real evidence (2001b, 297). "The intractable mystery that was religion," Boyer writes, "is now just another set of difficult but manageable problems" (2001b, 2). Research in anthropology, cognitive psychology, evolutionary biology, and linguistics, he claims, has revealed the factors at work behind cultural evolution, and cultural evolution is at the origin of religion (2001b, 298). On the basis of experimental studies and anthropological field work, Boyer makes the case for such a cultural evolution of religion and describes how a variety of cognitive factors can have brought it about in a number of articles (1996, 2000, 2001a) and especially in his book *Religion Explained: The Evolutionary Origins of Religious Thought* (2001b).

Boyer points out that people everywhere have had concepts of special beings with superior powers and knowledge, supernatural beings in the form of God or gods, spirits, the ancestors. "Religious concepts," in Boyer's terminology, are the concepts of supernatural beings that "matter" in people's lives (2001b, 137). The notion of an ancestor who is around and watching, who forbids certain behaviors and commands others, and who rewards or punishes depending on the response made is an example of such a religious concept. It is just such religious concepts of supernatural agents, concepts that matter, that Boyer proposes to explain through the mechanisms of cultural evolution.

Religion is said to have appeared with the "modern mind," and the modern mind to constitute a variety of specialized "cognitive inference systems" in communication with one another (2001b, 322). These mental inference systems, Boyer argues, are principally responsible for the cultural evolution of religious concepts (2001b, 322–23). They are largely responsible, in other words, for the evolutionary development of supernatural concepts through *cultural* selection, through acquisition and transmission in cultural processes. These inference systems, in his view, have also evolved but are biologically, rather than culturally, based; that is, they have been built in the human brain through *genetic* selection, through acquisition and transmission in biological processes.

Boyer claims that our present-day brains are prepared in advance to deal with relevant environmental information "because natural selection gave us particular mental predispositions"—that is, the specialized cognitive inference systems already mentioned (2001b, 3). Our brains evolved through genetic selection to act and react as they do in the interest of survival and reproduction (2001b, 118). Human evolutionary history shaped our inference systems to these ends as cognitive responses to problems that confronted our ancestors time and again. These recurrent problems are the environmental demands humans have always had to face: coping with dangers posed by human enemies and prowling animals, on the one hand, and promoting cooperation and collaboration with human allies, equally essential for human survival, on the other. In terms of evolutionary psychology, then, a cognitive inference system may be defined as an evolved capacity of the brain to handle "a limited aspect of the information available about our surroundings" (2001b, 98). Each such system provides "very smart inferences about that aspect," which is "why all these systems in the brain are called *inference systems*" (2001b, 98).

Boyer's central argument continues as follows. Our genetically selected "cognitive architecture," the network of mental inference systems, makes it highly probable biologically that a certain limited number of concepts or representations will be culturally selected rather than other variants. We've seen that for Boyer our cognitive inference systems originated in the interests of survival and reproduction, which is to say that they did not originate in a religious context of any sort. While our biologically evolved psychology is thus denied a specifically religious origin, Boyer insists that this psychology is nevertheless a readiness for "a small catalogue of culturally successful supernatural concepts" (2001a, 57; 2000, 195). All human beings are biologically equipped, he writes, to "easily acquire a certain *range* of religious notions and communicate them to others" (2001b, 3). In sum, according to Boyer, *biological* evolution gave the brain the *psychological* dispositions that shape *cultural* evolution: the evolution of the human brain by genetic selection issued in a brain design with certain cognitive inference systems, and these systems make it easy for the cultural selection of certain religious concepts of supernatural beings and their intervention in human lives (2001a, 71; 2001b, 133). It is these ideas, centering around cognitive inference systems, that will be explored in the remainder of the present discussion of Boyer's evolutionary psychology of religion.

The naturalistic, that is, Darwinian, account Boyer proposes means that no one, human or divine, designed religion (1994). No human being sat down and dreamt it up, invented it. Nor was it bestowed from on high in an awe-inspiring revelation. On the basis of the brain's genetically determined cognitive inference systems, religious concepts and practices resulted, rather, in Boyer's view, from the "repeated selective events" that constitute cultural selection, in a process of cultural refinement "during thousands of episodes when people told other people fantastic tales" (2001b, 310, 329). Those religious beliefs that passed the test of time are the relatively successful variants of the great many variants that have been produced by the human brain/mind, most of which have been modified or simply fallen by the wayside (2001b, 32).

The Construction of Religious Concepts
in the Individual Mind

Boyer says that the point of departure for acquiring concepts of supernat-ural beings is what other people say and do (2001b, 237). The information transmitted from others, however, constitutes not the religious concept it-self but "cues that lead people to build the concept" (2001a, 76). Much of the content of religious concepts is not directly transmitted from others at all, then, but is "reconstructed by each individual in the course of acquir-ing the concept" (2001b, 159). People are not told, for example, that spir-its remember past happenings or see what is going on around them. Here is where Boyer's pivotal cognitive inference systems come in. Through the activation of a specific inference system, Boyer says, the individual in-fers the mental workings of the spirits: namely that the spirits remember the past and see what is going on in the present. What people actually hear from others are things like "our ancestors are upset because we did not keep our side of the bargain" (2001b, 159–60). To make sense of such incomplete information, Boyer says, requires forming constructions, spontaneous inferences, about the mental events of the spirits involved. People thus assume that the ancestor is a person with a mind like their own, makes deals, knows what's going on, remembers, gets upset, and so on. Boyer comments, "People do not invent gods and spirits; they receive information that leads them to build such concepts" (2001b, 161). Mental inference systems, though instituted, as we've seen, for more pragmatic reasons, are already in place and ready to execute the constructive activ-ity required; they thus build the religious concept of a supernatural agent and a more complete conceptual framework (2001b, 40–42). All in all, then, concepts of supernatural beings, Boyer says, are not passed directly from brain to brain. They are "inferred rather than directly 'downloaded' from one mind to another" (2001a, 76). The brain's cognitive inference systems are said to be forever at work "reconstructing, distorting, chang-ing and developing the information communicated by others," thus mak-ing the best sense they can of such information as is provided from out-side (2001b, 33). Boyer remarks that processing the information received, producing inferences, and creating new information lead to a great vari-ety of religious concepts, to many variants (2001b, 39).

Boyer proceeds to say that experimental studies show that our brain's cognitive inference systems spontaneously categorize environmental ob-jects as persons, animals, plants, natural objects, or human artifacts (1996, 90; 2001a, 60–63). When the brain, on the basis of environmental cues, identifies something as, say, an animal, it naturally and spontaneously produces specialized inferences from the activated category "animal": this being was born of other animals of the same kind, it needs food to survive, it breathes, and so forth (2001b, 95–96). When we identify an ancestor, as above, as a "person," a specialized inference system (the intuitive psychology system; see below, "The Agency-Detection and Intuitive Psychology Inference Systems") is selectively turned on and, as already suggested, spontaneously applies all the attributes to the ancestor that go with being a person (2001b, 46, 101, 161). Properties are thus inferred "for free" from intuitive principles that belong to cognitive inference systems about what it means to be a person or to be an animal or whatever, thus rounding out and completing the limited environmental information available (2001a, 65, 76). Concepts of supernatural agency are easily acquired, stored, and communicated because of the tacit belief produced by the intuitive psychology system that spirits are agents belonging to the category "person," with minds that work like our own.

In sum, for Boyer, cultural phenomena such as religious concepts result from a process of selection always and everywhere occurring, and the selection process takes place in and through processes of interpretive construction and reconstruction—inference—principally in individual minds. The religious concepts taking shape in different individual minds are nevertheless said to resemble one another. Boyer says this is because the modern human mind/brain, consisting of genetically evolved inference systems, is the same always and everywhere, always and everywhere constructing and reconstructing religious concepts in similar ways (2001b, 40, 46–47). The reconstruction of remarkably similar religious concepts is the rule and not the exception in cultural history. The brain invents pretty much the same concepts of supernatural agents time and again. Concepts of invisible supernatural agents preoccupied with human behavior are found in all cultures.

Underground Belief-Making

The inference process central to Boyer's account of religious concepts is said to do its work largely unconsciously, in the "mental basement." A great deal of unreported "underground belief-making" takes place in the construction of supernatural agents. Beliefs simply show up, Boyer comments, without any evidence to back them up (2001b, 304–305). The beliefs *explicitly*, that is, consciously, showing up are intuitively produced by *implicit*, that is, unconscious, brain processes (2001b, 306). Indeed, people, in his view, often have the answer, that is, the explicit belief, without the question ever having been asked. People may believe, for example, in the immediate and effective presence of ancestors without ever asking, "*Do* our ancestors exist?" or "*Are* they around?" They simply assume they are—here is the inference process at work. No one sits down and consciously works out what it

means to be a spirit or an ancestor. The explicit belief in the ancestors' presence, in other words, is simply taken for granted, implicitly assumed. People believe that ancestors or gods exist or are around and are watching us
not on the basis of the relevant evidence, of which there is none, but because
such beliefs help them to complete and make sense of events, like a crop
failure, for which they have been given incomplete accounts, such as "The
ancestors are punishing us."

All in all, according to Boyer, implicit processes active in the mental basement create (infer) religious concepts, enable their communication, and
generate passion and commitment (2001b, 50). So far as the average person
is concerned, explicit beliefs simply happen. Boyer holds that only the tools
of cognitive science can help uncover the unconscious processes—that is,
the actively engaged cognitive inference systems, responsible for a conscious belief in supernatural entities. "Complicated systems are doing a lot
of underground work," he says, in such apparently uncomplicated beliefs
as "The ancestors will punish you if you defile their shrine" (2001b, 18–19).
Such routinely unnoticed activity, Boyer says, "goes a long way in explaining religion" (2001b, 88–89). In sum, Boyer proposes that diverse, specialized yet "exquisitely coordinated" cognitive systems, unconsciously going
about their complex work, account for religious concepts (2001b, 94–95).

Major Inference Systems

The mind/brain, we've seen, consists of cognitive inference systems: "lots
of specialized explanatory devices," each of which produces "very smart
inferences" about the limited incoming information that activates it
(2001b, 17, 96–100). We have seen that, in Boyer's view, inference systems
originally had nothing at all to do with religion and everything to do with
such things as staying clear of predators and successful social interaction.
These biologically evolved systems nevertheless have played, and continue to play, an enormous role in the cultural evolution of religion, as
we've seen, determining which religious concepts are likely to be selected
and to survive and which are not and, so, are likely to be forgotten or discarded. Some of the more important players in this evolutionary history
are the agency-detection system, the intuitive psychology inference system, the personal file inference system, the social exchange inference system, and the moral inference system.

The Agency-Detection and Intuitive Psychology Inference Systems

The related agency-detection and intuitive psychology systems are two
key inference systems (1996; 2000; 2001b, 122–23). The agency-detection
system monitors the aim-directed activity of both animals and humans

(2001b, 218). Detecting purposeful movement, Boyer remarks, was crucial for the survival of our ancestors, who had to be able to determine whether a given trajectory represented a preying animal, a stalking enemy, or wind-blown brush (2001b, 97). Moreover, our ancestors had to find food to eat, and so, their survival also depended on their ability to detect suitable prey, again, on the basis of characteristic movements. Our ancestors, then, simply had to be able to detect aim—purpose, agency, mind—in and through the movement of others. "Our evolutionary heritage is that of organisms that must deal with both predators and prey," Boyer comments, and so, it is hardly surprising that the brain has evolved the capacity to detect agency or mind (2001b, 144–46). In fact, overdetecting agency, that is, discovering agency where there isn't any, is said to have held a significant evolutionary advantage. The agency-detection system is "biased towards overdetection," towards "jumping to conclusions" (2001b, 145). This system, by overdetecting agency, thus doesn't take any chances when it comes to matters of life or death but is, so to speak, on a hair trigger: better safe than sorry!

The intuitive psychology inference system detects a particular sort of agency or mind—*personal* agency (2001b, 122–23). This system has the task of "reading" the mind of another person. It thus infers what other people are thinking and planning, what they think we are thinking, what they are feeling, what they are likely to do, and so forth, all of which are essential for successful social interaction (2001b, 104–45). Without human cooperation and collaboration in such undertakings as stalking prey and warding off enemies, Boyer says, human survival would have been simply impossible. Furthermore, inferring the mental states of our enemies, their purposes and likely moves, likewise serves survival. The evolutionary advantage of successfully reading other people's minds, their intentions, Boyer remarks, "triggered" the "extraordinary development" of the intuitive psychology inference system (2001b, 122–23).

The agency-detection and intuitive psychology inference systems are especially rich in the inferences they generate and, so, play an especially large role in Boyer's cultural-evolutionary account of the construction of religious concepts (2001b, 146). By overdetecting agency, the agency-detection system spontaneously finds supernatural agents where there are in fact none. Humans are naturally inclined, by reason of this system, to jump to the conclusion that there are agents behind, and involved in, the twists and turns of natural events, rain gods manipulating the weather, vindictive ancestors causing us grief, gods of the sea, sun gods, corn gods, fertility gods, wandering ghosts. Indeed, Boyer remarks that supernatural agency is overdetected everywhere, explaining all kinds of events. The fact that the concept of supernatural agents thus generates so many inferences makes for its evolutionary success.

The agency-detection system, designed in view of predation, discovers supernatural agents that do not exist, and the intuitive psychology system, designed to read human intentions, assigns intentions of a personal sort to these agents: gods, spirits, and ancestors are agents with minds just like our own. Supernatural agents are *personal* supernatural agents. Boyer points out that everything that goes with the category "person" now comes with the concept of supernatural agent (2001b, 143–44, 148; 2001a, 73). The concept of "supernatural person" is accordingly exceedingly rich in the inferences generated, again making for the concept's cultural selection. Gods are just like people, only on a much grander scale, and we "read" their minds just as we do those of other people. We find them to be vengeful, kind, loving, petty, generous, changeable, forgiving, partisan, moralistic, caring, and so on, just like people we know. Having all the characteristics we attribute to ourselves and other people, the concept of personal supernatural agents makes sense of many things others tell us, many things that happen around us, and many of the beliefs (inferences) that just come to us, as if from nowhere. This ability of supernatural agency to interpret incomplete and puzzling information, Boyer holds, is a fundamental reason why people believe.

The Personal File Inference System

The personal file inference system, Boyer says, keeps "'files' on every single person we interact with," thus helping us keep track of persons we are dealing with, friend or foe, ally or opponent, threat or no threat (2001b, 219). Knowing who is who is key to successful social interaction, and so, Boyer says, this system is at a selective evolutionary advantage. The personal file system, moreover, tracks others as distinct individuals with individual traits and histories of their own, recognizing faces and keeping tabs on "what just happened to them or what they just did" (2001b, 96–97). Upon being activated by the concept of a "supernatural person," the personal file system, designed to deal with other people, does similar work, identifying the various gods and ancestors, attributing the proper traits and roles to each, and keeping track of our history of relationships with them.

The Social Exchange Inference System

Boyer describes the social exchange inference system, which is important for smooth social interaction, as activated in situations where goods change hands. It delivers intuitions governed by the principle that every payout demands a commensurate payment. This system thus guides intuitions about the fairness required in the exchange of goods between human persons (2001b, 200–202). Religious concepts, Boyer remarks, abound in which gods and ancestors are engaged in social exchange with human beings, just as humans are with one another—striking bargains and entering into contracts (covenants). The activated social exchange system treats supernatural beings as exchange partners subject to fairness principles, just as it does other people. Gods are thus found to treat us well if we meet our obligations to them but to cause misfortune if we don't. A major theme of religion, then, has been that supernatural beings, like our fellow human beings, can be sources of both fortune and misfortune, depending on the quality of our dealings with them. Boyer points out that offerings are made to the gods, to spirits, and to ancestors the world over in order to win their favor and appease their anger. Boyer comments that behind sacrifice is virtually always the idea that misfortune can be avoided and good fortune assured if gods and humans are able to enter into a mutually beneficial exchange relation (2001b, 241).

The Moral Inference System

Boyer describes the moral inference system as "a specialized moral sense underlying ethical intuitions" (2001b, 179). The evolution of human beings as "a species of cooperators," he says, accounts for the ethical intuitions delivered by this system (2001b, 191). Supernatural agents, Boyer points out, are believed to be intensely interested in human moral choices and to be witnesses to moral action (2001b, 169–70, 173). People don't know why this is so but simply assume that a supernatural being or supernatural beings established the moral code and that gods or ancestors approve of some of our actions and disapprove of others. Boyer argues, however, that supernatural agency is not behind our moral intuitions and feelings; rather, the moral inference system developed out of the requirements of successful social interaction—that is, for purely pragmatic, wholly mundane reasons. Boyer says that it would be closer to the truth to say that the gods originate in our moral sense than to say that our moral sense originates in the gods. Concepts of gods and ancestors are said to succeed in cultural selection because of the sense they make, as their supposed originators, of the moral imperatives that announce themselves and confront us, command and bind us, but just appear, so to speak, out of nowhere. The ability of supernatural beings to explain our otherwise inexplicable moral sense—that is, their relevance in activating the moral inference system—gives the concept of these beings a selective advantage (see below, "Aggregate Relevance"). Boyer thus sees supernatural agents as "parasitic" upon the moral inference system—as they are upon other inference systems (see above, "The Agency-Detection and Intuitive Psychology Inference Systems," "The Personal File Inference System," and "The Social Exchange Inference System").

The Concept of Ancestors

Boyer sees death in the community as having played an important role in the cultural evolution of religious concepts. Dead bodies make a deep impression, inciting awe and fear and generating "rich inferences in a variety of different mental systems," and, so, they are "the object of great cultural attention and elaboration" (2001b, 226–28). Corpses incite different cognitive systems to "deliver incompatible intuitions" and, thus, are sources of confusion (2001b, 227). One system treats the dead body as mysteriously dangerous, a potent source of disease and contamination, while yet another represents it as still the person it was before death. Boyer remarks that the personal file system, identifying the dead person as the individual we knew, and the intuitive psychology system, still inferring the individual's personal status, in reciprocal communication with each other, "just cannot 'shut off'" but remain activated (2001b, 222–24). On the basis of previous experience, we infer certain things about the deceased as if he or she were still around (2001b, 223). Since the person, cognitively, is not "gone," the disposition of the dangerously threatening body presents a special problem. Death rituals come to terms with just this problem. These ceremonies do not owe their origin, then, to religious conceptions surrounding death or to any religious circumstance, in Boyer's view, but to conflicting inference systems, upon which they are parasitic (2001b, 226–28).

The resolution of this conflict between systems is, in Boyer's view, the paradigmatic supernatural concept of ancestors—the dead as processed by our inference systems, the dead as personal supernatural agent. The dead come to be seen as continuing to live on as individual agents with human minds, as persons. But they now live, invisibly, in separation from their bodies, which ritual has formally disposed of. Persons like ourselves, the dead are still effectively around, still actively involved with us and our fates. The concept of ancestor, Boyer remarks, is "the simplest and therefore most successful way in which concepts of supernatural agents are transmitted" and, so, is the most common concept of supernatural agents throughout the world (2001b, 227).

The Counterintuitive Character of Supernatural Concepts

The concept of ancestors, as people like ourselves, we've seen, gives rise to all of the many intuitive expectations that go with the category "person." In other words, religious ideas of supernatural entities like this one have "intuitive richness": they generate a lot of inferences. Intuitively rich concepts, Boyer asserts, are more likely to be recalled (replicated) and passed on (transmitted) and, so, to have "better survival potential" in the lengthy course of cultural evolution than those that do not (2001a, 73). A related factor said to favor cultural selection is the "aggregate relevance" of a concept. A concept has aggregate relevance if it jointly activates several different inference systems, making it easy to represent (2001b, 190; see below, "Aggregate Relevance"). The archeological evidence, Boyer comments, supports a further important element in the successful evolutionary history of supernatural concepts: the inclination of the human brain to attend to what is "counterintuitive" (2001b, 324). A concept is counterintuitive if it violates an intuitive expectation implied by the categorical identification of a being as, say, an animal or a person or a plant (2001a, 59–61). Religious concepts, Boyer claims, always include counterintuitive information (2001b, 64–65). Spirits are said to be persons and to be invisible. In violation of the intuitive expectation that we can see persons with our eyes, the concept of spirit is counterintuitive. Likewise, for a tree to overhear conversations is for it to violate what it means to be a tree. A counterintuitive tree with the sense of hearing, like a counterintuitive invisible person, demands attention, is recalled time and again, and makes a good story (2001b, 72–73, 129–30). Counterintuitive concepts are special, distinctive, fascinating, surprising, and attention grabbing, and so, they are at a selective advantage for acquisition, recall, and transmission in cultural evolution.

A concept can be counterintuitive, however, Boyer comments, only if all the other inferences that come "for free" with the relevant category continue to be run. An invisible person is still a person, and a tree with a mind is still a tree, with all that goes with being a person or a tree (1996, 91). A "good" supernatural concept thus continues to allow all the relevant inferences, all intuitive expectations, except the one excluded by the concept's specific violation (2001a, 87). All in all, the concept of an invisible person or an attentive tree, indeed, any "good" supernatural concept, is at a triple selective advantage in cultural evolution: eliciting standard categorical inferences, these concepts are inferentially rich; violating a standard categorical property, they are counterintuitive; and activating diverse inference systems, they have aggregate relevance, to which we now turn (1996, 91).

Aggregate Relevance

Boyer asserts that aggregate relevance, implied in much of the above discussion, drives the cultural transmission of religious concepts and, so, in his view, more or less explains why people believe (2001b, 314). A concept is said to have aggregate relevance, and thus ease of representation, if it jointly activates a variety of cognitive inference systems (2001b, 319). Only a select number of religious concepts actually reach aggregate relevance, "jointly activating inference systems for agency, predation, death, morality, social exchange, etc." (2001b, 324–25). This is why religions everywhere have certain features in common but not others. The concept of distinct supernatural agents—God or gods, ancestors, spirits—who are personally interested in us and actively engaged in our affairs excites diverse cognitive predispositions and, so, has aggregate relevance and appears everywhere (2001b, 164). All cultures thus have roughly the same supernatural entities. Praying to a supernatural agent activates the cognitive inference system related to verbal communication and social exchange. Promising the agent to be good from now on connects with people's social exchange and moral inference systems. Knowing that the agent is actively and personally engaged in our affairs and has certain intentions and a certain grasp of the situation brings the intuitive psychology inference system into play. Considering immoral behavior an offense against a supernatural agent engages the moral inference system. Realizing that a particular supernatural agent is displeased with our sacrifice involves the joint activation of the intuitive psychology, social exchange, and personal file systems. People thus have a variety of dealings with personal supernatural agents such as gods and ancestors (2001b, 312–13).

In sum, the concept of a "supernatural person," activating and being "distributed among" a number of different inference systems, has aggregate relevance (2001b, 312). The great many inferences—interpretive constructions—generated by the activated inference systems make sense of any number of puzzling and disturbing events and narratives in our world (2001b, 227). The concept is thus "intuitively plausible" and more likely to be recalled (replicated) and communicated (transmitted) to others, hence to "get built in human minds" (2001b, 298).

Religion Not in a Class of Its Own

Inference systems, as we've seen, are a purely natural outcome that arose through the genetic selection of the brain's physical dispositions as humans came to terms with recurrent environmental demands. Boyer says that these biological systems are responsible for the cultural selection of religious concepts, exactly as they are in the cultural selection of concepts in other areas of life. Religious concepts are not different from any other concepts (2001b, 311). Religion is not a special case; it does not constitute a class of its own. The brain's evolved dispositions for dealing with, among other things, predators and our fellow human beings are responsible for religion, which is simply a consequence or corollary of having the brains we do (2001b, 2). Religion is a likely event that Boyer says is natural to the human mind/brain and spontaneously occurs time and again (2001b, 322).

DANIEL DENNETT: *BREAKING THE SPELL*

Naturalistic Questioning of Religion

In his book *Breaking the Spell: Religion as a Natural Phenomenon* (2006), Daniel C. Dennett, professor of philosophy and cognitive scientist at Tufts University, questions the phenomenon of religion in its entirety. He defines religions tentatively as "social systems whose participants avow belief in a supernatural agent or agents whose approval is to be sought" (2006, 9). By this definition, there is no "religion" without supernatural agency, and so, institutions like Buddhism are excluded from consideration. Private or personal religion," highly esteemed by such psychologists as William James and Carl Jung, is anything but a "social system" and, so, by Dennett's definition is likewise ruled out. Positively, religion is seen to center on the invocation of gods "who are effective agents in real time," agents actively engaged in human affairs and human morality, in particular (2006, 11–12).

Dennett allows for the high-minded, perhaps atheistic, "nonjoiner," such as himself, whom he would call "spiritual" rather than "religious." Dennett places himself among those he calls "brights," people whose worldview has a naturalist, rather than a supernaturalist, character. "We brights," he writes, "don't believe in ghosts or elves or the Easter Bunny— or God. . . . We share a disbelief in black magic—and life after death. . . . 'I'm a bright' is not a boast but a proud avowal of an inquisitive worldview" (2003, 14). Dennett finds that religious people are prone to become indignant and resentful when questioning minds, such as his own, dare to investigate their beliefs. He considers such people to be under the influence of two "spells." The first spell is the taboo against a close investigation of religion. The second is the belief in "the life-enriching enchantment of religion itself" (2006, 17–18). If the first spell is broken, which Dennett is dead set on doing in his book, if religion is exposed to the light and carefully inspected, there is the very real possibility, he says, that the second spell, "belief in belief," will be broken as well. The first spell protects the second—thus its significance.

Dennett sees religion as a perfectly natural, scientifically examinable set of phenomena—no exceptions, no miracles allowed (2006, 25). By comparison with other natural phenomena, religions are very influential in people's lives. Dennett wants to know why this is the case, why religion commands such power over people, why it means so much to them. Indeed, he argues, religion is too important not to be investigated, and he makes it abundantly clear that objections from the faithful, however vociferous, will not deter him from his project. His book reviews, sometimes adopting, sometimes modifying, what he considers the best scientific analyses of religion currently available. He attempts to sketch the whole story of religion, hoping to get something on the table that is both testable and worth testing (2006, 103–104). He proceeds confidently, though aware that he is not above making mistakes.

Dennett, like Boyer, favors a Darwinian explanation of religion. Every last wonderful thing we treasure here on earth, he says, has been brought forth by reason of our planet's evolutionary history (2006, 53). "The apparent extravagance of religious practices," he writes, "can be accounted for in the austere terms of evolutionary biology" (2006, 93). People are said to pay a lot for their religions, dedicating themselves to them and even sacrificing their lives for them, curtailing their behaviors, building expensive temples, giving up valuable possessions, and generally expending huge amounts of time and energy in their service. Dennett comments that evolutionary biology shows that nothing as costly as that ever simply happens. Something or someone benefits from all the costly "design work" that goes into religion. He says that every "regular expenditure of time and energy has to be balanced by something of 'value,' and the ultimate measure of evolutionary value is *fitness*: the capacity to replicate (to reproduce or get copied or repeated) more successfully than the competition" (2006, 63, 69). The question, then, becomes, who or what benefits in religion? Whose fitness for survival is being furthered? The important point here is that this beneficiary may not be the religion's faithful but, as Dennett maintains, the religious beliefs and practices themselves (see below, "The Stewardship of Memes in Organized Religion"). Dennett points out, moreover, that for something to compete and survive, that is, for natural selection to occur, there need not be someone who knows what's going on and who orchestrates the whole process, even though, in retrospect, the outcome may appear to have been intelligently produced. Indeed, in what is called a "free-floating rationale," "blind, directionless evolutionary processes 'discover' designs that work" (2006, 59–60). Dennett contends that religions originated as folk religions in free-floating rationales endorsed by processes of natural selection.

Folk and Organized Forms of Religion

Dennett describes folk religions as those without written creeds or theologians or a hierarchy of officials. People's convictions at the stage of folk religions are vague and indeterminate. Everybody believes in the gods, Dennett says, but no one has ever stopped and worked out the details (2006, 161). Folk religions have no authors—conscious and deliberate authorship comes only later with the rise of organized religion—but result rather from "interdependent processes of biological and cultural evolution," from nothing but differential replication in which some variants are selected and others are left behind (2006, 114, 140). This is to say that free-floating rationales are at work in folk religions.

Folk religions, Dennett comments, "provided the cultural environment from which organized religions could emerge" (2006, 140). Religion in its organized form entails formalized beliefs and structures, theologians, dedicated buildings, and a cadre of hierarchically organized officials. Folk religion, called "unconscious" religion by Charles Darwin, was transformed into organized religion, "methodical" religion in Darwin's terminology, as culture developed and people became more reflective and got more involved (2006, 151). The free-floating rationales of folk religion came to be complemented, or even replaced, by consciously developed reasons (2006, 169). Religion thus became "more sophisticated, more elaborate, more of a production" (2006, 151).

Memes

Dennett cites the example of boatbuilders who, without giving it a thought, copy the designs culturally handed down from generation to generation. Slight variations may occur in the design, and from time to time one of these, representing an improvement or interesting innovation, will "engender a new lineage" (2006, 77–78). Dennett remarks that a mindless process such as this can, without drawing attention to itself and without intention, over a lengthy period, exquisitely shape cultural designs. A design that is *culturally* transmitted, like those used in boatbuilding, can thus involve a blind and directionless free-floating rationale, exactly like one that is *genetically* transmitted. In the two cases, Dennett remarks, there is design without a designer. And as in genetic transmission, the process works by differential replication, some variants getting repeated and others not. The more or less mindless cultural transmission, say, of boat designs, Dennett concludes "is a tempting parallel with the other transmission medium, the genes" (2006, 77). He writes, "This concept of cultural replicators, items that are copied over and over, has been given a name by evolutionary biologist Richard Dawkins (1976) who proposed to call them *memes*" (2006, 78). "Memes" are "bits of culture" that compete and reproduce the way genes do. Any culturally replicated item is a meme: words, a boat design, cooking methods, signals, games, buildings, hunting methods, a song, a dance, shaking hands, driving on the right, a rude gesture, and so forth (2006, 345). What is copied in both genes and memes is information. Dennett calls memes "packets of information." Exquisite designs are said to arise in the processes of cultural transmission, but they are able to do so through the very same "blind, mechanical, foresightedless" processes of natural selection (free-floating rationales) that have resulted in the excellent design of biological organisms (2006, 79–80).

Religious phenomena such as creeds (beliefs) and rituals (practices) are memes, designed in processes of cultural evolution and culturally transmitted from parent to child, the child generally adopting its parents' religion. Religions are thus seen by Dennett to be composed of memes, units of culture acquired, replicated, and transmitted in cultural evolution in accordance with strictly evolutionary principles. He argues that what is truly important for the strength of a religion is not uniformity of belief, which is becoming less and less common nowadays in any case, but uniformity of professing. Each act of profession is a cultural replication of the belief, and uniformity of meme replication is said to drive cultural evolution. In Dennett's words, "As long as the formulas get transmitted down through the ages, the memes will survive and flourish" (2006, 224–25). It matters not so much what people actually believe, then, but what they repeat, what they profess. Both formulas (creeds) and practices are publicly rehearsed—memes are replicated—in religion's rituals through group praying, singing, and dancing. Ritual divination, moreover, invites replication: getting an answer from divine powers helps people decide what to do next, thus solving a problem. Highly charged shamanic rituals are also likely to be replicated and selected over competing practices because of the "healings" they effect through their power of suggestion.

The Stewardship of Memes in Organized Religion

"The evolutionary design process that has given us religion," Dennett summarizes, involves the differential replication of memes, which "compose religion" (2006, 156, 184). Each religion is a complex of mutually compatible memes that has managed to survive in a process of natural selection. Dawkins has compared religious memes to viruses, thus suggesting that memes can proliferate regardless of the harm they do to their human hosts. In his book *The God Delusion* (2006), Dawkins expresses his doubts whether religion has any survival benefits for human beings at all. Instead, he attributes religion to a "misfiring" of a useful adaptation— namely a child's evolved tendency to believe its parents. Religious ideas, according to Dawkins, are viruslike "memes" that multiply—replicate— by infecting the gullible brains of children (Dawkins 1993, 34). Dennett asks, "To whose benefit?" Clearly, not to that of the child or the adult faithful, at least not in the first instance. The memes benefit, he answers, by proliferating. To proliferate, Dennett remarks, memes must, in competition with other memes, attract "hosts." Religion survives and flourishes, according to meme theory, by leaping from one human host to another. The human host, whose allegiance is captured by a meme, simply put, becomes the meme's servant (2006, 186). Like parasitic viruses that infect fish, even pushing them to suicide, Dennett says humans can become infected by an idea (meme)—a "mind virus" (Dawkins)—and go on to give up everything for the idea that has come to be lodged in their brains (2006, 4). Like a parasite, Dennett writes, "the Word of God" infects people's brains and gets them to carry it far and wide (2006, 6). The human stewards of the Word of God (meme), now the Supreme Good, Dennett remarks, will give anything to spread that Word, being as rational and calculating as they can in that endeavor (2006, 187). The Word has become number one, not the Word's human hosts. Through natural (evolutionary) means, Dennett says ideas are created and spread from mind to mind, pressing humans into their service, new powers and features being accumulated as things develop (2006, 6). It is not, then, that religion enhances human fitness, at least not necessarily. The self-reproducing constituents of a religion, the religion's memes, are the prime beneficiaries of religion's design features, not human beings (2006, 84–85). Indeed, the conviction that one's religion is the only path to anything and everything good can lead to an unconditional commitment to furthering the institution, regardless of the costs and outcome to the human carrier (2006, 176).

Once people become "stewards of their own favorite memes," Dennett says, an accelerating course of intentional improvements of the memes of religion takes place (2006, 187). Much of religion's design work is now seen to take place not through unintended and untended free-floating rationales (folk religion) but in the minds of individuals carefully pondering and debating ideas before deciding what is for the best (organized religion). Dennett, with Dawkins, thus sees culturally replicated memes as playing a central role in all religion, both folk and organized. All in all, Dennett is suggesting that in organized religion the folk religion's "wild" or self-sustaining memes became completely domesticated, acquiring individuals to serve them, fight their enemies, and exert every effort to assure their survival (2006, 170). Whereas the self-sustaining memes of folk religion, Dennett comments, exploit us whether we appreciate them or not, the domesticated memes of organized religion depend on the intentional assistance and cooperation of their human stewards for their propagation (2006, 170). Organized religion is thus, as characterized above, "more of a production." Blindly shaped free-floating rationales are thus supplemented and even replaced by rationales that are consciously thought out and argued over, rationales that are carefully designed by conscientious assistants (2006, 177).

Dennett remarks that countless revisions occur in the course of religion's cultural transmission. Religion is the evolved outcome of a great deal of working over and fine-tuning over the course of thousand of years, "with millions of its variants extinguished in the process" (2006, 292, 309). Religion's survival, Dennett remarks, is hardly surprising. Religion, he writes, has many appealing features and many protective features that serve to

keep these attractive features intact by defeating the competition and as-
suring loyalty (2006, 309). Dennett, as we've seen, thinks that memes, first
and foremost, serve their own survival. He nevertheless points out that the
memes of religion frequently serve, secondarily, to promote the group solidarity of their infested human hosts and thus serve their survival (2006,
184). He also recognizes that religious memes provide other incidental
benefits to their servants, such as bestowing meaning on life and giving
people an incentive to do great and good things. For others, however, Dennett finds religion's memes to be "toxic," to exploit "less savory aspects of
their psychology" and play on their weaknesses and shortcomings (2006,
310).

Dennett and Boyer: Culture and Psychology

Boyer's Skepticism on Memes

Dennett points out that Boyer has expressed skepticism about the usefulness of the notion of memes (2006, 379). Boyer, Dennett comments, holds
that a concept is not really simply "replicated" or "copied" at all, not
"downloaded" from mind to mind, from parent to child, for example, as
memes are said to be (see above, "The Construction of Religious Concepts
in the Individual Mind"). The presentation of a concept is said, rather, to
serve as a cue that triggers the production of something akin to it. Boyer
speaks of "construction" or "reconstruction" of the concept, not imitation
of what was heard. Dennett remarks that Boyer certainly sees culture as
evolving, but not directly, "not strictly by descent with modification," as
he does. Boyer describes religious concepts as already fundamentally implicit in the psychological inference systems of the hearers. Dennett remarks that Boyer prefers to focus "on the constraints and the biases discernible in the psychological mechanisms that people share," cognitive
inference systems, than on cultural units, memes (2006, 379–80). Boyer is
thus, according to Dennett, more interested in selective psychological
forces, which are biological (genetic) in origin, than in selective cultural
ones, in cognitive modules rather than memes (2006, 383; see above, "Why
People Believe: Genetic and Cultural Selection"). Dennett says he wants to
include both sets of forces. He wants to join a cultural account (through
memes) of cultural evolution to a psychological account (through cognitive inference systems) of cultural evolution, "to conceive of cultural evolution in terms of memes and in terms of the constraints of psychology,"
as well as of the interaction of both sets of factors (2006, 381). In sum, Dennett makes the case for a pivotal, but not exclusive, role of memes in the
cultural transmission of religious concepts. He argues that the similar concepts, for example, of Judaism and Christianity, may well be due to a com-

mon origin in the religion of Abraham, and thus to memes and their direct cultural transmission from mind to mind, generation to generation. On the other hand, an approach through cognitive inference systems explains why certain beliefs, rather than others, come to be initially selected, as well as why these beliefs are so easily communicated and transmitted: these systems constitute the mind/brain's natural aptitude for certain religious concepts as opposed to others. Dennett disagrees with Boyer about the enormous weight Boyer assigns to the constructive/reconstructive character of inference systems.

Endorsement of Boyer's Psychological "Fiction-Generating Contraption"

Following Boyer, Dennett traces the important religious concept of ancestors as "virtual persons"—"dead but still around"—back to conflicting inference systems, one of which Dennett calls the "intentional stance" (2006, 113). The intentional stance is essentially Boyer's "intuitive psychology inference system," the inference system said to lead to treating ancestors as persisting persons (2006, 108–12; see above, "The Agency-Detection and Intuitive Psychology Inference Systems"). Dennett refers to the intentional stance as a "Good Trick," "an evolutionary innovation that is so useful to so many different ways of life that it evolves over and over again in many different species" (2006, 109). Like Boyer, Dennett sees a related "hyperactive agent detection device"—discussed in the section on Boyer in terms of an "overdetection" of agency (see above, "The Agency-Detection and Intuitive Psychology Inference Systems")—as directly tied to the origin and perpetuation of supernatural concepts and to the finding of nonexistent gods and spirits behind nature's mysterious happenings (2006, 116). Dennett also accepts the important role Boyer attributes to counterintuitive concepts in the cultural success of religion (2006, 119; see above, "The Counterintuitive Character of Supernatural Concepts"). Dennett remarks that if we put these two psychological factors—the hyperactive agent detection device and the inclination to counterintuitive concepts—together, we get what Dennett calls a "fiction-generating contraption" (2006, 120). Such a contraption, Dennett remarks, can explain the myriad mythical creatures—demons, fairies, goblins, and the like—with which human imagination has populated the world. Dennett thus relies on Boyer's psychological approach, in addition to his own cultural approach, to help explain the cultural evolution of religion.

Both Boyer and Dennett believe that evolutionary science can, in principle, give a complete naturalistic account of religion. Both approach believers "from the outside," so to speak, through objective, third-person accounts of their behavior (see chapter 11, "Toward an Inclusive Cognitive

Neuroscience"). By excluding a serious preoccupation with first-person reports, in which believers describe their own personal, subjective experiences, both narrow the religious landscape. Dennett, for example, emphasizes the replication of memes, profession of belief, and behavioral religion. Some believers may well stop at mouthing their beliefs, thus failing to transcend the behavioral level. But others, as Gordon Allport rightly points out (see chapter 4, "Faith"), have questioned their beliefs, gone through doubt, come to terms with ambiguity, and attained a measure of mature, individual, and personal, internalized religion. Such believers are overlooked in an exclusively external investigation of religion.

The Spell of Belief in Belief

A powerful "belief in belief," the belief that religious belief is a good thing, something to be protected and furthered at all cost, is seen to accompany the stewardship of religious ideas in organized religion (2006, 196). Dennett says that people are glad that God exists because God is "the most wonderful of all things"(2006, 221). The faithful seem to Dennett to be in "romantic love" with their religion (2006, 251). They fear that morality will collapse and total chaos and meaninglessness ensue should religion disappear from the face of the earth. Many see belief in God as the only way to avoid eternal damnation in hell and, thus, to be of such enormous importance that they just have to share it with others. The faithful want everyone to believe. Dennett argues that such belief in belief in God keeps people from admitting the obvious: namely "that much of the traditional lore about God is no more worthy of *belief* than the lore about Santa Claus or Wonder Woman" (2006, 210). He points out that it is "obvious," of course, to the faithful of a given religion that the deities of every other religion are mere fabrications, man-made "idols." On this point, Dawkins is quoted as remarking that we are all atheists when it comes to all gods but one, the one we happen to believe in.

The Taboo against the Critical Investigation of Religion

Dennett remarks that belief in a providential God would be in danger of collapsing were its beliefworthiness seriously challenged (2006, 282). So, at all costs, he says, this must not happen; one must not question this belief. But, Dennett comments that, if beliefs are to be unquestionable, they must be incomprehensible, "downright unintelligible" (2006, 229). This then implies that even believers do not and, indeed, cannot understand their own beliefs; they "don't really know what they are professing" (2006, 246). Dennett sees this very incomprehensibility as a fitness-enhancing adaptation of a meme. Such an incomprehensible belief arouses wonder, attracting attention and leading to frequent rehearsal (replication) (2006, 230). To the faithful, mysteries are something to be in awe of, Dennett comments, not to be solved. Mysteriousness keeps mysteries going; mystery is a good thing. Furthermore, Dennett points out, whereas ordinary intelligible assertions are easily challenged, "typical, canonical religious beliefs cannot be tested for truth" (2006, 238). This untestability of the mysteries of faith, Dennett comments, "is as good as a defining characteristic of religious creeds" (2006, 238). Mysteries are to be taken on faith; one hears it is "insulting" and "demeaning" to inquire into matters "so sacred" (2006, 206–207). Sometimes this adaptation fails, however, and so, stronger measures are invoked: "Satan himself," one is gravely admonished, "is putting these doubts in your mind!"

The Intelligence of Mother Nature

Belief in God must remain unquestionable for it to remain invulnerable. Dennett is trying to break this very taboo against a close investigation of religion. He wants to make religion comprehensible, to find out what makes it tick. Science, he insists, can attain a rigorous understanding of religious concepts (2006, 261). He sees his own account of certain features of religion as preliminary, describing it as "a family of proto-theories" in need of further development (2006, 309). Dennett's survey of religious ideas ranges from the "blind, mechanical, robotic nature" of folk religion to organized religion and its "passionate defense and elaboration of the most exalted ideas known to humankind" (2006, 188). Evolutionary theorists, Dennett says, attribute to natural selection the design work that others attribute to a creative intelligence (2006, 243; see 1995). Darwin, he says, lets us see Mother Nature's intelligence "as a non-miraculous and non-mysterious—and hence all the more wonderful—feature of this self-creating thing" (1995, 185). Dennett does not locate the sacred in a person you pray or give thanks to but says he finds the world sacred (2006, 245). "There is humility, and awe, and sheer delight," he comments, "at the glory of the evolutionary landscape" (2006, 268).

REFERENCES

Boyer, Pascal. *The Naturalness of Religious Ideas: A Cognitive Theory of Religion.* Berkeley: University of California Press, 1994.

———. "What Makes Anthropomorphism Natural: Intuitive Ontology and Cultural Representations." *Journal of the Royal Anthropological Institute* 2 (1996): 83–97.

———. "Functional Origins of Religious Concepts: Ontological and Strategic Selection in Evolved Minds." *Journal of the Royal Anthropological Institute* 6 (2000): 195–214.

———. "Cultural Inheritance Tracks and Cognitive Predispositions: The Example of Religious Concepts." In *The Debated Mind: Evolutionary Psychology versus Ethnography*, ed. H. Whitehouse, 57–82. New York: Berg, 2001a.

———. *Religion Explained: The Evolutionary Origins of Religious Thought*. New York: Basic Books, 2001b.

Dawkins, R. *The Selfish Gene*. Oxford: Oxford University Press, 1976.

———. "Viruses of the Mind." *Free Inquiry* 13 (1993): 34–46.

———. *The God Delusion*. Boston: Houghton-Mifflin, 2006.

Dennett, D. C. *Darwin's Dangerous Idea: Evolution and the Meanings of Life*. New York: Simon and Schuster, 1995.

———. "The Bright Stuff." *Free Inquiry* 23 (2003): 14–16.

———. *Breaking the Spell: Religion as a Natural Phenomenon*. New York: Viking, 2006.

Index

Abbé Pire, 196
abhorrence of the mother, 281
Absolute, the, 21, 149, 269
absolute dependence, feeling of, 108
Adam, 179, 190, 197
Adler, Alfred, 132, 234
affective neuroscience, x, 301, 313–19
agency-detection inference system,
    335, 336–38, 339, 349
aggregate relevance, 339, 341–42
aggression, 159, 190, 229, 231, 271
alienation, 179, 198, 205
All, the, 206, 214–15
Allen, R. O., 263, 274
allocentric frame of reference, 323–24
Allport, Gordon, ix, 2, 62, 105–25, 128,
    255, 350; *Becoming*, 106, 125; *The
    Individual and His Religion*, 105, 123,
    124. *See also* Religious Orientation
    Scale
alpha rhythms, 318, 327
alternate states of consciousness, 319,
    327
ambiguity, coming to terms with, 124,
    350
ambivalence: toward the divine, 39;
    toward the father, 36, 38–39, 43, 45,
    46, 119

amygdala, 315, 325, 327
analytical psychology, 67, 102
ancestors, the, 332, 334–40, 342, 349
androcentric bias, 277, 278
androgynous becoming, 283
archaic heritage, 51, 55
archetypal feminine, the, 279
archetypal realms, 267, 270
archetypal thinking, 291
archetype of the self, 76–78, 81–84,
    88–93, 98. *See also* individuation,
    Jung's notion of
archetypes, 65–66, 68–91, 94–95, 98, 99,
    101; Frankl on, 244; Goldenberg on,
    290, 291, 293
art, 7, 47, 66, 233, 241; as transitional
    phenomenon, 254, 257–58
atheism, 5, 10, 119, 181, 219, 261
atheist, 119, 145, 157, 163, 196, 202, 214,
    219, 243, 250
atman, 96–97, 99, 176–78, 180, 186
atomism, 191, 302, 303
attentive self-awareness, 307, 309
Austin, James, x, 301, 311, 317, 318,
    319–28; *Zen and the Brain: Toward an
    Understanding of Meditation and
    Consciousness*, 319, 328; *Zen-Brain
    Reflections: Reviewing Recent*

Developments in Meditation and States of Consciousness, 319, 328
authoritarian religion, 196, 203–6, 220
availability factor, 262–63
awakening, 150, 175, 180, 187, 198, 217, 319, 320

basic needs, 132–34, 136, 140, 141, 147, 153, 159
basic trust, 244, 296, 297
Batson, Daniel, x, 251, 264–66, 274, 275
Becoming (Allport), 106, 125
Beers, William, 280
behaviorism, 106, 113, 114, 128, 158, 302
Being, realm of, 137–57
"being" orientation, 206–8
Being-cognition, 137, 138–40, 142–43, 146, 147–48, 150, 155, 158, 164
Being-love, 137–39, 146, 155, 156
Being-psychology, 146–47, 152–58, 159
Being-values, 128, 137–46, 147–49, 150, 153, 156, 157, 159, 160, 162, 163, 164
belief. *See* faith
"belief in belief," 343, 350
beliefs, 3, 79, 181–82, 255, 261, 264, 257, 265, 304; Allport on, 109, 111, 112, 119; Boyer on, 333, 335–36; Dennett on, 343, 344, 349, 350–51; Freud on, 39–40, 41, 53, 57, 58; Fromm on, 197, 203, 217, 255, 261. *See also* compromises, symptoms as; doctrines; faith
beneficiaries of religion's design features, 347
Benson, L., 263, 274
Between Belief and Unbelief (Pruyser), 255, 275
Beyond God the Father: Toward a Philosophy of Women's Liberation (Daly), 281, 298
birth and death, the twin phenomena of, 270
The Birth of the Living God: A Psychoanalytic Study (Rizzuto), 258, 275

body, the, 67, 157, 248, 252, 272, 298; as limited in space and time, 170, 269; as needing external control, 170–71, 172, 173, 187, 191; reclaiming, 290–95; as unity integrated into the universe, 173–74, 181, 184–85
Boyer, Pascal, x, 331–42, 344, 348–50, 351–52; *Religion Explained: The Evolutionary Origins of Religious Thought*, 332, 352
Brahman, 96–98, 99, 176–87, 192, 216
Breaking the Spell: Religion as a Natural Phenomenon (Dennett), 343, 352
brights, 343
Bucke, Richard, 33
Buddha, the, 29, 99, 207, 217, 221
Buddhism, x, 17, 167, 200, 209, 221, 301, 328–30, 343; Tibetan, and affective neuroscience, 313–19; Zen, and neuroscience, 319–28
Buddhist psychology, 314

Calvin, John, 217
care, ethic of, x, 287–90
cartography of the human psyche, 269–72
castration anxiety, 47, 48
categorical features of experience, 307, 309
Catholic Christianity, 87
Changing of the Gods: Feminism and the End of Traditional Religion (Goldenberg), 294, 298
Chinese religious thought, opposites in, 98–99
Christ. *See* Jesus Christ
Christian doctrine, 56–57, 88–93, 180–81, 190, 192
Christianity, 17, 110, 348; feminist psychology on, 278–79, 284, 285, 290; Freud on, 55–57, 61; Fromm on, 202, 203, 209, 216; Jung on, 87–88, 98; Watts on, 167, 174, 176, 180–82, 190, 192
cognitive neuroscience, x, 304
cognitive revolution, the, 302, 303
cognitive science, 305, 307, 336

collective unconscious, the, 66, 68–95, 101, 244, 271

Committed scale, 263

compassion, 29, 123, 195, 209, 214, 273, 286; meditation and, 301, 315–18, 325

completeness, life's goal as, 93, 201

complexes, 65, 82, 93

compromises, symptoms as, 48–51, 55, 58

compulsive behavior, 72, 245, 271; Freud on, 44, 47–52, 55, 57–58, 62; Fromm on, 203, 209–10, 217

conscience, 16; Allport on, 115–16, 117; Frankl on, 239–42, 243; Freud on, 45, 48, 50; Fromm on, 197, 198, 211, 212–13, 218, 220, 229. *See also* superego

consciousness, 183, 268; determining role of, in neural processes, x, 301, 302–4; field of, 1, 18, 176–78, 269; first emergence of, 197–200; meditation and the potentials of, 313–14, 317–19; modern, research, x, 266–74; role of, in neuroscientific research, 304–31. *See also* alternate states of consciousness; collective unconscious, the; cosmic consciousness; ego, the; kensho; mystical experience; nonordinary states of consciousness; peak experience, the; plateau experience, the; religious experience; subconscious, the; symbols, Jung on

Consensual scale, 263

conservative character of instinct, 61–62

consolation, religious, 34, 40

construction of religious concepts, 334–45, 348–49

contextual judgment, women's, 288

conventional feminine morality, 289

conversion, 148, 156, 246, 263, 304; James on, 17–19, 25

Copernicus, 31

cortical thickening, meditation and, 318

Cosmelli, D., 307, 309, 312, 328, 329, 330

cosmic consciousness, 33, 139, 159, 175, 185, 266, 269

counterintuitive character of supernatural concepts, 340–41, 349

creativity, 95, 127, 252, 253

credulity, 111–12

creeds, 14, 26, 86, 122, 156, 162, 344, 346, 351. *See also* doctrines

crucifixion, 89, 91–92, 180

Crumbaugh, James C., 230

cultural evolution of religion, 331–51

cultural selection of religious concepts, 331–33, 338, 339, 341, 342

cultural transmission of religious concepts, 69, 76, 99, 341, 345, 347, 348–49

daily-life practice, 320

Dalai Lama, the, 313, 314, 315, 317, 328, 329, 330

Daly, Mary, x, 281–83, 298; *Beyond God the Father: Toward a Philosophy of Women's Liberation*, 281, 298

Darwin, Charles, 31, 42, 345, 351, 352

Davidson, Richard, x, 301, 313, 315, 316–19, 328, 329; *Visions of Compassion: Western Scientists and Tibetan Buddhists Examine Human Nature* (with Harrington), 315, 328, 329

Dawkins, Richard, 345–47, 350, 352; *The God Delusion*, 346, 352

DeAngelis, T., 302, 303, 304, 328

death, 39, 78, 92, 180, 200, 232, 257, 260, 271, 285, 290; Boyer on, 340, 342; of Christ, 56, 179–80; Frankl on, 232, 235, 249; instinct (*see* destructive instincts); life after, 40, 53, 108, 204, 343; love of, 5, 215, 216, 220; and rebirth, the psychospiritual experience of, 267, 270, 271, 273; Watts on, 188–89, 190

defense mechanisms, 142, 197, 210

Deficiency: realm of, 145, 151, 152, 157; state of, 143, 146

Deficiency-cognition, 139
Deficiency-disease, 132
Deficiency-love, 138
Deficiency-motivation, 136–37, 139,
    159, 160
Deficiency-psychology, 157
delusions, religious doctrines as, 35,
    57–58
demand character, 141, 230
demythologization, 87
Dennett, Daniel, x, 331, 343–51, 352;
    *Breaking the Spell: Religion as a
    Natural Phenomenon*, 343, 352
Descartes, 61, 101, 171, 227
descent with modification, 348
desire, 2, 4, 8, 12, 255; Allport on,
    108–9, 110, 119, 121, 122, 128;
    Fromm on, 196, 198, 207, 209, 210,
    216; Oedipal, 42, 47, 50
desolation experience, 139
despair, 129, 142, 154, 232, 235
destructive instincts, 32, 59–61, 233
devil, the, 61, 190, 245, 285. *See also*
    Satan
differentiation, psychic, 73, 89, 90–91,
    92, 100
disbelief, 3, 111, 119, 120, 260, 343
discipline, necessity of, 116, 119, 128,
    132, 154, 209. *See also* daily-life
    practice
dissociability, primitive, 82
divided mind, the, 171, 190
divine, the, 243–46, 255–56, 296–97;
    Freud on, 39, 49, 52; James on, 11,
    13, 14, 19, 28–29; Jung on, 66, 79–80,
    82, 83, 100, 101; Maslow on, 128,
    160, 162; Watts on, 168, 179, 189,
    191
The Doctor and the Soul (Frankl), 223,
    249
doctrines, 14, 26, 86, 156, 162, 344, 346,
    357. *See also* beliefs; creeds;
    delusions, religious doctrines as;
    illusion, Freud's view of religion as;
    religious concepts
Donohue, M. J., 266, 274
double bind, 187

doubt, 4, 199, 265–66, 350, 351; Allport
    on, 111–12, 117, 119, 124
downward determinism, 302
dreams, noological dimension and,
    246
dualism, 61, 290, 303
A Dynamic Psychology of Religion
    (Pruyser), 255, 256, 275

Eastern religious thought, 96–99,
    167–92
ecofeminists, 286
Economic and Philosophical Manuscripts
    (Marx), 208
ego, the, 120, 123, 207, 214, 215, 235,
    236, 244, 269, 271, 297; Freud on, 31,
    33–35, 47, 61; Jung on, 65, 66, 73, 75,
    76–77, 79–81, 84, 89–95, 100;
    Maslow on, 137, 138, 142, 156, 159,
    164; Watts on, 169–72, 173–74,
    176–79, 181, 183, 184–86, 187,
    188–89, 191
egocentric frame of reference, 323–24
Egyptian Moses, the, 53, 64, 62
electroencephalogram (EEG), 305, 309,
    311–12; results and meditation, 316,
    317–18, 327
Ellison, Katherine, 313, 314, 317, 318,
    319, 328
emergent determinism, 302
emergent properties, 302–3
emotional disorders, 271
end-experiencing, 149
enlightenment, 192, 319–20, 321, 325.
    See also awakening
Enlightenment, the, 84, 125
epiphenomenon, 236, 268, 306
Erdmann, E., 303, 304, 328
Erikson, Erik, x, 277, 295–98
Eros, 32, 59–61, 62, 245, 279
escape from freedom, 199
eternal feminine, the, 282
eternal life, the doctrine of, 181
eternal Now, the, 186–87
eternity, 33, 71, 150, 187, 189
ethics, x, 21, 47, 51, 99, 280–81; Fromm
    on, 210–12, 220. *See also* morality

Eucharist, the, 57, 280
evil, 36, 40, 61, 108, 111, 257, 282, 285, 293; Fromm on, 197, 198, 211, 213; James on, 15, 17, 22; Jung on the inclusion of, in the self, 70, 77, 92, 93; Maslow on, 127, 128, 132, 140, 141, 143, 145, 153–54, 155, 158, 161, 164; Watts on, 168, 172, 179, 187, 189–90, 192
evolutionary biology, 332, 344
evolutionary psychology, 331–51
existential analysis, 236
existential phenomenology, 195, 249
existential vacuum, 234
experiential psychotherapies, x, 270, 271, 272–74
expiation of the primal crime, 44, 53, 56, 57
explanatory gap, 306–7, 312
explicit belief, 335–36
External scale, 264, 265
extrinsic religion, 105–6, 122, 123, 263, 264. *See also* immature religion
Extrinsic scale, 105, 263, 265

faith, 32, 130, 161, 182, 280, 281, 351; Allport on, 109, 111–12, 113, 121, 124; Frankl on, 235, 237, 243, 246, 247; Fromm on, 204, 207, 208; James on, 15, 16, 27, 28
Fall, the, 198, 200
father, the, role of in religion: Freud on, 32, 33, 34, 35–39, 42–57, 62; reactions to Freud on, 80, 119, 242, 247, 254, 261, 262, 279
father substitute, 43–45, 50, 55
feeling, the prerogative of, ix, 5, 6, 9, 23, 24, 25–26, 28, 29. *See also* passional nature, our
female inferiority, 278, 279, 281–82, 283
female sexual identity, 295
feminine evil, the myth of, 282
feminine mode, the, 295–98
feminism, 277, 280, 281, 286, 290, 292, 294
feminist analysts, 277, 278, 280
feminist critics, 277, 278, 279

feminist inclusivists, 277, 279, 280, 281, 286
Feuerbach, Ludwig, 32, 205
first-person methods, 305–13, 314, 318
fitness, evolutionary, 344, 347, 350
folk religion, 344–45, 347, 351
fourth force psychology, 158
Frankl, ix, x, 123, 162, 164, 223–49; *The Doctor and the Soul*, 223, 249; *Man's Search for Meaning*, 164, 223, 249
Franzmann, Majella, x, 284–86, 298; *Women and Religion*, 284, 298
free-floating rationales, 344, 345, 347
free will, 71, 111, 303. *See also* freedom
freedom, 65, 287; Frankl on, 227–28, 229, 231, 235, 236, 240, 241; Fromm on, 196, 197–99, 200, 204, 205, 211, 212, 215, 217, 218
Freud, Sigmund, ix, 31–62, 251, 254, 257, 261; Allport and, 110, 119, 120, 121; feminist psychology and, 277, 278–79, 280, 292–94; Frankl and, 224, 225, 226, 229, 232, 233, 235, 236, 244, 245; Fromm and, 195, 202, 203, 213, 215, 218; *The Future of an Illusion*, 41, 63; Jung and, 65, 72, 76, 80, 81, 101; Maslow and, 127, 128, 132, 153; *Moses and Monotheism*, 31, 51, 53, 63; "Obsessive Acts and Religious Practices," 48, 49, 51, 63; *Totem and Taboo*, 41, 45, 49–50, 63
Freudian physicalism, 292–94
Freudianism, orthodox, 158, 280
Fromm, Erich, ix, x, 128, 195–221; *Psychoanalysis and Religion*, 196, 221
frontal lobe, 321, 324, 326–27
full humanness, 134–35, 154
Fuller, A. R., 226, 249
functional autonomy, 109–10, 120
fusion: of Being-values, 141; of realms of Being and Deficiency, 150, 152, 157; of self and world, ix, 97, 141, 143, 147–48, 163–64, 209. *See also* plateau experience, the; relatedness
future, the, 102, 114, 154, 201, 204, 215, 304; Frankl on, 229, 234, 246; Freud

on, 32, 41, 58–59; Watts on, 172, 174, 186, 192

Gaia, 286
Geller, Jay, 278–79
gender differences, 287
gender reversal, 280
Genesis, 37, 81, 216
genetic selection, 331–33, 342
genetic transmission, 345
geneticism, 110
Gestalt: laws of organization, 173, 230, 303; psychology, 128, 230
Gilligan, Carol, x, 278, 286–90, 298; *In a Different Voice: Psychological Theory and Women's Development*, 286, 298
God: as archetypal manifestation, 78–81; the hidden, 243–46; humans as partners with, 27–28; as a possibility within human nature, 127, 196, 199, 200, 206, 207, 217, 220–21. *See also* Being-values; divine, the; God-image, the; God representation, the; illusion, Freud's view of religion as; pantheism; relativity of God, the; religion as historical truth; religious concepts; supernatural agents; Supreme Identity, the; supreme value; transitional phenomena; ultimate being
The God Delusion (Dawkins), 346
God the father, 56, 86–93, 281–83
God the Holy Spirit, 86–93
God representation, the, 258–63, 280
God the son, 86–93, 179, 281. *See also* Jesus Christ
Goddess movement, the, 277, 286, 294
Godhead, 90, 100, 178
God-image, the, x, 251, 263, 279, 280–81; Jung on, 81–83, 84, 90, 92, 101
gods, the, 8, 138, 141, 257, 267, 294, 339, 344; Freud on, 38, 39, 52–53, 54; Jung on, 67, 70, 79, 80, 82, 91
Goethe, Johann Wolfgang von, 45, 230, 235

Goldenberg, Naomi, x, 279, 290–95, 298; *Changing of the Gods: Feminism and the End of Traditional Religion*, 294, 298; *Resurrecting the Body: Feminism, Religion, and Psychoanalysis*, 290, 298
Goldstein, Kurt, 128, 165
Goleman, D., 313, 317, 328
"Good Trick," 349
grace, 17, 19, 148, 260
gradual enlightenment, 325
Great Self, the, 324
Griffin, E., 287, 298
Grof, Christina, 267, 273, 275
Grof, Stanislov, x, 251, 266–74, 275
Growth-motivation, 136–37, 152
guilt, 16, 171, 179, 204, 232, 257, 283; Freud on the sons', 43–49, 52, 56, 57; healthy, 115–16, 162, 213

happiness, 40, 174, 176; affective neuroscience and, 315, 316, 317; Frankl on, 223, 232–33; Fromm on, 204, 206, 211, 212, 217; James on, 15, 16, 17, 21; Maslow on, 144, 145, 150, 155, 159
Harrington, A., 314, 315, 328, 329, 330; *Visions of Compassion: Western Scientists and Tibetan Buddhists Examine Human Nature* (with Davidson), 315, 328, 329
"having orientation," 206–8
healthy-mindedness, 15–17
heart, role of the, 85, 235, 245; James on, 1, 4–5, 6, 29
heaven as attainment of Being-values, 156
Hegel, 198
Heidegger, Martin, 178, 249, 306
helplessness, human, 34, 36–40
hermeneutics: of recollection, 35, 220; of suspicion, 32, 35, 220
Higher Power, 17, 19, 21, 25, 27
hippocampus, 315
Hoffer, Erik, 264, 275
holism, 173, 174, 302–3. *See also* relatedness

holotropic breathwork, 268, 273–74
holotropic states of consciousness, 251, 266–74
holotropic therapy, 273–74
holy, the, 139, 157, 161, 162, 256, 257. *See also* sacred, the
Holy Spirit. *See* God the Holy Spirit
honesty, demand of, 269
Hood, R. W., 266, 275
Houshmand, Z., 316, 329
human well-being, inducing, 317–19
humanism, 124; Fromm's, 197, 210, 212, 217, 218, 220
humanistic psychology, 128, 158, 162
humanistic religion, 196, 206, 209, 211, 213, 218
Husserl, Edmund, 224, 226, 306
"hyperactive agent detection device," 349

"I," the, 183, 297, 322
"I-Me-Mine," the, 321, 322, 326
id, the, 31, 128, 236, 239, 315
ideal, the, 43, 121, 201, 204; Frankl on, 229, 230, 236; Maslow on, 129, 155, 156, 161
ideology, 80, 216
idolatry, 160, 182, 191; Fromm on, 198, 202, 203, 211, 216, 217
idols, 182, 196, 198, 216, 219, 350
ignorance, fundamental, 320, 322
Ikhnaton, Pharaoh, 53, 54
illumination, experience of, 23, 139, 149–50, 156
illusion, 320; the ego-, 169–70, 178; Freud's view of religion as, 35–41, 58, 62, 107, 111, 261, 278; Fromm's assault on, 195, 196, 197, 202, 208, 220; in object relations theory, 252–54, 256–58, 261
illusionistic sphere, 256, 257–58
image, psyche as, 66–67
imagination, the, 200, 292, 324, 349; Freud on, 35–37, 41, 62; Jung on, 69, 73, 75; Pruyser on, 256–58
immature religion, ix, 105, 120–21. *See also* extrinsic religion

impulse voices, 135, 153
In a Different Voice: Psychological Theory and Women's Development (Gilligan), 286, 298
Incarnation, the, 86, 88–93, 180
incest, 46, 203, 218, 220
incomprehensibility of religious beliefs, 350–51
Indian religious thought, opposites in, 96–97. *See also* Supreme Identity, the; Vedanta
individual, religion of the, 105, 107, 109, 110, 113–14, 118, 120–21, 123
The Individual and His Religion (Allport), 105, 123, 124
individuation, 149, 197, 199; Jung's notion of, 76–78, 84, 92, 93
infinite, the, 34, 83, 93, 107, 150, 157; Watts on, 176–80, 183, 185, 186, 188, 190–91
infinity, feeling of, 33
inner radar, 273
inner space, 295–96
insight-wisdom (*prajna*), 315, 320–21, 325
instinct, 23, 108, 110, 129, 145, 153, 154, 292; Frankl on, 224–27, 229, 233, 236, 237–38, 239, 244–45, 246; Freud on, 32, 39, 47, 48, 50–51, 58, 59–61; Fromm on, 197, 199–201; Jung on, 65, 66, 68–70, 72–73, 76, 77, 101
institutional religion, 49, 73, 106, 217, 247, 259, 296; James on, 1, 11, 13, 14, 18, 20, 26, 28–29; Maslow on, 155–56, 160, 161–63, 164. *See also* organized religion
intellect, the, 75, 113, 187, 196, 246, 272, 279, 292; Freud on, 41, 48, 58; James on, 2– 6, 14, 23, 24, 27, 28. *See also* reason
intentional object, 113, 226, 234, 247
intentional stance, the, 349
intentionality, 106, 113–15, 225–27, 233
intermediate area of experience, the, 252–54. *See also* transitional space
Internal scale, 264

intrapsychic character of human life, 61, 101, 226, 229, 234, 240

intrinsic religion, 105–6, 122–23, 264. *See also* mature religion

intrinsic requiredness, 133, 142, 175, 213, 230, 249

Intrinsic scale, 105, 263

intuitive psychology inference system, 335, 336–38, 342, 349

intuitive richness, 340

irrational, rights of the, 74–75

irreducible, the, 140, 302, 303, 306; Frankl on, 223, 225, 237, 239, 241, 242

Islam, 216, 290

isomorphism of self and world, 140, 143, 148

Jahve, 54, 55

James, William, ix, 13–30, 66, 248, 254, 343; Allport and, 105, 106, 124; Freud and, 33, 35, 62; Maslow and, 156, 164, 174, 191; "A Pluralistic Universe," 26, 30; "The Sentiment of Rationality," 4, 29; *The Varieties of Religious Experience*, 2, 9, 28, 30; "The Will to Believe," 2, 6, 8, 9, 23, 28, 29, 111

Jesus Christ, 29, 117, 207, 217, 321; in Freud's psychology, 56–57; in Jung's psychology, 82, 83, 87–93, 99, 101; in Watts's psychology, 179–80, 182, 192. *See also* God the son

Jewish morality, renunciatory, 278–79

Jones, L., 265, 275

Jonte-Pace, Diane, x, 277–81, 298

The Journals of A. H. Maslow, 128, 142, 145, 159, 165

joy, religious, 14, 19, 147, 154, 175, 190, 209, 246, 313

Judaism, 207, 216, 290, 348

Jung, Carl, ix, 2, 65–102, 124, 343; Feminist psychology and, 278, 279, 290, 291, 292; Frankl's psychology and, 224, 226, 244; Freud's psychology and, 33, 62, 63; Maslow's psychology and, 128, 132,

148, 153, 160; Watts's psychology and, 174, 175, 191

justice, ethic of, 286–88

Kabat-Zinn, Jon, 319

kensho, 320–25

Koehler, Wolfgang, 124, 125, 133, 230

Kohlberg, Lawrence, 286–87, 288, 289

Kojetin, B. A., 266, 275

Kristeva, Julia, 278, 280–81

latency, period of, 47, 51, 54–55

latent rationality, 98

law and authority factor, 262–63

Lazar, S. W., 318, 329

letting go, 214, 323

Levy-Bruhl, Lucien, 72

libido, 72–73, 79, 81, 97, 99, 100, 101

life task, 228, 231, 235, 237

lifeworld, 226, 227, 248

Lila: An Inquiry into Morals (Pirsig), 4, 30

Lindzey, G., 124, 125

lived experience, 239, 306

loathings and longings, 322, 325

Logos, 124, 229, 234, 245; Freud on, 32, 35, 41, 56, 58

logotherapy, 223, 234–36, 238, 239

longing for the father, 34, 38–39, 43, 52, 119

love, 19, 82, 121–22, 191, 207; as art, 208–9; as basic need, 132–33; conscience and, 240–41; as origin of superego, 45–46

"love and compassion" meditation, 301, 316, 317

lower mysticism, 22–23

LSD, 151, 168, 233, 266

Luther, Martin, 204

Lutz, Antoine, 305, 307–13, 318, 329, 330

macrocosm, 84, 110, 158, 181, 185

magnetic resonance imaging (MRI), 305, 318, 327

maladaptive self, 322

male anxiety, 282

male envy of women, 280

Malinowski, Bronislaw, 118

Mandala, 77, 82, 84

Man's Search for Meaning (Frankl), 164, 223, 249

Marcel, Gabriel, 243, 249

marginalization of women's religious experience, x, 284–85

Marx, Karl, 195, 198, 200, 208, 221; *Economic and Philosophical Manuscripts*, 208

masculine, the divine, 281–82

masculine character of religion, 279, 281–83, 284–85, 286–87

masculine God, the, 281–82, 283

masculine mode, the, 295–98

masculinity, superior psychological, 278–79

Maslow, Abraham, ix, 2, 33, 62, 123, 127–65, 302; *The Journals of A. H. Maslow*, 128, 142, 145, 159, 165

materialism, 10, 67, 95, 268, 302, 305, 306–7. *See also* objectivism; reductionism

maternal body, x, 292, 294

maternal Other, 298

maternal person, 296

matter, 67, 95, 183, 188, 197, 268, 282, 290, 303

mature religion, ix, 105, 106–7, 109–11, 114, 121, 123–24, 264–65. *See also* intrinsic religion

mature religious sentiment, the, 106–7, 109–11

McIntosh, D., 266, 275

meaning as the ideal, 229, 230, 236, 241

meaning of life, the, 78, 225, 228, 230, 231–32, 236, 241

meaningfulness, 79, 140, 231–32, 235, 237, 239

meaninglessness, 142, 234, 240, 350

meditation, 271, 273; Tibetan Buddhist, and affective neuroscience, x, 267, 301, 313–19; Zen Buddhist, and neuroscience, x, 267, 301, 319–20, 325–28

Meister Eckhart, 99–100, 208

memes, 331, 345–49, 350

memory, the self and, 186

Merleau-Ponty, Maurice, 28, 249, 306

metaguilt, 162

metamotivations, 137, 143

metaneeds, 136–37, 141, 143, 145, 153

metapathology, 145

methodical religion, 345

microcosm, 127, 148, 181, 185; Jung on the self as, 77, 83–84, 90, 98, 99, 101

microdeterminism, 302

Mind and Life Institute, 314

mind virus, 347

mindfulness meditation, 318, 325–26, 327

misogyny, 277, 278, 279, 280, 293

monad, 226

monkey mind, 327

monotheism, 39, 52, 53–55, 57, 203

moral development, women's, x, 278, 286–89

moral inference system, 336, 339, 342

morality, 4, 5, 94, 97–98, 190, 342, 343, 350; feminist psychology on, 280–81, 283, 292; Freud on the origins of, 39, 44, 45–46, 50–51, 57, 278–79. *See also* ethics; moral development, women's; moral inference system

morbid-mindedness, 15–17

More, the, 26, 31

Morris, R. J., 266, 275

Moses, 31, 53–55, 57, 62

Moses and Monotheism (Freud), 31, 51, 53, 63

music in breathwork, 273, 274

mystery, 20, 177, 192, 256, 332, 351; Maslow on, 130, 141, 147, 150, 162

mystical experience, 37, 62, 71, 117, 149, 163, 214–16; James on, 20–25, 27, 29; Watts on, 168, 173–76, 181–82, 183, 191–92. *See also* numinous, the; oceanic experience, the; peak experience, the; religious experience; Supreme Identity, the

"mystical identity" (*participation mystique*), 72, 73

myth, 14, 61, 62, 124, 153, 258, 267, 269, 270; feminist psychology on, 282, 292–93, 294; Jung on, 65, 69–71, 73–76, 77, 80–81, 84, 86–87, 91; Watts on, 175, 177, 178–80, 182, 191–92

natural selection, 332, 344, 345, 346
naturalistic account, 304, 333, 343–44, 349; Maslow's, 131, 134, 140, 149, 159
Nazism, 130, 151, 203, 204
near-death experiences, 271
need for the father's protection, 37–38
negative freedom, 199, 228
neo-Freudians, 195
neural coherence, 310–11, 315
neural integration, large-scale, 310–12
neurophenomenology, x, 301, 304–13
neuroplasticity, 314–15, 319
neuroscience, x, 301–30
neurosis, 95, 117, 120, 121, 202, 209, 210, 271; as deficiency disease, 132, 154, 164; noogenic, 234, 245; as private religion, 49, 202, 203, 245; religion as, 47–59
nihilism, 129, 158, 236, 249
Nirvana, 29, 216, 257
"no-I," state of, 226
nonordinary states of consciousness, 266, 268, 271, 272, 273
noological dimension of human life, the, 225–37; and religion, 237–46
numinous, the, 108, 178, 296–97; Jung on, 78–84, 86, 88, 92, 102

object relations, x, 251–63, 277, 278, 279–80, 281, 293, 294
objectivism, 62, 102, 158, 221, 231. *See also* materialism
"Obsessive Acts and Religious Practices" (Freud), 48, 49, 51, 63
oceanic experience, the, 32–35, 62
Oedipus complex, the, 42, 44–48, 62, 260, 261, 278, 279
omnipotent control, the child's, 252, 253

openness, human, 29, 107, 143, 191, 225–26, 242, 265
opposites, 22, 168, 189–90, 323; destructive and constructive instincts as cosmic struggle of, 59–61; Jung on, 67, 77, 81–82, 89–95. *See also* Chinese religious thought, opposites in; Indian religious thought, opposites in
oppression of women, 282, 291
orbitofrontal region, 327
organized religion, 14, 155, 160, 163, 203; Dennett on, 344–45, 346–48, 350, 351. *See also* institutional religion
original sin, 44, 56, 58, 128, 154, 179, 315
orthodoxy, 130, 203, 284
Orthodoxy scale, 365, 366
Otto, Rudolf, 78, 103, 108, 160, 165
outer space, 295
overconditioned psychic self, the, 321–23
overdetecting agency, 337, 349

pantheism, 1, 101–2, 167, 181, 244
parental figures, 261–63
The Parental Figures and the Representation of God (Vergote and Tamayo), 261, 275
Pascal, Blaise, 177
passional nature, our, 4, 5, 23
past, role of the, 110, 114, 174, 186, 229, 294, 322; Freud on, 31–32, 35, 47, 55, 57–58, 62
patriarchical religion, 279, 281–83, 286, 291, 294
peak experience, the, 33, 232, 233; Maslow on, 139, 147–52, 155–57, 159, 160, 163
perennial philosophy, the, 174, 180
perinatal level of the psyche, 268, 270–71, 272, 273
Perry, Ralph Barton, 7, 9, 30
personal agency, 337
personal file inference system, 336, 338, 339

personal religion, 11, 13–14, 20, 25, 156, 243

personal unconscious, the, 68

perspective, the role of, 230–31, 251

phenomena, 306, 307

phenomenology, 106, 113, 195, 306–7; Frankl on the use of, 223–26, 237, 248

Pirsig, Robert M., 4, 30; *Lila*, 4, 30

plateau experience, the, 149–52, 157, 159, 164, 175

Plato, 174, 290

play, 136, 295–96; as characterizing the intermediate area of experience, 253–60, 261; Watts on, 178–79, 180, 183–84, 187, 189, 191, 192

The Play of the Imagination (Pruyser), 255, 275

pleasure principle, the, 32, 59–61, 223, 232–34, 257

pluralistic approach, xi, 6–7, 29, 105

"A Pluralistic Universe" (James), 26, 30

polytheism, 39, 52–53

positive freedom, 199, 228

positivism, 1, 28, 31, 62, 258

positron-emission tomography (PET), 324, 327

postconventional feminine morality, 289

post-Freudian psychoanalysis, 292, 293

postnatal level of the psyche, 270, 271, 273

poststructuralist movement, the, 281

preconventional feminine morality, 289

prajna. See insight-wisdom

prayer, 26, 39, 49, 116, 260

predation, 336, 337, 338, 342

prefrontal cortex, 315, 316–17, 318

prejudice, 115, 122–23, 263, 265

prereflective understanding, 224, 232, 235, 238, 239

presupposition, xi, 102, 239, 248, 307

primal father, the, 42–56, 62

primal horde, the, 42

primary process, the, 35–36, 39, 152, 257

primary ties, 199, 201, 218

primordial images, 69, 70, 71, 75, 97. *See also* archetypes

productive orientation, 199, 202, 206, 208, 209, 212, 220

projection, 32, 108, 119, 204–5, 247, 282; Jung on, 72, 80, 88, 96, 97, 101

proofs for God's existence, 1, 24

Prophets, the, 14, 54

Pruyser, Paul, x, 251, 254–58, 275; *Between Belief and Unbelief*, 255, 275; *A Dynamic Psychology of Religion*, 255, 256, 275; *The Play of the Imagination: Toward a Psychoanalysis of Culture*, 255, 275

psychedelic drugs, 267, 268, 271

psychiatry, conventional, 268, 269, 270, 271

psychic self, the, 321–26. *See also* "I-Me-Mine," the

psychoanalysis, 105, 129, 255, 280, 292–93, 294; Frankl on, 229, 246, 247; Fromm on, 195, 209, 215, 218

Psychoanalysis and Religion (Fromm), 196, 221

psychologism, 101, 224, 235, 248

A Psychology of Ultimate Concern: Erik H. Erikson's Contribution to the Psychology of Religion (Zock), 297, 299

psychophysiological effects of meditation, 326–28

psychosis, 22, 35, 58–59, 75, 76, 79; Frankl on, 227, 237, 246, 247; Grof on, 268, 271–72, 273

psychosomatic disorders, 271–73, 274

psychospiritual transformation, 267–68

psychotherapy, 58, 225, 235, 246; experiential, x, 251, 270, 271, 273; Fromm on, 202, 209, 215, 218

Quest scale, 264–66

Raab, Kelley, 280

rationalism, 2, 23, 33, 79, 85, 124, 239

rationalization, 119–20, 215, 220

Rawlings, N. B., 313, 318, 329

Raynor-Prince, L., 265, 274

reality-testing, 252

reason, x, 23, 113, 153, 154, 257, 290; Frankl on, 239, 245, 249; Freud on, 32, 41, 56, 58; Fromm on, 196–97, 198, 200, 208, 210, 214; Jung on, 74, 75, 79, 85, 87, 94. *See also* intellect, the

rebirth, 17, 72, 220. *See also* death, and rebirth, the psychospiritual experience of

reductionism, 10, 28, 224–25, 231, 248, 251, 303, 305. *See also* materialism; objectivism

relatedness, 184–86, 206, 259, 279, 281. *See also* holism

relativism, 129, 211, 231

relativity of God, the, 99–100

"relaxation meditation," 327

religion, definition of, 32, 57, 107, 114, 182, 191, 200, 220, 254, 257; in evolutionary psychology, 331, 343, 344, 346; Frankl's, 237, 247, 248; James's, 13, 15, 25–26; Jung's, 66, 84–85; Maslow's, 155–56, 160, 162, 164

Religion Explained: The Evolutionary Origins of Religious Thought (Boyer), 332, 352

religion as historical truth, 41–59

religion of the son, 56

religion-as-end, 26

religion-as-means, 265

religion-as-quest, 265

religious concepts, 331–42, 348–49, 351. *See also* supernatural concepts

religious experience, 174, 280, 284–85, 296–98, 305; Fromm on, 197, 205, 206, 214–17, 219; James on, ix, 9–29; Maslow on, 155, 157, 160, 161, 162, 163. *See also* mystical experience

religious language, 117–18, 124, 283

religious need, 34, 196, 200–202

Religious Orientation Scale, 105, 263–66

religious representations of women, 285

Religious Viewpoints Scale, 264

remorse over killing the father, 43–44, 46, 47

replication, 344, 345–46, 350, 351

repression, 80, 108, 142, 169, 190, 224, 245; Freud on, 46–48, 50–52, 54, 57, 58–59; Fromm on, 209, 211, 212, 215. *See also* return of the repressed, the

res cogitans, 61, 101, 248

res extensa, 62, 171, 172, 183, 227, 248

responsibility, 13, 121, 158, 161, 185, 192; Frankl on, 235, 236–37, 243; Fromm on, 196, 198, 199, 212; Gilligan on, 287, 288, 289

responsibleness, 228, 231, 234–42, 246

Resurrecting the Body: Feminism, Religion, and Psychoanalysis (Goldenberg), 290, 298

resurrection, 56, 87, 90, 91–93, 180, 182

return of the repressed, the, 47, 48, 51, 52, 53, 55–56, 57–58, 59, 245

Ricoeur, Paul, 32, 35, 63, 220, 221

right hemisphere, 302, 323

rightness, the experience of, ix, 175, 191, 221

rites of initiation, 73, 267

ritual, 11, 74, 88, 267, 268, 340, 346; Allport on, 108, 116, 117; feminist psychology on, 278, 279–81, 285; Freud on, 44, 48–50, 53, 57, 58; Fromm on, 202, 203, 209–10, 220; Maslow on, 156, 157, 162

ritual divination, 346

Rizzuto, Ana-Maria, x, 251, 254, 258–61, 263; *The Birth of the Living God*, 258; *Why Did Freud Reject God: A Psychodynamic Interpretation*, 261, 275

Rodriquez, E. N., 311, 329

Ross, Cheryl Lynn, 280

Ross, J. M., 105, 125, 263–66

Ross, Mary Ellen, 280

Rta, 97, 99

Rudrauf, D., 308, 310, 311, 329

sacred, the, 185, 205, 267, 304, 351; Maslow on, 127, 128, 131, 135,

150–51, 157, 160, 161. *See also* holy, the
sacrifice, 54, 56, 89–90, 280, 339, 342
Saint Athanasius, 179
Saint Paul, 10, 40, 56, 57
saintliness, 19–20
salvation, 26–27, 56, 122, 156, 179, 204, 241
Sapp, G. L., 265, 275
Satan, 207, 351
satori, 320, 323
Scheler, Max, 223, 233
Schleiermacher, Friedrich, 108
Schoenrade, P., 264, 265, 274
science, 182, 231, 235, 278, 305, 309, 313–14, 316, 319, 349, 351; Allport on, 112–13, 117, 118; Boyer on, 331–32, 336; Freud on, 33, 35, 39, 41; Fromm on, 197, 208, 218; James on, 1, 4, 8–9, 10, 12, 14, 18, 23, 24; Jung on, 66, 70, 74–75, 86; Maslow's proposed expansion of, 127–31, 137, 142, 156, 161, 162; Sperry on, 302, 303–4
secondary process, the, 35, 152
secondary ties, 199, 204, 206, 218, 220
selectivity, human, 2, 6–9
self, the. *See* archetype of the self; Christian doctrines; God-image, the, Jung on; individuation, Jung's notion of; microcosm, Jung on self as; psychic self, the; self-actualization; self-image and morality; self-transcendence; Supreme Identity, the
self-actualization, 233; Maslow on, 128, 133–37, 144, 149, 151, 152, 154, 156, 159
self-actualizers, 136–37, 142–46, 149, 153, 155, 158
self-image and morality, 287, 290–91
self-regulation, psychic, 71
self-transcendence, 225–27, 228–30, 233, 241
Semantic Differential Parental scale, 261
"The Sentiment of Rationality" (James), 4, 29

"sex role socialization," 283
sexuality, 59–61, 65, 72, 108, 218, 229, 245, 285, 294
shadow, the, 68, 72
shamanism, 267, 346
Shear, J., 305, 306, 308, 328, 330
Siegel, Daniel, 314
sin, 16, 93, 189, 190. *See also* original sin
Singer, Wolf, 310–11, 329
skeptical approach, 3–5, 35, 111, 285, 319, 348
social exchange inference system, 336, 338–39, 342
social interaction, the role of, in evolution, 336, 337, 338, 339
specifically human, the, 69, 216, 261. *See also* noological dimension of human life, the
Sperry, Roger, x, 301, 302–4, 328, 329
Spilka, Bernard P., x, 251, 263–66, 274, 275
spirit, 14, 21, 269, 286, 336, 341; human, the, 235, 256, 273; Jung on, 66, 73, 77, 93–95, 100. *See also* God the Holy Spirit
spirits, 75, 80, 82, 349; Boyer on, 332, 334–35, 336, 338, 339, 341, 342
spiritual, the, 94, 153, 267, 272, 320
spiritual disorder, 154, 196
spiritual emergencies, 267–68, 271
spiritual life, the, 16, 95, 127, 153, 268
spiritual needs, 128, 133
split in human existence, the, 191, 199, 200–201, 209
spontaneity, ix, 71, 187–88, 245, 273; Maslow on, 136, 145, 146, 151, 155
stewardship of memes, the, 346–48, 350
Stover, D., 303, 304, 328
stress reduction, 274, 327
subconscious, the, 1, 17–19, 22–23, 25, 26–27
subcortex, 321
subjective object, the, 252–53
sublimation, 59–61, 73, 108, 110, 224, 245

subtractions of the psychic self, 322–23
sudden enlightenment, 324, 325
suffering, the meaningfulness of, 231–32
superego, 31, 45–46, 50, 61, 115–16, 213, 235, 242
supernatural agents, 332, 335, 337–38, 339, 340, 342. *See also* spirits
supernatural concepts, 332, 333, 340–41, 349. *See also* religious concepts
supernaturalism, 23, 31
The Supreme Identity (Watts), 175, 193
Supreme Identity, the, 33, 175–82, 190, 192
supreme value, 80, 100, 216, 219, 304
symbols, 181–82, 245, 254, 257–58; Jung on, 65–66, 69–79, 82, 84, 85–88, 95, 102
synchronized firing of neurons, 310–12
synchronized gamma-band activity, 304, 310–12, 313, 315, 317, 318
synergy of conscious and unconscious, 152

taboos of totemism, 42–45, 46, 50–51
talking cure, 294
Tao, 96, 98–99, 168, 187, 216
Taoism, 61, 98–99, 167, 184, 187
Taoistic noninterference, 138, 139, 152, 159
Taylor, Kylea, 273, 275
technologies of the sacred, 267
temperament, 108
tension-reduction, 35, 36, 59, 233, 248
theory of "I," Erikson's, 297, 298
theta rhythms, 318, 327
Third Force Psychology, 158
third-person methods, 305–13, 349
Thompson, E., 307–13, 329, 330
thought systems, the reality behind, 196, 197, 209, 214, 215–17, 220
Thurman, R. A. F., 328
Tibetan Buddhism, 313–19
Tibetan Buddhist meditation. *See* meditation, Tibetan Buddhist, and affective neuroscience

Tillich, Paul, 183, 214, 257
top-down view, 302
totem, 42–45, 52–53
Totem and Taboo (Freud), 41, 45, 49–50, 63
totem feast, 45, 50, 57
totemism, 42–53
Tracy, David, 191, 192
tragic triad of suffering, guilt, and death, 232, 234
transcendence: divine, 86, 242–48; as end-experiencing, 146, 157, 160; of self, 147–48, 156, 207, 225–43
transcenders, 159
transformation, 6, 109, 110, 195, 214, 267–68, 294; of the God-image, 67, 88, 258; Jung and psychic, 66, 72–73, 77, 88, 91, 95, 97, 99, 102; through meditation, 313–14, 315, 317, 319, 320, 326
transhumanistic psychology. *See* transpersonal psychology
transitional phenomena, 252–61
transitional space, 258–61. *See also* intermediate area of experience, the
transpersonal, the, 158
transpersonal level of the psyche, 269–70, 271–72
transpersonal psychology, 128, 158–59, 269, 271
Trinity, the, 86, 88–91, 93
trust in the ultimate, 227, 244
truth, 178, 182, 192, 249, 251, 257, 269, 281, 289, 291, 351; Fromm on, 196, 201, 202, 204, 208, 217, 218–19, 220; James on, 1–9, 17, 21–25, 26, 27, 28, 29; Jung on, 85, 86–87, 99, 107; Maslow on, 131, 134, 137, 139–44, 148, 150, 155, 156, 158, 164
twice-bornness, 16, 17, 19, 21, 26

ultimate being, 224, 237, 243, 240
ultimate concern, 214
ultimate meaning, 224, 237, 243–44, 246, 249
Ultimate Other, 297

ultimate reality, 112; Maslow on, 140, 142, 143, 148; Watts on, 181, 183, 191–92
unconscious, the individual Freudian, 270, 272
unconscious brain processes, 335
unconscious discrimination, 238
unconscious intelligence, 29, 71, 168
unconscious possession, 85
unconscious religiousness, 224, 243–46, 249
underground belief making, 335–36
unification, personality, 243–46, 249
uniqueness, individual, 77–78, 105, 109, 237
unitive consciousness, 149–52, 157–58, 159, 161, 164, 175. *See also* plateau experience, the
unmasking, xi, 62, 219, 235–36
unmotivated behavior, 136, 146–47, 157
unseen, the, 14, 189, 257, 291, 296
untestability of religious beliefs, 351
Upanishads, the, 21, 96, 98, 100, 176, 183
upward determinism, 302

valuelessness, contemporary, 129
values, 129–31, 132–34; the cognitive revolution and, 301, 303–4; life's essence as realizing, 225, 229, 231, 237; as rooted in human existence, 211–12, 214. *See also* Being-values
van Herik, Judith, 278–79
Varela, Francisco, x, 305, 306, 307, 308, 310, 311, 314, 328, 329, 330
The Varieties of Religious Experience (James), 2, 9, 28, 30
Vedanta, 175, 178, 180
Ventis, W. L., 264, 265, 274
verbal psychotherapy, 270, 272
verbal reports, 307–10, 311, 313, 318
Vergote, Antoine, x, 251, 261–63, 275; *The Parental Figures and the Representation of God* (with Tamayo), 261, 275
Vernon, E., 124, 125
Visions of Compassion: Western Scientists and Tibetan Buddhists Examine

Human Nature (Davidson and Harrington), 315, 328, 329

Wallace, B. Alan, 305, 306–7, 313–14, 315, 330
Watson, J., 266, 275
Watts, Alan, ix, 33, 62, 167–93; *The Supreme Identity*, 175, 193
Werme, P. H., 263, 273
Western science, 142, 313–14
Whitehead, A. N., 118
Whitman, Walt, 15
wholeness, attaining, 32, 127, 140, 267, 272; Jung on, 76–77, 82, 84, 90, 92, 95, 99
Why Did Freud Reject God: A Psychodynamic Interpretation (Rizzuto), 261, 275
wild memes, 347
Wilhelm, Richard, 66, 69, 72, 82, 87, 98, 99, 103
"The Will to Believe" (James), 2, 6, 8, 9, 23, 28, 29, 111
will to meaning, the, 228–34
will to pleasure, the, 232–34
will to power, the, 138, 232, 234
Winnicott, Donald, x, 251–54, 256–57, 258, 259, 260, 275, 279, 293
wise old man, the, 94
wish fulfillment, 85, 107, 118–19, 120–21, 255, 257, 259, 261, 278–79; Freud on, ix, 32, 35–38, 44, 46, 56, 62. *See also* illusion
women as dangerous, 284, 285
Women and Religion (Franzmann), 284, 298
wordlessness, subcortical circuits and, 321
words, the problem of, 117–18, 123, 156–57, 160; Watts and, 168–69, 170, 172, 174, 181, 182, 188
Wulff, D. M., 265–66, 275
wu-wei, 187

yes-function, 15, 20, 22
yin and yang, 61, 98, 99, 168
Yoga, 97, 267, 273, 327

Zajonc, A., 307, 329, 330
Zen and the Brain: Toward an Understanding of Meditation and Consciousness (Austin), 319, 328
Zen Buddhism, x, 150, 167, 187, 301, 319–28
Zen meditation. *See* meditation, Zen Buddhist, and neuroscience

Zen-Brain Reflections: Reviewing Recent Developments in Meditation and States of Consciousness (Austin), 319, 328
Zock, Hetty, x, 295–98, 299; *A Psychology of Ultimate Concern: Erik H. Erikson's Contribution to the Psychology of Religion*, 297